MW00991910

TODAY'S BEST
MILITARY WRITING

FORGE BOOKS BY WALTER J. BOYNE

Dawn over Kitty Hawk

Operation Iraqi Freedom:
What Went Right, What Went Wrong, and Why

Today's Best Military Writing: The Finest Articles on the
Past, Present, and Future of the U.S. Military (editor)

Today's Best Military Writing

THE FINEST ARTICLES
ON THE
PAST, PRESENT, AND FUTURE
OF
THE U.S. MILITARY

Colonel Walter J. Boyne,
USAF (Ret.)

A TOM DOHERTY ASSOCIATES BOOK
New York

TODAY'S BEST MILITARY WRITING:
THE FINEST ARTICLES ON THE PAST, PRESENT, AND FUTURE OF
THE U.S. MILITARY

Copyright © 2004 by Walter J. Boyne

All rights reserved, including the right to reproduce this book,
or portions thereof, in any form.

This book is printed on acid-free paper.

Book design by Mary A.Wirth

A Forge Book
Published by Tom Doherty Associates, LLC
175 Fifth Avenue
New York, NY 10010

www.tor.com

Forge® is a registered trademark of Tom Doherty Associates, LLC.

Library of Congress Cataloging-in-Publication Data

Today's best military writing : the finest articles on the past, present, and future of the
U.S. military / [edited by] Walter J. Boyne— 1st ed.
p. cm.
"A Tom Doherty Associates book."
ISBN 0-765-30887-8
EAN 978-0765-30887-0
1. United States—History, Military. 2. United States—Armed Forces—History.
I. Boyne, Walter J., 1929–

E181.T63 2004
355'.00973—dc22
2004047162

First Edition: September 2004

Printed in the United States of America

0 9 8 7 6 5 4 3 2 1

COPYRIGHT
ACKNOWLEDGMENTS

Preface copyright © 2004 by Walter J. Boyne.

"Lieutenant Andrew H. Foote and the African Slave Trade" by Spencer C. Tucker. Copyright © 2000 by Spencer C. Tucker. First published in *The American Neptune*, Vol. 60, No. 1. Reprinted by permission of the author.

"The F-15 Eagle: Origins and Development, 1964–1972" by Jacob Neufeld. Copyright © 2001 by Jacob Neufeld. First published in *Air Power History*, Spring 2001. Reprinted by permission of the author.

"No Master Plan: The Employment of Artillery in the Indian Wars, 1860–1890" by Major Prisco R. Hernandez, ARNG. Copyright © 2000 by *Field Artillery*. First published in *Field Artillery*, July/August 2000. Reprinted by permission of the author.

"Clarifying the Origins and Strategic Mission of the US Marine Corps Defense Battalion, 1898–1941" by David J. Ulbrich. Copyright © 1999 by the University of New South Wales. First published in *War & Society*, Vol. 7, No. 2, October 1999, pp. 81–109. Reprinted by permission of the author and the University of New South Wales.

"Birth of the American Way of War" by Thomas Fleming. Copyright © 2003 by *Military History Quarterly: The Quarterly Journal of Military History*. First published in *Military History Quarterly*, Winter 2003 issue. Reprinted by permission of PRIMEDIA Enthusiast Publications (History Group).

"More Than Numbers: Americans and the Revival of French Morale in the Great War" by Colonel Robert A. Doughty. Copyright © 2001 by

Army History First published in *Army History*, Spring 2001. Reprinted by permission of the author.

"Task Force Kingston" by Martin Blumenson. Copyright © 2000 by Martin Blumenson. First published in *Army* Magazine, January 2001. Reprinted by permission of the author and the Association of the U.S. Army.

"The Making of a Hero: What Really Happened Seventy-Five Years Ago After Lindbergh Landed at Le Bourget" by Lieutenant Colonel Raymond H. Fredette. Copyright © 2002 by Raymond H. Fredette. First published in *Air Power History*, Summer 2002. Reprinted by permission of the author.

"'Even in Auschwitz... Humanity Could Prevail': British POWs and Jewish Concentration-Camp Inmates at IG Auschwitz, 1943–1945" by Joseph Robert White. Copyright © 2001 by Joseph Robert White. First published in *Holocaust and Genocide Studies*, Vol. 15, No. 2. Reprinted by permission of the Oxford University Press.

"U.S. Army Chaplain Ministry to German War Criminals at Nuremberg, 1945–1946" by William J. Hourihan, Ph.D. Reprinted with permission from the U.S. Army Chaplain Corps, *The Army Chaplaincy: Professional Bulletin of the Unit Ministry Team*, Winter/Spring 2000.

"The Emerging Biocruise Threat" by Lieutenant Colonel Rex R. Kiziah, USAF. First published in *Air & Space Power Journal*, Spring 2003, pp. 81–94.

"The Looming Biological Warfare Storm: Misconceptions and Probable Scenarios" by Colonel (Dr.) Jim A. Davis, USAF. First published in *Air & Space Power Journal*, Spring 2003, pp. 57–67.

"Winged Cowboys: The Story Behind Air Mobility Command's Latest Biennial Rodeo" by Philip Handleman. Copyright © 2002 by Philip Handleman. First published in *Flightline*, Summer/Fall 2002. Reprinted by permission of the author.

"Defending Against the Non-State (Criminal) Soldier: Toward a Domestic Response Network" by Robert J. Bunker, Ph.D. Copyright © 1998 by the International Association of Chiefs of Police, 515 N. Washington St., Arlington, VA 22314. First published in *The Police Chief*, Vol. 65, No. 11, pp. 41, 44–49, November 1998. Reprinted by the permission of the IACP.

"Homeland Security Is a Coast Guard Mission" by Commander Stephen E. Flynn, USCG. Copyright © 2001 by the U.S. Naval Institute. First published in *Proceedings*, October 2001. Reprinted by permission of the U.S. Naval Institute, www.navalinstitute.com.

"Homeland Defense" by Adam J. Hebert. Copyright © 2001 by the Air Force Association. First published in *Air Force Magazine*, November 2001. Reprinted by permission from *Air Force Magazine*, published by the Air Force Association.

"What Can We Learn from Enduring Freedom?" by Dr. Milan Vego. Copyright © 2002 by the U.S. Naval Institute. First published in *Proceedings*, July 2002. Reprinted by permission of the U.S. Naval Institute, www.navalinstitute.com.

"Combat Search and Rescue: A Longer Look" by Colonel Darrel Whitcomb, USAF (Ret). Copyright © 2002 by Colonel Darrel Whitcomb. First published in *Air Power History*, Fall 2002. Reprinted by permission of the author.

"Pearl Harbor" by Barrett Tillman. Copyright © 2001 by Barrett Tillman. First published in *Flight Journal*, June 2001. Reprinted by permission of the author.

"Mortal Sting: How the USS *Hornet* Cured the Imperial Japanese Navy of Its 'Victory Disease'" by Edward L. Byrnes. Copyright © 2002 by Edward L. Byrnes. First published in *Foundation*, Fall 2002. Reprinted by permission of the author.

"No Gun Ri Revisited: Historical Lessons for Today's Army" by Brigadier General John S. Brown. Copyright © 2002 by *Army History*. First published in *Army History*, Spring/Summer 2002. Reprinted by permission of the author.

*This book is respectfully dedicated
to the men and women of the armed services of the United States.
Though few in number and tasked with the enormous responsibility
of defending our borders, protecting our interests abroad,
and seeing that justice prevails everywhere,
they carry on brilliantly in the service of our nation.*

CONTENTS

PREFACE

Selecting the articles that became a part of *Today's Best Military Writing* seemed to be an extremely difficult task at first—for a number of reasons.

The principal difficulty was that there were an extraordinary number of good articles to review over a wide variety of subjects. It soon became apparent that there is really a new and vital military culture in the United States, one that is probably unprecedented in history, and it is flourishing in the journals. It is evident from the number and the quality of the journals (as well as with the many military books that are published each year) that the armed services are staffed with many excellent writers who cover an almost endless variety of topics.

The depth of many of the articles was particularly interesting. Many of them called for the reader to be well informed on the subject being discussed, and many of them elicited a storm of responses in the "Letters to the Editor" columns that followed the appearance of the article.

In many ways, this active intellectual life was reflected in the conduct of Operation Iraqi Freedom (OIF), during which the top leaders of all the services operated at an extremely high level of proficiency. OIF was the first war in which the armed services of the United States operated so "jointly" and also the first war in which combined operations with our United Kingdom, Australian, and Polish allies worked so seamlessly. The effectiveness of joint and combined efforts was possible only because the leaders within the individual services were bright enough to be sure to work for the common good, rather than for the good of their own combat arm.

One of the problems I faced was reviewing—and selecting—articles that were out of the mainstream of my own interests. Oddly enough, this was most rewarding, for I read many fascinating articles that I would never have taken the time for ordinarily. Thus it was that I became interested in such diverse topics as the employment of artillery in the Indian Wars, Coast Guard operations in Homeland Defense, and the African slave trade. Each of the articles (and you'll find one on each of these subjects in the book) kindled a desire for further reading in the subject area, and I hope that this is one of the effects of this book— broadening the interests of its readers.

An interesting aspect of the decision process was examining articles that have already been awarded a distinguished prize. Early on, I made a determined effort not to be influenced by an award that had been made, and I was successful in doing so. Yet, as I carefully read the papers, it was soon evident why the prizewinners were selected—they were just too good not to win a prize, and too good not to be included herein.

Then this phenomenon led in turn to some major disappointments, for many excellent articles, which I would really like to have included, had to be left out—this year, at least—for reasons of space. With the material available, it would have been possible to create at least two, and perhaps three, volumes this size, all packed with excellent pieces. One saving grace was that two or three really excellent articles were often on the same subject, and the need to have a wide range of subjects meant that I could only choose the best one from the subject area, and then move on.

The articles you'll find in this edition of *Today's Best Military Writing* are, in my opinion, the very best selections from a highly competitive, highly talented field. I hope you enjoy them as much as I did.

TODAY'S BEST
MILITARY WRITING

SPENCER C. TUCKER

Lieutenant Andrew H. Foote and the African Slave Trade

On September 28, 1849, U.S. Secretary of the Navy William Ballard Preston ordered Lieutenant Andrew H. Foote to report to the Gosport Navy Yard and take command of the brig *Perry*, then fitting out for African service. Foote had twenty-seven years of naval service, the last nineteen as a lieutenant. Few had his experience at sea or his reputation for excellent seamanship.[1]

The *Perry* was part of an international effort to suppress the slave trade. Britain had borne the brunt of this burden. In 1807 Britain abolished the slave trade, and at the end of the Napoleonic Wars London had employed part of its navy in the task of halting traffic in slaves. British warships stationed off the west coast of Africa stopped and inspected vessels suspected of being slavers. On capturing such vessels, the Royal Navy returned the slaves to Africa and brought the crews to trial.

Ownership of slaves was legal in the United States, and the country was one of the world's principal slave-owning nations, but on March 2, 1807, Congress banned the importation of slaves as of January 1, 1808. The law provided for forfeiture of vessels and their cargoes, with

disposal of seized slaves left to the state in which the ships were condemned.

Congress strengthened this in an act in March 1819 that offered a
$50 bounty to informers for every illegally imported slave seized on
land or at sea. In May 1820 Congress empowered President James
Monroe to return illegal slaves to Africa. At the same time it declared
the foreign slave trade a form of piracy. In addition to the forfeiture of
vessels previously authorized, it provided the death penalty for Americans caught in the slave trade, but few U.S. warships visited the African
coast to enforce the ban.[2]

In order to halt the slave trade, Secretary of the Navy Seth Thompson (1819–1823) directed that ships of the Mediterranean squadron returning to the United States travel via the African coast and the West
Indies. This accomplished little, and in 1821 he ordered Lieutenant
Commander Robert F. Stockton to cruise against the African slave trade
in the schooner *Alligator*. Thompson also ordered Lieutenant Commander Matthew C. Perry in the schooner *Shark* to the Madeira and Cape
Verde islands. These efforts were largely ineffectual.[3]

Meanwhile, Royal Navy enforcement of anti-slaving measures was
hindered not only by the failure of the U.S. Navy to provide significant
naval strength off Africa but because, although most other nations had
granted permission to the British to search vessels flying their flags, the
United States steadfastly refused. This was the consequence of the
long and painful history of British searches of U.S. ships and impressment of seamen, one of the major causes of the War of 1812. Indeed,
while eschewing it in practice, the Royal Navy had never abandoned
the principle of impressment.

Even as strong an anti-slavery advocate as Secretary of State John
Quincy Adams (1817–1825) opposed granting the Royal Navy the right
to search American ships. When British Foreign Secretary George Can-
ning asked if there was anything more evil than the slave trade, Adams
said, "Yes, admitting the right of search by foreign officers of our vessels upon the seas in time of peace, for that would be making slaves of
ourselves." Strong Southern political pressure also worked against
enforcement.[4]

Such sentiment manifested itself in declining Congressional appropriations for suppression of the slave trade. In 1819 Congress authorized $100,000 for this work, but this shrank to $50,000 in 1823 and to
only $7,433.37 in 1839.[5]

As a consequence, most of the African slave trade was carried on in American-built vessels flying the Stars and Stripes. Swift American slave clippers immune from British search crowded the slave ports of Rio de Janeiro and Havana. Spanish, Portuguese, and Brazilian ships would often sail from Cuba or Brazil with false papers and an American on board who could pose as her captain if the ship were stopped by a Royal Navy vessel. By the early 1840s the situation was so bad that the governor of Liberia, Thomas Buchanan, claimed that the American flag was the chief obstacle to ending the slave trade.[6] In 1844 the American minister to Brazil reported:

> I regret to say this, but it is a fact not to be disguised or denied that the slave-trade is almost entirely carried on under our flag in American-built vessels, sold to slavers here, chartered for the coast of Africa, and these sold, or sold here—delivered on the coast. And, indeed, the scandalous traffic could not be carried on to any great extent were it not for the use made of our flag, and the facilities given for the chartering of American vessels to carry to the coast of Africa the outfit for the trade and the material for purchasing slaves.[7]

Such activity could be very lucrative. On her very first voyage the fast Baltimore-built *Venus*, which had cost $30,000, transported eight hundred slaves. They were then sold at a net profit of some $300 apiece, eight times the purchase price of the ship.

Mounting public pressure over the slave trade led President Martin Van Buren in 1838 to order that the U.S. Navy again patrol the West African coast. Although Secretary of the Navy James F. Paulding sent a number of small fast vessels there, little was accomplished in actually halting the traffic in slaves.[8]

In 1841 tensions over the stopping of American ships by Royal Navy cruisers led President John Tyler to declare in a speech to Congress that he recognized no difference between the rights of visit and search, and that if the British detained ships that turned out to be bonafide American they would be liable for damages. London, however, continued to press the United States to give up its ban on Royal Navy searches or to send a sufficient number of vessels to the African coast to investigate suspected slavers flying the American flag. Finally, the August 9, 1842, Webster-Ashburton Treaty, which also settled the long-running boundary dispute between the United States and Canada, provided for the maintenance of joint British-American squadrons to suppress the slave trade along the African coast. Each power committed itself to maintaining an African squadron mounting at least eighty guns. While the two squadrons would operate independently, they were to coordinate their actions to secure maximum effectiveness.

As a consequence of this agreement, in 1843 Congress provided funding for a much larger African squadron, initially commanded by Commodore Matthew C. Perry. His orders were to protect American commerce and suppress the slave trade carried out by Americans or under the U.S. flag. The same orders reminded Perry that Washington did not recognize the right of any other nation (*i.e.*, Britain) to visit or detain vessels belonging to American citizens.[9]

Foote's *Perry* was to join the African Squadron in 1849, commanded by Commodore Francis H. Gregory. It numbered five vessels mounting a total of seventy-eight guns, actually under the Webster-Ashburton Treaty minimum. The squadron had an immense area to patrol, from westernmost Africa at Cape Verde in Senegal to Cape Frio in southern Angola.

Given the paucity of its resources on station and the vast distances and problems involved, it is hardly surprising that the U.S. African Squadron took few slavers. By 1847 as many as 100,000 slaves a year were being shipped to the New World.[10]

While he was pleased to have his first command afloat and to be reunited with Gregory, who had been his first commanding officer, Foote was not excited about the prospects of African service. He even wrote to influential friends in Washington to try to get his orders changed to the Mediterranean Squadron. This was unsuccessful, and, as it turned out, Africa was an ideal assignment for the highly principled and staunchly Christian Foote.[11]

Foote knew the difficulties of African service. From any creek or estuary along five thousand miles of coastline slave ships might be loading their cargoes. Most slavers were fast sailing vessels, difficult to catch, and the West African coast was wild and inhospitable. Long known as the "white man's grave," it had fewer than one thousand whites, the vast majority of whom were traders restricted to the few coastal settlements. Searing heat alternated with torrential rains, ports of call were few, and crews ran the risk of contracting exotic diseases while in open boats on patrol.[12] As one naval historian has put it, "Hard work, yellow fever, frustration and adverse criticism were the usual rewards for African service."[13]

The *Perry*, rated at ten guns, had been built at the Norfolk Navy Yard and placed in service in October 1843. At 280 tons she was one of the faster vessels in the U.S. Navy. In and out of service throughout her life as a U.S. warship, she had already cruised off Africa. Armed with two 32-pounder long guns and six 32-pounder carronades, she had a crew of half a dozen officers and eighty seamen and Marines.[14]

The *Perry* sailed from Hampton Roads on November 27. Foote, who was one of the foremost advocates of naval temperance, was pleased that he had been able to get all crew members to sign the temperance pledge before sailing. The *Perry* made a fast crossing of the Atlantic without incident, although rough weather caused most of the officers and men to be seasick. The *Perry* joined the rest of the squadron at Porto Praya in the Cape Verde Islands on December 21. After reporting to Gregory in the Portsmouth, Foote oversaw preparing his ship for cruising off Africa.[15]

In early January 1850 British authorities at Porto Praya informed Commodore Gregory that American slavers were active along the coast south of the equator. This was below the normal American cruising area, and no U.S. warship had been in the area for three years. Foote and Gregory agreed that the *Perry* would spend at least five months off the coast and cruise as far south as 13° latitude. Foote's instructions called on him to intercept American slavers while protecting lawful U.S. vessels from search by other nations, to examine principal slave trading points below the equator, to cooperate with the Royal Navy where possible, to exercise his own judgment in other matters, and to be certain to look to the health of his crew.[16]

Foote was not optimistic, given his own rather precarious health and because he judged his ship poorly equipped for such a cruise. He had also discovered that his master and midshipmen were poor navigators and this forced him to take his own reckonings, which severely taxed his eyes, with which he had serious problems as a consequence of earlier service in the Mediterranean. Despite these difficulties Foote wrote that he hoped the cruise would be a chance for him to do humanity's work as well to "obtain a name" for himself.[17]

The *Perry* departed the Cape Verde Islands on January 9, 1850. Ten days later she arrived at Monrovia, Liberia, to take on provisions for the long trip south. Foote was also able to secure additional supplies from the sloop Yorktown, which was at Monrovia when she arrived.[18]

Founded in 1821 by the American Colonization Society with the aim of resettling blacks in Africa, the Republic of Liberia in 1850 was led by capable Virginia octoroon President Joseph J. Roberts. Foote arranged an exchange of visits, and when Roberts came aboard the *Perry* he welcomed him with a 21-gun salute. Monrovia's population was then two thousand and Foote was much impressed by what he saw there. Later he urged U.S. diplomatic recognition of Liberia and became an energetic supporter of the American Colonization Society. Convinced of the higher value of western civilization, and that whites had a duty to guide and uplift blacks, Foote saw that opportunity in Liberia, which offered the "freedom and incentives to higher motives of action . . . conducive to virtue." Christian missionaries could help by spreading the Gospel and introducing public education. Foote's visit to Monrovia was influential in shaping his attitude toward blacks, and he believed that, despite having begun their lives in bondage, blacks had "capacity beyond what we are inclined to admit."[19]

After her brief stop at Monrovia the *Perry* sailed south. She reached St. Philip de Benguela, the southernmost point of her sailing station, forty-one days later, on March 7. During the passage the Americans stopped and boarded three vessels, all found to be legal traders.

Foote's health had now worsened. In addition to problems with his eyesight, he developed headaches and lumbago and often was unable to leave his bed.[20]

He was also having problems with several of his officers, most notably First Lieutenant William B. Renshaw. Although Foote was not opposed to corporal punishment, he preferred to influence the crew through example and religious instruction, and Renshaw and others disagreed with this approach. Foote wrote in his journal on January 29, "I am determined however to carry out my own system wherever I do command."[21]

Foote was handicapped in his operations because St. Philip de Benguela was hopelessly removed from Porto Praya. Counting the stop at Monrovia, it took the *Perry* two months to reach there. The distances involved left little time on station before the brig would run short of water and provisions and have to return to Porto Praya. In a report to the Navy Department he argued unsuccessfully for a more southerly base closer to the center of slave trading activities.[22]

On arriving off the Portuguese settlement of St. Paul de Loanda, Foote learned that American merchants were conducting a growing trade in the region in dye-stuffs, gums and palm oil. This American financial stake was actually greater than that of the British, French, or

Portuguese, all of whom had squadrons along the southern African coast and consuls to protect their interests.[23]

Foote wrote to the Navy Department to recommend that the United States establish a permanent African coastal presence both in "one or two men of war" and diplomatic personnel. He also spelled out how slave running was being conducted in ships with two sets of papers, one American and the other Brazilian. The ship would originally have been American, sold in Latin America but retaining her original papers. She would sail to Africa with an American captain and crew and legitimate cargo. There the identity would change. Usually a Portuguese or Brazilian captain and crew would come on board along with the cargo of slaves. The ship would then sail with the American papers, which could be presented if stopped. If in the rare chance that a slaver was stopped by a U.S. warship, her captain would show the legitimate foreign registration.[24]

Although Foote publicly expressed his approval of the U.S. stance on refusing British captains the right to search American flag ships, in private he was troubled by it, especially when he learned the way slavers were using the American flag, as in the case of the barque *Navarre*, boarded by H.M.S. *Firefly* on March 19 "when under American colors, and captured under Brazilian colors." He believed that his government's approach had put the country "on the side of the slave traders."[25]

British captains were glad to have a U.S. warship in the area and they approached Foote about cruising with them. He agreed, and the *Perry* soon headed for the area around Ambriz, a notorious slave port, there to patrol with several British warships. Most of the time the *Perry* operated with the steam frigate H.M.S. *Cyclops*, commanded by Captain George F. Hastings. Foote stopped and checked all ships flying the U.S. flag and used his boats in shore to search for slavers and slave collection points. The boats were on occasion away for a week or more.[26]

Such work was difficult and took a toll on Foote's health. Forced to spend much of the time in bed in his cabin, he became convinced he was near death. The duty also affected his crew; several applied for reinstatement of their grog ration, although he managed to talk them out of it. He continued to have problems with Renshaw, who had by now alienated much of the crew and the other officers.[27]

Foote must have been greatly cheered by the arrival in early April of the sloop *John Adams*, another ship in the American squadron, which then joined the *Perry* in patrol. This did not last long; the *Perry* was low on supplies and water and soon sailed for Prince's Island in the Gulf of Guinea to rendezvous with the flagship *Portsmouth*.

The *Perry* arrived at Prince's Island on April 27, and Foote immediately reported to Gregory. The cruise had lasted 107 days: eighty at sea and the remainder at anchor at various points along the coast. Gregory commended Foote for the discharge of his duties, but with the *John Adams* running short of provisions he ordered Foote to secure needed stores from the flagship and return to Ambriz.[28]

The brief stay on Prince's Island did wonders for Foote's health. He enjoyed several restful days ashore, eating fresh food and being able to bathe. He also persuaded Gregory to take on Lieutenant Renshaw as his flag lieutenant, which he reported had an immediate calming effect aboard the *Perry*.[29]

Gregory's new instructions were the same as before, with one notable exception. The commodore was unhappy with reports of the British detaining suspect American flag vessels and then threatening to hand them over for search by American warships. Gregory wanted Foote to assert U.S. authority. If a British captain decided to detain a suspected American ship he must do so on his own authority and not think he could rely on U.S. Navy connivance.[30]

Foote disagreed. He believed that the American flag was only "prima facie" and not "conclusive proof" of nationality. While it would be wrong for the crew of a British warship to stop an American vessel and search her, no matter her cargo, this did not apply to a ship that was not American and was falsely flying the flag.[31]

Foote's boarding instructions, however, followed Gregory's orders:[32]

> If a vessel hoists the American flag—is of American build, has the name and place of ownership in the United States registered on her stern, or has but a part of these indications of her nationality— you will on boarding ask for her papers, which papers you will examine and retain, if she exacts suspicion of being a slaver, until you have searched sufficiently to satisfy yourself of her real character. If the vessel be American and doubts exist as to her character you will detain and bring her to this vessel, or if it can be done more expediently, you will dispatch one of your boats, communicating such information as will enable me to give specific directions, or to visit the vessel in person.
>
> If the vessel be a foreigner, you will on the moment of ascertaining the fact, leave her, declining even the request of the captain

to search, or to endorse her character as it must always be borne in mind that our government does not permit the search and detention of American vessels by foreign cruisers, and is consequently particular to observe towards the vessels of other nations the same line of conduct, which she exacts from foreign cruisers toward her own vessels. You will also remember that our squadron is on this coast solely for the protection of American commerce, and for the suppression of the slave trade as far as it may be carried on by American citizens, or under the American flag.

The *Perry* returned to her station off Ambriz. After boarding several vessels, all of which turned out to be legal traders, on June 6 Foote got lucky, probably because no U.S. Navy vessels were expected in the area for some time. At 3 p.m. that day a lookout on the *Perry* spotted a large ship standing in for Ambriz. An hour later the *Perry*, which had no colors flying, overhauled the ship, which had "Martha, New York" painted on her stern. Her captain, believing the brig to be a Royal Navy vessel, shortened sail and promptly hoisted the American flag. Foote then sent Second Lieutenant (Acting First Lieutenant) Madison Rush to board her.

As Rush's boat rounded the stern of the *Martha*, her captain, Henry M. Merrill, recognized the U.S. naval uniform and promptly ordered the U.S. flag hauled down and the Brazilian flag raised in its stead. When Rush demanded the ship's papers, Merrill said he had none. At the same time a lookout on the *Perry* saw men aboard the *Martha* throw something over-board and Foote sent another boat to retrieve it. It turned out to be the captain's writing desk, containing the log and papers identifying Merrill as a U.S. citizen and stating that the majority owner of the vessel was another American, living in Rio de Janeiro.

There were no slaves yet aboard, but all the equipment for the dreaded "Middle Passage" from Africa to the West Indies or the United States was in place, including a fully laid slave deck, 176 water casks filled with one hundred to one hundred fifty gallons each, one hundred fifty barrels of farina, and several sacks of beans to keep the human cargo alive during the passage. She also carried four hundred spoons, four boilers for cooking, and thirty to forty muskets.

Foote had ordered Rush to hold the ship to the first flag she raised. Captain Merrill protested that his vessel could not be searched or seized while she was under the Brazilian flag. Foote's response was that he would then seize his ship as a pirate vessel for sailing without papers. Merrill then confessed that his vessel was indeed a slaver and that he had expected that night to take on board eighteen hundred slaves and would have been at sea before daybreak.

Merrill begged him not to, but Foote ordered the *Martha*'s 35-man crew placed in irons. He sent the ship to New York under Rush, along with Acting Lieutenant Maurice Simons and a prize crew of twenty-five men, there to be condemned and sold. In New York Merrill jumped bond and escaped punishment; his first lieutenant was convicted and sentenced to two years in prison. The rest of the crew, being foreigners, were released. The capture of the *Martha* earned Captain Hastings' congratulations. He told Foote that he had given the slave trade "the heaviest blow" it had received since he had been on the African station.[33]

The rest of the *Perry*'s cruise was uneventful, although the men had to work harder than before now that their numbers were reduced by a third. Foote himself was buoyed by his triumph and busied himself with the daily operations of the brig. He was pleased that the crew retained a positive attitude despite the difficult conditions and added work.[34]

When at their next meeting Gregory praised Foote for the efficiency and hard work of his reduced crew, Foote saw an opening and attributed it to his methods of discipline and especially to a grog-free environment. The imperfect nature of this system of discipline may be seen, however, in that the same week Foote ordered two of his crewmen flogged, one for drunkenness and the other for smuggling alcohol aboard ship.[35]

In early August the *Perry* returned to Loanda for a prearranged meeting between Foote, Gregory, and British squadron commander Commodore Arthur Fanshawe. On August 15 Fanshawe arrived in the *Cyclops*. The three men met to see if they might resolve their differences regarding searches of possible slavers. Fanshawe claimed that all vessels taken by the Royal Navy were at least partially Brazilian. He also said that, had any of them clearly been U.S. vessels, the British would not have interfered with them. Gregory argued that the British had indeed interfered with bona fide U.S. merchant ships, and that even if they were involved in illegal trade these ships were off limits to the British. The U.S. Navy would be responsible for U.S. ships involved in the slave trade. As he put it, "we choose to punish our own rascals in our own way."[36]

Foote took no part in the discussions. It would have been inappropriate for him as a junior officer to have questioned his commander in such a matter, but he was clearly unhappy with Washington's position regarding searches. As he put it in his journal, "I had little or no sympathy for them & rather than had them escape was gratified that the English had captured them." Foote would have preferred that U.S. warships had taken them, but until the *Perry*'s service no U.S. warship had been off the southern African coast in at least two years. The United States had not even lived up to its obligation to maintain an 80-gun squadron on anti-slavery patrol.[37]

The meeting between the British and American commanders was interrupted on August 18 with the arrival of a British merchantman with news of a suspected slaver in Ambriz, less than a day's sail away. The Royal Navy had boarded her in the belief that she was Brazilian; on learning that she was American, they requested a U.S. Navy warship. Gregory immediately dispatched Foote to investigate.

Foote was able to intercept the suspected slaver, which proved to be the brigantine *Chatsworth* of Baltimore. Her papers seemed to be in order, but her crew was entirely foreign with the exception of her young American captain. Foote was certain the *Chatsworth* was a slaver and instructed Renshaw to sail her to Loanda for disposition. There he explained to Gregory his reasons for seizing her. Her cargo included one hundred bags of farina, jerked beef, and casks and barrels sufficient to carry water for a large slave cargo. She also carried a quantity of plank sufficient to build a slave deck. A letter from the reputed owner of the ship, written in Portuguese, instructed the American captain that he was to leave the ship whenever he was directed to do so by an Italian supercargo by the name of Francisco Serralunga, who seemed to be the final authority on the ship. The *Chatsworth* was also known to have shipped a cargo of slaves on her last voyage and she had been apprehended at one of the most notorious locations for slaving. Although Gregory agreed with Foote that the *Chatsworth* was probably a slaver, he nonetheless ordered her released, concluding there was insufficient evidence to gain a judgment in a U.S. court.[38]

At the end of August Gregory returned to Porto Praya; before departing he told Foote that, much as he regretted this decision, no other ships were available and the *Perry* would have to resume her patrol duties along the southern African coast. On August 24, 1850, the brig began her third cruise in the area.

Foote had not forgotten about the *Chatsworth*, and he now attempted a ruse in hopes of catching her in slaving. The *Perry* originally sailed south from Loanda, but once she was out of sight of land Foote ordered a new course to the north for Ambriz. Again he caught the *Chatsworth* off that port and conducted a thorough search of her, but he could find no evidence of slavery activities. When on September 5 Foote again departed Ambriz he left behind some men in the brig's cutter to keep the *Chatsworth* under surveillance.[39]

Foote then sailed the *Perry* north to the Angolan port of Ambrizete. Believing it would be to the benefit of an American-owned factory there, Foote went ashore to meet with the queen of the area. He tried to impress on her the advantages that would accrue from "trading with our people with gum, copper, bronze, instead of permitting her own people to be sold as slaves for the purchase of goods." The queen complained about warships, and especially their boats, chasing her fishing boats and taking their catch, "the principal support of her people." Foote assured her that the U.S. Navy was forbidden to do this and that "we were her friends and the friends of her people." He concluded that occasional visits with native authorities would help increase U.S. trade.[40]

When the *Perry* again returned to Ambriz, Foote learned that four thousand slaves had been gathered to be shipped from the area. Determined to prevent this, on September 11 Foote ordered the *Chatsworth* seized. To assure that this time the charges would stick, Foote secured statements from legitimate traders in the area that the ship had earlier been engaged in slaving activities and that her owner in Rio had admitted that he was ordering her on another slaving voyage.

Foote informed Gregory that he could prove the *Chatsworth* carried two sets of papers: one U.S. and the other Brazilian. He also managed to secure a confession from the ship's master of her true mission. Italian supercargo "Serralunga," who was ashore inspecting the slaves to be loaded when the vessel was seized, protested what he described as an illegal seizure and asserted that no U.S. court would ever condemn the vessel for slave running. He also threatened Foote with $15,000 in damages; Foote said he was willing to run that risk. Almost certainly "Serralunga" was Theodore Canot, a prominent figure in the African slave trade known as "Mr. Gunpowder" for his violent rages. Foote believed he was the real owner. Ignoring his threats, Foote sent the *Chatsworth* to Baltimore under Acting Sailing Master (passed midshipman) Edmund Shepherd and Midshipman Oliver P. Allen, where after a prolonged trial in district court she was indeed condemned as a slaver. Foote believed she was a greater loss to the African slave trade than the *Martha*.[41]

In defying his commanding officer's earlier judgment and possibly embarrassing him, Foote risked his naval career; he had also laid himself open to possible personal financial ruin. The *Chatsworth* incident clearly shows Foote's determination to pursue a course he believed morally correct, regardless of possible personal consequences.

The rest of the *Perry's* cruise was without incident, and on September 19 Foote ordered her to sail for St. Helena in the South Atlantic. During the passage to the island the *Perry* chased down one vessel, which turned out to be a Portuguese brig. On October 10 she arrived at Jamestown, St. Helena, for what would be a ten-day stay and a well earned rest for the crew.

Foote established a cordial relationship with the British authorities on St. Helena, although he did press his case in the matter of several vessels the British captured. He held that because these ships carried false U.S. papers, they should be considered as under U.S. Navy jurisdiction. The British may have thought this a matter of ego or cash incentive for Foote, but it was for him purely a legal issue. Privately he acknowledged that much of American African trade was indirectly bound up in the slave trade, and he never doubted British motives. As he concluded, "I really believe . . . that the British officers generally mean to do right & act liberally in the suppression of the slave trade. Our flag has been much abused & I do wish that an arrangement might be made by which all slavers might be taken by any nation."[42]

After a passage of ten days from St. Helena the *Perry* arrived at Loanda. After several days there she resumed cruising off Ambriz in the company of the *Cyclops*. Foote was able to report to Secretary of the Navy William A. Graham that after the capture of the *Chatsworth* there were "no suspicious American vessels on the Coast."[43]

At the end of December his ship's food and stores almost depleted and his crew reduced in half by the need to man the captures, Foote ordered the *Perry* to return to Porto Praya. By then he and two young acting lieutenants were her only remaining officers. The *Perry* had been almost constantly on station an entire year, during which time she had sailed some twenty-one thousand miles. In reflecting about the cruise in his journal, Foote expressed pride in his accomplishments. Without doubt it had been the most taxing year of his life, but "with God's blessing" he had handled a difficult and responsible diplomatic and naval assignment well and accomplished much for himself, for the Navy, and for his country.[44]

On January 8, 1851, the *Perry* dropped anchor at Porto Praya. Foote fully expected that Gregory would order him and his ship home. He and his men were worn out, and the *Perry* was now in serious need of repairs. Concerns about his ship were real. Even before leaving the United States he had pointed out that the *Perry* had been rushed back into service without the overhaul she should have received after her previous cruise. Within a month of her sailing, on December 22, 1849, Foote had written a long letter to Chief of the Bureau of Construction Equipment and Repair Commodore Charles Skinner enumerating numerous complaints: the *Perry* was leaking badly, her copper was worn out, and much of her rigging needed to be replaced. Now, more than a year later, he could add to that list the need of a new suit of sails and new wood and iron fittings.[45]

Instead, Gregory, who had few ships and a vast area of responsibility, ordered Foote to embark on another Angolan cruise. Foote believed this could be a death sentence, and it led him to an explosion of anger and an indiscretion that almost caused Gregory to order him home without his ship.[46]

The unstated and real cause of problems between the two men was Foote's anger at seeing his ship the only active member of the squadron and Gregory's refusal to order the brig and her crew home. In order to make up the serious shortage in his own officers, Foote requested that officers on the flagship be transferred to him. He especially wanted Lieutenant William M. Porter as his executive officer. Protocol and common sense dictated that he first informally ask Porter and then Gregory before making a formal request. A misunderstanding led to a series of sharp notes between Foote and Gregory. Foote even asked that he be relieved of his command to plead his case personally before the secretary of the navy. To his credit, Gregory worked to defuse the situation by assuring Foote of his full confidence, support, and friendship. Foote then accepted Gregory's remarks as proof of vindication.[47]

Foote, assisted by two additional officers, one of them new First Lieutenant Porter, and some men to make up for those sent home in two prize crews, now prepared the *Perry* for yet another cruise below the equator, including installing a new suit of sails provided by the sailmaker on the Portsmouth.

The *Perry* left Porto Praya on February 20 and arrived off Ambriz twenty-two days later. Her third cruise off the southern Africa coast was uneventful. British officials at Loanda informed Foote that there was now little slavery activity in the area. Only one slaver had been taken since January. Foote then sailed his brig north to the vicinity of the mouth of the Congo River, another active point for the slave trade, where he again cooperated with the British squadron. The new British commodore told him that joint British-American efforts had virtually ended the slave trade on the southern coast. As the *Perry* represented almost the entire American effort in that regard, Foote must have been pleased.[48]

The more relaxed nature of the third cruise was reflected in a second visit to St. Helena, beginning on May 29. Later Foote allowed his crew liberty in Elephants' Bay along the African coast south of the Congo River, where the men fished and hunted. Foote hoped to shoot a few rare tropical birds as specimens for the Philadelphia Academy of Science, but apparently the men were not sufficiently good shots to accomplish this.[49]

After a stop at Monrovia on June 30 the *Perry* returned to Porto Praya. Foote was disappointed that no U.S. warships were in the port and no orders to return home. The *Perry* was now leaking badly and her rigging and iron work had further deteriorated. Foote was particularly anxious to sail the Atlantic in the summer; a winter crossing might prove disastrous for the brig in her weakened state. Morale was low and discipline had sharply deteriorated. There was a corresponding increase in punishments, and a number of crew members petitioned Foote for restoration of the grog ration. Foote noted in his journal that even the officers were affected and "in a great state of excitement and indignation at Commodore Gregory."[50]

New squadron commander Commodore Eli LaVallette, who had sailed a few days earlier, left word that Foote was either to wait at Porto Praya or to proceed to Funchal, Madeira. Foote elected for the latter. The *Perry* arrived at Funchal on August 8 and spent six weeks there. Shore liberty greatly improved morale.

Foote was, however, furious when he learned that Gregory, without personally inspecting the brig, had informed his successor that she was fit for additional service. Although the nimble *Perry* was the only one of Gregory's ships suitable for extended coastal work against slavers, Foote was justified in his conclusion that for the past two years she had been the only vessel in the squadron actively employed.[51]

Leaving Madeira on September 20, the *Perry* arrived at Porto Praya on October 1. Finally, on November 12 Commodore LaVallette arrived at the port, came aboard the *Perry*, and informed Foote that he had just received orders dated June 17 to send her home. Foote and his crew now worked quickly to prepare the *Perry* for what would now be a hazardous winter Atlantic crossing. On November 15 the crew hoisted anchor. The *Perry* sailed out into the Atlantic, accompanied by cheers from seamen on the other ships of the squadron. Foote wrote in his journal: "Thus adieu to the coast of Africa. . . . I shall never perhaps in life be called upon to act again so responsible a part on my own judgment."[52]

The Atlantic crossing was without incident and accomplished in twenty-six days. On December 23, 1851, the *Perry* tied up at the Brooklyn Navy Yard. She had been gone twenty-five months and had traveled 40,500 miles.[53]

Foote spent the next four years ashore, the longest such period since he had joined the Navy. Tired and spent, he was no doubt pleased to receive an official letter of thanks from Commodore Gregory and new Secretary of the Navy James C. Dobbin.[54]

Foote's achievements had indeed been remarkable. His crew had stopped and boarded seventy vessels. They had seized only two of these, but they were among the most important slavers taken in this period and both actions had been upheld by U.S. courts. Put in perspective, during the period 1843–1857 the U.S. African Squadron took only nineteen vessels, of which only six were condemned. Foote's tally was a third of the total.[55]

It is also remarkable that not one crew member died during the *Perry's* two years in African service; the death rate for the British squadron during the period was five percent. Foote attributed the excellent health of his crew to not allowing the men to stay on shore at night and their lack of a grog ration.[56] Although he and his men were disappointed that they never received prize money for the two African captures, Foote had the satisfaction of having established his reputation both as an energetic naval commander and accomplished seaman. He claimed this was worth more to him than any financial gain.[57]

Foote, who was promoted to commander in December 1852, now flung himself into reform activities. He visited Washington to lobby Congress for an end to the spirit ration. In his free time he was a frequent public lecturer on topics as temperance, improving conditions for sailors, and support for overseas missionaries.[58] He was also in the forefront of efforts to end the slave trade. Although a northerner and a Whig, he had never been an abolitionist and regarded Southern slavery as rather benign, but he returned from Africa convinced that the way to end slavery was to support efforts at colonization in Liberia. He joined the American Colonization Society and became one of its most ardent backers. In speeches he told of his firsthand knowledge of the effectiveness of the Liberian experiment. He was impressed with Liberia's leaders, especially President Roberts, and he was convinced that the country would soon become rich with an economy based on agriculture, mining, and trade. Liberia could be a beacon for the rest of Africa. Privately he expressed the view that if he were black he would want to live in Liberia. Even if they were no longer slaves, blacks in America would still be in bondage to the white power structure and white racial attitudes.[59]

Foote was particularly concerned over the possibility that the American African Squadron might be disbanded. There was much talk in Congress that U.S. warships were no longer necessary off Africa and that the squadron was a financial drain. Secretary of the Navy Graham was one of those who favored disbanding the squadron and allocating its vessels elsewhere. Foote opposed this in a letter to Graham, in public speeches, and on trips to Washington that included conversations with Senator John M. Clayton of Delaware and even President Millard Fillmore.[60]

In April 1853 Foote received a letter from Navy Captain James L. Lardner of the *Dale*, who had just returned from Africa where his ship had captured two slavers. Lardner criticized the squadron's activities, noting that it seemed that "many of our naval officers are more afraid of slavers than the rascals are of them." This lack of action, he believed, had led to an increase in slavery activities, much to the shame of the United States Navy and the American flag.[61]

Lardner's letter may have been the final impetus for Foote, but in mid-1853 he began work on what would be his first and only serious writing effort, a book about Africa and the activities of the U.S. Navy African Squadron. He saw it as a means to persuade those in government to continue the effort to suppress the African slave trade and to publicize Liberia. He also hoped to secure personal recognition. Increasingly concerned about his health and aware that because of the seniority system he might finish his naval career as a commander, Foote saw the book as his possible legacy. He had ample time to write; his only Navy duties during this time period were to serve as judge advocate in courts martial of three officers held at nearby navy yards.[62]

In 1854 Foote published *Africa and the American Flag*. The book is a well-written account in which he stresses the contrasts of his African experience. It also is sometimes quite eloquent, as in this passage:[63]

> It is difficult in looking over the ship's side to conceive the transparency of the sea. The reflection of the blue sky in these tropic regions colors it like an opaque sapphire, till some fish startles one by suddenly appearing from beneath, seeming to carry daylight down with him into the depths below. One is then reminded that the vessel is suspended over a transparent abyss. There for ages has sunk the dark-skinned sufferer from "the horrors of the middle passage," carrying that ghastly daylight down with him, to rest "until the sea shall give up its dead," and the slaver and his merchant come from their places to be confronted with their victim.

The first two-thirds of the book treats African geography, botany, climate, zoology, and culture of western Africa, and Western efforts, including those of the United States, to halt the slave trade. Foote relied heavily on records of the American Colonization Society and secondary works by other authors. This section contains much conjecture, but it also contains a history of Liberia and operations of the American Colonization Society.

The last third of the book, its most important part, is the record of his own experiences in Africa with the U.S. squadron, in which he detailed efforts to suppress the slave trade. In it he praised the Colonization Society and made a strong argument for maintaining the U.S. African Squadron. He argued that the squadron was necessary in order to protect a growing American trade with Africa from both slavers and illegal searches by Royal Navy warships. He also pointed out that the U.S. squadron had helped reduce the slave trade because slavers could no longer hide behind the U.S. flag immune from British search. Finally, the squadron would assure the continuing success of Liberia and the spread of Christianity in Africa. Problems for the squadron could be alleviated by moving its base from Porto Praya closer to the actual U.S. cruising station and adding fast steamers.[64]

Foote made clear the horror of the slave trade and heaped contempt on those who profited from its great human misery. One day they would have to answer to God for "the theft of living men, the foulness and corruption of the steaming slave-deck, and the charnel-house of wretchedness and despair."[65]

It is hard to tell the exact impact of the book on decision-making in Washington. Foote did send copies, along with covering letters, to influential friends in the capital, and during Congressional debate on the African Squadron, Senator Clayton read from a letter Foote had written. But sentiment in favor of maintaining the squadron had grown when, the year before, new Secretary of the Navy Dobbin had come out in favor of its continuation. As it turned out, Congress did not change the status quo; the African Squadron continued.[66]

Navy officers, educators, leaders in the colonization movement, Protestant clergy, and newspapers across the country praised Foote's book, which was soon also published in London and established Foote as a leading figure within the African colonization movement.

On January 18, 1855, Foote addressed the annual meeting of the Board of Directors of the American Colonization Society. In his remarks he supported legislation to deny consular sea-letters to American vessels sold abroad if they were bound for Africa. The ease of obtaining these had enabled many slavers to claim American nationality. He also argued for continued close cooperation between the Royal and U.S. Navies as vital in intercepting suspected slavers, and he suggested that if there was to be any modification in the Webster-Ashburton Treaty that it should take the form of specifying the inclusion of small, light draft steamers in the American squadron. The Society then adopted a resolution supporting continuation of the Webster-Ashburton Treaty in its entirety and keeping the African Squadron on station and at full strength, rendering it more efficient by the inclusion of small steamers. The board also authorized publication of Foote's speech as a pamphlet; it appeared that same year under the title, "The African Squadron: Ashburton Treaty: Consular Sea Letters." Undoubtedly Foote's efforts helped sway the Congressional decision not to end the Webster-Ashburton Treaty.[67]

The African cruise changed Foote, and its mission remained a passion. He continued to speak out for African colonization and vigorous U.S. action to suppress the slave trade. In July 1859 he sent Secretary of the Navy Isaac Toucey a long letter on the subject, in which he reiterated the reasons for vigorous enforcement. He argued for a supply depot to support operations off the southern African coast and, in contrast to many of his fellow officers, for vigorous cooperation with the Royal Navy as the best way to end the trade. He also believed that a strong U.S. presence off the African coast would help promote the success of Liberia. He saw his own best chance to secure a niche in history as being in suppression of the African slave trade, and he hoped to help accomplish this in command of one of the Navy's new light-draft steamers.[68]

Foote's lobbying for an African Squadron billet was unsuccessful. Shortly after the Civil War began he received command of the U.S. Navy flotilla in the West and won the Union's first great victory in February 1862 by capturing Fort Henry on the Tennessee River, which won him promotion to admiral. He also participated in the Union victories at Fort Donelson and Island No. 10. However, a wound received in the attack at Fort Donelson, illness, and the strain of his work all took a toll. In April he left the Mississippi Squadron to recover. Even then African service remained in his mind. In July 1862, when he wrote Secretary of the Navy Gideon Welles to request extended leave, he asked: "When the rebellion is crushed and a squadron is fitted out to enforce the new treaty for the suppression of the African slave-trade, I should be pleased to have command."[69]

It was not to be. Returning to active service as head of the Bureau of Equipment and Recruiting, Foote was then named to command the South Atlantic Blockading Squadron. Andrew Foote died in New York City on June 26, 1863, of Bright's disease while waiting to take up his command. While he is principally remembered for his duty in China and his Civil War service, the assignment of which Foote was most proud during his long career was his command of the brig *Perry* in helping to halt the African slave trade.

JACOB NEUFELD

The F-15 Eagle: Origins and Development, 1964–1972

*A*s the war in Southeast Asia escalated—particularly after air-to-air
*combat operations over North Vietnam intensified—U.S. Air Force
leaders saw clearly that the service needed a new air superiority fighter. After
USAF officials initiated studies in 1965 aimed at defining such an aircraft, a
lengthy concept formulation phase ensued, during which emerged the important
theory of energy maneuverability. In 1969, after the Air Force was authorized
to proceed with the project, contract definition studies got under way; industry
competition followed, and by year's end the winning contractor was selected. Led
by Maj. Gen. Benjamin N. Bellis, the Air Force overcame opponents, critics, and
bureaucracy to produce the world's premier fighter.*

That Central Bird

The Air Force owed its very existence to the principle of centralized
control of air resources by a separate service commander. This doctrine's chief value lay in its flexibility to exploit the combat situation
while managing air resources economically. Given no cost limits and a

reduced tactical force structure, the Air Force predictably selected multipurpose rather than specialized aircraft.

Inflation and the war in Southeast Asia, however, paved the way for low-cost, specialized aircraft. Accordingly, in October 1965, the Air Force moved to acquire Navy A-7s for close air support until it could develop its own A-X candidate for this mission. Besides satisfying the penchant of the Office of the Secretary of Defense (OSD) for commonality and averting forfeiture of the close air support role to the Army, this stratagem helped the Air Force to make a case for replacing its aging F-4 fleet by the mid-1970s. Indeed, the Air Force's advanced tactical fighter concept, the F-X, began life as the best combination of air-to-ground and air-to-air capabilities. These features, plus its short takeoff and landing (STOL) capability, won the F-15 initial funding support for design studies.

However, because diverse interests within the Air Force wanted to stamp their particular imprint upon the aircraft, the F-15 emerged as a highly compromised design that stood little chance of gaining approval. In addition, the Air Force—faced with keen competition from the Navy for funds—had to overcome the OSD Systems Analysis staff's campaign to replace tactical air's inventory of large, sophisticated aircraft with smaller, less costly ones.

In a masterful stroke, the Air Force in the spring of 1968 adopted air superiority—the *sine qua non* of aerial combat—as the best way out of its dilemma. South Vietnam's "permissive environment," the Air Force argued, had lulled OSD into pursuing the mistaken policy of "assuming" air superiority in weapon system development. But the air war over North Vietnam had already shown that even older MiGs could outclass sophisticated but less maneuverable U.S. fighters. Only by hurriedly installing an aerial gun in the F-4 did the USAF manage to keep an air-combat edge. Furthermore, the Air Force emphasized the folly of assuming air superiority over Europe—a region of more vital concern to the United States. The Moscow Air Show in July 1967 forcefully brought this point home when the Soviets paraded a half-dozen new fighters for Americans to evaluate and contend with in the years ahead.

In the summer of 1968, the Air Force rallied behind a new slogan: "To fly and fight." It applied a 40,000-pound weight limit on the F-15 and pointed the design toward an uncompromised air superiority fighter. Significantly, the design yielded a bountiful "fallout" capability: at little extra cost, the F-15 could carry enough fuel, armaments, and avionics to perform a host of air-to-ground missions as well. In short, the Air Force advertised air superiority, while in fact developing a worthy successor to the F-4. The F-15 became "that central bird" the Air Force needed for flexibility under its centralized control doctrine.

The Air Superiority Mission

After the Korean War, President Dwight D. Eisenhower adopted a policy of nuclear deterrence that relied primarily on strategic air power and downgraded the conventional mission of tactical fighter aircraft. For example, the Century series fighters (F-100 through F-111) were increasingly designed for use against strategic targets in nuclear war rather than for tactical air combat.

Although air superiority remained the "prerequisite" for conducting air operations, the emphasis had shifted to penetration over maneuverability; bomb load-carrying capacity over armament; and alert status over sortie rates. As Air Force Vice Chief of Staff Gen. Bruce K. Holloway noted in 1968, "The tactical fighter became less and less an air superiority system and more and more what was once called an attack aircraft."[1]

This shift in emphasis ignored the political and geographic limitations that had shackled the Far East Air Forces in Korea. The USAF now promoted attacks on "airfields and parked aircraft . . . fuel and ammunition dumps, maintenance facilities and command and control centers" as "the most lucrative method" of gaining air superiority.[2]

But the linkage of tactical fighters and air superiority was not without its proponents, and one of the most determined advocates of air superiority was Maj. Gen. Arthur C. "Sailor" Agan. Upon becoming Air Staff Director of Plans in July 1964, Agan found that many Pentagon officials believed that the dogfight and aerial guns were relics of the past and that missiles would dominate future air battles. Army members of the Joint Staff in particular questioned the effectiveness of all tactical fighters and argued that surface-to-air missiles (SAMs) would impose unacceptable losses on fighter aircraft.[3]

But Agan, a former World War II P-38 pilot and group commander who flew forty-five combat missions over Europe, was convinced that high performance fighter aircraft would survive and remain the key to successful ground operations. Unfortunately, the Air Force had acquired two new multipurpose fighters—the F-4C and the F-111—and was in no position to ask for development of another fighter.

The Office of the Secretary of Defense, particularly Secretary Robert S. McNamara's Systems Analysis staff, favored purchasing large numbers of small, inexpensive attack aircraft for the tactical air forces.[4] McNamara's staff measured the effectiveness of air superiority, close air support, and interdiction "by their impact on the force ratio between opposing land forces, and thus . . . the land/air 'trade-off' would be a decisive factor in sizing U.S. tactical air forces."[5] Agan and the Air Staff did not oppose this approach, but they believed that in wartime little could be done without first achieving air superiority and argued that the United States should acquire the best possible fighters in the world.

Although Agan failed to convert OSD officials, he managed to persuade Chief of Staff Gen. John P. McConnell that a new fighter was needed. Agan drafted a policy statement on tactical air superiority that McConnell circulated Air Force-wide in May 1965—after combat operations over North Vietnam had begun—recognizing the Air Force's requirement "to win air superiority."[6]

The War's Impact

OSD became interested in acquiring new fighters only after it became clear that USAF aircraft providing close air support for South Vietnamese troops were obsolete and dangerous. But in January 1965, McNamara allotted only $10 million in fiscal year 1966 to modify existing USAF tactical aircraft. He also directed the Air Force to consider developing a new fighter "optimized for close support and useful in ground attack" and instructed the service to assume tactical air superiority in their planning for Vietnam.[7] This instruction disturbed Secretary of the Air Force Eugene M. Zuckert and Air Staff officials.[8]

Meanwhile, an Air Staff group, chaired by Lt. Col. John W. Bohn, Jr., had been working since August 1964 to critically assess USAF reliance on high-performance tactical fighters. Completed in late February 1965,[9] the Bohn study recommended that the Air Force acquire a mix of high- and low-cost aircraft as the most economical way to strengthen the tactical force. For the support role, the study narrowed the candidates to the lightweight, comparatively inexpensive F-5 and the Navy A-7.[10]

McConnell subsequently advised Zuckert that the Bohn study showed the folly of assuming air superiority, citing recent Defense Intelligence Agency estimates that new Soviet interceptors posed a threat beyond the capability of existing U.S. forces to counter. He argued that air superiority required fighter aircraft to survive attacks by both enemy interceptors and antiaircraft weapons.[11] For the close air support mission, he proposed bringing a mix of lower-cost aircraft into the Air Force inventory.

Zuckert forwarded the Bohn study to OSD and recommended the Air Force be authorized to purchase two wings of F-5s as an interim measure while beginning work on a medium-cost tactical fighter for the 1970s. Zuckert told McNamara that the proposed new fighter would also have "significant air-to-air fighting capability."[12] Meanwhile, an Air Staff study completed in June 1965 under the direction of Col. Bruce Hinton concluded that the A-7 would be the best close support aircraft if the Air Force could assume air superiority. However, Hinton's group questioned that assumption and recommended the Air Force select an improved version of the F-5—not the export model.[13]

Aware of Air Staff disagreement about the A-7 vs. the F-5 and noting OSD's indecision on the matter, Zuckert chose not to press for the latter until the Air Force had crystallized its position on tactical forces.[14] Another important reason for delay was to enable the Air Staff to undertake a detailed examination of the proposed medium-cost F-X (fighter experimental).

F-X Working Group

In April 1965, Dr. Harold Brown, Director of Defense Research and Engineering (DDR&E), lent his support to the official Air Force position, agreeing to the interim acquisition of the F-5 and authorizing development of an F-X.[15] Thereupon, Lt. Gen. James Ferguson, Deputy Chief of Staff for R&D, established an Air Staff work group, to conduct prerequisite studies for an F-X to cost between $1-2 million each, with a production run of 800 to 1,000 aircraft. The contemplated fighter would possess "superior air-to-air, all-weather, and aided-visual-ground attack" capabilities. It also was envisioned as a single-seat, twin-engine fighter stressing maneuverability over speed. The F-X's initial operational capability (IOC) was 1970.[16]

DDR&E representatives told the F-X group it could obtain study funds only if the F-X was presented as a multipurpose fighter; any attempt to depict it as a specialized combat plane would fail.[17] This view was shared by elements of the Air Staff.[18] Supporters of an air superiority fighter, including Generals Ferguson and Jack J. Catton, Director of Operational Requirements, therefore decided to disguise the F-X as a multipurpose fighter and emphasized air-to-ground capability over air-to-air. In August, the Air Force requested and later received $1 million for parametric design studies for the F-X under the Close Support Fighter funding line.[19]

Meanwhile, Air Force complacency over tactical air superiority had begun to evaporate after two F-105s on an April 4 bomb run over North Vietnam were shot down by several supposedly obsolete MiG-15s or -17s.[20] The episode rekindled interest in tactical air superiority,[21] lent added urgency to the F-X effort, and prompted Ferguson to seek cooperation from the field. On April 29, using the same guidelines established for the Air Staff's concurrent F-X studies, he directed the Air Force Systems Command (AFSC) to undertake studies of a multipurpose fighter with a STOL capability.[22]

The requirement for a STOL fighter attracted the attention of Col. John J. Burns, Assistant Director of Requirements, Headquarters, Tactical Air Command (TAC). Burns, who had been a member of the Bohn group and was an ardent air superiority advocate, pounced on the STOL requirement and immediately drafted a position paper for a lightweight day air superiority fighter.[23]

Gen. Gabriel P. Disosway, a World War II fighter pilot commander, took over TAC on August 1. He immediately reviewed Burns' work. In October, he sent to the Air Staff a qualitative operational requirement (QOR) that emphasized TAC's interest in an "aircraft capable of out-performing the enemy in the air." Challenging the notion that only a multipurpose fighter could gain OSD and congressional approval, it specified a lightweight day fighter in the 30,000- to 35,000-pound range. The requirement also called for equipping the new aircraft with a radar capability similar to the F-4s, with both infrared and radar missiles. TAC also emphasized the need for maneuvering performance and high thrust-to-weight ratio; but because of temperature limitation, it lowered the maximum speed requirement from Mach 3.0 to 2.5—a change that would save between 35 and 40 percent of the total cost, or $4.5 versus $2.5 million per copy.[24]

The Pivotal Decision

During the summer and fall of 1965, the Air Force continued to wrestle with the F-5 versus the A-7 issue. OSD, particularly Systems Analysis, was still enamored of the "commonality" principle, wherein the Air Force and Navy would possess a combined tactical force comprised of F-111, F-4, and A-7 aircraft. In July, McNamara directed OSD and the Air Force to begin a joint study to select either the F-5 or A-7 for the close air support role in Vietnam. At the same time, but on a lower priority, he endorsed the Air Force's prerequisite work on developing the new F-X fighter.[25] Meanwhile, Brown—who as DDR&E had backed the F-5—reversed his position after being named Secretary of the Air Force, a position he assumed on October 1. In November, he and McConnell proposed acquiring eleven squadrons (264 aircraft) of A-7s. Although criticized in some Air Force circles as a capitulation to OSD, the decision to buy the A-7 was in fact a sensible compromise that ultimately gained approval for the F-X. Agan recognized this point and endorsed the decision. The F-X could now be justified as a "more sophisticated, higher performance aircraft . . . an air superiority replacement for the F-4."[26]

F-X work statements—which had previously aimed at the production of a medium-cost, multipurpose aircraft highlighting close air support—now called for an aircraft with the "best combination of air-to-air and air-to-ground characteristics."[27] More than mere semantics, this revision permitted the Air Force to launch a major effort to acquire a new fighter. Secretary Brown had opened the door to the F-X and, more importantly, he emphasized the air-to-air mission and the need to expand the tactical force.

Meanwhile, Disosway and his colleagues in the United States Air Forces, Europe (USAFE) and the Pacific Air Forces (PACAF) held firm to the TAC view that designing the F-X to accommodate both air-to-air and air-to-ground missions would severely jeopardize air superiority. Disosway and his fellow "four-stars," Generals Holloway and Hunter Harris, urged Chief of Staff McConnell to endorse air superiority as the primary mission of the F-X, with secondary missions being considered a bonus from the aircraft's superior design.[28]

Disosway and his operations advisers believed that, given the limitations on the employment of tactical air power—such as the enemy sanctuaries that existed during the Korean and Vietnam Wars—the only way the Air Force could meet the challenge posed by lightweight, maneuverable Soviet fighters in the 1970s was to design a superior, uncompromised air combat fighter.[29]

Nevertheless, Headquarters USAF decided to continue to study the case for a fighter capable of both the air superiority and ground attack missions. Ferguson, who became AFSC commander in September 1966, asked Disosway to await the results of parametric design studies that had begun in March. Ferguson personally opposed the parametric study requirement, but believed the results would substantiate the case for an air superiority fighter.[30]

Concept Formulation Phase (CFP)

In December 1965, the Air Force had sent requests for proposals (RFPs) to thirteen aircraft manufacturers for the initial F-X parametric design studies. Three winning contractors drew up some 500 proposed designs and in July 1966, the Aeronautical Systems Division (ASD) selected the one it considered the best for an air-to-air and air-to-ground aircraft.[31]

Indeed, the emphasis on the multipurpose features of the F-X dominated the parametric studies. ASD's goal was to develop an aircraft with sufficient capability to offset the alleged Soviet superiority in maneuverability while maintaining the U.S. edge in range. What emerged was a proposed F-X weighing more than 60,000 pounds to accommodate all the avionics and armaments packages. In this F-X, the Air Force would get a very expensive aircraft resembling the F-111 but which, in no sense, would be an air superiority fighter.[32]

Energy Maneuverability

Ferguson and his development planners sensed that the F-X requirements were "badly spelled out." They persuaded Disosway to modify his requirements, thanks in large part to the work of Maj. John R. Boyd. In October 1966, Boyd joined the Tactical Division of the Air Staff Directorate of Requirements. When asked to comment on the "Representative F-X design," he summarily rejected it. A veteran pilot of the late 1950s and author of the air combat training manual used by the Fighter Weapons School at Nellis AFB, Nevada, Boyd was well qualified to assess fighter aircraft. In 1962, while completing an engineering course at Georgia Tech, he had studied the relationships between energy and energy changes of aircraft during flight and devised a method to measure aircraft maneuverability—the ability to change altitude, airspeed, and direction.

Boyd continued his energy maneuverability (EM) studies at his next station, Eglin AFB, Florida. There he met mathematician Thomas Christie, and in May 1964 they published an official two-volume treatise on energy maneuverability.[33] That year, the EM theory was brought to the attention of members of the Air Staff, including Generals Agan and Catton.

Although the EM theory did not represent anything new in terms of physics or aerodynamics, it led Boyd and Christie to devise a revolutionary analytical technique that permitted fighter "jocks" to communicate with engineers. The EM theory expressed in numbers what fighter pilots had been trying to say for years by moving their hands. It also permitted planners and developers to compare competing aircraft directly and to demonstrate the effects of design changes on aircraft performance. Finally, the theory could be used to teach pilots how to exploit their aircraft's advantages over that of the enemy.[34]

Meanwhile, working within the Tactical Division, Boyd began applying the EM theory to the F-X, projecting how the aircraft would perform in the critical maneuvering performance envelope—the subsonic and transonic speeds up to Mach 1.6 and altitudes up to 30,000 feet. He then asked TAC, ASD, and the study contractors to provide tradeoffs between range, structural requirements, and on-board equipment. Then, by comparing configuration changes for fixed and variable wing sweeps, Boyd designed a model that would demonstrate the effects of specific requirements on the F-X design.[35]

By the spring of 1967, through the efforts of Boyd and others, a 40,000-pound F-X aircraft was "popped out." Its proposed engine bypass had been lowered to 1.5, thrust-to-weight increased to .97, and top speed scaled down to a range of Mach 2.3 to 2.5. During the various design tradeoffs, Boyd challenged the validity of ASD's drag polars (lift versus drag charts) and argued that lower wing loadings on the order of eighty pounds/ft^2 would be more appropriate for the F-X design. Pursuing his research into drag polars, he later examined the effects of optimizing propulsion, configuration, avionics, and weapons for the fixed and variable sweep-wing designs. His calculations of these tradeoffs pointed to 0.6 as the "best" engine bypass ratio and to a sixty to sixty-five pounds/ft^2 wing loading. The design studies incorporated into the final F-15 configuration confirmed these values.[36]

Concept Formulation

The F-X formulation phase continued through the spring and summer of 1967. By March, a three-part concept formulation package (CFP) and a technical development plan (TDP) had been drafted, specifying the F-X rationale, cost, and development schedule. In August, Secretary Brown submitted to OSD a revised cost proposal for the F-X as the Air Force's recommended new tactical fighter candidate to replace the F-4. He noted the Air Force's tactical force structure for the mid-1970s—limited to twenty-four wings by OSD—included thirteen F-4, six F-111, and five A-7 wings, respectively oriented to perform air superiority, interdiction, and close air support missions. Brown now argued for the paramountcy of air superiority, without which the other missions would be either impossible or too costly, and for the need to protect ground forces against enemy air attack. He noted that although the multipurpose F-4 Vietnam workhorse was a capable air-to-air fighter, its continued effectiveness was doubtful. U.S. intelligence in March 1967 had projected that by the mid-1970s approximately half the Soviet tactical aircraft inventory would consist of modern fighters said to excel the F-4 in air combat.

While Soviet fighter designs stressed range and payload, U.S. tactical air superiority in the Korean and Vietnam Wars was attributed to "superior pilot skill and better armament and avionics." These advantages were not expected to prevail in a conventional war in Europe, given the likelihood of encountering well-trained Soviet pilots. Moreover, the Soviets were increasing their maneuverability edge and significantly improving their missile and fire-control systems. The Air Force cautioned in August that it could no longer "rely on pilot skill alone to offset any technical inferiority of U.S. aircraft. . . . To win an air war against Soviet forces it is essential that U.S. pilots be given the best aircraft that technology can afford."[37]

According to various Air Force analyses, little improvement could be expected from modifying existing aircraft such as the F-4, F-111, YF-12, A-7, and a U.S.-West German V/STOL design. Additionally, the cost of such an effort would be extremely high, approaching that required to develop a completely new fighter. Brown conceded that additional study was required to refine the F-X characteristics.

In a memorandum to McNamara, Brown reiterated that there were several unresolved areas involving the "Representative F-X." Brown also foreshadowed the commonality issue by predicting that certain components and subsystems of the F-X and the Navy's VFAX fighter could be made interchangeable. He was less optimistic about the possibility of using common airframe assemblies for the two planes.[38]

The Commonality Issue

By the spring of 1965, there was a general consensus in the Air Force and Navy that the TFX (F-111) would not meet the needs of both services, and in October the Air Force and Navy independently issued operational requirements for multi-mission fighter aircraft. Anticipating that OSD might impose a new commonality requirement on them, the services from the outset "agreed to disagree" about operational requirements.

In May 1966, McNamara ordered a joint review of the commonality issue.[39] Conducted over the next eighteen months, the review confirmed that the needs of the Air Force and Navy could not be met by a single airframe. The Air Force emphasized maneuverability performance through low wing loading; the Navy was more concerned with mission versatility, such as extended loiter time for fleet air defense.[40] The differences that emerged during the joint study convinced some in the Air Force that they were in direct competition with the Navy for money to support development of a new fighter.

An Air Force Position Emerges

Sensing that the Navy was about to promote its new aircraft as an air superiority fighter, and convinced that the Air Force could produce a better design, Disosway decided the time had come to settle the controversy within the Air Force between the multipurpose and air superiority advocates. In February 1968, he issued TAC Required Operational Capability (ROC) 9–68. The document cited two new threats in justifying its call for an air superiority fighter. First, the MiG-21, exploiting its ground control interception advantage, continued to trouble USAF fighter pilots in Vietnam—where the air-to-air combat ratio between U.S. and North Vietnamese aircraft was about 2.5 to 1. Secondly, the Soviets had displayed several new fighters at the July 1967 Moscow Air Show, and one of these—the Foxbat—was regarded as superior in speed, ceiling, and endurance to existing and projected U.S. counterparts (including the "Representative F-X" described in the summer 1967 CFP).

Both Headquarters USAF and TAC wanted a new fighter, but the multipurpose advocates believed it best to present the F-X as a successor to the F-4, whereas the air superiority proponents were equally convinced that only their approach could defeat the Navy's bid. At any rate, by early 1968, the air superiority advocates had gained the upper hand. A decisive factor favoring the air superiority school was that Generals Disosway and Holloway occupied key positions at the same time and fought persistently for their viewpoint. However, the fear that the Navy would walk off with the prize unless the Air Force decided to "speak with one voice" united the factions.[41] In May, McConnell explained the Air Force position to the Senate Armed Services Committee: "There were a lot of people in the Air Force who wanted to make the F-X into another F-4 type of aircraft. We finally decided—and I hope there is no one who still disagrees—that this aircraft is going to be an air superiority fighter."[42]

Meanwhile, the Navy had undertaken to improve its fighter's energy maneuverability characteristics whenever the Air Force did so. Dissatisfied with the VFAX, its replacement for the F-111B model of the TFX, the Navy decided to cancel it and tacitly accept an unsolicited bid from Grumman Aircraft to develop a more competitive fighter. Designated the VFX—it subsequently entered the inventory as the F-14 "Tomcat"—the Navy's proposed aircraft combined previous multi-mission requirements, including air superiority, in two variant designs—the VFX-1 and the VFX-2. The Navy now argued that the VFX could match the F-X performance and was also adaptable to both carrier- and land-based operations.

Clearly, the Air Force's task was to counter Navy strategy by presenting an air superiority fighter uncompromised by secondary mission requirements. One compromise remained, however: the F-X had to accommodate Sparrow missiles to shoot down the high-flying, high-speed Soviet Foxbat.

In May 1968, McConnell assigned top priority to the F-X program and designated January 1, 1969, as the target date for implementing contract definition.[43] This meant strengthening the F-X program office at Wright-Patterson AFB, Ohio, and providing all available manpower and other resources.[44] Further encouragement came from Dr. John Foster, the new DDR&E, who predicted that the F-X would get OSD approval by September 1968. AFSC's vice-commander, Lt. Gen. Charles Terhune, stressed the importance of running an exemplary program to gain support for the F-X from the Nixon administration, which would take office in January 1969.[45]

By the spring of 1968, DDR&E accepted that its commonality drive had failed. Still, Foster recommended that the Air Force and Navy conduct a joint engine development program—the one item both services had agreed upon. However, in June, Assistant Secretary of the Air Force for R&D Alexander Flax told AFSC to proceed with a unilateral program because he considered commonality "dead." To unify the effort, the Air Force appointed Brig. Gen. Roger K. Rhodarmer as liaison for F-X activities. He proceeded to select a staff of fighter pilots, including Colonels John Boyd and Robert Titus and Maj. John Axley, to help him sell the F-X program. Rhodarmer's task was twofold. First, he had to achieve a unified position within the Air Force, specifically by resolving outstanding differences. This was no mean task, since TAC and ASD continued to clash over such basics as the F-X's maximum speed, energy maneuverability, and structural loads. Second, he had to steer the F-X documentation through OSD and Congress.[46]

Point Design Studies

Meanwhile, in August 1967, the Air Force had solicited bids from seven aerospace companies for a second round of studies. These "point design" studies sought to establish a technical base for the F-X proposal, refining the F-X concept in four areas: (1) validating the aircraft's performance in wind tunnel tests; (2) matching propulsion requirements against performance; (3) examining the preferred avionics and armaments systems; and (4) studying the effects of crew size. All investigations were completed by June 1968, at which time a composite Air Force team, headed by Col. Robert P. Daly, assembled at Wright-Patterson AFB to "scrub down" the results and rewrite the concept formulation package.[47]

CFP Supplement

Although many high-risk, high-cost items remained, the point design studies and scrub down proved fruitful. In August 1968, the Air Staff issued a supplement to the CFP. There was no longer any ambivalence about the Air Force's air superiority doctrine. Thus, the CFP supplement stated that:

> It is sometimes held that air combat of the future will assume an entirely different complexion than that of the past. The Air Force does not share that contention. To the contrary, tactical applications of air superiority forces will remain essentially the same for the foreseeable future.[48]

The war in Southeast Asia had taught the Air Force that smaller-sized aircraft could better escape radar and visual detection; thus, the supplement specified a one-man crew for the F-X but retained a two-man trainer version. The wing planform remained open, although the "Representative F-X" described a swing-wing rather than a fixed-wing design. The major subsystems—engine, radar, and gun—would be selected on a competitive flyoff basis. While the Air Force did not resolve some of the difficult issues, it decided to stress the air superiority aspects of the F-X and relegated air-to-ground capabilities to a secondary or bonus status.

In mid-August, McConnell approved the F-X source selection plans and the joint Air Force-Navy engine development program. Brown's endorsement came the next month.[49]

The final task in the concept formulation phase was to write an F-X development concept paper (DCP). Prepared by DDR&E's staff with Air Force assistance, the DCP described the F-X as "a single-place, twin-engine aircraft featuring excellent pilot visibility, with internal fuel sized for 260 nm design mission and . . . a balanced combination of standoff [missiles] and close-in [gun] target kill potential." The one-man crew decision, validated during the point design studies, was predicated on the ability of a single pilot to perform nearly all missions assigned. The penalties for adding a second crewman, including 5,000 to 6,000 pounds of extra weight at a cost of $500,000 per aircraft, were considered unacceptable. The twin-engine design was selected because it featured faster throttling response, commonality with the F-14, and earlier availability.[50] The most ambiguous features, however, involved the F-X radar and avionics packages, which were lumped together as "flexible vs. specialized counterair capability." Thus, the choice was between a smaller, lighter aircraft that would be difficult for the enemy to detect and a larger aircraft like the F-X that could more easily detect an enemy aircraft. Although selecting the latter, the Air Force left open a final trade-off until sometime during the contract definition phase.[51]

Cost estimates changed again because of a revised aircraft buy. The Air Force's future tactical force had been restructured to twenty-nine wings, including nine F-4, five F-X, seven F-111, and four A-7 and four A-X (later A-10) wings. This plan required only 520 aircraft.[52]

DCP 19 F-X Program Costs*	($ millions)
Development cost	1,078
Investment cost	4,059
Flyaway cost per aircraft	5.3
Operating costs (10 years)	2,991
Total system cost	8,128

* The unit cost of an aircraft can be very confusing because of the misleading terminology used. *Flyaway cost* represents the basic cost of an aircraft without R&D, spares, initial production and support costs. *Unit production cost* omits costs for R&D. *Unit program cost* includes the unit production cost plus all R&D, test and evaluation, ground support, training equipment, spares, and depot tooling. For example, *Air Force Magazine*, June 1971, p 30, cited the F-15 flyaway cost at $6.2 million, unit production cost at $7.6 million, and unit program cost at $10 million. [Memo, Hansen to Seamans, subj: Congressional Hearing Resume, 22 Jul 69.]

Prototyping Rejected

The final issue in the F-X DCP was whether to pursue contract definition or prototyping for aircraft procurement. Foster supported the Air Force's request to begin contract definition immediately.[53]

Actually, the Air Force position on this issue had grown out of a "sense of urgency" because of the challenge from the Navy's VFX and the inauguration of a new president who would make the usual changes in OSD's civilian leadership. The F-X airframe would be purchased via the total package procurement concept, but higher risk subsystems would undergo competitive prototyping. On September 28, 1968, Deputy Secretary of Defense Paul H. Nitze approved contract definition of the F-X.[54]

These efforts demonstrated that, although differences remained within the Air Force, outwardly it could present a unified stand. The Air Force had won approval to develop a new fighter, the F-X becoming the F-15; marshaled its resources toward that goal; and established a central office in Washington to deal with whatever problems arose.

Contract Definition

On September 30, 1968, the Air Force launched the F-X contract definition phase by soliciting bids from eight aircraft companies. Fairchild-Hiller, General Dynamics, McDonnell Douglas, and North American responded. Boeing, Lockheed, Grumman (which had won the F-14 contract in February 1969), and Northrop had participated in the concept formulation effort but did not submit bids. On December 30, Flax announced the award of $15.4 million in contracts for contract definition to all bidders except General Dynamics. The three bidders were asked to submit technical proposals—including the projected cost of the aircraft and a development schedule—by the end of June 1969.[55]

As contract definition began, a question arose over the number of competitors the Air Force should maintain and for what length of time. In February 1969, the new Secretary of the Air Force, Dr. Robert C. Seamans, issued guidelines to enable him to eliminate one of the three contractors by April and another by September.[56] Foster, on the other hand, believed that a more extended period of competition might decrease the final cost of the F-15 development contract.[57]

A New Contracting Philosophy

Meanwhile, a rising tide of public and congressional criticism over the enormous cost overruns in the C-5A program forced the Air Force to reconsider its plan to procure the F-15 under the fixed-price "total package" concept used for the huge cargo aircraft. ASD commander Maj. Gen. Harry E. Goldsworthy pointed out to Ferguson that the proposed F-15 integrated system would be a major challenge to an industry that had little recent experience in developing an air superiority fighter. Moreover, he maintained that cost estimates for an aircraft yet to be designed were highly unreliable.[58]

Goldsworthy advocated some kind of production commitment during the competitive phase of the program but only if it also protected the contractor against unreasonable financial risk. As a corrective, he recommended relying on a cost-type arrangement for the development phase with a fixed-price incentive provision to govern the production phase.[59]

Selling the New Approach

If the Air Force seemed satisfied with the Goldsworthy procurement method, OSD was not. Through the spring and early summer of 1969, Seamans pressed OSD for its approval.[60] Foster, however, continued to oppose anything other than a fixed-price contractual arrangement.[61]

Meanwhile, Deputy Secretary of Defense David Packard had not made a decision. At a crucial meeting with Seamans in June, he conceded it was unrealistic to delay further the setting of a price for the F-15.[62]

With OSD delaying its authorization, Seamans was forced to withdraw his original February 1969 guidance to the contractors regarding the proposed production schedules and to ask them to provide ceiling-price estimates that the Air Force might invoke at its discretion. He also asked the contractors to propose a set of demonstration milestones that they would be committed to reach so as to "provide technical confidence in the program." These milestones, which were to prove central to the new weapon system acquisition approach, would be negotiated with the successful bidder.[63]

Foster, who continued to insist that a fixed-price arrangement was the only approach he would support, recommended another round of design studies to reduce the F-15's requirements and realign the aircraft's flyaway costs to the $5.33 million figure specified in the DCP.[64] Though opposed to his reasoning, the Air Force offered to ease some of the aircraft's air-to-ground mission requirements.[65] On June 27, with contract time running out, Seamans appealed once again to Packard, who finally gave the Air Force the go-ahead.[66]

The F-15 contract negotiations, conducted during November and December 1969, involved a total of six contracts with three airframe companies. Each company also signed contracts with two engine manufacturers. The idea was to have all these contracts in force, pending the Air Force's selection of an airframe builder and then the engine developer. In effect, the Air Force obtained commitments without having to wait for the results of the competitions. Although Foster continued to provide "informal direction" to the F-15 program office, the new contracting method remained intact.[67]

The F-15 Program Office

In August 1966, several years before contract negotiations began, the Air Force had established an F-X special projects office at Wright-Patterson AFB to oversee development of both the F-X and A-X close air support aircraft. The office, which first came under ASD's Deputy for Advanced Systems Planning, was initially headed by Col. Robert P. Daly with a staff of seventeen.[68]

Following OSD's approval of the F-X DCP in September 1968, the System Program Office (SPO) was reorganized in October and assigned to the Deputy for Systems Management for both operational and administrative support. A number of internal changes occurred at this time, including setting up divisions for configuration management, program control, procurement and production, and test and deployment. By July 1969, the F-15 development and procurement program was considered the model for both the Air Force and OSD.

On July 11, 1969, Brig. Gen. designee Benjamin N. Bellis became the head of the SPO. Bellis was one of the Air Force's most experienced managers, with service dating back to 1947. He had made his reputation in the development field with the Matador and Atlas missiles, managed the F-12/SR-71 aircraft development project, and served as ASD Deputy for Reconnaissance and Electronic Warfare. Bellis had written the Air Force 375-series management regulations, acquired a warrant as a procurement specialist, and earned advanced degrees in aeronautical engineering and business administration.

In October, the F-15 office became a "Super SPO." Bellis now reported directly to the AFSC commander, bypassing ASD. He reorganized the SPO, assuming total responsibility for program management, including the engine, armaments, and avionics systems and he made the Joint Engine Program Office (JEPO) a component of his office.[69]

Bellis reorganized his directorates into procurement and production, test and deployment, configuration management, integrated logistics support, program control, systems engineering, and projects. The latter was responsible for insuring that vital components—airframe, avionics, and armaments—were developed and available when needed.[70]

Bellis was also authorized to select the best personnel available to join the F-15 project. In a short time, his handpicked staff grew to about 230 people—half military and half civilian. The prestigious F-15 assignment attracted many experienced, highly competent people. Moreover, because Bellis was keenly interested in the career advancement of his staff, he was able to build a tightly-knit and well-motivated group.[71]

Bellis' staff also included liaison officers from TAC, Air Training Command (ATC), and Air Force Logistics Command (AFLC). They would provide close coordination with the user commands so that the first F-15 wing could become fully operational at the end of the development and testing phases. A systems application panel brought together veteran TAC pilots to make sure the F-15 would remain a "fighter pilot's plane."[72] Finally, Bellis established a straight arrow group to guard against improper conduct between SPO personnel and the F-15 contractors.

Some aspects of Bellis's management caused controversy. He was sometimes overly secretive in managing the F-15 office. Bellis believed that he alone was responsible for program management and brooked no outside interference. His tough stance at times embittered his relations with officials in the Air Force Secretariat who were authorized to monitor the F-15 program. During the source selection phase in the late summer and fall of 1969, he complained about the intensive scrutiny from various agencies. As a result, Secretaries Seamans and Packard instructed Air Force and OSD officials to operate strictly through the F-15 SPO in their work.[73]

Management Facelift

The F-15 reorganization marked the beginning of a thorough housecleaning of Air Force management procedures. Under congressional pressure because of the unhappy C-5A experience, Defense Secretary Melvin Laird decided that a presidential blue-ribbon panel should examine Department of Defense (DoD) procedures. However, because the development problems could not wait, Secretary Packard conducted his own assessment. Concluding that "total package" was not working, he undertook to make extensive changes. He eliminated unessential staff layers in decision-making; improved cost-estimating procedures; and placed greater emphasis on prototyping, i.e., "flying before buying."

In April 1969, anticipating the need to improve the Air Force weapon-system acquisition process, General Ferguson decided to centralize program control. He advised ASD that all configuration changes for the F-15 "affecting the mission, increasing the weight or target cost, and impacting the schedule" would be approved by a triumvirate including himself, General Ryan, and Lt. Gen. Marvin L. McNickle, the Deputy Chief of Staff (R&D).[74] Next, Ferguson convinced Seamans and Ryan to reorient the Air Force management philosophy. The first step was to get the Air Staff out of the management "business" by shifting the Program Element Monitor (PEM) function to AFSC. Effective August 1, 1969, this action freed the Air Staff to "focus on policy and plans," and enabled AFSC to monitor the program through the new F-15 SPO.[75]

The new reporting channel—from Bellis to Ferguson to Ryan and Seamans—was called the Blue Line. It fulfilled the Air Force's desire to reduce "the number of review echelons."[76] The AFSC program monitor, known as the Assistant for F-15, assumed the duties previously assigned to Rhodarmer during the F-15 advocacy stage and also served as the Washington area focal point for all F-15 matters. The monitor briefed the Air Staff monthly on the F-15's progress while Bellis presented quarterly briefings and written reports—known as Selected Assessment Reviews—to Seamans, Ryan, and other top officials. This arrangement insured tight program control and released the F-15 SPO to concentrate on day-to-day management activities.[77]

These streamlined procedures, which closely paralleled Secretary Packard's views on weapon system management, account for the harmonious relationship that existed between OSD and the Air Force on the F-15 program.

Source Selection

On July 1, 1969, Fairchild-Hiller, McDonnell-Douglas, and North American submitted technical proposals and on August 30, their cost proposals. The Source Selection Evaluation Board (SSEB), headed by General Bellis, then evaluated these bids, examining eighty-seven separate factors under four major categories—technology, logistics, operations, and management. They rated the competitors in each category and, without making a recommendation, submitted the raw data to a Source Selection Advisory Council (SSAC), comprised of representatives from the user commands and chaired by ASD commander Maj. Gen. Lee V. Gossick. The council then applied a set of weighting factors that they had defined in June 1969, before the start of the evaluation. Although rating the contractors in the four major categories, the council, too, did not select a winner. Instead, it forwarded the scores through the Air Staff to Secretary Seamans, who, as Source Selection Authority (SSA), had the final decision.[78]

Project Focus

During this evaluation, Secretary Packard directed the Air Force to make a final review of the F-15 program requirements. He acknowledged that the review, called Project Focus, would delay the F-15 IOC, but believed this compromise would be worthwhile if it avoided costly mistakes.[79] Packard also clamped a $1 billion per year spending limit on the F-15 program and directed that Project Focus be completed by mid-November 1969 to avoid disturbing the source-selection process.

Foster, too, wanted to more thoroughly evaluate the contractor proposals. Citing the F-111 and C-5A competitions as examples of programs that had suffered from inadequate evaluation, he stated that last-minute changes were the cause of their problems. Foster warned that F-15 cost estimates had already exceeded the September 1968 DCP threshold and asked the Air Force to control escalating costs.[80]

Meanwhile, the Air Force had acted promptly to meet Packard's call for a program review. Bellis established a Program Evaluation Group (PEG),[81] which quickly suggested a long list of items to reduce F-15 costs by more than $1.5 million per aircraft. The cost review continued throughout the F-15 project and a subsequent General Accounting Office (GAO) report in July 1970 credited it with about $1 billion in savings.[82] In December 1969, encouraged by the work of Project Focus, Packard authorized the Air Force to go forward with the F-15 development.[83]

McDonnell Wins

Secretary Seamans, having announced the award of the F-15 contract to McDonnell-Douglas on December 23, 1969, estimated that the development phase, including the design and fabrication of twenty aircraft, would cost $1.1 billion.[84] Donald Malvern, McDonnell's F-15 general manager, reported that the firm had already spent 2.5 million man-hours in winning the F-15 contract. His team of between 200 and 1,000 people had worked for two years examining over 100 alternative designs with thousands of variations. From an economic standpoint, the F-15 contract "saved" one third of the company's 33,000 jobs in the St. Louis, Missouri, area. The F-15 contract also promised to increase McDonnell's sagging commercial airliner sales and absorb the slack of lowered F-4 production.[85]

Air Force Weathers Congressional Scrutiny

Before and after the award of the contract to McDonnell-Douglas, the F-15 competition was the target of congressional and media scrutiny. One of the thorniest issues concerned disclosure of the Air Force's source selection criteria. In July 1969, John R. Blandford, chief counsel for the House Armed Services Committee (HASC), asked the Air Force to reveal this information. Assistant Air Force Secretary Philip N. Whittaker argued that complying would compromise "business confidentiality."[86] Even when the competition was completed, Whittaker parceled out only selective bits of information to Congress.[87]

A November 22 *Armed Forces Journal* article charged that the Air Force had illegally withheld disclosure of the F-15 source selection weighting factors from the contractors.[88] Representative Otis Pike (D-N.Y.), a critic of defense spending, brought the case to the House floor. Seamans stated that the Air Force *could* furnish the weighting factors, but that such action was "in no sense mandatory." He also reminded his critics that the selection criteria had been established on June 2, 1969, *before* the contractors had submitted their proposals. Though further explaining the source selection process, he did not divulge the requested criteria.[89] The Air Force position in this case was later vindicated through a GAO investigation that found itself "in full agreement with the Air Force."[90]

The Subsystems: The Engine

Although USAF officials had rejected a prototype competition for the F-15 airframe contract, they readily pursued this approach for the airplane's subsystems, including the engine, radar, and short-range missile. A prototype competition among several contractors would reduce program costs and risks. System contractors were to be selected on the basis of proof-testing and demonstration of subsystem prototypes.

In December 1967, the Air Force and Navy agreed to conduct a joint engine-development program.[91] They would develop a high-performance afterburning turbofan Advanced Technology Engine (ATE), drawing upon the experience gained in the development of the lift-cruise engine of the U.S.-West German V/STOL and Advanced Manned Strategic Aircraft (AMSA) bomber programs. Developing the ATE emerged as the main problem in an otherwise exemplary F-15 program.[92]

From the start of the project, the Air Force and Navy disagreed about its management. In early 1968, the Air Force proposed establishing within one service a joint engine program office (JEPO). This proposal reflected the Air Force's single-management concept for the F-15 program and had precedent in other joint projects. On the other hand, the Navy favored single-source procurement and creation of a joint executive committee to oversee separate project offices in each service.[93]

The situation reached an impasse. The issue was partially resolved in April 1968, when Foster named the Air Force executive agent to manage the Initial Engine Development Program (IEDP), but he left open his decision on management of the final development phase.[94]

At the end of August, OSD authorized the award of two eighteen-month contracts totaling $117.45 million to General Electric and Pratt & Whitney.[95] Jointly funded by the Air Force and Navy, the contracts authorized each company to build one prototype for each service. The purpose was not merely to develop different engines, but to fulfill each service's thrust requirements. Since the Navy's proposed aircraft was heavier than the F-15, it required a larger engine. Both the Air Force and Navy engine models were to be designed. However, since the Navy planned to use the TF-30 engine in their F-14 prototype, the services agreed that only the Air Force engine model and some components of the Navy model would be built initially.[96]

In February 1970, after reviewing the technical and cost proposals and design substantiation data submitted by the two engine contractors, the Source Selection Evaluation Board designated the Pratt & Whitney design as "clearly superior to the General Electric System." After the source selection authority—Secretary Seamans—also chose Pratt & Whitney, that company received the formal award on March 1, authorizing the Air Force and Navy to sign separate engine contracts with it.[97]

The Air Force engine model, designated the F100-PW100, was an augmented twin-spool, axial-flow gas turbine that delivered more than 22,000 pounds of thrust and weighed less than 2,800 pounds. Using the same "common core" as the F100, the Navy version of the ATE, the F401-PW400, generated over 27,000 pounds of thrust and weighed under 3,500 pounds. The two engines differed in the fan, afterburner, and compressor sections. The addition in the Navy model of a "stub" compressor in front of the main compressor increased the engine airflow but, by raising its weight, lowered the engine thrust-to weight ratio.[98]

In November 1970, because of F-14 funding cuts, the Navy pared its engine request in fiscal years 1972 through 1974. In the spring of 1971, the Navy further cut its order to fit the lagging F-14B airframe schedule. Then, on June 22, a new Navy decision to buy 301 F-14As—the model that used the TF-30 engine—canceled the remaining engines and voided the joint Navy-Air Force engine production contract.[99]

Earlier, in February 1971, Pratt & Whitney projected a $65 million cost overrun in the engine funding for fiscal year 1973. Although the JEPO stood fast then, advising the contractor that no more funds were available, these new circumstances forced the Air Force to rewrite its own engine production contract. The new agreement raised Air Force costs by about $532 million. Under this revised program, development milestones for the F401 engine slipped from February to December for the preliminary flight rating test (PFRT), from February to June 1973 for the military qualification test, and from June 1972 to mid-1974 for the delivery of production models.[100]

The ATE also suffered from several technical problems. At the start of the development program, there were two compressor designs: the primary aerodynamic compressor Series I, and the advanced aerodynamic compressor Series II. In October 1970, both services favored Series I because it was lighter and on schedule. However, by mid-1971, when it appeared that Series I would not meet its full production requirements, the services revived Series II. The Air Force eventually installed Series I in its first five test aircraft and Series II in all remaining test aircraft and in its F-15 and F-14B production models.[101]

In February 1972, the YF100 (Series I) engine passed its PFRT milestone on schedule, in time for the first F-15B flight in July. The Air Force rated Series I superior in thrust-to-weight, fuel consumption pressure ratio per stage, and turbine temperature levels. Meanwhile, in August 1972, the Air Force suspended the Military Qualification Test (MQT) testing three times for the Series II engine—an early warning of the many engine troubles to come in 1973.[102]

Other Subsystems: Radar and Armament

The F-15's remaining subsystems were open to competitive development. After soliciting industry bids in August 1968, the Air Force selected Westinghouse Electric and Hughes Aircraft in November to develop, produce, and test models of the attack radar subsystem. McDonnell-Douglas, the airframe contractor, was responsible for selecting the winner of the twenty-month competition after night testing and evaluating both radar prototypes. The Air Force wanted a lightweight, highly reliable advanced design suitable for one-man operation. The radar's capabilities were to include long-range detection and tracking of small, high-speed objects approaching from upper altitudes down to "tree-top" level. The radar was to send tracking data to a central on-board computer for accurate launching of the aircraft's missiles. For closing dogfights, the radar was to acquire targets automatically on the head-up display so that the pilot would not have to accomplish this manually.[103] In July and August 1970, McDonnell-Douglas conducted more than 100 flights to test competing radar units aboard its modified RB-66 aircraft. With Air Force approval, McDonnell awarded Hughes Aircraft the radar contract in September.

To cut costs, the Air Force ordered another thorough "scrubdown" of the F-15 requirements. Starting in July 1970, a panel headed by Maj. Gen. Jewell C. Maxwell reviewed the avionics and armaments, focusing on three items: (1) the Tactical Electronic Warning System (TEWS), whose development cost the panel favored separating from the F-15 program; (2) Target Identification Sensor—Electronic Optical (TISEO), a device for target identification beyond visual range; and (3) the AIM 7-E-2 missile, a backup for the AIM-7F Sparrow. The Air Force adopted the panel's recommendation to eliminate the last two systems.[104]

The F-15's armament included both missiles and an internal cannon. The Air Force added the gun on the advice of veteran pilots and Vietnam returnees as well in light of the Israeli success with cannon in the June 1967 Six-Day War. Though the primary gun for the F-15 was the M61 Vulcan (a 20-mm Gatling-type cannon used in Vietnam), the Air Force also began a long-term project to develop a 25-mm cannon using caseless ammunition. In the spring of 1968, it selected Philco-Ford and General Electric to design a prototype of the advanced gun, designated the GAU-7A Improved Aerial Gun System. The $36 million fixed-price competition ended in November 1971, when Philco-Ford won the contract.[105]

The Air Force also proposed to equip the F-15 with a new short-range missile (SRM) for use against maneuvering fighters at close range. But in September 1970, the Air Force canceled the SRM because of rising costs, agreeing with the Navy to substitute an improved version of the Sidewinder missile.[106]

Dissent and Decision

Despite USAF attempts to stem criticism of the F-15, basic differences arose inside and outside the Pentagon over the kind of aircraft to acquire. The Air Force was especially sensitive to criticism because of competition with the Navy to get funds for an air superiority fighter. Having established the F-15's basic requirements, the Air Force decided to "speak with one voice" and not tolerate any dissent. Nevertheless, criticism of the F-15 made the Air Force reexamine the project and design an aircraft markedly superior to the one it had promoted at the beginning of the program.

One proposed alternative to the F-15, dubbed the F-XX, was the brain child of Pierre M. Sprey of Systems Analysis. He believed that ASD engineers, responding to TAC's exorbitant requirements and paying little heed to cost, had produced a design that was too expensive, incorporated high-risk technology, was unnecessarily complex, and would not achieve its advertised air superiority performance. Sprey's alternative was a 25,000-pound, single-seat, one-engine fighter with a high thrust-to-weight ratio and an estimated 25 percent greater range than the F-X. The Air Force and Navy were not impressed. They rejected the proposed lightweight fighter because it lacked range for missions deep in enemy territory and could not carry the requisite avionics for countering enemy defenses. Finally, the services argued that only the F-15 and F-14 could counter the high-speed, high-altitude Foxbat.[107]

But Sprey was not alone in advocating a lightweight fighter. Several members of the Air Staff, aided by dissident Navy fliers, designed a lightweight fighter alternative to the F-15 and, in August 1969, submitted their proposal to General Ryan. Suppressing the proposal, F-15 advocates used the episode to unify the Air Force position on the air superiority fighter.[108]

As later events showed, Sprey's F-XX idea, though having considerable merit, was ill-timed. His criticism only united the Air Force and Navy against him because they were too far along in their advocacy to turn back to the "drawing board." Although by no means the last challenge to the F-15 and F-14 programs, it set the stage for their defense. A critical factor here was OSD's inflexibility on the tactical air force structure. Because they could not shake OSD force size limits, both services preferred to develop aircraft that were as versatile as possible.

F-15 vs. Foxbat and the F-14

In urging development of the F-15, the Air Force was pressed to explain the aircraft's alleged "inferiority" to the Soviet Foxbat. Basically, industry sources claimed the F-15 could not defeat the high-speed, high-altitude Foxbat (Mach 3+ at 80,000 feet) and urged scrapping the F-15 program. Rhodarmer's team, however, convinced Congress that, in terms of maneuverability, the F-15 was superior to any existing or projected Soviet aircraft. They noted its superior maneuverability in air combat, emphasizing the F-15's decided edge in such key dogfight factors as wing loading and thrust-to-weight ratio.[109]

	F-15	Foxbat
Thrust-to-weight	1.1	.78
Wing loading (pounds/ft²)	65	98

Critics of the F-15 prodded the Air Force to look at other aircraft. But the Air Force eventually concluded that the F-15's maneuverability, radar, and "shoot-up" Sparrow missiles could defeat the Foxbat. Describing the Foxbat as a technological threat only, the Air Force remained convinced of the F-15's ability to "out-fly, out-fight, and out-fox the rest."[110]

In authorizing development of the next generation tactical fighters, OSD generally presented the F-15 and F-14 as noncompetitive aircraft. The F-14 would provide the Navy with a long-range missile capability (AWG-9 Phoenix) for fleet air defense, with the F-14 variants performing "other fighter roles"; the F-15 was to achieve for the Air Force overall air superiority. In the spring of 1969, General McConnell and Adm. Thomas Moorer, Chief of Naval Operations, agreed to toe the OSD line—namely, that the two aircraft were intended for different missions. Whenever the issue did arise, the Air Force highlighted the F-15's maneuverability advantage and the mission differences between it and the F-14.[111]

Modifications and First Flight

Criticism of the F-15's design assumptions obliged the Air Force to re-examine the aircraft's design more critically and "scrub out" extraneous requirements. In particular, the role of the National Aeronautics and Space Administration (NASA) as a consultant during the source selection and its independent laboratory evaluation uncovered certain deficiencies that might otherwise have gone unnoticed. Between the time of its contract award and the spring of 1971, the F-15 had undergone a number of major design changes. The F-15 made its ceremonial debut on June 26, 1972, at McDonnell-Douglas's St. Louis plant. Painted "air superiority blue" and christened the Eagle, it was hailed as the first U.S. air superiority fighter since the F-86 appeared two decades earlier. The F-15's flight test program was launched on July 27 with a 50-minute maiden flight over Edwards AFB, California. With all systems working "as expected," and piloted by Irving L. Burrows of McDonnell-Douglas, the Eagle attained 12,000 feet and about 320 miles per hour. The flight-test program continued on schedule without any significant problems through the 1,000th flight in November 1973, by which date the F-15 had flown above 60,000 feet at speeds over Mach 2.3.[112]

MAJOR PRISCO
R. HERNANDEZ, ARNG

☆ ☆ ☆ ☆ ☆ ☆ ☆ ☆

No Master Plan:
The Employment of
Artillery in the
Indian Wars, 1860–1890

Although there are many studies on the employment and effectiveness of Field Artillery during the American Civil War, there are few detailed studies of its use in the many campaigns the US Army conducted against the western Indians in the second half of the 19th century.[1] Furthermore, military writers often prefer to focus on campaigns and battles that demonstrate brilliance in planning and execution or in which cherished principles are validated. Most of these factors are absent in the case of artillery employment in the Indian campaigns.

Artillery employment in the west was haphazard, at best, and was not based on well-developed doctrine or solidly conceived planning. Nevertheless, these operations are worthy of careful study because we learn not only from successful or brilliant operations but, perhaps, even more from those that fall short of the ideal. This article examines the Indian wars and extracts lessons that may prove to be valuable today.

Artillery Equipment, Organization and Doctrine

In the mid-19th century, American artillery doctrine and practice were modeled on professional European doctrine and practice, especially French.[2] Artillery doctrine emphasized the use of massive firepower to destroy or severely weaken enemy infantry or cavalry formations in preparation for an attack or to attrit the enemy when in the defense. This doctrine was used with relatively minor modifications during the great clashes of the Civil War.

Compared to the European style of warfare represented by formal set-piece battles with thousands of combatants on each side, the Indian wars approximated modern low-intensity conflict and even peacekeeping and peace-enforcing operations.[3] Indeed, many of the Army's operations were conducted to round up and return recalcitrant Indians to their assigned reservations or to protect settlers or friendly tribes from attack by hostile bands.

The standard battlefield pieces were the 12-pounder smooth-bore "Napoleon" and the 10-inch Parrott "rifle."[4] These large pieces were very effective in set-piece battles, and their carriages offered adequate battlefield mobility. Smaller pieces also were in use. They supplemented the fire of their larger counterparts and some, like the "mountain howitzers," were intended for use in restrictive terrain or where heavy loads presented too great of an impediment to tactical mobility.

The lighter pieces belonged to the horse or light branches of the Field Artillery. However, the veteran batteries of light or horse artillery that had distinguished themselves greatly in the Civil War were disbanded, victims of the post-war budget reductions and general war-weariness among the public.[5]

All these pieces were used by artillery forces west of the Mississippi. In addition, the artillery deployed several Gatling guns. These were considered light artillery pieces rather than machineguns.

In the western campaigns, artillery was allocated piecemeal to support cavalry or infantry formations. The most common practice was to attach a two-piece section of guns or howitzers to a cavalry or infantry regiment. Given these arrangements, junior artillery officers commonly operated in isolation from any higher artillery headquarters.

Tactical and Operational Environment

The style of warfare practiced by western plains and desert Indians was radically different from the formal European model. It was characterized by ambush, rapid maneuver, hit-and-run tactics, dispersion, avoidance of the enemy's strength and a lack of discrimination between soldiers and civilians. Thus, when fighting its western campaigns, the US Army relied mostly on its mounted arm for operational and tactical actions, while the infantry guarded major forts and installations, which secured lines of communications and supply.[6] In addition, artillerymen were often pressed into service as infantrymen or cavalrymen as the situation demanded.[7] Paradoxically, in many instances, artillery pieces were served by hastily trained infantry or cavalry soldiers, not by artillerymen.[8]

In the western plains, mountains and deserts, the role of the artillery was problematic. Soldiers soon recognized that the fire and thunder of even a small howitzer made a big impression on Indians whose experiences with firearms had been limited to small arms. The usual shocking psychological effect of artillery was intensified due to the cultural disparity of the antagonists.[9]

However, even the lightest artillery was a hindrance to movement over the vast arid western spaces, and its logistical requirements were a heavy burden on the Army's strained and barely adequate supply and transportation system.[10] Nonetheless, operational level commanders included artillery pieces in their campaign plans more for their value as "firepower insurance" and the availability of the pieces than because they followed a well-developed plan of employment founded on sound doctrine. The actual tactical employment of the pieces rested in the hands of a small group of junior artillery officers who had to adapt quickly to the situation at hand and improvise solutions to novel tactical problems.

Tactical Employment of Artillery in the West

The following is a discussion of some of the most notable combat actions that pitted artillery against western Indians and several engagements in which artillery might have turned the tide of battle if it had been employed.

Adobe Walls

In 1862, Kit Carson, then a colonel of New Mexico volunteers, led a punitive expedition against the southern plains tribes who had been raiding into eastern New Mexico and southeastern Colorado. The expedition included two troops of cavalry, a battalion of infantry and two small mountain howitzers.

Carson's troops were led by Ute and Jicarilla Apache scouts, blood enemies of the Comanches, and their allies. Carson came upon an Indian encampment near the headwaters of the Canadian River in the Texas panhandle. The troopers attacked the camp but found themselves surrounded by a large group of Comanche, Kiowa and Cheyenne warriors. The outnumbered troopers sought refuge in Adobe Walls, a ruined trading post, and organized a defense against persistent attacks by the plains warriors.

At this point in the battle, Colonel Carson's two howitzers played a decisive role.[11] Their fire broke the back of the plains warriors' charge, but it could not destroy them once the braves decided to disengage. The artillery's success was strictly defensive.

APACHE PASS

Also in 1862, a similar type of action occurred at Apache Pass in eastern Arizona. This time, a large band of more than 700 Apache warriors under Chiefs Mangas Coloradas and Cochise ambushed a column of 126 California militiamen under Captain Thomas Roberts in a narrow mountain defile. The initial Apache volley severely disorganized the column, causing some casualties and scaring the animals.

Artillerymen managed to move the two mountain howitzers to both sides of the trail, unlimber them and get them into action. Their fire dispersed the attackers, causing some casualties among the Indians. The Apaches sought cover among the rugged boulders and kept up an accurate harassing fire. The artillerymen then loaded explosive shells, which burst over the heads of the Indians, forcing them to withdraw uphill. Later, the Apaches mounted an evening attack on the soldiers. It failed largely because of the fire of the two howitzers.

Despite a successful defense, the initiative remained with the attackers who retained the ability to disperse, regroup and resume combat on their terms. Nonetheless, the howitzers arguably saved the column from annihilation, considering the Apaches outnumbered the soldiers about seven to one, had chosen the terrain well and had achieved surprise.

This limited defensive success of artillery against Indians unaccustomed to heavy caliber fire was significant as it showed without a doubt that artillery gave soldiers a tremendous survivability advantage even in the most disadvantageous of tactical situations.

BOZEMAN TRAIL

Purely defensive, also, was Colonel Henry B. Carrington's employment of howitzers to cover woodcutting and foraging parties that sallied forth from Forts Kearney, Laramie and other posts guarding the Bozeman Trail in Wyoming in 1866. On several occasions during Chief Red Cloud's War, these parties were attacked by Sioux warriors in sight of the forts. The howitzers saved many a soldier's life as the surprised warriors dispersed under their fire.[12]

ENCOUNTER WITH CRAZY HORSE

Also in 1866, when Captain William J. Fetterman sallied forth to pursue Chief Crazy Horse's braves in reckless disregard to his orders and without artillery support, he paid for it with his life and the total annihilation of his 80-man command.[13] His actions and motivations eerily foreshadowed those of General George Armstrong Custer a few years later at the Little Big Horn.

CUSTER AND EVANS ON THE STAKED PLAINS

In 1868, General Phillip Sheridan ordered a winter campaign against the southern plains tribes. Establishing a pattern for future western campaigns, Sheridan ordered three converging columns on the Indians' winter campgrounds in the largely unexplored barren wilds of the *Llano Estacado* (the Staked Plains) of the Texas panhandle.[14] In November, Major Andrew W. Evans moved northeastward from New Mexico into the Texas panhandle while Lieutenant Colonel George Armstrong Custer set out from Fort Dodge, Kansas, on a southwesterly route that took him to Camp Supply in Indian Territory and on to the Washita River. The third column proceeded from Colorado. The campaign resulted in two major engagements: one involving Custer's column, the other Evans'. A comparison between the actions of both commanders is instructive.

Custer's column consisted of virtually the entire 7th Cavalry Regiment with no infantry or artillery support. Although there were several howitzers available at Fort Dodge and at least one at Camp Supply, Custer chose not to take them.

After weathering a severe snow blizzard, his scouts came upon the winter encampment of Chief Black Kettle of the Southern Cheyenne at the Washita River just east of the Staked Plains. Custer divided his forces into four groups and attacked the village from various directions. His troopers surprised the Indians, burning their lodges and inflicting many casualties.

However, the noise of battle attracted many warriors from neighboring camps. These warriors harassed the 7th Cavalry from a distance, following the soldiers and menacing the supply trains. As time passed, more and more warriors gathered, sniping at the tired troopers and threatening to cut off their line of communications.

Under these circumstances, Custer was forced to withdraw. By conducting a circuitous night march he was able to escape northeastward toward Camp Supply.

Major Evans followed the old Adobe Walls trail through the Staked Plains along the Canadian River. He led a combined arms column of cavalry, infantry and a battery of four mountain howitzers.

After weeks of fruitless searching, his men noticed they were being tracked by Indians. Evans sent a detachment under Captain Tarleton to chase them off. The Indians drew the soldiers into an ambush. Tarleton, heavily outnumbered, dispatched a courier to ask for reinforcements.

Evans immediately dispatched a "flying column," consisting of a cavalry troop and a section of two howitzers, followed shortly thereafter with the main body and the rest of the artillery. Artillery fire dispersed the Indians, allowing the troopers to pursue them to their camp.

Again, the fire of the howitzers quickly persuaded the Indians to flee and abandon their lodges and prized possessions, including many horses. It would be a hard winter for them.

Evans' success was firmly secured by his howitzers. The following morning, he withdrew in good order after destroying the Indian camp.

Although both engagements were successful, in one case an entire regiment of cavalry was forced to withdraw under considerable pressure from the Indians, while on the other hand, a combined arms column was able to consolidate and reorganize, stave off attacks and withdraw at its leisure. Custer was able to achieve surprise but was forced to withdraw under pressure. Evans, on the other hand, turned the tables on the Indians and retained control of the battlefield. The difference in their situations was that Evans' howitzers provided him an overmatching firepower advantage that gave him a strong measure of force protection "insurance."[15]

THE LAVA BEDS

Guns, howitzers and mortars were taken into action against the Modocs of California. The Modoc War of 1872–73 was a six-month campaign fought over some of the most forbidding terrain in the west. The Modocs, led by Chief Kintpuash (aka, "Captain Jack"), retired to the rugged Lava Beds of northeastern California and defied the Army until they were starved out of their inhospitable refuge. The fighting resembled trench warfare rather than the war of movement common to most of the western theater.

The forces mustered against the Indians included mountain howitzers and small Coehorn mortars. The howitzers proved to be largely ineffective in the rugged terrain, which restricted mobility and offered ample cover and concealment to the Indians. The mortars were able to reach into "dead space" but were limited by their lack of proper sighting and the constant sniping of Modoc sharpshooters, which prevented accurate observation and adjustments of fires.

In addition, the pieces were manned by green units made up largely of untrained recruits. This resulted in some unfortunate incidents, such as soldiers panicking under the Modocs' incessant sniping and abandoning their guns.

However, when observers were able to adjust fire on Captain Jack's suspected hideout, they forced him out of his Lava stronghold. The Indians became disheartened when faced with a seemingly random and unstoppable rain of destruction from the sky.

Interestingly, artillery soldiers proved to be the deciding factor in this war. The artillery batteries, even when acting as mounted infantry, proved to be the most disciplined and effective troops in the campaign. Fittingly, they were the ones that finally captured Captain Jack and put an end to this bitter war.

Cedar Creek

Colonel Nelson Miles, the commander who brought the Indian wars to a close, customarily included howitzers in his columns. Miles, a pragmatic realist, appreciated the huge psychological and firepower advantage these pieces gave his soldiers when facing mounted Indians.

In his winter campaign of 1875–76, Miles carried his guns concealed within supply wagons.[16] This increased their effectiveness tremendously as their fire came as a total surprise to the Indians.

At Cedar Creek, Montana, Miles encountered Chief Sitting Bull's Sioux. They gave battle. During the ensuing fighting, his three-inch ordnance rifle cooperated with the long-range rifle fire of the infantry to keep the warriors at bay and disperse them, inflicting serious casualties. Captain Simon Snyder, who directed the gun during this engagement, later wrote in his diary, "I had charge of the artillery; which did excellent service, as it appeared to completely demoralize the enemy and kept them at a respectable distance."[17]

Wolf Mountain

Similarly, when attacked by large groups of Sioux warriors in the area of the Wolf Mountains, Miles brought his guns into action with telling efficiency. This time he surprised the mounted Indians by waiting until they pressed their charge. At the last moment, he uncovered the artillery wagons and fired canister from a Napoleon and a three-inch ordnance rifle. The effect was devastating.[18]

In his memoirs, Miles noted that "the Indians could not stand artillery."[19] Miles' appreciation for the value of artillery in the west led him to request that the War Department field a modern breechloading mountain howitzer. His request was approved, and he received a steel Hotchiss gun for testing at his post in Montana.[20] It was to see service within a few months.

The Nez Perce War of 1877

This war included some actions in which artillery figured prominently. Hostilities broke out when the southern band of the Nez Perces defied government orders to abandon their ancestral lands in Oregon's Wallowa Valley. Government troops under General Oliver Howard were tasked to subdue the defiant Indians.

The Nez Perces under Chiefs Joseph and Looking Glass numbered only some 150 warriors accompanied by about 550 older men, women and children.[21] Despite their small number, the Indians fought an impressive defensive campaign over extremely forbidding terrain, keeping many larger regular Army units at bay for almost four months.

Howard's command consisted of more than 2,000 infantry, cavalry and artillery soldiers, militia volunteers and Indian scouts. At the beginning of the campaign, his complement of artillery included no less than six guns, a battery of mortars and several Gatling guns.[22] Most of these lagged behind once the Indians began their retreat. The Army fought at least six major engagements in this campaign of which only two proved to be clear battlefield victories.[23] Artillery figured prominently in three of these.

At the Clearwater stream in northwestern Idaho, the Indians fought a defensive engagement that lasted for two days. Soldiers of the Fourth US Artillery under Colonel Marcus Miller of Modoc War fame figured prominently in this action. The Indians understood the significance of the artillery and attempted to silence it by concentrating their fire on the gunners. The Redlegs stood to their guns and poured effective canister and shellfire on their opponents, enabling the soldiers to stand firm and eventually dislodge the Nez Perces.[24]

Another engagement occurred when Colonel John Gibbon marched against the Nez Perces from his post in Fort Raw, Montana. At Big Hole in the Bitterroot Mountains of southwestern Montana, he found the Indians and attacked their lodges in a dawn assault. The Indians rallied and conducted a fierce defense. In this fight, Nez Perce warriors captured Gibbon's only howitzer and disabled it. They were then able to disengage and make good their escape.

Gibbon erred when he didn't bring the howitzer forward with the assaulting troops. It couldn't support his assault and, at the same time, lacked infantry or cavalry support. Gibbon's actions are puzzling because he had written a manual for artillerists in 1863 where he advocated using the artillery in conjunction with the other arms.[25]

This skirmish also proved that the Nez Perces understood the value of artillery and concentrated their efforts against it. The taking of the gun was a tribute to their bravery and acute tactical sense.

By late September, the Nez Perces, tired, hungry and decimated, had, nonetheless, repeatedly contained and outwitted a much larger and better-equipped army. Their valiant odyssey was cut short by Colonel Miles only about 40 miles south of the Canadian border. His mixed column of cavalry and mounted infantry included a Napoleon and his new Hotchiss gun. Miles surprised the Indians in their lodges, but his assault was brought to a halt by the usual accurate Nez Perce marksmanship. Some braves occupied prepared rifle pits while others ensured the safety of their women and children.

Miles' artillerymen improvised by digging up the ground to the rear of their pieces, sinking in the tailpieces and elevating the guns in order to achieve a higher trajectory against the entrenched Indians.[26] Their high-angle fire caused some casualties and held the Indians at bay, but it did not prove decisive.

The engagement was inconclusive; both sides sniped at each other for a few days without either being able to press the attack or withdraw. Resistance finally ceased with the arrival of the main body under the command of General Howard. These reinforcements convinced the Nez Perces of the futility of further resistance. The campaign ended on a poignant note when Chief Joseph surrendered his rifle to General Howard exclaiming: "From where the sun now stands, I will fight no more—forever."[27]

Tactical Analysis

As has been shown, artillery was commonly used in attacks on Indian encampments. This isn't the place to comment on the morality or appropriateness of these actions. Suffice it to say that they were controversial, even in their own day. Both Generals Sherman and Sheridan considered attacking Indian villages in winter an integral part of their campaigns of attrition.[28] On the purely technical level, they only confirm the destructive power of artillery against a massed target.

Artillery was used by Major Evans against the Comanches and Kiowas at Soldier's Creek. Some years later Colonel Miles employed artillery against the Sioux. Most of the engagements in the Nez Perce campaign were fought when the Indians defended their camps against the Army. Finally, artillery was employed in the last tragic act of the Indian wars. At Wounded Knee, the 7th Cavalry and its attached battery of four Hotchiss breechloaders killed and wounded more than 200 Sioux, including many women and children.[29]

Perhaps the true battlefield significance of Field Artillery in the western environment may be judged by comparing those engagements in which it was present to those where it was lacking. The Custer and Fetterman debacles were the worst defeats the Army suffered in the western campaigns against the Indians. Both were inflicted upon units whose commanders were recklessly overconfident, disobeyed or very liberally interpreted their orders and were lacking in artillery. Given similar tactical situations, it is possible that without artillery firepower other engagements, such as those at Adobe Walls, Apache Pass and Evans' fight at Soldier's Creek, could have been just as disastrous.

Lessons for Today

What can today's Redlegs learn from the experiences of the Field Artillerymen who fought in the Indian wars? First and foremost, military forces that operate without clear, practical doctrine oriented to the battlefield realities they will likely face do so at their peril. They are forced to make-do with a continual search for immediate *ad hoc* solutions to critical battlefield situations. Although history shows that American soldiers have been great tactical improvisers, reacting to new challenges with flair and imagination, the lack of a doctrinal framework in the friction-fraught environment of battle recklessly invites disaster.

In the case of the Indian wars of the second half of the 19th century, the problem wasn't an absolute lack of doctrine. A highly developed doctrine based on European models existed and was practiced and modified to suit the realities of the great American Civil War.

The problem was that the Indian campaigns lay outside the accepted parameters of "civilized warfare." The Indian wars were regarded variously as "policing the frontier," conducting expeditions against "renegades" or "punishing raiders." All these types of actions were considered unworthy of serious military thought and, consequently, were thought to be outside the pale of the "major and minor" tactical practice of the period. The underlying stream of thought seems to have been that professional military officers should have no trouble overcoming bands of "half-naked savages."[30]

This is eerily similar to the situation we face today. US Army units are called upon to conduct operations against warring factions that don't follow the model of war against a duly constituted nation state. Similarly, the Army possesses an adequate and battle-tested doctrine. However, there is a tendency to equate this doctrine to more abstract and, presumably, unalterable principles of war. I suggest that the appropriate response isn't to make doctrine fit a procrustean theoretical framework, but to tailor it to more specific likely theaters of operations.

Collectively, we prefer to think and write about Desert Storm, and even World War II rather than about Grenada, Mogadishu, Haiti, the Balkans, et al.[31] Again, commonly heard comments, such as "the Army is not a police force," "we're not in the disaster relief business," etc., fail to accept the most likely operational realities and leave us unprepared for them.[32]

The fact is that even a cursory study of American military history reveals that small conflicts of all descriptions far outnumber "real" high- to mid-intensity wars fought between "nation states." The problem, then as now, is a lack of appropriate theater-specific doctrine. This is especially critical as it pertains to the role of Field Artillery and firepower support in general.

Clearly, the formulation of doctrine is a central element of strategy and isn't the exclusive purview of artillerymen or even of the Army as a whole. But as the coordinators of the fire-support battlefield operating system (BOS), artillery officers must make their voices heard at every step of the doctrine writing process.

Second, artillery employment must be an integral part of the operational commander's overall campaign plan. In the Indian campaigns, artillery was included in the plans more as an afterthought or because a particular asset was readily available than as part of a well thought-out plan of action.

The sole exception to this practice appears to have been Nelson Miles, who not only included artillery and infantry in his columns, but also attempted to maximize the element of surprise by concealing the pieces in covered supply wagons. Significantly, Miles included infantry in his mixed columns to exploit the firepower advantage of the infantry rifle and to protect his supply trains.[33] The pragmatic and efficient Miles presents a stark contrast to the overconfident and romantic Custer who derided both infantry and artillery support, assuming he would conquer solely through his cavalry's elan.

Third, artillery is almost always a tactical "heavy hitter." Whenever artillery firepower can be effectively brought to bear, it can decisively alter the balance of combat power. Even relatively light pieces are "heavy hitters" in a light environment. This battlefield reality was clearly demonstrated whenever light pieces were brought to bear against the Indians. In such an environment, artillery provides a significant measure of force protection insurance against threats but only if it is kept at the ready. Now, as then, the ability of Field Artillery to harm the enemy at a distance gives the force with the artillery a marked advantage.

The protection Field Artillery provides to infantry and cavalry is an enormous contribution to their morale and operational effectiveness. As Robert Scales observes in his book *Firepower in Limited War,* "Bold strokes across the map mean little in such [guerrilla] wars. Occasional maneuver by battalions is the practical limit. The purpose of supporting firepower should be to amplify the destructive power of a limited maneuver force and to protect it against catastrophic losses in the field."[34]

On the other hand, the offensive decisiveness of Field Artillery is directly tied to its deployment capabilities and the rapidity with which it can be "unlimbered" and brought into action. Many of the tactical possibilities and limitations of Field Artillery that emerged during the Indian wars remain true today in similar operational environments. Today's technology offers much greater operational and tactical mobility, but to maximize these capabilities, the artillery commander must be proactive and anticipate where his pieces may be most effectively deployed.

Finally, in common with many other chapters in US Army history, it was the junior officer or NCO on the ground that made a difference. By quickly appraising the situation and reacting energetically to the tactical problem at hand, these junior leaders made the best out of bad situations, sometimes turning the tide of battle in their favor. This type of energetic, decisive action at the small unit-level has been, and continues to be, a distinctive strength in the American Army.

Nonetheless, the penchant for improvisation and clear thinking in critical situations should never serve as a substitute for foresight and detailed planning. Now, as then, the wise artillerist must ensure his voice is heard at all stages of the planning process—operational, tactical and in the conduct of battle. Only then can the Army maximize the true potential of artillery while minimizing its limitations.

DAVID J. ULBRICH

★　★　★　★　★　★　★　★

Clarifying the Origins and Strategic Mission of the US Marine Corps Defense Battalion, 1898–1941

Purpose and Scope

'Remember Wake!'[1] The ringing battle cry helped to rally a nation. From 8 to 23 December 1941, some 400 US marines from the First Defense Battalion held Wake Island against insurmountable odds. They repelled Japanese amphibious, air and sea attacks, only surrendering when their situation became untenable. The marines at Wake proved to some extent the defense battalion's tactical merits.[2]

Before Pearl Harbor, these units also complemented the amphibious assault units to form what could be considered the US Marine Corps' strategic dual mission: supporting the US Fleet by the seizure and defence of advanced island bases. Their particular uses evolved over time from coaling stations to submarine bases and finally to air bases.[3] Advanced base theory provided the conceptual Framework; and in 1939 the defense battalion became the application.[4]

Using recently declassified records from the National Archives[5] this article argues that advanced base theory and the defense battalion consistently played integral roles in America's Pacific strategy prior to

the Second World War. From the turn of the century until the Japanese attack on Pearl Harbor, the Corps' highest priority gradually
shifted from base defence toward amphibious assault. Yet this shift did
not necessarily marginalise defense battalions.

Some historians of the Marine Corps have discussed base defence
theory and defense battalions in a positive light. Little debate exists
about the base defence's importance for America's Pacific strategy from
1898 until to the early 1920s.[6] During the years thereafter, the defensive component of the Corps' dual mission receives less and less historical coverage. Those historians who do examine the defense battalion
in a positive light often fall short of presenting the unit's full strategic
significance in the pre-Second World War context. My research ex-
pands on this line of thinking by placing the defense battalion in context as an essential part of America's pre-war Pacific strategy.[7]

However, despite accepting advanced base theory as the conceptual foundation for defense battalions, other historians of the Marine
Corps pay scant attention to these units. Theirs is the established view
which, if the units are mentioned at all, most often portrays defense
battalions in two ways. First, defense battalions are downplayed in
favour of the Marine divisions, the units which fulfilled the amphibious assault part of the Corps' dual strategic mission. In this interpretation, amphibious assault almost seems to be projected backward in time
before December 1941 as the Corps' overwhelmingly primary mission.
Second, the defense battalions' actual importance is sometimes muddled by unclear historical explanations of their theoretical and practical
roles in pre-war strategy. The reader may become confused by conflicting representations of strategy and operations in prewar and wartime contexts.[8] At any rate, defense battalions get lumped together
with 'special units' such as raider, barrage balloon, and parachute battalions. Presumably, according to the accepted view, the 'skilled' personnel in all these units would have been better assigned to Corps'
amphibious assault units.[9]

The fact that defense battalions and other units siphoned off
above-average marines from the amphibious assault units is not dis-
puted here. Likewise, there is no argument over the fact that by the late
1930s amphibious assault theory had certainly found its practical application in the Marine division. For present purposes, the key issues are
those generally accepted interpretations and explanations of defense
battalions. Both issues can be better understood by determining
whether the allocation of manpower and other resources to defense
battalions made sense in the pre-Second World War strategic context.

On one level, the established view's focus on amphibious assault may be warranted because of the crucial offensive role played by the Marine divisions during the Pacific War. These units occupied a highly visible place as the conflict developed; conversely, defense battalions saw much less conspicuous wartime action. Nevertheless, on another level, the period of high visibility of amphibious assault refers to a time long after the attack on Pearl Harbor—not before it—and therefore is of limited utility in understanding prewar Marine Corps history.

The aim of this article is to clarify, if not correct, the established historical interpretations and explanations about Marine defense battalions by analysing their role in the Corps' dual strategic mission as well as in the preparations to perform that role. These units claimed a long pre-history and consistently retained a prominent place in context of America's prewar Pacific strategy. Even in 1941, defense battalions remained the Corps' second highest priority directly below the amphibious assault units and, consequently, could not be viewed as marginal or marginalised units.

Base Defence Theory 1898–1933

Defense battalions were not created in a vacuum in 1939; on the contrary, their origins can be traced as far back as the turn of the century. Prior to 1898 marines had traditionally served in a small Marine Corps as seaborne soldier and constabulary security. Victory in the Spanish–American War propelled the United States of America into great power status and transformed the Corps' role in naval strategy.[10] Adhering to Mahanian principles, naval planners realised that an American fleet could dominate the seas only if a network of bases existed. Controlling islands like Guam, Wake and Midway meant controlling trade routes and communication lines; some island bases were expected to be used as coaling stations. With these needs in mind, the United States Navy's General Board charged the Marine Corps with defending America's outlying bases. Thus the theory of advanced base defense was born.[11]

Between 1910 and 1917 the Corps formed the Advanced Base Brigade and established an Advanced Base School. During base defence manoeuvres on Culebra in 1914, the brigade successfully fortified the island, harassed the attacking flotilla, and repulsed an amphibious assault.[12] Initially, planners envisioned a single Marine unit that could either defend or seize an island base. Colonel John Lejeune, later Commandant of the Marine Corps from 1920 to 1929, even believed that the advanced base force could also easily be adapted to base seizure. This dual role for the single unit proved impractical because base defence weapons and equipment were too cumbersome to be sent ashore in a quick amphibious assault. Although by the beginning of the First World War the Corps had been acknowledged as ideally suited for base defence, neither the Navy nor the civilian government allocated the resources to the Corps necessary for the deployment of forces or fortification of island bases.[13]

Marine participation in the First World War did little to influence directly the evolution of the base defence concept. But the outcome of that war definitely affected base defence in a strategic necessity. In the postwar draw-down the Advanced Base Brigade was replaced by the Marine Expeditionary Force (MEF), a new unit with both defence and assault functions. But, without exercises or equipment, the MEF did not constitute a viable fighting force. Simultaneously, in the 1920s, a very significant strategic need for base defence arose in the Pacific Ocean because Japan emerged as the major threat to America's strategic and commercial interests in the Far East.[14]

While drawing up contingency plans for a war against Japan, US Navy planners had to find a way to defend US bases and seize those of the Japanese. The Marine Corps presented itself as the logical choice for both defensive and offensive operations and found its *raison d'être* in this dual mission: seizure complemented defense.[15]

In 1921 Marine Major Earl H. Ellis laid out the details in his two definitive works on Pacific naval strategy. His *Navy Bases: Their Location, Resources, and Security* as well as his *Advanced Base Operations in Micronesia* affirmed the Corps' place in the US Navy's strategy. Because Ellis envisioned an offensive war against Japan, the amphibious assault component grew in relation to base defence. Still, when marines captured bases, these same bases had to be held against potential counterattack, a very real danger. Base defence thus played a significant role even in an offensive campaign.[16] Ellis was not alone in promoting defensive and offensive advanced base operations; many Marine and Navy personnel concurred that marines should perform both operations.[17]

The two Ellis reports immediately found applications in America's strategy. The Five Power Treaty of 1922 prohibited the US from fortifying bases in the western Pacific and thus limited America's ability to respond to Japan's threat in the region.[18] American strategists reacted by formulating the coloured plans to fight wars against potentially hostile nations—Japan's designation being 'Orange'. After a Japanese attack in the opening round of a conflict, the 1926 ORANGE Plan anticipated 'an offensive war, primarily Naval, directed toward the isolation and exhaustion of Japan, through offensive operations against her naval forces and economic life'.[19] Specifically, the US Fleet would sail westward, crush the Japanese fleet in cataclysmic battles, relieve the beleaguered Philippines, and strangle the Japanese home islands. The ORANGE Plan directed the Corps to defend and seize island bases in support of the fleet's operations.[20]

The interservice report 'Joint Action of the Army and Navy' of 1927 concurred with the ORANGE Plan on the Corps' dual mission. The Departments of the Army and the Navy designated the Corps' 'fundamental' duties as follows: 'land operations in support of the fleet for the initial seizure and defense of advanced bases and for such limited auxiliary land operations as are essential to the successful prosecution of the Naval campaign'.[21] Emphasis within such a campaign was placed on the marine units' strategic mobility. Taken together, the ORANGE Plan and 'Joint Action of the Army and Navy' report echoed Ellis, not to mention the great naval theorist Alfred Thayer Mahan.[22]

Obtaining operational readiness still entailed overcoming many obstacles. Republican-directed reductions in the 1920s and the Great Depression in the 1930s caused fiscal hardship for the Corps. The US military as a whole was slashed to the barest necessity. The Corps' strength steadily sank to its lowest level in 1936, with 17,239 officers and men.[23] To make matters worse, stagnation of promotion and pay plagued the Corps until the late 1930s. At the same time, Japan began increasing its offensive capabilities and building an East Asian empire.[24]

Base Defence Theory Becomes Reality, 1933–1939

With the election in 1932 of former Assistant Secretary of the Navy Franklin D. Roosevelt as President, the Corps' prospects improved. Carl Vinson, a Democrat from Georgia, also assumed the Chairmanship of the House Naval Affairs Committee in the Democratic landslide in 1932. Marine Reservist Melvin J. Maas of Minnesota served as the ranking minority member of House Naval Affairs and consistently helped increase the Corps' level of preparedness. In Roosevelt, Vinson, Maas and others, the Marine Corps finally found, powerful patrons in the White House and Congress who looked sympathetically on the seaborne services' fiscal woes. Nevertheless, the American public remained unwilling to tolerate substantial military budget increases for most of the decade.[25]

A year later, the Navy created the Fleet Marine Force (FMF). It would eventually evolve into a viable fleet support unit. Regarded by many Marine Corps historians as primarily fulfilling an amphibious assault mission, the FMF's mandate actually included both base defence and seizure components.[26] In a 1934 article in the *Marine Corps Gazette* titled 'The Fleet Marine Force,' Marine Lieutenant Colonel Ralph S. Keyser explained that the FMF had been specifically designed for the 'establishment and protection' as well as the 'seizure and denial' of advanced bases. Keyser was not alone in his contention that the FMF was both offensive and defensive; official and unofficial contemporary Marine Corps and Navy sources as well some Marine Corps historians also point to this dual role.[27] Yet, despite the call for such a base defence unit on paper, no unit specifically designed for this mandate existed in 1933.

Also in 1934, students and faculty at the Marine Corps Schools (MCS) also compiled the *Tentative Manual of Landing Operations*. According to this text, the FMF would support the fleet 'by land operations in the seizure, defense, and holding of temporary advanced bases'. During the Navy's campaign, seized bases would have to be occupied by a Marine detachment securing 'temporary bases' against counterattack. As the campaign progressed, an Army unit was expected to replace the marine base defence unit if the base became a 'permanent base'. The Marine unit would then be free to follow the campaign's next movement.[28] Island bases on Wake, Midway and Guam may also seem to be 'permanent' in nature and therefore within the Army's responsibility. But, Navy planners clearly considered island bases like these to be advanced bases and therefore the Corps' responsibility to safeguard.[29] Perhaps the best way to understand the difference between 'temporary' and 'permanent' bases would be to think of temporary bases as those bases in relatively immediate danger of enemy attack. Permanent bases, on the other hand, lay further back from the combat area and therefore were expected to be garrisoned by the Army (see Appendices 1, 2 and 4).[30]

While marines hammered out base seizure and defence techniques, international tensions escalated as Japan expanded in Manchuria, violated treaties on arms limitations, and left the League of Nations. American strategists recognised that the possibility of a war with Japan loomed ominously on the horizon. The new situation necessitated a fresh set of war plans. Amidst these ever-changing circumstances, the

Corps struggled to sustain its offensive and defensive niches in the new war plans. For instance, in the report 'Joint Action of Army and Navy, 1935', the Corps was subsumed within the Navy's proposed function as America's only seaborne service. This report failed to mention any of the Corps' 'general functions', but that did not diminish the genuine strategic need for the Corps' special offensive and defensive capabilities. Consequently, the Corps used both base defence and amphibious assault as means to retain its identity as a seaborne service (see Appendix 1).[31]

Marine planners believed that the Corps could ill afford to neglect the base defence and amphibious assault mandates in America's Pacific strategy, just as the nation's Pacific strategy could not exclude those mandates. So, when recommending revisions for the above 'Joint Action of Army and Navy, 1935', Marine Corps Commandant Ben H. Fuller called for a verbatim restatement of the Corps' functions as found in the 'Joint Action of Army and Navy, 1927'. He claimed that amphibious assault and base defence were 'valuable' and 'essential' contributions to a successful campaign. Neglecting to mention marine units in these capacities, Fuller complained, would also be a 'disadvantage' to the Corps in 'development, planning, procurement, and training for war'. Two intertwined themes can be seen in Fuller's recommended revisions: first, the Navy had to be reminded that base seizure and defence fulfilled certain strategic requirements; and second, the Corps had to be reaffirmed as a 'coordinate element of national defense'.[32]

As the 1930s drew to a close, America's strategic position in the world looked more and more dismal. On paper, war plans existed to deal with a Japanese conflict. While few steps had been taken to increase operational readiness, the FMF did make some strides toward training amphibious assault units and improving its landing techniques. Nevertheless, no unit specifically designed for bases and no significant construction projects on island bases existed. To rectify this situation, the US Navy convened the Hepburn Board in December 1938. After examining the difference between theory and reality, the Board strongly recommended that island outposts including Guam, Wake, Palmyra, Johnston and Midway be fully developed and equipped as bases for submarines, aircraft and surface vessels. Board members saw the development of these advanced bases as a strategic imperative for both deterring Japanese expansion in the western Pacific and allowing America to react to Japanese movement. To hold the islands against Japanese air, sea and amphibious assaults, the Hepburn Board called for the Marine Corps to form 'defense detachments' much like the Advanced Base Brigade

20 years before. By early 1939, then, the Corps found itself firmly en-
sconced as the Navy's base defence and amphibious assault force.[33]

In accordance with the Hepburn Board's recommendations, advanced defence base theory coalesced into naval strategy with the advent
of the Marine Corps defense battalion in autumn 1939. It is noteworthy that bringing a bona fide base defence unit on line completed the
FMF's dual support mission as originally conceived in 1934.[34] The appropriations bill before Congress in early 1939 included only funds to
build up Guam; however, the Navy began planning fortification and
construction for several island bases in the western Pacific. In addition,
the Navy designated the tentative size and armament of the defence
detachments to be stationed on the island bases.[35]

Defense battalions fitted the Navy's strategic priority for base defence perfectly. They possessed 'zero tactical mobility' but could be rapidly transported across an ocean with only two days' notice. These units
also added self-sufficiency to their strategic mobility.[36] Because of indef-
inite periods of isolation and the logistical challenges of resupply, Marine First Lieutenant Robert D. Heinl, Jr, argued that defense battalions
should receive 'as least as much' ammunition as assault units. His perspective was noteworthy because he later served in two defense battalions and with amphibious assault units. After the war, Heinl also wrote a
history of the Corps which reveals many of his personal perspectives.
Other Marine and Navy planners hoped that the US Pacific Fleet would
relieve a besieged island base before the logistical situation became desperate.[37]

Theoretically composed of about 1000 heavily armed leathernecks,
defense battalions could repel air, sea and land attacks. Although modest in manpower, they boasted truly impressive firepower: six Navy
5-inch guns, 12 3-inch AA guns, 48 .50-calibre machine guns, and
48 .30-calibre machine guns. Heavier 7-inch guns might also be included among the artillery. The proportion of marines per heavy
weapon in a defense battalion was much greater than in the conventional FMF amphibious assault unit of similar size. In fact, the unit's
weaponry approximated the firepower of a light cruiser.[38]

Japan protested against the Hepburn Board's recommendations—
especially the fortification of Guam and other western Pacific islands.
The Japanese planners clearly recognised the strategic significance of
US bases in the western Pacific. They hoped to use the various western
Pacific islands as a defensive buffer against American intrusion. Thus,
Japanese strategy essentially mirrored US strategy.[39]

The Defense Battalions' Niche in America's Pacific Strategy, 1939–1941

While plans existed for deploying defense battalions and fortifying island bases, few steps were actually taken toward the end of achieving the plans' goals. Pathetically insufficient manpower and equipment hampered the Corps' combat readiness. Admiral Harold Stark, Chief of Naval Operations (CNO), tried to free personnel for service in defense battalions. He contemplated replacing marine units at naval stations with Army units as well as transferring marines from amphibious assault units to defense battalions. Stark's most surprising possible means of manning the units involved transferring marines from the FMF's amphibious assault units to defense battalions. Even with such high-level sanction, wringing appropriations from a tight-fisted Congress remained a perennial challenge. The Corps required more funding to fulfil its dual mission.[40]

The outbreak of war in Europe in 1939 constituted a major watershed for the Corps and America's military as a whole. As President Roosevelt declared a 'limited national emergency', strategic planning ceased being a hypothetical exercise. Coordinating coalition warfare on multiple fronts made the ORANGE Plan obsolete and subsequently required more flexible contingency plans. In replacing the ORANGE Plan, American strategists tried to predict every possible wartime scenario in formulating the five new RAINBOW Plans. For example, one version called for America to defend the western hemisphere unilaterally; a different version called for France and Britain to fight Germany on the Continent while the US concentrated on defeating Japan in the Far East. Whereas the various RAINBOW Plans changed strategy for America's Navy and Army, the Corps' dual mission of base seizure and defence remained constant.[41]

With overriding threats in Europe and in the Far East, justification of the need for base seizure and defence forces and material ceased to be a major issue. Expansion of the American military as a whole emerged as the new major issue: how much and how fast? The Corps' public relations machine quickly exploited the increased interest in preparedness. In all forms of media, marines touted their service as America's 'first line of defense'. The Corps' publicity efforts cleverly highlighted the defensive component for publicity purposes; non-aggressive rhetoric played well with the American public still heavily leaning toward isolationism.[42]

The reality of unpreparedness also persisted. Supplying either assault or defence missions severely stretched the Corps' already meagre resources. Allocation of men and material for the both halves of the strategic dual mission was impossible.[43] As of June 1940, only a fraction of 'on order' ammunition had been obtained. For projectiles above .50-calibre, an average of 2.5 units of fire were on hand' and 4.5 units were 'on order'. This was a small fraction of the 22.5 units of fire required for full combat readiness. 'On order' items due by 1942 failed to match the FMF's total material and ammunition requirements. Even in this time of need, defense battalions still occupied a significant enough place among the Corps' priorities to justify distribution of weapons and ammunition.[44]

The Corps could not have expanded quickly without help from international disappointments like France's unexpected collapse and Britain's desperate situation. The dismal global scene raised the American public's desire for military preparedness. The elections of 1940 marked another watershed for the Corps. No longer did the President or sympathetic Members of Congress feel hamstrung by isolationist voters. As America's isolationist tone gradually shifted to a non-belligerent interventionist tone, the defense battalions, the Corps and the American military as a whole were beneficiaries.

Because of the constantly changing international situation, America's military planners began formulating yet another set of strategies to deal with the Axis threat. Building on the obsolete ORANGE Plan and RAINBOW 5 Plans, the CNO wrote his so-called 'Stark Memorandum'. Stark submitted the final version of this memo to the Secretary of the Navy on 12 November 1940, less than two weeks after Roosevelt's re-election. In the event that America entered the war, Stark's series of contingency plans, the last of which was named Plan DOG, called for a concentrated effort against Germany. Meanwhile, American forces would conduct a 'strategic defense' against Japan which included maintaining a picket line along the Malay Barrier and making 'limited' or 'tactical' offensives in the central Pacific. Plan DOG eventually formed the basis for the American-British Conference (ABC-1), the blueprint for the defeat of the Axis powers drawn up in early 1941.[45]

Although the new war plans de-emphasised the Navy's role in the Pacific, the Corps figured heavily as the defensive and offensive forces for operations in Plan DOG and the ABC-1 talks. This was especially true of a the anticipated 'strategic defense' in which island bases would periodically change hands back and forth between adversaries. Both American and Japanese forces would make air, sea and land assaults on the opponents' island bases as well as their naval forces in the vicinity.[46]

Advance base theory had clearly achieved a high priority in the Navy's strategic plans. Defense battalions then lacked only a large enough share of the Corps' resources to be raised to combat readiness. A memo dated 10 January 1941 from Admiral R. E. Ingersoll to Commandant Thomas Holcomb confirms base defense's place in the Corps and the Navy's priority list. Ingersoll writing on behalf of the CNO stated:

> It is the desire of the [CNO] that the [Commandant] take the necessary steps to provide for the organization and equipment of six (6) additional Marine Defense Battalions, the project to take first priority after completion of the organization of the two Marine Divisions.[47]

Hence, although Ingersoll did prioritise the Corps' personnel with amphibious assault units ranked ahead of base defense units, the two divisions neither eliminated nor marginalised the defense battalions' mandate (see Appendix 2).

Correspondence between high-level Marine and Navy personnel indicated still more speculation about the possibility of forming 'Separate Infantry Battalions' to serve as combat support for defense battalions (see Appendix 3). When ranking all the Corps' priorities later in 1941, the FMF's two divisions always occupied the highest place followed immediately by defense battalions. Marine aviation units and shipboard units still remained in lower priorities than amphibious assault and base defence.[48]

By March 1941 seven defense battalions had been formed, and the defense battalion on Midway had received its full complement of marines. While encouraging at face value, only five of the seven defense battalions 'could be considered as being reasonably well trained and prepared to carry out the mission of defending small bases against minor raids'. A 'minor raid' was considered an attack coming from small enemy flotillas and assault forces, not unlike the forces which would eventually attack Wake Island. The two units lacking 'certain major items' depended on the Army to furnish its equipment. According to one estimate, bringing the defense battalions to full readiness would take four months—until July 1941.[49]

The FMF's two divisions also faced severe shortages. These two amphibious assault units possessed only 50 per cent of their manpower and 40 per cent of their required equipment. A report on the FMF's deficiencies predicted a 16-month delay until July 1942 before 100 per cent manpower could be achieved in the two divisions. Conversely, the defense battalions' 'speed of attainment' was only four months, a full year shorter than the two divisions designated as amphibious assault units. This indicates some sense of urgency concerning the real value of defense battalions, in absolute terms and in terms relative to the amphibious assault forces.[50]

Available manpower lagged far behind actual demand. As the Corps neared 50,000 officers and men in April 1941, its 'Plan for Expansion' called for subsequent growth to 75,000. Yet, the Corps perpetually included less than 50 per cent of the strength required by American war plans.[51]

Because of the alarming gains made by the Axis powers, America's industrial mobilisation and military expansion accelerated in 1941. The Lend–Lease Program created another level of competition for scarce resources. For example, American industrial backing was a boon for Britain but also exacerbated the already severe shortages in material in the US itself. As for manpower, employment opportunities in manufacturing siphoned off many potential recruits. Young men could obtain safer, more lucrative employment than joining the military. The resulting recruitment and procurement difficulties caused intense competition among the services. Yet, despite all the other opportunities for employment, the Corps still recruited young men who wanted 'to be marines'.[52] Whereas stagnation of pay and promotion had been a difficulty for more than 20 years, the Corps faced two new challenges: attracting men with the physical qualifications to be marines and then training the green recruits to be leathernecks.[53]

Inside the Marine Corps, the distribution of limited resources among its multiple responsibilities yields much evidence for the importance of defense battalions. Sufficient quantities of men and equipment simply did not exist. Several cases in point illustrate the frustration faced by the Corps' leadership as they robbed Peter to pay Paul.

Scarcity of experienced commissioned and non-commissioned officers increasingly plagued the Corps. Filling the marine divisions and defense battalions, let alone amphibious units such as the two Marine divisions, became problematic in 1941. Defense battalions required a more flexible tactical command structure than amphibious assault units. For example, the defense battalions were expected to function autonomously during an enemy's attack. As of 30 November 1941, 5264 marines were serving in six defense battalions; this amounted to 20 per cent of the 26,560 marines in the entire FMF. Of these 5264 marines,

4399 from five defense battalions were on post outside the continental United States, whereas a paltry 489 marines from the Second Marine Division had been stationed outside the continental US.[54] With a finite amount of manpower available for assignment in any unit, these figures were much too high for units considered by planners to be strategically unimportant. Defense battalions were not the only units which devoured scarce manpower; formation of Marine Aircraft Groups compounded the Corps' current manpower shortages.[55]

The defense battalions' significance may also be seen through the eyes of the officers corps. Marine planners considered assigning colonels to command defense battalions because of the need for flexibility and autonomy. A chance for independent command would also have enticed officers into requesting transfer to these base defense units. Lower ranking officers undoubtedly made such requests. In any case, with the severe shortage of experienced officers in 1940 and 1941, the mere mention of using a senior officer such as a colonel to command a defense battalion testifies to this unit's importance.[56]

The quality of the officers assigned to defense battalions caused much concern as manpower allocation became more problematic. Service in defense battalions required specialised mathematical skills for radar operation, anti-aircraft direction, and coastal artillery direction. Not every marine possessed these skills. In the mid-1930s, the Marine Corps Schools (MCS) devoted a considerable amount of course work to advanced base defense including part of one class and another entire class. Specifically, the 'First Year Class' entailed study of 'command and staff functions of . . . independent units . . . including the seizure, occupation and defense of advanced bases'. For more advanced students, the 'Base Defense Weapons Class' covered 'technical and practical' issues such as the tactical use of base defense weapons. The 'Base Defense Weapons Course' lasted a full year and trained marines like Major James P. S. Devereux who, in December 1941, commanded the ill-fated leathernecks on Wake Island. By the late 1930s, the MCS 's curriculum had shifted to more emphasis on amphibious assault training but still included a significant component on advanced base defense.[57]

Regardless of the emphasis of a particular MCS course, information and techniques could be used simultaneously by both base defense and amphibious assault officers. This cross-fertilisation probably indicated mutual inclusiveness between defensive and offensive techniques and activities. For example, after graduating from the 'The Basic School' in 1938, Robert D. Heinl crossed over between defensive and offensive assignments. From 1938 to 1939, he served on the USS

Tuscaloosa and excelled at directing 5-inch gunfire. In 1939 Heinl transferred to the 4th Defense Battalion and later to the 13th Defense Battalion. Still later, he distinguished himself as a naval gunfire support
expert at Iwo Jima. It is important to note that Heinl did not attend the
MCS's 'Base Defense Weapons Course'. Yet, presumably, he gleaned
valuable lessons from both halves of the Corps' dual mission. Heinl
drew diverse experiences from serving in both base defense and amphibious assault units. He also wrote several articles and reports which
helped articulate the Corps' dual mission. In the previous discussions
about manpower distribution and the educational system in the Corps,
the defense battalions drew so many 'skilled' personnel for a very good
reason: Navy and Marine planners expected these units to fulfil the vital strategic mission of advanced base defence.[58]

Despite fiscal and organisational challenges, elements of the 1st Defense Battalion were finally stationed on Midway, Wake and Palmyra
by July 1941. While these new developments represented encouraging
steps, reality can be seen the US Navy's 'Are We Ready III' report of
September 1941. It replied to the question in its own title with a negative answer. The Corps stayed 50 per cent below its then authorised
strength. The ammunition supply looked no better. On average, the
two marine divisions and all six defense battalions possessed less than
five units of fire.[59]

In addition to shortages in manpower and ammunition, defense
battalions lacked .30 and .50-calibre machine guns as well as aircraft
support and radar sighting equipment. The shortage of machine guns
especially disturbed everyone from marines on the island bases to
Admiral Husband Kimmel, Commander in Chief of the Pacific Fleet
(CINCPAC). In one of several reports to CNO Stark, Kimmel
pleaded: 'I do think that the few machine guns required by these [de-
fense] battalions should be spared from other activities and I hope
that the ammunition situation will be remedied very shortly.[60] The
CINCPAC had hard choices to make with limited resources; the fact
that he desired to get the most basic weapons to the defense battalions stationed in the Pacific testifies to these units' significance. Kimmel's urgent requests did not bring much help for the marines
stationed on islands such as Wake, Guam and Midway. Sufficient
weapons, ammunition and equipment did not exist—not for the
Corps, the Navy or the Army.[61]

Little could be done to speed America's armament. The sluggish
wheels of democracy turned very slowly (see Appendix 4). Less than
2 months before the Japanese attack on Pearl Harbor, items 'on order'

were expected to take three to ten months to bring the defense battalions to full combat readiness. Stop-gap measures such as dispatching anti-quated aircraft to Wake and Midway did little to raise combat readiness.[62]

Conclusion

The established historical view portrays the US Marine Corps defense battalions in two ways: it may muddle the explanation for this unit's role in the Corps' dual strategic mission; or it may devalue the defense battalions for depleting the manpower and equipment available for am-phibious assault units and thus undermine the Corps' overall level of readiness. Admittedly, much of the impetus for defense battalions came from outside the Corps and possibly from a minority within the Corps. Likewise, defense battalions certainly did draw manpower and resources from the Marine divisions.[63] Yet, when these statements are re-examined in light of recently unearthed documentation, the only plausible conclu-sion could be that defense battalions played a significant role in prewar plans and thus justified large manpower and equipment allocations. As heir to the advanced base theory, the US Marine Corps defense battalion remained an essential fixture in America's war plans.

US military operations and strategy before the Second World War cannot be measured according to operations and strategy during the conflict. Strategy and operations were two different animals—made that much more so by vastly disparate prewar and wartime contexts. Because the Japanese attack on Pearl Harbor drastically changed America's strate-gic situation, much of prewar planning had to be scrapped, at least in the short term.[64]

Appendices

APPENDIX 1

/declassified/   11 May 1936

FROM: The Major General Commandant
TO: The Chief of Naval Operations
SUBJECT: Recommended revision of Joint Action of Army and Navy, 1935
REFERENCES: (a) Joint Action of Army and Navy, 1935
              (b) Joint Action of Army and Navy, 1927
ENCLOSURES: (A) A suggested revision of reference (a).

1. The publication, Joint Action Army and Navy, 1935, recently distributed by the Department, treats the Marine Corps in a manner which is fundamentally different from the treatment in the 1927 edition. In the 1927 edition the Marine Corps was considered as a coordinate element of national defense, and its general functions were listed separately. In the 1935 edition the Marine Corps was considered "an integral part of the sea forces" and no Marine Corps general functions were specifically listed.

2. It is understood that there was no intention in this revision to curtail the general functions of the Marine Corps or to change the policies heretofore in effect relative to its development, planning, procurement and training. Nevertheless the wording of the 1935 edition is possible of an interpretation which may seriously affect the future usefulness of the Marine Corps.

3. Specifically two important functions of the Marine Corps, listed as shown below in the 1927 edition, do not appear to be properly covered in the 1935 edition:

   GENERAL FUNCTIONS OF THE MARINE CORPS

   (a) For land operations in support of the fleet for the initial seizure and the defense of advanced bases and for such limited auxiliary land operations as are essential to the prosecution of the naval campaign.

   (b) For emergency service in time of peace for protection of the interests of the United States in foreign countries.

Both of these functions are, in the 1935 edition, listed under Army functions and are *not* listed under Navy functions.

4. In the seizure and temporary defense of advanced bases, the Marine Corps can, it is believed, make its most valuable contribution to a naval campaign. The Marine Corps considers this function its primary mission and feels assured that its forces will be used by the Navy in this capacity to the limit of their capabilities. Considering the important purpose of this publication, the failure to provide, specifically, for this as a naval function, may react seriously to the disadvantage of the Marine Corps in the future development, planning, procurement and training for war.

5. The Navy has, from the organization of this Republic to and including the present time, exercised the function of landing its forces in an emergency in foreign countries in time of peace for protection of the interest of the United States. The Navy will undoubtedly continue to do so when the emergency so requires. It is therefore believed that this function should be specifically provided for under the Navy functions.

A failure to do so may in the future lead to misunderstandings, possibly leading to undesirable controversy.

6. There is the possibility also that the omission of paragraph 9, Chapter III, (1927 edition), leaves the right of the Marine Corps to operate shore based aircraft open to challenge. It is believed, however, that the statement that "neither service will attempt to restrict in any way the means and weapons used by the other services" gives sufficient reassurance that this question will not be raised.

7. In order that the subject may be clarified and important naval functions be specifically provided for, the Marine Corps strongly recommends:
   (a) That modifications, substantially as shown in enclosure (A), be included in the next revision of "Joint Action of the Army and Navy."
   (b) That the Marine Corps be advised by letter that it is the interpretation of the Navy Department that the functions of the Marine Corps as specified in the 1927 edition of this document remained unchanged.

ENCLOSURE (A)

CHAPTER 1.

6. General Functions of the Navy.

   1. General Functions of the Navy in peace and war.
      (1) — (2) —
      (3) To support the national policies and commerce of the United States and to provide forces for emergency service in foreign territory in support thereof.
      (4) —

   b. Additional General Functions of the Navy in war.
      (1) — (2) —
      (3) To seize, establish and to defend, until relieved by Army forces, advanced naval bases; and to conduct such limited auxiliary land operations as are essential to the prosecution of the naval campaign.

Source: History Amphibious File 38, Marine Corps University Research Archives.

APPENDIX 2

/declassified/   10 January 1941
FROM: The Chief of Naval Operations
TO: The Major General Commandant

SUBJECT: Organization of the Additional Marine Defense Battal-
                  ions.
REFERENCE: (a) MGC Confidential Serial 475440 dated 9 December
                  1940.

1. It is the desire of the Chief of Naval Operations that the Major General
   Commandant take the necessary steps to provide for the organization
   and equipment of six (6) additional Marine Defense Battalions, the project to take first priority after the completion of the organization of the
   two Marine Divisions. The necessary authorization and funds should be
   obtained from Congress at the earliest practicable date.
2. The Bureau of Ordnance is taking steps to recondition forty-one (41)
   7"/45 caliber guns and to equip these weapons with mechanical data receivers. The guns will be available for use by the new Defense Battalions. The Bureau of Ordnance will also prepare plans for concrete firing
   platforms for 7"/45 caliber guns.
3. The new Defense Battalions should be equipped with the new Army
   90 m/m, 37 m/m, 30 m/m, and .50 caliber anti-aircraft guns, insofar as
   these weapons can be made available by the Army, and estimates for funds
   should be drawn on this basis. In view of the shortage in these weapons,
   arrangements will probably have to be made to utilize temporarily such
   weapons as can be made available.
4. The Chief of Naval Operations concurs with the Major General Commandant relative to the employment of 7"/45 caliber gun at more permanent bases, rather than as normal equipment for defense battalions
   for use in the moving situations.

                                              /signed/
                                              R. E. Ingersoll
                                              Acting

Divisions of Plans and Policies War Plans Section 1926–1942, Box 4,
Record Group 127, National Archives and Records Administration.

APPENDIX 3

/declassified/

PLAN FOR EXPANSION OF THE US MARINE CORPS,
REPORT AND RECOMMENDATIONS
BY THE GENERAL BOARD,
MAY 6, 1941

Enclosure (A)

Report on Expansion of the US Marine Corps

1. The approved US Naval Policy includes the following:
   "To maintain the Marine Corps in such strength as to provide the requisite Fleet Marine Force and detachments for other purposes."
2. The strength of "requisite Fleet Marine Force" depends upon the overseas operations the Marine Corps is expected to undertake in war. The Joint Action of the Army and Navy states as follows:
   (a) "Land operations by the Navy are proper only when immediately auxiliary to or in support of normal Navy functions."
   (b) "The Marine Corps is an integral part of the Navy in war."
   In this same publication "General functions of the Navy in war" include
   (c) "To seize, establish and defend until relieved by Army forces advance naval bases and to conduct such limited auxiliary land operations as are essential to the prosecution of the naval campaign."
3. In order to carry of the functions of the Marine Corps in an overseas campaign, the Fleet Marine Force has been organized and is intended to include the following:
   (a) Marine Divisions for the seizure of advance naval bases;
   (b) Defense Battalions, Separate Infantry Battalions and Balloon Battalions, for the defense of advance naval bases;
   (c) Base Depots for support and supply of the Marine Divisions;
   (d) Aircraft wings for close cooperation with ground troops in the seizure of advance naval bases;
   (e) Base Defense Aircraft Groups to assist in the defense of advance naval bases, and
   (f) Base Air Detachments for maintenance of Aircraft Wings and Defense Air Groups.
   […]

The Fleet Marine Force

5. The Marine Division is the main subdivision of the Fleet Marine Force and its organization at present follows in general the lines of the Army triangular infantry division, with the exception that certain special troops, such as tank and parachute units, are attached to the Marine Division, whereas in the Army these are included in the Corps. There is a close approximation of weapons in the Marine and Army Divisions except that all weapons of Marine Infantry Regiments and of Light

Artillery units can be man-handled. Land transportation facilities for the Marine Division are included to support offensive operations up to 25 miles inland, but due to problems of sea transport they are kept at a minimum, and are but a fraction of those provided the Army Division.

6. The Marine Division, Table I, comprises 673 commissioned officers, 56 warrant officers, and 14,522 enlisted men of the Marine Corps, as at present organized.

7. The composition, organization and strength of the Marine Division are submitted to the General Board by the US Marine Corps appear to the satisfactory for the overseas landing operations. The question as to the number of Marine Divisions necessary has been fully discussed and while it appears that a major war conducted in both the Atlantic and Pacific might require three Marine Divisions, most of the probable operations can be carried through successfully with one Marine Division full supported as it would be by a Naval Attack Force. As present there are no Army organizations organized or trained for overseas landing operations for the seizure and occupation of a naval advance base and the nature of these operations is such that Marine Divisions with the special equipment and training will be essential for their effective conduct.

8. Even were there a number of Army Divisions organized and trained for the seizure of advanced naval bases it would still be essential that there be available to the Navy for immediate employment in an emergency, fully equipped, fully trained and always ready for active service, at least two Marine Divisions.

9. It is recommended, therefore, that two completely equipped and manned Marine Divisions be provided as soon as practicable [. . .] it is further recommended that there be obtained as soon as possible the equipment required for a third Marine Division [. . .]

10. The Defense Battalion is set up to provide defense forces at outlying bases against raids and minor attacks by aircraft, surface craft and landing forces, when defense forces are not provided by the Army or when the defense will be taken over by the Army after the base has been secured. Defense Battalions are in addition to the Marine Divisions, because the continuance of an overseas campaign many readily require the projection of landing force operations to other areas for the seizure of additional bases, and the Marine Divisions should not be depleted to provide troops for the defense of bases or positions occupied and thus lessen their effectiveness for future operations. Furthermore, the Defense Battalion includes weapons such as heavier guns

and anti-aircraft guns, that are not included in the Marine Division, because they are not primarily offensive weapons and would tend to lessen the mobility of the Marine Divisions.

11. Two general types of Defense Battalions are in contemplation, which may be designated Light and Heavy, dependent upon the types and numbers of weapons required to be employed. The difference in the two types is primarily due to the inclusion in the Heavy Defense Battalion of more and heavier A.A. machine guns and of 6-inch instead of 5-inch emplacement guns. The Light Defense Battalion consists of 34 commissioned officers, 6 warrant officers and 799 enlisted men of Marine Corps. The Heavy Defense Battalion consisted of 37 commissioned officers, 6 warrant officers, and 920 enlisted men of the Marine Corps. The composition, organization and strength of these Defense Battalions as submitted to the General Board by US Marine Corps, is consider satisfactory for the purposes intended.

12. Full consideration has been given to the number of Defense Battalions required and it is recommended that a total of 8 Defense Battalions, 4 Light and 4 Heavy, be organized as soon as possible and maintained in full strength. It is further recommended that the equipment necessary for 4 additional Heavy Defense Battalions be obtained and stored in emergency conditions require later organization of more Defense Battalions.

13. Separate Infantry Battalions are for the purpose of augmenting the Defense Battalions at an advanced naval base against minor raids. It is considered probable that in war most of the Defense Battalions will require infantry support, and it is not advisable or desirable to deplete the Marine Divisions of infantry for this purpose. The Separate Infantry Battalion consists of 34 commissioned officers and 815 enlisted men of the Marine Corps.

14. Consideration of total strength and of probable employment appear to require 8 of these Battalions and it is recommended that 8 Separate Infantry Battalions be organized as soon as equipment and personnel can be made available. [. . .]

19. The Base Defense Aircraft Group is contemplated for assignment to a advance naval base to augment the Defense Battalions and Separate Infantry Battalions by providing aviation for the defense.

20. While it is expected that naval advance bases seized and consolidated will be garrisoned by Army troops, there will be a period wherein these bases must be defended by Marines and during this period Marine Corps aviation must be included in the defense forces. The Marine Aircraft

Wing should not be depleted for this purpose as it will probably be required for further operations of the Marine Division. [. . .]

Source: General Records of the Department of the Navy, General Board Subject File 1900–1947, GB 432, Box 135, Record Group 80, National Archive and Records Administration.

APPENDIX 4

Secret   Pearl Harbor, T. H., 2 December 1941
FROM: Commander-in-Chief, United States Pacific Fleet
TO: The Chief of Naval Operations
SUBJECT: The Defense of Outlying Bases

[. . .]

5. It is not completely clear whether or not the Navy Department has in mind that the Army will ultimately relieve the Marine Defense Battalions. If so, it is assumed that such action would be taken in order to have those battalions and their equipment available to garrison positions taken by assault in the Marshalls and Carolinas. Should such assumption be correct, it is pertinent to note that transports, *trained* assault troops, etc., are not now available to make the seizures. Moreover, the local Army authorities are not only short of anti-aircraft equipment, but of most other armament necessary for the defense of an advanced island base. If the Marine Defense Battalions were withdrawn at this time it would be necessary to leave behind most of their equipment, and they would have none for use elsewhere.

6. To clarify the current situation to some extent, certain information and considerations that may not otherwise be readily available in the Department are mentioned below:

(a) Army is not only lacking AA guns for outlying bases, but has a serious shortage at Oahu. In has insufficient suitable guns for replacing the Marine 7" and 5" guns without weakening the defense of Hawaii. By taking 155 mm guns from Hawaii the Marine 5" guns might be replaced but the 155 mm guns would either cover a limited arc or else their mobility would be lost.

(b) Army can spare no .50 caliber machine guns but can supply rifles and .30 caliber machine guns.

[. . .]

(e) Army has personnel available in sufficient numbers to reenforce or relieve the Marine Defense Battalions. The Marines have been organized, equipped, and trained for work of this particular character.

They are already established, habited to the mode of life, and experienced in fitting their activities to accord with the various other naval activities in these outlying places. It is no reflection upon the Army to say that their units would require considerable time to acquire the proficiency in this specialized work that the Marines already have.

(f) In emergency, Army personnel might replace casualties or reenforce Marines, but it would, for the very obvious reasons, be highly preferable to have other Marines available for that purpose.

(g) No spare armament for defense battalions is available. In fact, some deficiencies in equipment for existing battalions exist [. . .] Armament and equipment for any new defense battalion has not been assembled.

(h) The bases are being developed to facilitate fleet operations. Irrespective of the source of defense forces, various other naval activities will continue at these outlying bases. Placing the defenses in Army hands would bring difficult problems of command relationships. Such problems would not, of course, be insurmountable, but would be avoided if the Marines are not replaced.

[. . .]

12. If, during the progress of the war, enemy positions are taken and require garrisons they should, of course, be defended by Marine Defense Battalions. It would be preferable to have Marine battalions with full equipment available for such duty without disrupting the defense of existing bases. At present, our Advanced Bases should be defended by the most competent personnel available, viz, the Marine Defense Battalion. If our progress in the war has brought more advanced positions under our control, then the most seasoned and experienced personnel should be in the more exposed positions; and the present Advanced Bases, by virtue of our forward movement, would be less liable to enemy attack, could be manned by less skilled personnel. Even so, it would be better to have new Marines rather than the Army to take over their defense, but the Army should be ready and qualified to do so. In any event, the battalions projected into the new bases must have their full equipment without withdrawing that in the present bases.

13. The forgoing discussion has had particular application to Midway, Wake, Johnston, and Palmyra. The situation as to Samoa is not greatly different [. . .]

[. . .]

19. It is recommended that:

(a) Deficiencies in armament at existing Advanced Bases, and in existing Marine Defense Battalions, be remedied as rapidly as possible [. . .]

(b) Fourth Defense Battalion and proposed new Defense Battalion be maintained as mobile battalions in Pearl Harbor in accordance with existing plans; and that the organization and acquirement of equipment for this new defense battalion be expedited;

(c) At least two additional defense battalions be organized and equipped at San Diego, with plans to use these battalions those mentioned in (b) above garrisoning positions captured in the Marshalls;

(d) An understanding with Army be reached now that in case Army takes &over defense of Advanced Bases, command of such bases will remain with Navy [. . .]

(e) Commitments to further island developments in the Central and South Pacific be held to a minimum as to number and logistic requirements,

(f) No plans be made for relieving Marine Defense Battalions or air units until Army has organized, equipped and trained for coordinated action suitable units for taking over.

[. . .]

H. E. Kimmel

Source: Hearings Before the Joint Committee on the Investigation of the Pearl Harbor Attack, 79th Congress, 1st Session, Part 15, November 1945 to May 1946 (Washington: GPO, 1946), 2480–4.

THOMAS FLEMING

Birth of the American Way of War

Excitement swirled on the decks and in the holds of the seventy-ship American fleet as it approached the city of Veracruz on March 5, 1847. The 12,250 soldiers on the transports uneasily eyed the huge fortress of San Juan de Ulloa, guarding the ample harbor. Everyone was acutely aware that they were about to embark on an epic struggle in the footsteps of the first conqueror of Mexico, Hernando Cortez. They did not know that they were going to do something even more important—invent the American way of making war.

Aboard the steamer *Massachusetts* was the six-foot, four-and-a-half-inch commander of the expedition, Maj. Gen. Winfield Scott. Know to his men as "Old Fuss and Feathers," Scott loved military pageantry. Nothing pleased him as much as a dress uniform. He loved to put on full regalia for inspections, reviews, and similar ceremonies. But he was about to demonstrate that he was much more than a parade-ground soldier.

Scott conferred with the naval commander in charge of the United States blockade of the Mexican east coast, Commodore David Conner, and together they selected a landing site. Time was of the essence.

Veracruz had to be captured swiftly, before the yellow fever season began. The dreaded *vomito* could decimate Scott's army, which was already far below the strength he had been promised by President James K. Polk.

On March 9, the infantry transferred from the transports to lighter draft naval vessels and entered a stretch of water sheltered by Sacrificios Island, about two miles south of Veracruz, beyond the range of the heavy guns of the San Juan fortress. There the first wave of fifty-five hundred men, commanded by swaggering Maj. Gen. William "Haughty Bill" Worth, transferred to a fleet of "surf boats" designed by General Scott. These early landing craft had high protective sides and ample room for about fifty soldiers. They were light and easily rowed by sailors from the fleet.

With Haughty Bill in the lead aboard a small cutter, the boats headed for the Mexican shore at 6 P.M. Aboard the fleet's ships bands played "Yankee Doodle," "Hail Columbia," and the "Star Spangled Banner" while everyone watched tensely. Off the beach, U.S. Navy warships stood ready to bombard if Mexican opposition appeared. Two guns from the San Juan fortress hurled projectiles toward the boats, but they did not even come close. As the cutter grounded, General Worth leaped from her bow, sword in hand, the first man ashore. His troops were not far behind him. They swiftly formed into companies and seized thirty-foot-high sand dunes a few hundred yards inland. Not a bullet was fired at them.

Behind Worth's men came another division under Brig. Gen. David E. Twiggs. They were followed by the army's third division, under the command of Maj. Gen. Robert Patterson. By 10 P.M. almost twelve thousand men were ashore without the loss of a single soldier. It was the first but by no means the last evidence of what headwork—Winfield Scott's term for mental effort—could accomplish in a war.

Scott's men soon advanced on Veracruz. Even in this preliminary step, headwork was visible. Scott sent Patterson's division, composed of volunteers, forward to build a road through the shifting sand. After a few miles of backbreaking work, Twiggs' division advanced down this already constructed road and began building an extension that completed the ring of men and guns around the city. Next came trenches and emplacement of gun batteries. Meanwhile, the Americans cut off Veracruz's water supply. All this took the better part of two weeks.

Scott now called on the Mexican commander, General Juan Morales, to surrender. He refused, hoping Scott, possibly spooked by the oncoming yellow fever season, would order a frontal assault. Morales had more than four thousand men manning the fortress of San Juan and numerous other bastions in Veracruz. He was confident that he could make the Americans pay a very high price for a victory.

Scott vetoed a frontal assault, even though Haughty Bill Worth practically demanded it. Seven months earlier, Worth, fighting under Maj. Gen. Zachary Taylor, had led an attack on the Mexican city of Monterrey in which 488 Americans were killed or wounded—nearly a fifth of their army. They had captured the city in three days, although there was no need for such urgency. Worth made this spurious success the basis of his argument with Scott.

Worth (and Taylor) personified the old-fashioned approach to generalship—the matter-of-fact acceptance of high casualties. It is interesting, and quite possibly no accident, that Scott kept Worth and his division behind at Collado Beach, near the landing site, where he set up his headquarters. He may well have feared that Worth would undertake a frontal assault on Veracruz without waiting for orders. The two men had served together in the War of 1812, and Scott knew the hunger for glory that gnawed at Haughty Bill's soul.

In a written reply to Worth's call for a frontal assault, Scott admitted the importance of quickly forcing Veracruz's surrender. But he still thought that headwork rather than storming was the right choice. Scott pointed out that an attack would take place at night and would involve the massacre of the Mexican garrison as well as many noncombatants. He found "the horrors of such slaughter . . . revolting." He also feared it would cost "two thousand of our best men." Since he had received only half the men promised to him, "how then could we hope to penetrate in the interior?"

At the same time, the sixty-year-old Scott knew how to play the daring leader in order to inspire his men. When he sailed from Lobos Island, two hundred miles north of Veracruz, where he had ordered his Regulars and volunteers to converge, he stood on the prow of *Massachusetts* in his dress uniform while soldiers and sailors cheered him. During the preparations for the siege of Veracruz, Scott was inspecting the lines when he saw some curious soldiers climbing up on the parapet to get a look at him. He ordered them back into the trenches. "Don't expose yourselves!" he said.

"But General—you are exposed," one of them called.

"Oh," Scott said. "Generals can be made out of anybody, but men cannot be had."

———

On March 23, Scott opened a bombardment on Veracruz from sea and land. With the continuing cooperation of the navy, he brought ashore some heavy guns from the fleet to add additional punch from the land side. These iron monsters fired thirty-two- and sixty-two-pound balls that wreaked havoc on roofs and walls, opening a fifty-foot breach on the southern side of the city. Mortars added a rain of high explosives that started fires and stirred panic in civilians and soldiers. Mexican guns responded but did little damage to the American batteries, which Scott's engineers had protected with numerous sandbags.

After three days of punishment, General Morales sent out a flag of truce. The following day Veracruz surrendered. Not a man in Scott's army had been killed. Wounded totaled only sixty-seven. Four men in the American naval battery, manned by sailors, died from a single cannonball. It was an incredibly small price to pay for the "Gibraltar of Mexico."

Impelled by dread of the *vomito*, Scott quickly organized his army for a march into the interior. He set up a city government in Veracruz and appointed General Worth the governor. The commander in chief made an elaborate attempt to conciliate the Mexicans. He attended Sunday mass at Veracruz's cathedral and issued a proclamation declaring that the American army was prepared to pay fair prices for food, mules, and horses. "Americans are not your enemies," he declared. They were "only the enemies of those who misgoverned you and brought you into this unnatural war."

This too was good headwork. With barely ten thousand men—he had to leave a fifth of his army behind in Veracruz—Scott could not hope to conquer a country of seven million people unless he persuaded a large number of them that the Americans came as friends.

Conciliation was one of the few ideas about the Mexican War that Scott shared with President Polk. The general's lifelong rivalry with Democrat Andrew Jackson had led him to embrace the tenets of the Whig Party, forerunners of present-day Republicans. In fact, his enthusiasm for the party had impelled him to publicly endorse their 1844 presidential candidate, Henry Clay. During the first year of the war, President Polk, who had won the election by a whisker, had conspicuously ignored Scott, the U.S. Army's commander in chief. Polk let Maj. Gen. Zachary Taylor take charge of the fighting.

"Old Zach" had won three victories and cleared northern Mexico of enemy troops, but the Mexican government stubbornly refused to ask for terms and ignored Polk's attempts to negotiate. Finally the desperate president, under growing political fire from Whigs and restless

Democrats, turned to Scott and gave him orders to march to Mexico City and "conquer a peace."

Although profoundly uneasy about Polk's trustworthiness (several times Scott spoke anxiously about being caught between his military enemies firing on his front and political enemies fusillading his rear), Scott tackled the challenge with élan and thoroughness. A very intelligent man, his study of war had convinced him of the importance of planning and careful preparation.

One of his first moves was to acquire a first-rate staff, many of them West Pointers destined to win fame in a later war. They included Captain Robert E. Lee and Lieutenants Joseph E. Johnston, P.G.T. Beauregard, and George McClellan. As inspector general he chose Lt. Col. Ethan Allen Hitchcock, who had been on the West Point faculty for many years.

Scott had been catapulted to fame by his victory at Chippewa during the War of 1812. There he demonstrated a talent for thinking as well as fighting that did much to rescue the reputation of the American army in that poorly planned war. Americans had relied on hordes of semitrained militia to overwhelm the enemy. Outnumbered British Regulars routed them with dismaying ease.

The July 5, 1814, battle near the Chippewa River in Canada was a conscious attempt to lure the British army into fighting American Regulars. Brigadier General Scott had spent much of the previous year drilling and training his regiments. The British, expecting to find militia, were startled by the Americans' coolness under fire and the precision with which they executed Scott's commands. His tactics were modeled on the duke of Wellington's system in Spain—a solid line opposing an enemy who advanced in columns. Scott added a few touches of his own, splitting his regiments into battalions that advanced on the left and right so they were able to fire with devastating effect on the British flanks. Light artillery ably supported this flanking fire. By the time Scott shouted the order for a bayonet charge, the British were so demoralized they fled to the safe side of the Chippewa, leaving 515 dead and wounded behind them. The victory made Scott an instant national hero. The country resounded with pealing church bells and vibrant hosannahs.

With Veracruz secured, Scott ordered General Twiggs to advance up the Mexican National Highway to Jalapa, roughly halfway to Mexico City. Haughty Bill Worth, who expected the honor of commanding the army's vanguard, was mortally offended. But Scott ignored his protest, this time with a soothing bromide about rotating honors in the army. Twiggs' selection may also have been a covert payback for Worth's attempt to embarrass Scott into a frontal assault on Veracruz. That was Worth's opinion, which he made no attempt to conceal.

Twiggs was not an improvement on Worth, as far as headwork was concerned. A bull of a man with a Jehovah-like beard, he was known to his soldiers as "Old Davey the Bengal Tiger." Scott had a low opinion of his brainpower, but he admired his ability to get a maximum effort from his men, especially when "he cursed them out of their boots."

In Mexico City, meanwhile, the leader of the national government, General Antonio Lopez de Santa Anna, was convinced that he could destroy Scott's army long before it neared the capital. Santa Anna had been running Mexico off and on for thirty years, alternating between the roles of dictator and president. An astute self-promoter, he had used the loss of a leg in an artillery duel with the French to bolster his image as a savior ready to suffer and die for his country.

Forced to flee a revolution in 1845, the general had persuaded President Polk to let him return, supposedly as a man committed to making peace. No sooner had he appeared in Mexico City than he called for all-out war against the gringos and became the supreme leader again. Gathering an army of twenty-five thousand men, he headed north, hoping to annihilate Zachary Taylor, who had unwisely disobeyed orders and advanced from Monterrey to the isolated town of Buena Vista with an army from which Scott had withdrawn all the Regulars. Relying heavily on his West Point–trained artillerymen, Taylor managed to beat off the assault at a heavy cost. Santa Anna returned to Mexico City proclaiming a victory.

This verbal agility enabled the general to assemble another army, which he confidently declared would destroy Scott's troops by taking advantage of the formidable terrain through which the National Highway passed. Santa Anna was thinking in particular of the rugged countryside about forty miles below Jalapa, dominated by Cerro Gordo—Fat Mountain. It was also known as El Telegrafo because it had been used in the past to send primitive messages from its seven-hundred-foot-high crest to the mountains beyond it and thence to Mexico City. About a mile in front of Cerro Gordo on the right were three steep cliffs that an attacking army would have to surmount before tackling the slopes of Fat Mountain itself. Other cliffs overlooked the Rio del Plan, a turbulent river that made it impossible for an enemy to turn the right flank.

Santa Anna's only worry was his left or northern flank. There, however, he was reassured by men who knew the locality that not even a rabbit could traverse the wilderness of solid chaparral cut by invisible ravines and small hills. A large flat-topped hill, La Atalaya, frowned about half a mile northeast of Cerro Gordo, adding an anchor to this flank. Santa Anna was so confident that the chaparral was impenetrable, he ignored advice to fortify La Atalaya; he decreed, on the contrary, that a twenty-four-man outpost was more than sufficient. As a precaution, on the crest of Cerro Gordo he built a large observation tower, which he topped with a Mexican flag.

To defend this favorable ground, Santa Anna had gathered about twelve thousand troops—many of them paroled by Scott at Veracruz on the promise that they would not fight again. It was an unstable army, short of provisions and even of water, most of which had to be hauled from the Rio del Plan on mules. But they had forty-three pieces of artillery and the assurance of their general that the gringos would have to attack up the National Highway, making them easy targets for guns of all sizes.

Santa Anna's prediction would have come true if the American army's strategy had been left to David Twiggs. Old Davey had marched his men at a killing pace through the sandy lowlands. Nearly a third of the ranks had been forced to drop out, and a number had fallen prey to Mexican guerrillas. But the rest had rejoined the army by the time Twiggs crossed the National Bridge over the Antigua River and marched another ten miles to Plan del Rio, a village about ten miles below Cerro Gordo. There he exchanged random shots with retreating Mexicans who had apparently considered making a stand at the National Bridge.

Twiggs' scouts reported a large number of Mexicans on Cerro Gordo. Undeterred, Twiggs pushed forward, confident that he could disperse them as he had (so he thought) chased off the defenders of the National Bridge. In actuality, they had wisely decided to fall back to Cerro Gordo because the river was easily forded to the north and south of the bridge. As Twiggs' men approached Fat Mountain, they met a hail of bullets and cannonballs. Hastily retreating out of range, Old Davey ordered his engineers, Lieutenants Beauregard, Johnston, and Zealous B. Tower, to reconnoiter the situation. They soon reported that the entire Mexican army was on Fat Mountain. Twiggs announced his intention to attack them within three days.

His men, including the engineers, were appalled. They all had a low opinion of General Twiggs' brainpower. Their division numbered only twenty-six hundred men, a squadron of dragoons, plus two batteries of light artillery and some heavier guns. Many soldiers began writing farewell letters to wives and sweethearts.

They were temporarily rescued by the arrival of Maj. Gen. Patterson with the second division of the army. A politician without pretensions to military expertise, Patterson was skeptical about attacking without Scott's approval. But he was running a fever and took to his bed, leaving Twiggs still in command. Old Davey announced they would attack the next day, April 14. His plan amounted to military suicide. He was going to throw most of his force at Santa Anna's right, where he had mounted batteries on the three formidable cliffs. Twiggs ordered the batteries taken at bayonet point.

Lieutenant Beauregard, meanwhile, had been exploring the Mexican left. Clawing his way through the chaparral, he had found a path that led to the top of La Atalaya, within easy cannon shot of Cerro Gordo. He reported this discovery to Twiggs, but it made no impression on him. In his tent, the ailing Patterson was having second thoughts. He summoned Beauregard and asked him what he thought of Twiggs' battle plan. The nervous twenty-nine-year-old West Pointer diplomatically replied that he was sure it would work, but it was risky. He suggested concentrating their whole force against Cerro Gordo, and only making a demonstration before the three batteries on the right.

Patterson, not relishing a confrontation with Twiggs, claimed he was too sick to get out of bed and sent Beauregard to Old Davey with orders to change his mind. Knowing the Bengal Tiger's temper, Beauregard decided to leave Patterson out of it and offered the alternate plan to Twiggs as his own idea—which it was, to a large extent.

Twiggs pondered for a moment and solemnly replied it was too late. He had issued the orders, and changing them would confuse and possibly unnerve the soldiers. "Don't you think we will succeed anyhow?" Twiggs growled.

"Certainly sir," Beauregard said, adding a murmur about making sure all the risks were in their favor. So much for headwork, as far as Twiggs was concerned.

To everyone's relief—and possibly with some urging from the diplomatic Lieutenant Beauregard—Patterson dragged himself out of his sickbed at 11 o'clock that night and resumed command. He promptly canceled the attack until Scott arrived. The commander in chief rode into camp the next day around noon along with Captain Robert E. Lee and Colonel Hitchcock.

Scott was greeted with almost hysterical cheers by the uneasy soldiers, who saw him as their salvation from Twiggs. Not far behind

Scott was the third division of the army. He quietly gave his approval to Patterson's cancellation of the attack and ordered Lee to take charge of a reconnaissance aimed at avoiding a frontal assault.

Beauregard reported to Lee his preliminary exploration of the Mexican left, and the captain decided to see what he could find on his own. Accompanied by a soldier guide named John Fitzwater, the black-mustachioed Virginian headed into the chaparral. Working his way down a long, tree-choked ravine, Lee began to believe that some sort of road could be constructed.

After several hours of slogging, Lee and Fitzwater emerged into a clearing around a spring. A well-trampled path ran southward. Lee realized they were behind the left flank of the Mexican army. Suddenly he heard voices. He and Fitzwater dived behind some fallen trees as a group of Mexican soldiers headed for the spring.

The enemy drank and stood around discussing the Yanquis; several sat down on a tree trunk, within three feet of the sweating Lee. One man stepped over the trunk and missed Lee by inches. These visitors were replaced by others who kept Lee and Fitzwater immobilized until darkness fell. Insects tormented them, but they endured their bites in painful silence.

In the pitch-black night, Lee and his guide groped their way back down the ravine to headquarters and reported their findings. Lee admitted his conclusions were rudimentary. Another officer who had explored the same area was also hopeful but wary. Scott said he was in no hurry. In the salubrious air of the highlands, his army was out of reach of yellow fever.

The next day, Scott sent Lee out with a detachment of pioneers who began cutting a road through the chaparral. This time the captain gave the spring a wide berth but pushed on much farther to the northwest. Scott had told him his goal was a turning movement that would cut the road to Jalapa, trapping the Mexican army. Lee did not go as far as the road—that might have invited a large-scale enemy counterattack—but he got close enough to see it and the town of Cerro Gordo. He returned confident they could spring the trap when the Americans attacked. By the end of the day, the pioneers had hacked out a passable road, good enough to tolerate wagons and even artillery. It was christened the Trail.

The time for action had arrived. Scott gave Twiggs the honor of leading the flanking movement, with Lee serving as his guide to supply the brainpower. The commander in chief attached a brigade of volunteers under Maj. Gen. James Shields to bolster Twiggs' numbers. At

4:30 A.M. on Saturday, April 17, Old Davey led his men up the National Highway onto Lee's Trail. It took them four hours to advance four miles to La Atalaya, which Scott wanted them to occupy with a company of Regulars.

Thanks to their observation tower on Cerro Gordo, the Mexicans detected the American movement around their flank. They met Twiggs' occupying company with a storming party that surged up the opposite slope of La Atalaya. The pugnacious Twiggs committed Colonel W.S. Harney's entire brigade to hold the hill. This they did without difficulty—but someone in the brigade made the mistake of asking Old Davey how far they should go.

"Charge 'em to hell!" Twiggs bellowed, before Lee could intervene. The men poured down the northwest slope after the retreating Mexicans and followed them halfway up the steep side of Cerro Gordo— until they were stopped by sheets of musket bullets and numerous cannon balls. Not a few men went down. The rest took cover behind rocks and trees until darkness enabled them to retreat to La Atalaya.

Twiggs' old-fashioned generalship inadvertently helped conceal Scott's intentions. At the end of the day, Santa Anna concluded he had beaten off the Yanquis' main attack, and he spent the night celebrating another imaginary victory. The Americans, meanwhile, were hauling artillery along the Trail.

Lieutenant Ulysses S. Grant, serving ingloriously as a regimental quarter-master (also known as superintendent of mules) in Worth's division, nevertheless appreciated the difficulties that Lee and his fellow engineers encountered in the process. He later described how the cannons were laboriously lugged over the rough terrain: "Artillery was let down the steep slopes [of the ravines] by hand, the men engaged attaching a strong rope to the rear axle and letting the guns down, a piece at a time, while the men at the ropes kept their ground on top, paying out gradually. In like manner the guns were drawn by hand up the opposite slopes."

These same guns were manhandled up the slopes of La Atalaya that night in the darkness, under Lee's supervision. Fresh troops had been sent to perform this task while Twiggs' men got some badly needed sleep. But the apparently tireless Captain Lee worked all night after sharing the heat and exhausting efforts of the day. On the summit of La Atalaya, he took charge of emplacing the guns and preparing them for action in the early morning.

By now, Scott assumed surprise had been lost. So he decided to combine a turning movement with a frontal assault. Lee was given the task of leading two brigades—Shields' and Colonel Bennet Riley's—deep into the Mexican rear to cut the National Highway. The rest of Twiggs' division assaulted Cerro Gordo from the flank, while other regiments attacked the center. On the American far left, another brigade was given the task of assailing the three batteries on the cliffs.

As the sun rose, the American battery on La Atalaya erupted, blasting the startled Mexicans on Cerro Gordo. Up the slopes swarmed Twiggs' shouting, cheering soldiers. In the center, the men of Patterson's division were performing with similar élan, well supported by other American heavy guns. Only on the left were things not going well. There, a volunteer brigadier general named Gideon Pillow ignored the advice of his West Point guide and chose a route to his jumping off point that exposed his men to enfilading fire from all three batteries. Adding to the disarray, Pillow claimed he was "shot to pieces" when a bullet hit him in the arm, and he retreated to his tent.

As Patterson's and Twiggs' men swarmed onto Cerro Gordo's heights to fight hand to hand with the Mexican defenders, Lee's two brigades erupted onto the National Highway, led by the indomitable captain. A Mexican battery momentarily repulsed one brigade, but the sight of Americans pouring out of the chaparral was too much for the jittery Mexican infantry. "The Yanquis! They have come out to the road. Every man for himself!" they screamed and ran for the river on their right. The cry swept through the army and up the slopes of Cerro Gordo, where it had a similar unraveling impact.

Soon the batteries on the Mexican right were abandoned, making an attack by Pillow's flustered regiments superfluous. On Cerro Gordo and elsewhere, Mexicans surrendered by the hundreds, while many more fled. Santa Anna leaped onto a mule and escaped in the wake of his disintegrating army. He abandoned not only an overflowing money chest but also a spare wooden leg. Displaying the passion for souvenirs that would soon become the American soldiers' hallmark, an Illinois volunteer company seized the leg and shipped it to Chicago, where it was displayed for many years. When someone driving Santa Anna's gold-encrusted coach drawn by six white mules tried to flee up the highway, it was riddled by Lee's blocking force.

The victory was total. The Mexican army had evaporated. Scott captured more than three thousand enemy soldiers. Mexican casualties could only be estimated, but they left about twelve hundred dead and wounded on the field. Their escape route was splattered with the blood of more wounded. Scott's casualties were thirty officers and 387 men—of whom only sixty-four were killed.

When the firing subsided, Scott rode forward with a few staff members. The elated soldiers swarmed around him, and the general shook hands with them and called out his congratulations. As their numbers grew, he made a brief speech to his "brother soldiers." It ended with the declaration that they had "a claim on my gratitude for your conduct this day which I will never forget."

At Cerro Gordo, and in a preliminary way at Veracruz, Winfield Scott, with his commitment to headwork instead of a reliance on raw courage, invented the American way of war. Its hallmarks are careful reconnaissance, flanking movements, and a heavy reliance on artillery. The goal has been a small casualty list.

A few months later, at the Battle of Contreras in the Valley of Mexico, Scott repeated the Cerro Gordo performance, again with the help of Robert E. Lee. This time Santa Anna thought his left flank was protected by a lava field called the Pedregal that stretched for miles through a seemingly impassable desert of rock and scrub brush. Lee explored it and returned with a sketch of a possible road. Scott put five hundred men to work on building it in rain-swept darkness. The result was a flank attack that swept the Mexicans out of Contreras in seventeen stunning minutes.

Scott's small army astounded the civilized world by pushing on to capture the capital of Mexico and force the Mexicans to negotiate peace. In his dispatches, Scott repeatedly praised the West Point aides who contributed so much to the headwork side of this amazing performance.

Scott's formula has recurred repeatedly in battles American generals have fought since the Mexican War. There is little doubt that when Thomas J. "Stonewall" Jackson proposed to Robert E. Lee his risky forced march around the Union flank at Chancellorsville, Lee remembered Cerro Gordo and Contreras as he gave the idea his approval.

Ulysses Grant, ex-mule skinner of Cerro Gordo, also remembered the flanking movement as a recipe for victory. In the series of battles that began in the Wilderness in 1864, Grant constantly shifted his forces leftward, trying to get around the Confederate flank. Lee, the man who had helped Scott invent that way of war at Cerro Gordo, just as constantly shifted men and guns to prevent this from happening, until the two armies were occupying dozens of miles of trenches, stretching from Richmond to Petersburg.

Grant accepted the stalemate before Richmond because it enabled

William Tecumseh Sherman to apply the Cerro Gordo solution to the entire Confederacy. Striking into the exposed Southern flank, Sherman invaded Georgia and performed a pas de deux with another soldier who had studied tactics under Scott, Joseph Johnston. Sherman repeatedly eschewed a frontal assault for a sideslip around either flank, which the astute Johnston expected and countered by shifting his army to meet each movement.

But when the Confederate government replaced Johnston with reckless John Bell Hood, a frontal assault man who thought like a reincarnation of Old Davey the Bengal Tiger Twiggs, the Confederate Army of Tennessee was soon decimated, and Sherman's path from Atlanta to the sea was virtually unopposed. In a few months Lee was faced with collapsing civilian morale as well as envelopment from the rear.

Fifty-three years later, when the American army's offensive stalled in the mud of the Argonne, General John J. Pershing had the wits—and courage—to admit he had badly underestimated the power of massed German machine guns and artillery, and turned to the brightest general in his entourage for an answer. That general was the fat, overage Hunter Liggett, who was fond of saying that what made a good soldier was the stuff above the collar, not below it. Headwork again.

Liggett reorganized Pershing's army, clearing up serious problems of coordination at the front and chaos in the rear, where more than a hundred thousand stragglers were wandering. Liggett ordered the infantry to substitute flanking movements for frontal assaults on machine-gun nests, and applied a variation on Cerro Gordo's tactics to the battlefield as a whole. Divisions on the American left were ordered to apply relentless pressure to the German line, forcing the enemy to shift troops he could not spare to defend that part of the battlefield. Liggett, meanwhile, concentrated a massive amount of artillery on his real objective: the German center. On November 1, 1918, when the Americans resumed the offensive, the combination of a stunning cascade of high-explosive shells and new infantry tactics tore a huge gap in the heart of the German line, forcing the instant retreat of both wings and an accelerating rout that made the armistice on November 11 an inevitability.

In World War II, the breakout from Normandy was a Cerro Gordo replay, with the addition of a new weapon to supplement the artillery: the bomber. While British General Bernard Montgomery pinned down German armor in front of Caen, General Omar Bradley sent six divisions smashing into the strategic road center of St. Lô, preceded by a twenty-five-hundred-plane armada that dropped four thousand tons of bombs on the German defenders. Pouring through the gap, the Americans swiftly overran Brittany while other armored columns raced toward Paris. Hitler, stubbornly refusing to retreat, attempted a counterattack that ended in a classic envelopment. The Fifth and Seventh Panzer Armies were trapped in the Falaise-Argentan pocket and virtually annihilated, opening most of France to the Allied armies.

Six years later, when war erupted in Korea, the ultimate flank attack was executed by the general who had led the assault against the German center in the Argonne and had exhibited a rare talent for sideslipping around enemy island strongpoints in the South Pacific: Douglas MacArthur. In the fall of 1950, MacArthur's main army was pinned against the tip of the Korean Peninsula, around Pusan, under relentless attack by North Korean divisions. Scraping together a task force over the objections of the Joint Chiefs of Staff, MacArthur landed at Inchon, far to the north of Pusan, and executed an envelopment that turned the North Koreans into scurrying fugitives.

Vietnam did not lend itself to this kind of clever deception. But Desert Storm saw the headwork generals back in charge of the battlefield. While U.S. Marines attacked frontally to pin down the Iraqi left, General Norman Schwarzkopf's armored, airmobile, and airborne divisions executed a brilliant turning movement that soon had them around the enemy right flank and racing deep into their rear. The demoralized Iraqis surrendered by the thousands. American casualties were negligible.

If Old Fuss and Feathers was looking down on any of these shows from the groves of Valhalla, he was undoubtedly smiling. His descendants had continued to make headwork and firepower as important as courage in the American order of battle.

COLONEL ROBERT
A. DOUGHTY

More Than Numbers:
Americans and the Revival
of French Morale in the
Great War

Of the contributions made by American forces to the Allied effort in World War I, the most important may have been the Americans' role in reviving French morale. Arriving in June 1917 after the failure of the Nivelle offensive and amid a spate of mutinies within the French Army, the Americans initially did little to reassure French soldiers in the trenches, but their eager entry into battle against the German offensive in March 1918 soon contributed significantly to restoring French morale and assuring Allied victory. Without this assistance, the French Army might have disintegrated and the Germans emerged victorious.

Though historians often note the importance of American troop strength and industrial power, especially in the erosion of German resolve, they rarely give the Americans much credit for reviving French morale.[1] British historian John Keegan's recent book, *The First World War*, exemplifies this view. While Keegan highlights the appearance of the Americans in the title of his final chapter, "America and Armageddon," he largely discounts their military significance. Keegan emphasizes the Americans' large numbers, but he neglects their contribution to the fighting and the impact of their combat successes on the revival of French determination and hope.[2] Indeed, he largely dismisses the U.S. Army's contribution by repeatedly mentioning its lack of professionalism and competence and by neglecting its achievements on the battlefield. Instead, using the colorful language that makes his books appealing to so many readers, Keegan merely explains in a general way that the Germans were "confronted with an army whose soldiers sprang, in uncountable numbers, as if from soil sown with dragons' teeth."[3]

Keegan's line of interpretation, which tends to minimize the importance of the French and Americans in the final phase of the war and to inflate the role of Sir Douglas Haig's British forces, is one to which British authors have long adhered. The roots of this view go back to the war itself, when the British bridled under the tutelage of the French in the first years of the war and demanded greater credit for Allied successes later for shouldering a larger part of the war's burden, and its casualties, in the Somme and Passchendaele offensives in 1916 and 1917.[4] After the war, the complexity and significance of the British effort emerged as important themes in the British official history which Brig. Gen. Sir James Edmonds and his colleagues compiled.[5] Not immune to pressure from high-ranking officers who had served in the war, Edmonds crafted the volumes in the official history to present a favorable view of senior British commanders and exhibited what Canadian historian Tim Travers has called a "bias in favor of Haig and his GHQ."[6] Moreover, Edmonds fired broadsides at the French official history for its alleged failure to give sufficient credit to the British.[7] Whatever the shortcomings of the British official history, Edmonds's work provided the foundation for many historians' understanding of the war and influenced most of them—including Americans—to give the British the lion's share of credit for Allied success in the latter phase of the war.[8]

In his book on World War I Keegan relies excessively on Edmonds's work and its derivatives. While making ample use of recent works about the Eastern Front, he uses few French sources and remarks that the French official history, "though detailed, is desiccated in tone."[9] He also focuses more on British battles than those fought by the armies of other nations. The reader of his book learns far more, for example, about the British at Neuve-Chapelle than the French in Champagne, even though the battles in Champagne were far larger and more important. The reader thus views the Great War through the prism of the British experience and learns little about either the fragility of the French Army in 1917–1918 or the significance of the American contribution to restoring the will of the French soldier to fight.

Even though American soldiers served more frequently with the French than the British in World War I, American historians have long viewed the Great War primarily through the eyes of British participants and the works of British authors.[10] Many have relied on works published in London to expand their understanding of the war beyond the American experience, and they have rarely used French sources or archives. More comfortable with English- than French-language materials, they often have worked in the Public Records Office in London, but few of them have conducted research in the massive holdings of the Service Historique de l'Armée de Terre at the Château de Vincennes in Paris. Moreover, American historians have rarely used the French official history, even though it includes important documents pertaining to the service of American units in the war.[11]

Of the numerous holdings in French archives that shed light on the American contribution, the most significant may be the reports submitted by the postal service during the war. In brief, the French censored the letters written by soldiers during the war to prevent their revealing secret information—locations of units, plans for upcoming operations, casualties, etc.—in their letters to their loved ones. As the postal officials read the letters, they quickly realized they could obtain valuable information about French soldiers' morale, and they soon began submitting regular reports to senior military leaders. These reports tell us a great deal about French perceptions of the Americans and thus illustrate the effect the Americans had on the French.

When the United States severed diplomatic relations with Germany in early February 1917, French confidence, according to the postal reports, briefly soared. The report of 15 February noted, "The mass [of the soldiers] think that an ally of this importance would not join our side if Germany was not at the end of its rope."[12] Ten days after the United States declared war on 6 April, however, French General Robert Nivelle launched an ill-fated attack against the German lines along the Chemin des Dames north of the Aisne River. The attack cost the French over 134,000 casualties without producing the anticipated breakthrough. Whatever optimism had existed before the attack quickly dissipated.[13]

The soldiers' discontent soon boiled over into mutinies, particularly in the units involved in the failed April offensive, and dispirited French soldiers even began to question the benefit their nation would derive from American military support.[14] The postal authorities reported on 1 May, "Many [soldiers] think that the entry of America into the war, while giving us numerous advantages, will prolong the war at least a year and, by the relief of workers [who will be replaced by Americans], send thousands of French to their deaths."[15]

According to Guy Pedroncini, who has written the standard work on the subject, the most violent phase of the mutinies occurred between 1–6 June, when for the first time French soldiers shot or beat to death their fellow countrymen, perhaps as many as six. In fact, most of the acts of indiscipline that resulted in court-martial convictions occurred during this brief period.[16] French morale, both civilian and military, had apparently collapsed, and the French Army seemed on the edge of disintegration. Amid the turmoil of these mutinies, the psychological effect of the Americans' arrival in mid-June could not have been more opportune. When General John J. Pershing debarked at the Gare du Nord in Paris on 13 June, the French Army had just weathered the most violent phase of the mutinies, and the high-ranking civilian and military officials who met him did now know if the soldiers' anger would subside or surge.

Though the effect of Pershing's arrival on French soldiers was not yet apparent, his appearance immediately heartened the citizens of Paris. In his memoirs the American general wrote:

> Dense masses of people lined the boulevards and filled the squares. It was said that never before in the history of Paris had there been such an outpouring of people. Men, women, and children absolutely packed every foot of space, even to the windows and housetops. Cheers and tears were mingled together and shouts of enthusiasm fairly rent the air. Women climbed into our automobiles screaming, "Vive l'Amérique," and threw flowers until we were literally buried. Everybody waved flags and banners.[17]

When Pershing met General Philippe Pétain on 16 June, the French general-in-chief emphasized the importance of the American presence and said, "I hope it is not too late."[18] Recognizing the fragility of the situation, Pershing told Washington the French could "hold on until spring" but warned that, if the French government failed to support its army, "the latter will lose its morale and disaster [will] follow."[19]

To prop up sagging French morale, Pétain personally visited numerous units, including perhaps as many as ninety divisions. During these visits he spoke to groups of soldiers and sought to reassure them by describing the strategic situation and the enormous resources of the United States and by asserting the inevitability of France's victory with the United States as an ally.[20] He also issued a pamphlet entitled "Why We Fight"[21] and distributed a memorandum on the strategic situation that concluded, "France can expect with reasonable confidence a victorious peace that is indispensable to it and that it deserves because of its heavy sacrifices."[22] Though the relationship between Pershing's arrival in Paris on 13 June and the decline that had begun a week earlier in the number and severity of mutinies cannot be precisely measured, Pétain's words and the Americans' arrival must both have contributed to the restoration of discipline in the French Army.

Despite the enthusiastic reception Pershing received in Paris and the end of the mutinies, the promise of American involvement did not fully restore French soldiers' morale immediately. Indeed, hope declined further as German successes on the Eastern Front, combined with the recent revolution in Russia, threatened to permit the Germans to shift more forces to the Western Front, a situation that seriously worried French troops.[23] The French military mission in Russia had provided detailed reports outlining the worsening situation that developed there following the overthrow of the tsar and the establishment of a provisional government in Petrograd in March 1917.[24] Though French soldiers initially perceived events in Russia as "democratic" and "anti-German,"[25] more realistic and ominous insights came from the French military mission. It reported that General Mikhail Alexeyev, the Russian commander-in-chief, had been obliged to assemble his army group commanders for a meeting with representatives of the provisional government and a committee of workers and soldiers. The military mission also reported that the Germans had sent emissaries to talk to the Russian soldiers about peace.[26]

Two weeks before Pershing arrived in Paris, another report from Petrograd described the situation there as "calm anarchy" and observed, "The [Russian] officers remain passive, the men do whatever they want."[27] On 24 July the French mission, terming the existing situation a "debacle," mentioned some of the efforts by the Russians to reestablish discipline.[28] Subsequent reports from Russia described the situation in bleak terms, observing the collapse of morale, the breakup of units, the abandonment of defensive positions, and significant German advances into Russia.[29] Although the Bolsheviks did not begin formal peace negotiations at Brest-Litovsk until December 1917 and only in April 1918 signed a treaty effecting Russia's withdrawal from the war, the Allies quickly recognized the changing strategic equation. In late July 1917 Allied military leaders met to discuss alternatives if the Russians left the war, and, as Pershing noted in his memoirs, "the opinion prevailed in the conference that Russia was practically eliminated as a military factor."[30]

Coupled with the impending loss of Russia as an ally, the outbreak of mutiny left the French Army extremely vulnerable. A postal report in early June emphasized French soldiers' concern about Russia and observed, "Russia inspires great mistrust."[31] Even though the official bulletin that the French Army circulated as a newspaper among its soldiers said little about the turbulent events in Russia before 6 June,[32] the soldiers managed to follow events on the Eastern Front carefully, and some even called for a revolution in France or an immediate end to the war.[33] Recognizing that French soldiers were near their breaking point, the Army's high command identified the Russian revolution as one of the principal external causes of the mutinies.[34] Though the mutinies in France waned after the first week of June, the French Army remained the weak link in Allied defenses, as Pétain acknowledged to Pershing when the two met privately in early July. Though not mentioning the mutinies, the French general, who knew his soldiers as well as or better than any other commander in the war, expressed concern about a revolution breaking out in France and observed, "Such an outcome . . . would permit the Germans to dictate the terms of peace instead of the Allies."[35]

As the Russian Army disintegrated, the arrival of the first Americans gave the French some reason for hope. French soldiers soon realized, however, that the Americans were not well prepared for high-intensity warfare, leading the French to become more critical, uncertain, and discouraged. The postal report for late November observed, "The Americans are judged intelligent and easy to train, strong and generous; they are criticized for having little discipline, for liking champagne and women too much, [and] for being a bit presumptuous."[36] When France's High Commissioner in the United States, André Tardieu, stated publicly that the Americans would not be ready until 1919, the attitude of French soldiers worsened.[37] The French high command also had reservations about the Americans and noted in a strategic assessment, "It will be dangerous to hasten the entry of American divisions into the front."[38]

By mid-December, the French high command noted a "crisis of pessimism" among the soldiers and cited as major factors events in Russia and German propaganda.[39] Pétain had painted a bleak picture of the strategic situation at the first meeting of the Comité de Guerre convened by Prime Minister Georges Clemenceau earlier that month.[40] The situation would, however, become even more daunting, as French intelligence reported in March 1918 that the number of German divisions on the Western Front had increased to 188 from 157 two months earlier.[41] Even the arrival of more Americans could not halt the decline of French morale during the winter of 1917–1918. In mid-February 1918 the postal report emphasized the growing doubts among French soldiers about the Americans and their "anxiety" about whether U.S. cooperation would "shorten the war or prolong it."[42] The late-February morale report observed, "The depth of weariness [in French soldiers] is obvious."[43]

That the Americans could indeed help to shorten the war first became apparent to French soldiers as the Allies struggled to respond to the German spring offensive in March 1918. After Pershing met with Prime Minister Clemenceau and Generals Ferdinand Foch and Pétain on 28 March and announced his willingness to commit all available troops to the fight, the hopes of French soldiers rose as they watched the Americans go into action. Though the format and method of compiling the report on morale changed during this crucial period, comments about the Americans became more and more positive as the weeks passed. The postal report of 6 April stated, "The units that are in contact with the Americans (Second, Eighth, Sixth Armies) have a more and more favorable assessment of our new allies. . . . Rapport between French and Americans is cordial everywhere."[44] While the report of 5 May was critical of the performance of the British in the initial phase of the German spring offensive, it emphasized the courage of the Americans under fire and the value of their presence in strengthening the confidence of French soldiers. That report included a statistical analysis of the positive factors influencing French morale, as mentioned in their correspondence, and the "cooperation of the Americans" ranked higher than any other.[45]

The Americans' presence and participation in the fighting had an even more positive effect in subsequent weeks. While expressing concern about the "fatigue" of French soldiers, the report of 15 May emphasized the "cordial" relationship between the French and Americans. It also praised the soldierly qualities of African American soldiers, observing that "they are considered 'well trained and well disciplined.' They establish very good relations with our troops. The units charged with providing training for these new allies are struck by their 'good will' and by their desire to do well. . . . They are above all very dedicated."[46] A few weeks later even more positive comments appeared, relating this time to American troops in general: "Our soldiers establish very cordial relationships with these allies; they value the good appearance of their men, their valiant conduct under fire, the audacity of their aviators; they admire the strength and quality of their equipment."[47] Adding to the kudos for the Americans, the senior engineer officer in French Second Army emphasized the greater confidence of his troops and observed, "The sight of numerous Americans, their willing participation in operations, sustains this confidence."[48]

In early June 1918 the Americans' most visible entry into battle occurred along the Marne River. In his postwar memoirs, Jean de Pierrefeu, a French staff officer who worked at Pétain's headquarters, painted a vivid picture of the Americans moving toward Belleau Wood, Vaux, and Château Thierry:

> Amidst enthusiastic civilians, they passed in interminable columns, tightly packed in trucks, feet in the air, in extraordinary positions, some perched on the tops, nearly all bare-headed and unbuttoned, singing their national songs at the top of their voices. The spectacle of this magnificent youth from across the sea, these youngsters of twenty years with smooth faces, radiating strength and health in their new uniforms, had an immense effect. They offered a striking contrast with our regiments in soiled uniforms, worn by the years of war, with our emaciated soldiers and their somber eyes who were nothing more than bundles of nerves held together by a heroic, sacrificial will. The general impression was that a magical transfusion of blood was taking place. Life was returning in floods to revive the half-dead body of France, which was almost drained of blood after four years of innumerable wounds. No one said anything about these soldiers not being trained, about their having only courage. . . . When one looked at this event in the broadest sense, one perceived the presence of gushing, untiring force that would overcome everything because of its strength.[49]

No one saw the effects of the "magical transfusion of blood" better than French field army commanders. The Second Army commander emphasized in early July the increase in French morale: "Some of our men already have begun to envisage the possibility of a fifth winter in the war, but it should be noted that this eventuality does not seem to depress their morale, for they are persuaded that victory will not escape us."[50] In mid-July, on the eve of the combined Franco-

American offensive between the Marne and Aisne Rivers near Soissons which gave the Allies the initiative and began the series of operations that would result in Germany's defeat, the Sixth Army commander, who had several U.S. divisions under his command for the operation, stated, "One can see that the military situation will in the near future turn to the benefit of the Allies, thanks to the resources that America has liberally placed in the service of the common cause. The continual arrival of new, robust, combative troops with an abundance of matériel reassures our men and arouses their highest hopes."[51] Two weeks after the recapture of Soissons, the commander of Seventh Army remarked on the importance of that counteroffensive in changing the attitude of his soldiers from "somber" to "clear enthusiasm."[52] At the same time the Second Army commander reported, "The current morale of the troops is splendid. . . . Their confidence is based on the continued success of the operations under way, the value of the High Command, [and] the cooperation of our allies, the Americans above all. The combative qualities demonstrated every day [by the Americans], their almost inexhaustible reserves, and their prodigious effort sustain all the hopes [of the French soldiers]."[53]

Even more positive reports came in subsequent weeks. The Second Army commander reported in September: "The continued arrival of American troops, who have already proved their combat value, gives all our soldiers complete confidence in our forces, and at the same time a certitude of result. The soldiers discuss only the date of the decision, which most expect to achieve in the coming spring." He added, "Confidence in victory remains absolute."[54] Also in September the commander of Eighth Army reported, "The uneasiness which existed several months ago has completely disappeared. Everyone believes that with the powerful cooperation of the Americans the battle against Germany can result only in its defeat."[55] A month later, the Eighth Army commander highlighted improved morale and emphasized the boost coming from the Americans' contribution. He concluded, "The morale of all the units of Eighth Army has never been better."[56]

As one reads these reports, one cannot help but be struck by the profoundly positive effect the Americans and their military contributions had on the morale of French soldiers. Again and again one reads about the numerous Americans arriving in France and about the great pleasure French soldiers had in watching and helping the Americans prepare for combat. Many of the reports, such as the Eighth Army's report of 14 October 1918, note the importance of all of France's allies in the final phases of the war but emphasize the enthusiasm and abilities of the Americans.[57] Clearly, the reports on morale offer important evidence about the contribution of the Americans to the Allied victory and suggest that their importance came from far more than mere numbers.

Though saying the Americans won the war exaggerates their contribution, it is clear that the fortuitous arrival of the Americans helped Pétain keep his army in the trenches and resume offensive operations. Had the Americans arrived a few months later, or had Pershing not offered all his forces to the Allies on 28 March 1918, the outcome of the war could have been significantly different. The task Pershing faced between 13 June 1917, the date of his arrival in Paris, and 28 March 1918 was an incredibly difficult one given the complexity of organizing, equipping, and training the American army and transporting it to Europe. The success that Pershing's forces achieved on the battlefield is truly one of the most remarkable military accomplishments of the twentieth century, one that derived not only from the numbers of his forces but also from the quality and aggressiveness of his officers and soldiers. Clearly, the effect the Americans had on the outcome of the war came from far more than their confronting the Germans "with an army whose soldiers sprang, in uncountable numbers, as if from soil sown with dragons' teeth." While the doughboys did not win the war for the Allies, France might have collapsed and the Allies lost had the Americans not entered battle energetically and effectively a year after declaring war.

MARTIN BLUMENSON

★　★　★　★　★　★　★　★

Task Force Kingston

He looked younger than his 22 years. Or perhaps he seemed younger because I expected a man who had a bullet hole in his shirt, a rip in the leg of his pants—torn by a shell fragment—and a bullet crease across the top of his helmet to look tough, hard-bitten and old. He was boyish.

He was too young, I thought, to be the commander I was looking for, too young to have accomplished one of the impressive achievements of the Korean War. How could this lieutenant have commanded captains?

I met him in Korea in the summer of 1951 when I was visiting the 32nd Infantry. The regiment had recently come out of the line and was in bivouac for a week or so of rest. I was there for a few days doing some interviewing about an action of interest to my historical section.

At the regimental headquarters I came to know pretty well the operations officer, Maj. Frederick Lash. When I finished my assignment and was ready to go back to Seoul, I went over to the S-3 tent to thank him for his help. That's when I learned about Kingston.

The idea came to Lash as an afterthought. We were shaking hands when he mentioned it. "By the way, Lieutenant," he said, "have you ever heard about Task Force Kingston?"

I never had.

"You might look into it sometime," he suggested. "It's a little on the odd side."

I was curious, but only mildly. Lots of people had good stories. Still, I respected Lash. I had enjoyed his hospitality. And his offhand, under-played manner provoked my interest. "What's it about?" I asked.

We went over to the mess tent for a cup of coffee, and he told me. He had been the battalion operations officer during the action and had been part of it.

The story had its intriguing aspects. It wrote a glowing sentence in the official record of the Korean War. Not many young second lieu-tenants had that to their credit.

"Where is this guy Kingston?" I asked.

"He's with Company K," Lash said, waving a hand vaguely. "They're bivouacked over the hill there."

I decided I might as well stay another day. "Can I get over there all right?"

"Sure, it's not far."

It wasn't far by an infantryman's reckoning. Lash gave me direc-tions, said he'd put my driver up another night and telephoned the company I was coming.

My jeep could go only part of the way. Then I climbed a trail up one of those steep Korean hills. If the company hadn't sent a soldier to meet me at the top, I'd have been lost. The soldier guided me down the slope and across a meadow where a baseball game was in progress. We reached a stream, and my guide, being polite, held the swinging foot-bridge steady as I crossed. On the opposite shore I found myself in a grove of trees, and there Company K had pitched its tents.

It was peaceful there that summer morning. Walking through the meadow had been hot, but among the trees it was suddenly cool. The sound of water in the stream did not hurt the illusion any. Nor did the distant cries of the baseball game.

The first sergeant of the company was sitting outside his tent working bareheaded at a table. He looked young. (I found out later he was 19.) His table was full of mail, and he was printing words and dates across a lot of unopened letters—words like *deceased, missing, 51st Evac Hosp.* I still remember a pile of pink envelopes; I could almost smell the faint perfume. The letters were neatly bound with a piece of string, the top one addressed to a private by his wife who, from the number of letters, had written faithfully every day. Across the face of the envelope, the sergeant had printed the word *deceased* and a date.

The sergeant directed me to the officers' tent. There I found 2nd Lt. Robert C. Kingston. He was reading a book under a tree, looking for all the world like a kid home from college for summer vacation. He seemed shy when I introduced myself. He wasn't too happy when I asked him to tell me about his task force. But he said he'd try.

We talked most of the day despite some interruptions. It was his 22nd birthday, and aside from the other company officers who sat with us from time to time, visitors came strolling in. Even the battalion commander came by to wish him many happy returns. Lash showed up. Everyone had some excuse to explain his being there, like pretending to be on an inspection trip. It was obvious they had come to pay their respects. The cooks had a cake for him at dinner.

After it got dark, the company officers had their party for Kingston. They were nice enough to invite me to join them and spend the night. We gathered in the tent where a brand-new bottle of whiskey had been saved for the occasion. Somebody played the accordion; someone had taken the trouble to go all the way to Seoul to borrow it so Kingston could have music on his birthday. It was a pleasant evening.

The sound of voices outside the tent awakened me the next morning. It was quite early, but no one else was in the tent. The officers were outside arguing.

"I'll go," Kingston was saying. "It's my turn to go."

"Why don't you be sensible?" someone asked. "You don't have to go."

"Use your head," someone else said. "You don't have to do everything."

"I'm going," Kingston said.

"What for?" someone shouted. "What the hell are you trying to prove?"

"Shut up," another voice said. "He doesn't have to prove anything. All he's got to do is stay here."

"Listen, Bob," a calm voice said, "it's foolish for you to go out on this patrol. You don't have to. You've only got a few more weeks to stay here. Take it easy. You're practically on your way home."

"I'm going," Kingston said. "Jack is new, and he needs the experience. I'm taking him along."

"I'll take Jack," someone said.

"I can go myself," Jack said. "I'm not a baby."

"You're coming with me," Kingston said.

There was sudden silence. Kingston came into the tent. I was up by then, putting on my boots. He went to his cot and from underneath pulled out his helmet, the one with the crease across the top. He put it on his head, waved at me and left.

He was gone by the time I got outside. Two of the officers who had been arguing with him were still there. I asked what was going on.

"The goddam fool," one of them said. "Someone spotted some Chinese over the ridge, and battalion told us to send a platoon up the valley to clean them out. Kingston says it's his turn to go. So he went."

"No one could stop him?" I said rather uselessly.

They didn't bother to answer.

"Imagine," the other officer said, "imagine getting it in a rear area like this."

I was suddenly miserable. I went down to the mess tent and had some coffee. I had planned to leave right after breakfast, but I couldn't.

All morning long I sat outside the tent brooding. I fussed with my notes, but all I could think of was how Kingston was pushing his luck. A hole in his shirt, a shell fragment through his pants, a crease across his helmet.

The hours dragged interminably. The shade under the trees was somehow gloomy. No one was playing baseball in the meadow. The first sergeant was sitting at his table outside his tent, and for some ungodly reason he was wearing his helmet. He didn't look 19 years old any more.

I finally saw the troops coming down the slope of the hill just before noon. They straggled across the meadow. They looked tired, beat. I searched among them for Kingston. I couldn't find his figure. Or Jack's.

Putting my notes away, I hurried down to the company headquarters. The men came across the swaying bridge and headed for their tents. A solitary figure walked toward the headquarters to check in. It was Kingston's platoon sergeant.

I was sure the worst had happened until I noticed the first sergeant—he wasn't wearing his helmet. Someone was singing in the mess tent. A couple of soldiers were tossing a baseball back and forth as they headed toward the meadow. The grapevine had been working. I should have known everything was all right even before I saw the two men coming down the hill.

Kingston and Jack were late because they had first reported in at battalion. The platoon had rounded up one Chinese soldier. No one had been hurt.

Lunch was a cheerful meal. I departed soon afterward.

I still didn't have the whole story on Task Force Kingston, but after seeing him and the effect he had on the people around him, I was determined to get it. It took me several weeks to look into the official records of the campaign and to find the people who could supply a few missing pieces. By then I had a pretty good idea of Task Force Kingston, what it had done and why it was unique.

The time was late November 1950. The North Korean army had been defeated, and its remnants were streaming north in retreat. The United Nations troops were in pursuit, advancing toward the Yalu River, the northern boundary of Korea. Gen. Douglas MacArthur, who liked impressive terms, named the movement a "compression envelopment," which didn't really mean anything. The war, then called a police action, seemed about to end. Reaching the Yalu was a formality, like rounding the bases and touching home plate after hitting the ball out of the park. The troops talked of being home by Christmas, or at least in Japan. They didn't know yet about the Chinese communists.

The Buffalo regiment of the 7th Division—the 17th Infantry—was driving north to the Yalu along a main road leading to the village of Hyesanjin, the last community this side of Manchuria. Fifteen miles to the west the 3rd Battalion of the 32nd Infantry was moving along a parallel road leading to Singalpajin. Once at the Yalu, the 17th was to march west from Hyesanjin to Singalpajin; the battalion of the 32nd was to push westward to meet marines coming north from Chosin Reservoir.

This was the plan, but it never materialized. Chinese troops were massing, and they were about to disrupt more than these local arrangements. No one knew this, however, when Lt. Kingston was called to the battalion command post on the evening of November 21, 1950.

The place was Wondokchang, 32 miles south of the Yalu. From Wondokchang the road runs north for 10 miles to Samsu, 12 more to Yongsong-ni and finally 10 more to Singalpajin.

The 3rd Battalion, besides being temporarily short one rifle company guarding a power plant, was operating all by itself. Forty-four miles north of the regimental headquarters, it was rather alone in enemy territory and somewhat in a vacuum. No one had much information about friendly neighboring forces. No one knew much about enemy forces that might be nearby.

Though beaten, though streaming north to sanctuary in Manchuria, the North Korean troops had a nasty way of turning to fight when cornered. They were still dangerous; and though a major offensive was out of the question, their deadly weapons were ambush, the unexpected trap, sudden flank attack.

Reluctant to plunge ahead into the unknown, the battalion commander gave Kingston the mission of spearheading the advance. Kingston was to reconnoiter and, if possible, take Samsu. To help Kingston and the 33 men in his platoon, the battalion commander gave Kingston seven tracked vehicles (from the 15th Antiaircraft Artillery Battalion). Kingston's command thereby became a task force.

The vehicles were half-tracks. Four of them mounted twin-forties—two rapid-fire 40-mm guns. Three had quad-fifties—four caliber .50 machine guns tied together. Designed to fire at planes, the guns were nevertheless effective against targets on the ground. They put out a tremendous volume of fire. They were practical also because the men of Kingston's infantry platoon could ride on the carriages that mounted the guns.

The vehicles and their crews were commanded by a first lieutenant named Allen. Though Kingston was a second lieutenant and therefore junior to Allen, Kingston commanded the task force. This was odd, but not the rationale: Allen's function was to support Kingston; the guns were in support of the infantry.

Of the three enemies in Korea—the weather, the terrain and the North Koreans—the weather was probably the worst. If the sun was shining, the temperature in winter might get up to 20 degrees below zero; 30 and 40 below were more normal.

The troops wore everything they could manage—woolen long johns, two pairs of socks, cotton pants over wool trousers, pile jacket over wool shirt, parka with hood, trigger-finger mittens with wool insert, scarves around their heads under their helmets to protect their ears. Anyone who was sitting or standing was usually stamping his feet to keep them from getting numb.

The cold affected equipment. Motors had to be started every hour and run at least 15 minutes. Men had to shoot their weapons periodically to be sure they worked. They had to build fires in empty 55-gallon drums and put them against mortar base plates to keep the metal from crystallizing and snapping. Artillery shells did not always detonate completely when fired.

Living, simply keeping alive in the cold, was enough of a job without having to worry about the terrain and the enemy. Yet these, too, were dangerous. The ground was covered with snow, a dreary landscape almost bare of growth. Streams were frozen so thick the ice could support tanks. The single road to Samsu was narrow. It wound through mountains, across the face of cliffs, along the edge of a gorge. A skid could mean death.

Across the road the North Koreans had rolled boulders down from the hills. Kingston's vehicles were able to get past four of these rock slides by maneuvering around them or pushing the rocks aside. A fifth obstacle near a destroyed bridge caused some trouble.

The column had to back up several hundred yards to a place where each vehicle could plunge off the side of the road. Each in turn teetered uncertainly for a second or two before dropping off the embankment and skidding into a frozen field. The column crossed the field, then a frozen creek and finally found a place where the vehicles could get back on the road. But first some timbers from the bridge had to be used to make a ramp.

All this took time. Whenever the vehicles halted, men had to be sent out to the front and flanks as outposts. Kingston's task force was all day moving the 10 miles to Samsu.

Still, no enemy troops had been seen. Not until the task force was within sight of Samsu did the first hostile fire sound that day. Several shots rang out in the town.

Kingston immediately halted the vehicles, told the infantrymen to dismount. They waited, listening for more evidence of the enemy's presence. Only silence. So they slipped into town, a village of about 50 houses, bombed-out, burned, bullet-riddled. The place was deserted, without a living thing, not even a dog. The shots? The bodies of four civilians lay in the school yard, probably murdered upon Kingston's approach.

Waving in the vehicles and setting up an all-around defense of the town, Kingston radioed battalion he was there. Soon after dark, trucks carrying the rest of Company K and battalion headquarters arrived in Samsu.

That night the operations officer, Capt. Lash, called Kingston into the command post. "You'll continue your advance tomorrow," Lash told him.

"How far?"

"All the way."

Kingston's face showed his surprise. "The Yalu?"

Lash nodded. "Think you can make it?"

Kingston grinned. "Are you kidding? Sure, I'll make it."

It was no choice assignment, and it wasn't going to be easy. For the next three days Kingston's task force started from Samsu toward Yongsong-ni each morning and had to turn back each afternoon. The reasons were the same: terrain, weather and North Korean troops.

The road was narrow, with a cliff most of the way along the right side, a drop-off to a river on the left, high ground on both sides, giving the enemy the opportunity to keep the task force under surveillance and fire. The weather stayed cold, and the men were miserable. Rock slides, defended roadblocks, sudden fusillades of fire obstructed the task force. Snow flurries kept planes from flying in support. Ice on the road kept the vehicles to a crawl. Artillery shells from Samsu seemed to have no effect on the enemy.

Darkness came early on the third day, and the drivers had to use their blackout lights to get back to Samsu. The men were suddenly tired, disgusted with an operation that seemed to be getting them nowhere. Kingston found himself swearing under his breath.

He reported in to battalion headquarters, where he saw the battalion commander. "No casualties, but we lost a quad-fifty. It tipped over into a ditch."

"You didn't leave anything in the quad-fifty, did you?"

It was a routine question, but Kingston flared. "What the hell do you think I am?" He recovered at once. "I'm sorry, sir. We stripped it: ammo, spare parts, gas, the works."

There was a silence between them before the colonel spoke. "You all right?"

"Yes, sir." He nodded to add emphasis. "Just mad."

"You want to try it again tomorrow?"

"You bet I do, Colonel."

"You need anything else?"

He had already gotten more troops added to his task force: a jeep mounting a machine gun; a tank belonging to the 7th Reconnaissance Troop; a squad, then a platoon, from the 13th Engineer Combat Battalion and under a first lieutenant named Donovan; a forward observer, Lt. Trotter, from Battery C, 48th Field Artillery Battalion, whose job it was to direct the fire of howitzers emplaced at Samsu; a tactical air control officer, Capt. Jiminez, whose job was to bring in planes to bomb and strafe.

But Kingston asked for and received another tank, more jeep-mounted machine guns, some mortars. This brought his command to more than a hundred men.

With this strength he blasted through on the following day to Yongsong-ni, a collection of 30 houses, most of them burned. But it took a firefight, an air strike and several casualties to get the troops through the town.

Kingston reported his arrival to battalion by radio. "I'm going on," he told Lash.

"Watch your step. We just got some intelligence information. There's about a battalion opposing you."

"You want me to stop?"

"No, but be careful. I've just sent you up some heavy mortars."

"Can you send me more troops?" He meant infantry.

"Not right now. Maybe later."

About a mile beyond Yongsong-ni, the road ascends. The incline starts gradually, becomes increasingly steep. It rises finally to a mountain pass, a defile overshadowed by high ground on both sides.

At the bottom of the rise, the task force ran into North Korean fire. Rifle and machine-gun bullets swept the road, wounding several men, among them Lt. Allen, the antiaircraft officer.

From the ditches where the infantry took cover, from the carriages where the crew members huddled behind their guns, the men of the task force put out a tremendous volume of fire. The tanks blasted the high ground at virtual point-blank range. Yet the North Koreans refused to give way.

It was difficult to see the enemy troops, the elusive figures behind boulders. Mortar shells began to drop in and around the Americans, some artillery came in, but it was impossible to locate their positions.

"Trotter!" Kingston shouted. "Get some shells up here." Trotter was already on his radio, calling for artillery support.

"Jiminez!" Kingston roared.

"OK, OK," Jiminez yelled back. "I'm getting the planes now." His radio operator had been wounded, and he had taken over the squawk box.

The heavy mortars arrived in the person of Capt. Harry Hammer, who commanded a platoon. He had loaded his men and weapons into trucks at Samsu, then drove on ahead in his jeep. At Yongsong-ni, hearing the sound of gunfire, he walked on to find Kingston taking shelter behind one of the twin-forty carriages. Hammer crouched beside him. "I have 70 men and four mortars on the way up," he told Kingston.

"Set them up," Kingston said, "and get some shells up here."

Hammer hurried back to Yongsong-ni to speed the movement.

The mortars didn't help. Neither did an air strike by four Corsairs, which gave such close-in support that one bomb showered dirt over a few of Kingston's men. A small stone cut his lip.

Sending Sgt. Wayne O. Wood and a squad of men to outflank enemy positions on high ground turned out to be an impossible maneuver. Enemy machine guns cut them down.

Kingston yelled to his own machine gunners to keep working. He noticed Sgt. Templin firing his jeep machine gun even though he lacked cover, Sgt. Emerick working his 60-mm mortars from the ditch.

Despite the fact that every man in the task force was shooting, the opposition was too strong. "I'm breaking off," he told Lash over the radio. "I'm taking too many casualties." He was bitterly disappointed; he had not fulfilled his promise. But to keep at it didn't make sense at the price he would have to pay.

Though it was ticklish work to disengage, Kingston at last moved his men back to Yongsong-ni, where he organized defensive positions.

Not long afterward, more reinforcement arrived. Lash had sent up a rifle company and an artillery battery for attachment to the task force.

The rifle company posed a problem. It was Company I, and the commander not only outranked Kingston but was an infantryman, too. Though Hammer and Jiminez were also captains, their position under Kingston could be rationalized by the fact that they were in support of Kingston's infantry; but the infantry captain did not exactly fit that category.

"Kingston," the company commander informed him, "I'm taking command of the troops in Yongsong-ni." This was usual practice.

"OK, Captain," Kingston said. "You're the senior commander in town. You're the commander of Yongsong-ni."

Cold, tired, angry, Kingston was spooning a supper of cold beans out of a can. His cut lip hurt.

"How about the task force?" Kingston asked. "You also in command of Task Force Kingston?"

"I suppose so. You have any objections?"

"What did battalion say?"

"They said to come up and reinforce you."

An incoming shell crashed into the wall of a building nearby, the sole wall of the building still standing before the shell demolished it.

"Hammer," Kingston shouted, "get your men on that."

A few more rounds came in from a single gun, then the fire ceased. No one was hurt. The only damage was to a tire on a truck, shredded by shell fragments.

Later that evening, as Kingston huddled around a bonfire with several of his men, the rifle company commander came by. "Want to talk to you," he told Kingston.

They walked off a few yards from the men. "Listen," the captain said, "as far as I'm concerned, this is your task force. You have the mission. I'm here to reinforce you, and I'll support you. You need anything, you let me know."

Surprise kept Kingston silent a moment. "You sure you want it that way?"

The captain was sure.

"Thanks," Kingston said. Then his voice became crisp. "I'll tell you what I think we ought to do. Much as I want to get there, I think we ought to rest the men tomorrow. Let them write some letters home, clean their weapons, get some sleep, three hot meals. I'll check it out with battalion. Is that OK with you?"

The captain nodded. "Fine. Go ahead."

Since battalion had no objections, the men got their day of rest. The only activity came from the Artillery and the heavy mortars, which fired some harassing missions.

The following morning Kingston gathered his vehicles and his platoon of riflemen together to lead the advance. Company I would follow on foot.

Before the column started, two more officers showed up. One was a major from the Buffaloes, the 17th Infantry—no one in the task force ever found out his name; his job was to "coordinate" the contact at Singalpajin. The other was Capt. Ed Wild, battery commander of the howitzers supporting Kingston. Officially, he was there to "coordinate" the forward observers, but really all he wanted to do was spit in the Yalu.

Kingston's impatience to complete his mission and cover the 10 miles to the Yalu was obvious. And contagious. It spread to the men of the task force now numbering around three hundred men, including the anonymous major, three captains and several first lieutenants.

The day of rest had worked wonders. The men were in high

spirits. "Let's go!" Kingston shouted, waving his arm in a wide forward motion and springing aboard a quad-fifty carriage.

The vehicles rumbled forward, the crews firing an occasional few rounds to keep their weapons in working order, the infantrymen shooting from time to time to keep their rifles operating. No enemy fire came from the mountain pass. Part way through the defile, two dead North Korean soldiers lay in the road, one on a stretcher. Three engineer soldiers, after checking the bodies to be sure they were not booby-trapped, rolled them out of the way.

At the top of the pass, across eight miles of bleak countryside, lay the Yalu River gorge and the cliffs of Manchuria, clearly visible. Though he still could not see the river itself, Kingston had a feeling of elation.

The task force reached a small destroyed bridge, and the vehicles halted while the engineers set about to repair it. Some men set fire to haystacks in a nearby field to keep warm. At one of the fires, a hand grenade fell out of someone's pocket and rolled into the flames. The explosion killed one man, wounded eight. Among those wounded was Trotter, Kingston's forward observer. Capt. Wild radioed back to his battery to tell Lt. Jim Hughes to get forward as fast as he could.

When the bridge was repaired, the task force continued without incident until the road ended at a gap. The road there was notched into the face of a cliff, and North Koreans had demolished part of the ledge. This was serious, for it meant a long repair job for Donovan and his engineers. The vehicles were immobilized.

Impatient to keep going, Kingston consulted with the rifle company commander. No enemy troops were in sight. There was a good chance that the way to the Yalu was open. "I'll take my platoon down the cliff and strike cross-country," he told the captain.

"Fine, I'll come with you."

Along with him came his forward observer, Lt. Robert Stein; Hughes, Kingston's forward observer; Wild, the battery commander; and the unknown major.

Descending the cliff to a wide plain, they picked up the road again. It was a small force now, for casualties over the past few days had drastically cut the size of Kingston's platoon. He placed seven men under Sgt. Vanretti in the lead to act as point. Then came Kingston and the group of officers. Following were eight men under Sgt. King, a cool, levelheaded type.

They walked a few miles toward the cliffs of Manchuria, toward the Yalu gorge and the river they still could not see. Around a curve in the road they came upon the village of Singalpajin. The road ran through a large flat field bounded on three sides by a loop of the Yalu gorge. Along the left side of the road, a row of undamaged houses marked the outskirts of town.

Vanretti held up his hand to signal halt. He sent four men to the first house to make sure it was empty. Kingston waved King forward and directed his men to the right of the road to cover Vanretti and his group.

The first two houses were unoccupied. Everyone was moving forward when a volley of rifle fire suddenly descended on Kingston's group. A bullet wounded Stein in the arm. Stein, Wild, Hughes and the company commander dived into a drainage ditch alongside the road. Kingston remembered passing a small culvert; he sprinted back and jumped into it. The major followed.

When the fire subsided, Kingston raised up from the culvert and yelled to King to deploy off the road into the field on the right. Even as he shouted, the four officers burst from the ditch and sprinted to the first house. Stein was holding his left arm. Bullets kicked up the snow around them, but they made it to the house and disappeared inside. What the hell! Kingston said to himself. Then he figured they needed the shelter to fix Stein's wound.

He noticed the major's face. The officer was gritting his teeth in pain.

"What's the matter?" Kingston asked.

"Sprained or broke my ankle."

A soldier from Vanretti's group crawled down the ditch to the culvert to find out what Kingston wanted done. Kingston told him to help the major to the rear. Both men crawled off. Kingston inched forward to get in touch with Vanretti and the point.

He found Vanretti and his five men taking cover in the ditch. King's men meanwhile were coming forward on the other side of the road, moving one at a time in short rushes. The enemy seemed holed up in the fourth house of the town, a building larger than the rest. It was perhaps 40 yards away.

"What'll we do?" Vanretti asked.

"I'll get King to cover us," Kingston said. "You take two men and work your way up on the left of the house. The rest of you men cover them from here. When you're in position, Vanretti, I'll run straight at them and try to get their attention. You move in on them. Thirty minutes ought to do it. But be sure to wait for me."

Vanretti nodded. He pointed to two men and started crawling out of the ditch, across the field. The two men followed. Kingston sent a man across the road to tell King what to do, and rifle fire soon started to beat against the house. Kingston crawled down the ditch to get out of the line of fire of his own men.

When 30 minutes had passed, Kingston leaped out of the ditch and started running, heading straight for the house. He had a grenade in his right hand, his rifle in the other. He whooped and yelled as loud as he could. Out of the corner of his eye he could see Vanretti and the two men with him spring to their feet and run toward the house. The crust on the snow was hard. Though it supported Kingston at first, the crust cracked as he picked up speed, then broke. The faster Kingston tried to run, the deeper his feet sank through the crust. He felt he was moving at a walk, his feet floundering in the snow. Vanretti too seemed to be walking, painfully slowly. Kingston's breath came in large gasping sobs. His eyes stung from tears brought on by the cold, and he closed them for a few seconds as he ran. He heard the whang of bullets close to him. Having covered half the distance, he felt he could go no farther. He was breathing in great aching gasps. With what seemed to him his last ounce of strength, he flung the grenade toward the house. He was watching it arch through the air when something hit him hard on top of the head, spun him around, knocked him down.

When Kingston opened his eyes, Vanretti was bending over him. "You're all right," Vanretti was saying in a gentle, imploring voice.

"You're all right. You're going to be all right. You got to be all right."

He noticed that Vanretti was holding a helmet with a bullet crease across the top.

"You're all right, Lieutenant," Vanretti urged. "You're going to be fine."

Kingston sat up, blinking his eyes, still not altogether coordinated.

"We got them," Vanretti said. "That grenade came in perfect."

"Anybody hurt?"

"Not a one, nobody."

"How many were there? In the house."

"Five. We got them. We thought they got you."

A body of troops came walking around the curve in the road. It was Company I, which soon cleared the rest of Singalpajin. Not many North Koreans were there. The bulk of the battalion that had opposed Kingston at the defile had apparently crossed the frozen Yalu into Manchuria.

During the day everyone managed to get to the edge of the gorge to look at the frozen sheet of ice that was the Yalu. Several men, among them Wild, descended to the riverbank to spit into the river.

The road on the cliff was repaired, and the vehicles descended into town. The troops set up camp for the night. Hearing the sound of motor convoys across the river in Manchuria, they discussed the rumor that Chinese troops were entering Korea to oppose the United Nations forces. It was November 28, and they did not know that the Chinese had already intervened in the war. The marines had already been hurt at Chosin Reservoir.

The next morning a radio message from battalion informed the troops at Singalpajin that plans had been changed. They were not to wait for the Buffaloes. Instead, they were to return to Samsu. A general withdrawal from North Korea was under way.

During the grim days of retreat that followed, the fact that Task Force Kingston had reached the Yalu seemed like an incredible dream of small import. No one congratulated the men or their leader. Yet of all the American units that had tried to get to the Yalu, only two made it—the 17th Infantry and Task Force Kingston. The Buffaloes arrived there first and got the publicity. All Task Force Kingston got was a sentence in the official record. And the satisfaction of having completed the assigned mission. Behind the accomplishment was the personal triumph of a 21-year-old second lieutenant.

I met Fred Lash again several years later, this time in the Pentagon. He was a lieutenant colonel. After making known our mutual pleasure at the encounter, we retired to a coffee bar for a few minutes. The talk turned to Kingston.

"Did he make it home OK?" I asked.

Lash assured me that Bob Kingston got home to Brookline, Mass., all right.

The mention of a particular place startled me. For the first time I realized that, aside from what Kingston had done in Korea, I didn't know much, if anything, about him. "It never occurred to me," I told the colonel, "to ask him where he was from. Or anything about himself."

He shrugged. "Why should you? I don't know much about him myself."

"Tell me something," I said. "Maybe you can clear up something that has always bothered me."

The colonel waited.

"Tell me about the command setup on Kingston," I said. "Part of it never quite made sense."

He smiled. "It *was* odd. It was a peculiar command setup."

"Hammer told me no one ever questioned the fact that Kingston was the boss. But really, when you sent Company I up to Yongsong-ni, didn't you mean for the company commander to take over?"

Lash laughed. "That's a low blow. Officially, according to the records, we put the company commander in command of the task force. But since the task force had already been in existence about a week and was being mentioned in the situation reports, the periodic reports and the journals, we didn't change the name of it."

"Well, who was in command the last day when the troops reached the Yalu?"

"Officially? Or actually?"

"I guess you've answered it. All right, tell me why you sent Company I up to Kingston? Why not Company K? K was available, wasn't it?"

Lash laughed again. "You've hit one of my darkest secrets. But I'll tell you. I figured that if Kingston's company came up to reinforce him, he would revert to being simply a platoon leader in that company. But since Kingston's platoon was not an organic part of Company I, Kingston had a good chance to remain in control."

"You figured it would work like that?"

Lash was modest, too. "Well, maybe not so clearly as that."

"But it worked."

"Yes, it worked out fine. Any command situation works out fine when you have good men."

"You don't mean just Kingston."

"I mean the commander of Company I, too. He was a good officer, and he deserves a lot of credit."

"Hammer, Allen, Donovan and the rest of them also, I suppose."

"Right," Lash said. He paused for a moment before adding thoughtfully, "But mostly Kingston. The others crystallized around him."

I didn't know whether *crystallized* was exactly the right word, but I certainly understood what he meant.

Epilogue

by Colonel John M. Collins, U.S. Army (Ret.)

Second Lt. Robert Charles Kingston had already landed at Inchon and fought his way up the Korean peninsula before he took that incredible trek to the Yalu River without even a hand-drawn strip map to guide his group for the last 23 miles. That feat, which remains unique in the annals of the U.S. Army, was merely the first among many exploits that have made "Barbwire Bob" a Special Forces icon and a role model for young infantry officers ever since.

Capt. Kingston's 1959 efficiency report described a dedicated warrior whose "total hopes, dreams and aspirations reflect a single-minded devotion to military service found in few officers of any rank." Well said. His 37-year active duty career featured 29 years with troops, nine campaigns as a lieutenant during combat in Korea, seven more as a field-grade officer in Vietnam and 15 years of command at every commissioned level, from a rifle platoon in Company K of the 7th Infantry Division's 32nd Regiment to U.S. Central Command, which embraced 19 countries within its area of responsibility. He accumulated more than 50 awards and decorations along the way, including the Distinguished Service Cross, three Distinguished Service Medals and two Silver Stars.

Other honors include induction into the Infantry Officer Candidate School, Ranger and Special Forces Halls of Fame. Special Forces Chapter XIII bears his name in Korea, where he commanded a waterborne raider detachment that conducted covert missions in 1951 before he successively became an instructor in the Ranger Department at Fort Benning, Ga.; an unconventional warfare planner with U.S. Army Europe; senior advisor to the South Vietnamese Ranger High Command; an operations officer with the Studies and Observation Group; commanding officer of the 3rd Special Forces Group at Fort Bragg, N.C.; commanding general of the John F. Kennedy Special Warfare Center; and a founding father of Delta Force. Former Congressman Dan Daniel (D-VA), a principal architect of legislation that originated the U.S. Special Operations Command in 1986, saw "only one four-star general with the requisite special operations experience [to take charge]. That is Bob Kingston"—who, because of bad timing, had mandatorily retired the previous year. "The ideal solution," Daniel continued, "would be to recall him to active duty," but that proved infeasible.

Assorted Secretaries of Defense, Chairmen of the Joint Chiefs of Staff, Service Chiefs, other commanders in chief, members of Congress, foreign dignitaries and admiring subordinates consistently praised Gen. Kingston. When former Army Chief of Staff Gen. Edward C. (Shy) Meyer pinned on Bob's third star, he said, "If I ever go to war again, I want this man on my flank." Special operations forces in Vietnam, by voice vote, declared Bob "the man I'd most like to have in a foxhole with me and the man I'd least like to have as an enemy." A sergeant who served with Bob in the 1st Battalion, 35th Infantry, at Pleiku summed up enlisted views with these words: "He was the bravest and the best, a born leader who saved a lot of our lives."

LIEUTENANT COLONEL RAYMOND H. FREDETTE, USAF (RET.)

The Making of a Hero: What Really Happened Seventy-Five Years Ago, After Lindbergh Landed at Le Bourget

The dramatic story of Charles Lindbergh's arrival in Paris after a suspenseful flight of 33½ hours from New York on May 21, 1927, has often been told, beginning with the dispatches of the reporters whose do-or-die assignment was to interview him as soon as he landed. They all failed. Moments after he touched down on the grassy field at Le Bourget, the flier disappeared. The press found him hours later at the American Embassy in the personal custody of the ambassador, Myron T. Herrick. Lindbergh, so the story goes, had been rescued from the crowd that had bolted out on the field and engulfed his plane as he landed.

In his book about the flight, *The Spirit of St. Louis*, Lindbergh credits two French airmen, he identifies only as Detroyat and Delage, for saving him from the mob. After being hustled into a hangar, he recalls he was later taken to the military side of the field at the order of a French officer, Major Weiss. While there he was visited by Ambassador Herrick who decided on the spot to take him to the embassy as his guest. In light of many other accounts of his tumultuous reception, Lindbergh's own version in a brief afterword omits many telling details. But even when he could not be completely candid, he felt compelled to be very specific. "We passed Dugny, Stains, Saint Denis, and entered through the Saint Ouen gate," he remembers of his ride from Le Bourget "over bumpy side roads" into the city.

Lindbergh was on his way to achieving an incandescent fame that even today, after man has conquered space and landed on the moon, has yet to fade completely from the popular mind. In explaining this phenomenon, no little credit is due to Ambassador Herrick. At that pivotal moment in the pilot's life, Herrick sheltered him, groomed him and, after giving him a crash course in modesty and tact, presented him to the world with all the prestige he commanded as an American ambassador much beloved by the French. Such was his popularity that they likened him to Benjamin Franklin, our envoy to France at the time of the American Revolution.

Still handsome and energetic at over seventy years of age, Herrick had previously served as ambassador to France early in World War I. In September 1914, when swiftly advancing German troops threatened to take Paris, the French government and the entire diplomatic corps were evacuated to Bordeaux, except Herrick. He insisted on staying behind to protect American citizens as well as the art treasures of the capital. He vowed he would raise the Stars and Stripes over the Louvre, and go out to meet the Germans personally if they marched in. Although Paris did not fall, the French never forgot the ambassador's act of defiance.

The flight of an American plane from New York to Paris in May 1927 struck Herrick as yet another alarming intrusion. If successful, he feared it would have a "lamentable effect" on the already strained relations between the two countries. Earlier that month, two French fliers, Charles Nungesser and Francois Coli, had taken off from Le Bourget for New York. Their success would have won them the $25,000 Orteig Prize for the first non-stop flight between Paris and New York. Some French newspapers even published joyful accounts of the arrival of the two airmen at the Battery in lower Manhattan. When the reports proved false, and it became clear that the French plane had disappeared, the mood in Paris turned from exultation to anger. The press accused the U.S. Weather Bureau of having withheld weather data in favor of the transatlantic fliers who were poised to take off from New York. American tourists were jostled on the Champs Elysées, and a hostile crowd reportedly had torn down a U.S. flag outside an American newspaper office.

Herrick sent an urgent cable to Washington warning that no American plane should attempt a transatlantic flight "until an appropriate time has elapsed." The ambassador, as had everyone else, expected Commander Richard E. Byrd would be the first to leave aboard his trimotor, the *America*. With his considerable financial banking, Byrd was seen as the most likely winner of the so-called Atlantic Race.

"Who in the devil is Charles Lindbergh?" was the reaction in Paris as the news of his takeoff from New York was received. After the disappearance of Nungesser and Coli, his solo flight seemed all the more foolhardy. Herrick again cabled Washington for confirmation that "le fou volant" was indeed on his way, and then left the embassy to attend the championship tennis matches between French and American players at St. Cloud. When questioned by the press, he seemed uninterested in the American pilot no one seemed to know. In truth, his flight in progress was just about the last straw for the ambassador.

Among his concerns was the pending execution of two Italian immigrants, Sacco and Vanzetti, in a Massachusetts prison. Convicted of killing a payroll guard in a holdup, the pair had been the object of violent demonstrations in Europe; many believed they were being persecuted for their political views. At the time of the trial, a package addressed to Herrick had seriously injured his valet when it exploded as he opened it. The ambassador was now receiving threatening letters, warning that he would also die if Sacco and Vanzetti were executed. His residence, as well as the embassy, were under heavy police guard. Herrick was also anxious about a convention of the American Legion to be held in Paris that summer. The Legionnaires were known to be rowdy, and some Americans residing in the city were arranging to leave during the event because of the tense anti-American atmosphere.

Although Herrick insisted he had "no plan of any kind regarding Lindbergh," he virtually took over the reception for him at Le Bourget. Weeks earlier, Commander Byrd's sponsors had sent an advance man to Paris to work with a Franco-American committee that was organizing a grand welcome. These arrangements were quickly revamped in the event Lindbergh made it across the Atlantic. As one embassy insider noted later, it was felt he might be "placed in a situation here where one remark could have international complications. . . ."

The revised plan called for keeping Lindbergh away from reporters until he could be primed on what to say, so as not to offend French sensibilities after the loss of Nungesser and Coli. On landing, he was to taxi up the airport terminal between two rows of policemen reinforced by troops. Once there, he would be escorted directly from his plane to the upper level of the terminal for a brief welcoming ceremony. Admission to a fenced-in area in front of the building was to be limited to individuals with "complete official documents," which did not include reporters.

These arrangements did not concern the Paris bureau chief of

The New York Times, Edwin L. James, who had plans of his own. Before Lindbergh left New York, his St. Louis backers had negotiated a contract with the paper for the exclusive rights to his story. The *Times'* managing editor, Frederick Birchall, then cabled James "to isolate" Lindbergh the moment he landed before other reporters could reach him. As James recalled, his "elaborate preparations" included "a fine automobile ready to bring the aviator back to the capital to give his own story. . . . Oh, it was a wonderful plan."

Back home, the editor of the *Chicago Tribune* somehow learned of the scheme, and he in turn promptly notified his own Paris bureau chief, Henry Wales. A crusty veteran of the city's press corps, Wales was not about to lose out to a competitor on the Lindbergh story. "I could see his arrival," he indignantly recalled. "Jimmy James and his staff would take possession of Mr. Lindbergh—kidnap him, if necessary; hide him in some hotel; milk his story to the last detail. With the yarn safely in type, they'd invite the rest of us to meet the hero. . . ."

Wales was on close terms with Herrick, having written speeches for him, and he alerted the ambassador who acted quickly to beat James at his own game with the help of French officials. As William Shirer of *Berlin Dairy* fame, then a cub reporter working with Wales, notes in his memoirs, "the police and Major Pierre Weiss, commandant of Le Bourget military field . . . worked out a last-minute plan with Ambassador Herrick for a reception."

Major Weiss actually commanded only the bomber unit of the 34th Aviation Regiment, that was based on the opposite side of the field from the civilian air terminal. The major's help was key to a plan to "rescue" Lindbergh even before James and his reporters could get to him. Early that morning, a Saturday, Weiss was observed busily making preparations and giving orders to his men for the arrival of the American pilot. As ensuing events would show, they were to seize him right out of the cockpit as he landed, and keep him in custody at least overnight. By that time, he could be coached by Herrick before meeting the press. With the crowd kept at a distance, a bogus flier, appearing extremely fatigued, even on the verge of collapse, would appear briefly at the air terminal. It was arranged to have a doctor, an American, on hand with his kit and a blanket roll. "He'll naturally be exhausted when he arrives," anticipated the physician. "I positively won't let him do any talking tonight."

Seemingly uninvolved in all this, Herrick attended the tennis matches at St. Cloud for a second day. Late that afternoon, a messenger from the embassy rushed up to him in the president's box and handed him a telegram. Lindbergh had been sighted over Ireland. On receiving the news, the ambassador and his party were observed leaving for Paris "in disarray." "I hardly even dared to expect his arrival," Herrick later disclaimed. "I merely went to the flying field on the chance that he would be successful in his attempt and I wanted to be on hand to congratulate him."

On arriving at Le Bourget, Herrick realized he was facing a very difficult, if not impossible, situation. As word spread of the American flier making it safely across the Atlantic, thousands of Parisians clogged the roads leading to the airport. They crowded about the terminal and noisily filled the small restaurant inside. The police guarding the restricted reception area out front became so hard pressed that they accepted "any card that had your picture on it."

Ambassador Herrick, at least, found himself in full command with all the assistance French authorities could provide. The crowd, the chief of the Paris police informed him, was the largest since "the peace parade. I've sent for five hundred more police, Your Excellency." The Elysée Palace sent a military aide, Colonel Denain, to act on behalf of the French president, Gaston Doumergue, at the airport. "All help and courtesy will be extended to Mr. Lindbergh," announced the Foreign Office. . . . "Sufficient police will be on hand to guard him against any demonstration."

Lindbergh landed after dark shortly after 10:20 P.M., settling softly like an exhausted carrier pigeon as he neared the ground. In his book, *The Spirit of St. Louis*, he complains about the poor lighting and "jolting into blackness" until he finally stopped, and then swung around "to taxi back toward the floodlights and the hangars." He never reached them. Once he was safely on the ground, some lights were purposely turned off and he was beaconed away by military searchlights to a spot a half-mile from the terminal where Major Weiss and his soldiers were waiting to pounce on him.

According to the flier's account, his first words on landing were, "Are there any mechanics here?" Ironically enough, the man who claimed to have been first to reach the plane was a mechanic by the name of Fernand Sarrazin. No ordinary mechanic, he was, in fact, the chief of aircraft maintenance for C.I.D.N.A. (Compagnie Internationale de Navigation Aerienne), an airline based at Le Bourget. Sarrazin was obviously out there to take charge of the plane; it was to one of the company's hangars that the *Spirit of St. Louis* was taken later that evening.

Without disclosing why he did so, Sarrazin said he walked out of his hangar onto the field at about ten o'clock, the time Lindbergh was expected to arrive. He watched as the American landed and taxied toward him. As he recalled, he barely had time to shout, "Ici Paris, Le Bourget," before some soldiers pulled up in automobiles. "They got a hold of Lindbergh, or rather I should say they kidnapped him, so quickly was this done without any regard for the safeguarding of the plane. Consequently, I remained with the machine."

By some similar coincidence, Hank Wales, Herrick's informant about the *Times* plan, and Shirer were also out in that particular area of the field. They saw the flier touch down in the half-light, and then turn to taxi in their direction. "By luck," wrote Shirer without explaining their good fortune, "he stopped a few yards from where Wales and I were standing." Wales recognized Major Weiss in full uniform shouting to Lindbergh to cut his engine, while his men "were pulling and twisting at the door to the cabin of the slowly moving plane." The flier's first words, said Wales, were not about mechanics, but an admonition to the soldiers as the door swung open: "Careful there; don't break it." Once the *Spirit of St. Louis* came to a full stop, Wales saw "the sergeants reach inside and seize Lindbergh." Realizing he was about to be carried off, the flier reached out as far as he could and managed to slam the cabin door shut.

About this time, James and two of his *Times* reporters reached the scene of the melee. They had gone out at dusk and walked along the police lines stretching out from the terminal until they thinned out. Huddled together, they then waited behind the glare of a large flare for Lindbergh to arrive. After he landed, James and his party, unlike Wales and Shirer, had to run several hundred yards to reach the plane. "We could see he was struggling," James recalled, after Lindbergh was pulled from his cabin. "He fell to the ground once and then he was on the shoulders of a dozen men."

Lindbergh, in his book, makes no mention of the soldiers who descended on him like commandos. Instead, he remembers the surging crowd, fearing it would do serious damage to the plane. "Within seconds my open windows were blocked with faces," he writes. Only after he "decided to get out of the cockpit and try to find some English-speaking person, who would help me organize a guard to hold back the crowd," does he recall being grabbed by "dozens of hands" as he emerged.

The thousands who had been waiting, many of them for hours, were puzzled on seeing the gray-white monoplane land in the shadows and then taxi away from the terminal. The crowd may have sensed it would be denied seeing the American pilot, and the sight of the figures of James and his party running toward the plane evidently sparked a stampede. A human wave crashed through "the very strongest fences, some seven feet high, with spikes on the top," and rushed out on the open field. Looking over his shoulder, James saw "countless bobbing heads between us and the flares. . . ."

The unexpected surge of the huge crowd gave credence to the story that Lindbergh's "rescue" was an impromptu affair; it also greatly complicated the reception Herrick had planned at the terminal. As Wales described it, while Lindbergh was being "spirited into an army hangar, a bogus aviator was rushed through the crowd to be presented to the Ambassador." The man acting as a double for Lindbergh was a Parisian haberdasher named Jean Claude d'Ahetze. Although he did not look much like the American flier, he was tall and spoke some English. Standing by on the field when the plane landed, he said he thought it was an incoming mail flight until he saw the words, "Spirit of St. Louis" on its nose.

Garbed in a leather jacket, the young Frenchman reached in through the open cockpit window and pulled Lindbergh's helmet off his head, even before his plane came to a complete stop. Since he likely would be photographed, he needed an American-styled helmet that was different from French flying gear. Conceivably, d'Ahetze could have taxied the *Spirit of St. Louis* to the terminal. Although not a pilot, he had served as an aviation mechanic during the war.

Lindbergh effectively denies any such encounters with d'Ahetze, or with Sarrazin, the mechanic, not to mention Major Weiss who was observed shouting to him to cut his engine (*Coupez! Coupez!*). "No one reached my plane," he said categorically, "until I had turned back toward the hangars, cut the switches, and the wheels had stopped rolling." Lindbergh was much less certain as to what happened to his helmet. As he recalls in his book, "my helmet had somehow gotten onto the head of an American reporter. Someone had pointed to him and called out, '*There is Lindbergh! There is Lindbergh!*' The crowd had taken over the reporter and left me free."

In the confusion, d'Ahetze in his leather jacket and wearing the flier's helmet may himself have been mistaken for Lindbergh. In any event, he in turn lost the helmet, which wound up on the head of Harry Wheeler, a young American in the crowd. Much as he tried to break loose, he was hoisted up on the shoulders of a small group of men and carried away toward the airport terminal.

According to d'Ahetze the youth was taken for Lindbergh, having been "designated as such by some French officers who, in the meantime, cleverly concealed the real Lindbergh." Herrick's own recollections were more consistent with the account of a "rescue," and a spontaneous one at that. A year or so later, he said: "This man turned out to be a New York

Herald reporter . . . to whom Major Weiss had given the helmet with orders to take it to me. This was done to deceive the crowd and get them clear of Lindbergh and his ship. The ruse succeeded, and it only goes to show how quickly aviators have to think and act."

Tall and blond-haired, Wheeler certainly looked like Lindbergh, but he was not a reporter. He was a Brown University student on a summer tour of Europe. His clothes torn and disheveled, he was still struggling as he was carried up to the upper level of the terminal where Herrick, clutching a bouquet of red roses, and other officials were waiting to receive the hero. Describing the scene as one that provided "the only comedy of the evening," William Shirer relates:

> " 'But I'm not Lindbergh, Mr. Ambassador,' he insisted.
> 'Of course you are,' Herrick replied, holding out the roses.
> 'I tell you, sir, I'm not Lindbergh,' the young man repeated.
> 'My name is Harry Wheeler. Everyone got confused because of this,' and he held up the crumpled helmet . . .
> 'If you're not Lindbergh, then where is he?' the ambassador asked.
> 'Some French officers took him to a hangar on the other side of the field while that crazy mob was almost killing me.' "

Although essentially correct, Shirer's account had to be written from hearsay, because no reporters were admitted to the upper level of the terminal. He was also writing from hindsight because Wheeler had no way of knowing at the time where Lindbergh had been taken. As for Herrick, he hardly could have expected the real Lindbergh to appear at the terminal. Confused by the switch of doubles, he was reassured when d'Ahetze arrived in the wake of the small group that had brought in the American student. He informed Herrick that his "son" had landed and that he had seen the plane. Determined not to be cheated out of his moment of glory, d'Ahetze then regained possession of the helmet.

"I opened the window and wild with joy showed the crowd Lindbergh's helmet," he recounted. "It was at that precise moment that I was mistaken for Lindbergh. I wore a leather coat, my hair was tousled. The mob cheered me as surely no man was ever cheered. . . . Finally, I realized the mistake, withdrew, and gave Lindbergh's helmet to Ambassador Herrick."

D'Ahetze never did say that he acted as a stand-in for Lindbergh. Obviously not wanting to implicate Herrick, he claimed to have done little more than appear at the window with the helmet. Yet, one eyewitness, John P. V. Heinmuller, saw the entire charade carried out as planned.

Heinmuller, later president of the Longines-Wittnauer Watch Company, was allowed on the upper level of the terminal as an official observer of the National Aeronautic Association. He had hastily sailed for Europe fully expecting another entrant in the transatlantic race, Clarence Chamberlain, flying the *Columbia* with the plane's owner, Charles Levine, as his passenger, would be the first to reach Paris. Instead, he arrived in the French capital just in time to see Lindbergh land at Le Bourget. He had no reason to believe that the "tired flier" at the terminal was not Lindbergh.

"I was lucky to be admitted, through the aid of Comm. Weiss," Heinmuller wrote home four days later. "Only Lindbergh, the official physician [who fully expected to find his patient in a state of complete exhaustion], and a few high officials were admitted to the upper floor. . . .

After the physician had pronounced the flier's condition satisfactory, he was escorted secretly through a side door with a French military coat worn over his flying suit to help hide his identity. The crowd outside, not knowing he had gone, kept calling for Lindbergh's appearance. . . ."

Herrick's problem was to placate the crowd and persuade it to go home. He sent his son, Parmely, out waving the helmet, and he also was mistaken for Lindbergh. Herrick himself then appeared and "offered the leather helmet to the French people like a scalp." Finally, the lights in the terminal were turned off for a time to convince the crowd that Lindbergh had left.

D'Ahetze, at least, recorded his name for posterity in what was unquestionably the most momentous landing in aviation history. Officials of the Paris Aero club were with Herrick at the terminal with a landing certificate, attesting to the flier's arrival at Le Bourget. The document was important in laying claim to the Orteig Prize, but Lindbergh was not there to sign it. The officials were finally persuaded he had, indeed, landed upon being shown his helmet with the label of its Boston manufacturer sewn inside. Acting as a proxy, d'Ahetze signed the certificate along with a few others, as did Lindbergh the next day.

The French haberdasher, Herrick always insisted, was merely the man "who delivered to me Lindy's helmet," but he evidently felt obligated to him for more than that act alone. A year later, the ambassador wrote to Lindbergh, on his behalf. "What he would like," communicated Herrick, "is an autographed picture of yourself and, in view of the fact that he gave me the means of verifying your landing that memorable evening, I take the liberty of placing his request before you. . . ."

D'Ahetze apparently did not get a picture. In 1933, when Lindbergh returned to Paris for the first time since his flight, the haberdasher appealed directly to him by letter. Writing "in my poor language," he identified himself as "the first man who speak [sic] with you after your memorial flying—thirty-three hours—when your spirit [plane] run in the grass at Le Bourget—21 May!! and I took your helmet on your head myself. Do you remember . . .?" Even in the case of d'Ahetze, Lindbergh was not inclined to respond to requests for autographed pictures.

D'Ahetze ended his letter by identifying himself as a "Friend of Michael Detroyat," a name that Lindbergh would come to know well. One of the two acknowledged "rescuers," Detroyat had led the assault in getting the flier out of his cockpit. A sergeant who spoke some English, he was promoted to lieutenant shortly thereafter. A skillful pilot, Detroyat met Lindbergh again in Europe in the thirties, and also in 1940, when he came to the United States with a French mission seeking to purchase American warplanes. So far as it can be determined, Detroyat never spoke for the record on what transpired that night at Le Bourget, nor did he question Lindbergh's account when asked to read the manuscript of his book before its publication in 1953.

The other "rescuer," George Delage, was not a soldier, but Detroyat may have recruited him for his better command of English. A commercial pilot based in England, he flew between London and Paris with a French airline, Air Union. Although Delage does not appear to have ever spoken for the record either, he also believed he was owed a favor for his role at Le Bourget. Some two years later he wrote to the flier asking, "May I recall to you the circumstances of our first meeting?" What Delage wanted was Lindbergh's help in getting employment as a pilot with some airline in the States. Receiving no reply, he wrote Lindbergh six months later, again apparently to no avail.

Acting together, Detroyat and Delage took custody of Lindbergh after the soldiers pulled him out of his plane. As improbable as it was that two English-speaking Frenchmen in that immense crowd should reach him at the same time, Lindbergh claims that is just what happened. "Two French aviators," he writes, "the military pilot Detroyat and the civil pilot Delage, found themselves close to me in the jam of people. . . . I spoke no word of French; my new friends but little English. . . ." Lindbergh had little choice but to go along with them. "With arms solidly linked in mine," he continues, "I began moving slowly, but unnoticed through the crowd." He does not say that his escorts sought to disguise his appearance. Lindbergh was made to remove his flying suit, and Delage handed him his own Air Union jacket to put on.

If Lindbergh felt indignant about this, it was nothing compared to his concern about his plane. "I should not try to get back to it," he remembers being told. "They were determined about that—there was no mistaking their tones and gestures. They laughed and shook their heads as I protested, and kept pointing to the car." Delage had a small Renault, which was much less conspicuous in driving the flier away than an army vehicle. As Lindbergh recalls, they went to "a big hangar" where he "was taken to a small room on one side. My friends motioned me to a chair and put out most of the lights—so I would not be discovered by the crowd."

Lindbergh's account corroborates the notion that he was rescued from the mob. It also raises the question of why, instead of hiding the flier, Delage did not keep on driving beyond the airport to a place where he would be safe, such as a hotel, just as James of the *Times* had planned to do. In any event, the stop at the hangar does give Lindbergh an opportunity to introduce Major Weiss, who up to this point is not mentioned in his narrative. Detroyat left, the flier goes on, "to search for an officer of higher rank." It appears the sergeant had some trouble finding one until "in the midst of the crowd, he came across Major Weiss.... The Major could not believe that I was sitting in a hangar's darkened room. 'It is impossible,' he told Detroyat. 'Lindbergh has just been carried triumphantly to the official reception committee.'" The incredulous major, the flier continues, came to the hangar with Detroyat, and "on seeing me insisted that I be taken to his office on the military side of Le Bourget—about a mile away. So we climbed into the Renault again, and drove across the field. Then, it was Major Weiss's turn to go out and search for higher officer."

After Detroyat and Delage had taken charge of Lindbergh at the plane, Weiss threw a cordon of police and soldiers around the machine until it could be taken to Sarrazin's hangar. The major then joined Herrick and the other officials at the terminal. Had the reporters not seen him directing the "rescue," no one would have been the wiser. When Weiss was summoned to the telephone, it could only have been Detroyat calling to inform him they had arrived with Lindbergh at the military section of the field. D'Ahetze who happened to be standing nearby the phone at the terminal, confirms in his account, "Commandant Weiss learned that Lindbergh was safe." In turn, he informed Herrick who decided he would like to see his "son" that night, and the major immediately left to set up a meeting.

Colonel Denain, the military aide sent by the Elysée Palace, was also called to the phone at the terminal. This time, the eavesdropper was the Belgian air attaché serving in Paris, Baron Willy Coppens de Houthulst. A famous ace who had lost a leg in the war, Coppens was a colorful figure noted for his devilish sense of humor. He also spoke English, which was perhaps one reason why he was at the terminal. "Yes, he has arrived, but we do not know where he is," Coppens heard the colonel say. "I was waiting until I had seen him before telephoning. Please give my apologies to the President . . . How did you find out? Ah! Weiss. Yes, I see. North Block. . . ."

Coppens kept his plane in a hangar in the North Block along with those of the bomber unit commanded by Weiss. Concluding that Lindbergh had been taken there, the attaché quickly left and drove across the field without lights. When he arrived at the rear of the hangar where Weiss had his office, the attaché ran into some soldiers guarding the entrance. Being in uniform, he was allowed to go in. Lindbergh, he was told, was not in Weiss's office, but in a tiny room at the end of a hallway. A soldier was posted at the door. On seeing the tall, boyish American who had just flown the Atlantic, Coppens was at a loss of words. Looking forlorn, the flier was still wearing Delage's uniform jacket on which were pinned some military ribbons.

"I see you have the French Military Medal," Coppens jested in accented English. "That's too wonderful!" Unsmiling, Lindbergh replied the jacket did not belong to him, and added with some anger, "They have already taken my helmet!" He then pulled a slip of paper from his wallet. On it was written the name of a small Paris hotel. He asked Coppens about it, wondering "if it might not be too expensive?" The flier had been told he would be met on landing by *Times* reporters, but he was not one to leave anything to chance. So far, he had been proven correct. He had yet to speak to correspondents from the *Times*, or any other newspaper. Coppens was struck by Lindbergh's cool composure, recalling that "his face—was it due to fatigue?—conveyed no emotion whatsoever, neither joy nor enthusiasm."

Barely ten minutes after Coppens saw Lindbergh, there was some rushing about in the hallway. Major Weiss was telling the soldiers that the American ambassador was coming and to prepare for his arrival. The flier, Herrick noted later, had been found only after "a diligent search. It was not until one o'clock that we discovered him in a little adobe building on the far side of the field with his rescuers."

Weiss escorted Lindbergh from his room and led him outside where a line of soldiers had been hastily drawn up as an honor guard. They stiffened to attention as a large, chauffeured car drove up with Herrick, Colonel Denain, and a few other French officers inside. The ambassador undoubtedly expected to find a grubby, oil-stained pilot barely able to stand from fatigue. As it was, he was completely taken

aback when he saw the fair-haired youth waiting impassively with
Weiss and the soldiers. Emerging from the car, "the old man reached
out and embraced his compatriot *a la mode de chez nous*," observed Coppens. Visibly moved, Herrick was heard to mutter, "A kid! He's just a
kid!"

Lindbergh was much relieved to see the American ambassador.
From the brusque treatment he had received, he was convinced he was
in some sort of trouble. He had explained to his French keepers who he
was and showed them his passport. "I was a little worried about that,
since I had no visa," he conceded. "But I received mostly smiles and
laughter in reply." Being made fun of was annoying, but all he could do
"was just wait and let events develop."

"When I greeted him he handed me his three letters of introduction with a happy smile," recalled Herrick. "One [was] addressed to me,
one to Mr. Houghton [the U.S. envoy in London], and the third, I forgot to whom." Once inside, the ambassador was shown a room where
the French "were making up a cot for their guest." Chairs were brought
in so they could sit down, but Lindbergh said he preferred to stand.
"Thank you," he declined. "I have been sitting." Herrick was taken by
the dry-witted response. "I was so captured by his sense of humor, his
smile and his general appearance," he went on, "that the thought then
first occurred to me to ask him to become my guest at the embassy. . . .
I immediately took him by the hand and said: 'My boy, come with me; I
am going to take you home and look after you.' His face lighted up and
he said: 'Are you?'"

The warm invitation was not unlike countless others the flier received from farmers while barnstorming, or from Mr. Conkling, the
kindly postmaster of Springfield, Illinois, when the weather turned
bad on the mail run to Chicago. A home-cooked meal and a wide bed
in the spare room upstairs was usually more comfortable, and cheaper,
than staying in a hotel in town. But that night at Le Bourget, it would
have been better for Lindbergh if he had stayed at the airport, and
slept on the steel cot which the soldiers were readying for him. Come
morning, he could have made his own plans and been on his way in a
few days. The flier was about to become a pawn, and his whole life
would be changed to a degree far beyond the significance of his solo
ocean journey.

Major Weiss, who was quite prepared to keep Lindbergh at Le
Bourget, delivered his prize to the American ambassador. The flier's
biggest concern now was his plane, and what had happened to it. As
they were about to leave, Herrick recalls Lindbergh saying he wanted to

go "fix the windows of my ship, for these Frenchmen will not know how to do it. Before I could restrain him . . . he dashed out." The flier tells a different story, stating "a discussion in French followed" his request to see the plane. He says he was told not to worry. The *Spirit of St. Louis* was not badly damaged, and he could inspect it after he had slept.

"Well, how do you feel about it, Captain?" Herrick asks solicitously in the flier's account. "I argued that I wanted to get some items from the cockpit, and to show how to put the windows in." Lindbergh claims he was driven back to the "Air Union hangar" where "my *Spirit of St. Louis* has been placed inside." After "a careful inspection," he was satisfied "no serious damage had been done. A few hours of work would make my plane airworthy again." Never one to concede injury, Lindbergh was trying to minimize what could not be completely denied, as revealed in photographs taken of the plane.

The pictures also established that it had been taken to the C.I.D.N.A. hangar. "I must say," states Sarrazin, the chief mechanic, "I did not see Lindbergh again during the course of that memorable night. . . . Since the plane suffered quite a bit of damage—the fabric on the fuselage and control panels torn out, the empennage thrown out of line, the tail skid twisted—the fuselage and control surfaces had to be completely recovered. . . ." The French were adamant about not showing the plane until it had been restored, but their concern was not so much about upsetting Lindbergh. Ambassador Herrick had warned them that any harm befalling the flier or his machine would arouse hostile American feelings against France.

When Lindbergh bolted out of the door in search of his plane, his "rescuers" ran in pursuit and brought him back to Herrick. "Instead of taking him to his ship, they bundled him immediately into their car and started off to Paris by roads known only to them," confirms the ambassador. "I did not see him again until I got to the embassy some hours later."

Major Weiss went along with Detroyat and Delage in the overcrowded Renault. Aside from assuring that Lindbergh would reach the embassy, the French officer added the dignity of his rank to a brief ceremony that took place enroute. An impromptu affair, it had all the earmarks of having been suggested, if not ordered, by Ambassador Herrick. Once in the city, Lindbergh and his escort made a visit at the tomb of the Unknown Soldier at the Arc de Triomphe. While it is doubtful the flier fully understood the significance of the site, much less cared on his third night without sleep, Weiss recorded the event in highly grandiloquent terms.

"Lindbergh asked us to stop," reads an article he wrote shortly thereafter. "He walked to the tomb and bowed in silence. Only three of us witnessed this historic scene, in which the conqueror of the Atlantic stood over the grave of that other conqueror, shedding a leaf from the still fresh crown on his brow. No spectacle of such solemn grandeur has been seen in this generation." Weiss said nothing about his "rescue" of Lindbergh at Le Bourget.

Coppens, the Belgian attaché, had followed the Renault in his own car into Paris. As they drove up the Champs Élysées, he saw Delage pull over in front of the Claridge Hotel. The doorman went inside and returned with some flowers he collected from the empty tables in the dining room. At such an early hour, they were the only ones available to place on the tomb of France's Unknown Soldier. Lindbergh himself mentions no such floral tribute. "My friends took me through the arch," he relates, "and I found myself standing silently with them at the tomb. . . . They wanted my first stop in Paris to be at the Arc de Triomphe, they said."

Barely a few hours later, the Paris newspaper, *Le Matin*, reported in bold headlines how an exuberant crowd had greeted the flier at Le Bourget with cries of "Vive Lindbergh! Vive l'Amerique!" Another front-page story informed Parisians of his moving early morning visit to the Arc de Triomphe "to salute the Unknown Soldier." Back in the States, the *St. Louis Post-Dispatch* noted editorially shortly after the flight that, while "on his way into Paris in Ambassador Herrick's automobile," Lindbergh "requested that the prearranged route into the city be changed so as to permit him to lay a wreath on the tomb of the French Unknown Soldier. Tired and exhausted as he was, he achieved by this little act . . . added respect and appreciation not only for himself but the nation he represented. . . . America has reason to be proud." Evidently, Herrick still had contacts in St. Louis where, as a young man, he had worked briefly as a reporter.

The ambassador himself credited Lindbergh with ending "one of those periods of petulant nagging and quarreling between the French and ourselves. . . . Within ten hours after Lindbergh landed at Le Bourget all these clouds were rolling away. . . ." Fearful there might not be "another Lindbergh to drop out of the sky to help us . . . next time bickering starts up," Herrick could only hope "we might have sense enough to invent one just for the occasion."

Some correspondents were not above doing a little inventing of their own that night, as they faced Sunday edition deadlines without having seen Lindbergh. John Pickering of the *Paris Herald* ran three miles from Le Bourget before finding a taxi for the rest of the trip back to his office. "Christ, what a story!" he exclaimed on arriving. "I practically had my hands on him. Then, presto! He's gone. First guy to fly it, and not a single word from him. We're high and dry."

Hank Wales of the *Chicago Tribune* was not so hard pressed in covering the big event. Acting as if he knew all along that Lindbergh would not be speaking to anyone on arrival, Wales proceeded to write an imaginary interview with him at plane-side.

" 'Am I in Paris?' " he quotes the flier on landing.

" 'You're here,' I told him, as the mob jabbered in French. . . ."

Wales noted how Lindbergh, a strict teetotaler, "gulped down a swallow of brandy from a flask one of the French pilots offered, and it seemed to revive him."

For his "Lindbergh exclusive," he received a $500 bonus from his newspaper, a considerable sum at the time. Other envious correspondents accused Wales of having written his imaginative dispatch earlier that afternoon. "Wales was on excellent terms with Herrick," recounted Waverley Root of the *Chicago Tribune*'s Paris edition," and it wouldn't have been beyond him to acquaint Herrick with what he intended to write and make sure there would be no denial of it. Indeed, he might even, as a friend of the ambassador, have served as a sort of unofficial adviser on what angles it would be politic to persuade Lindbergh to stress . . . in the interest of French American amity."

"We reporters suffered the tortures of the damned," echoed James of the *Times*. He nonetheless managed to turn in "a slick professional job" telling how Lindbergh appeared at the terminal after being rescued from the crowd. In a follow-up article, James pointed an accusing finger, not at Herrick, but the reception committee for "deeply planning" to snatch Lindbergh on landing so "that those *New York Times* reporters did not do any 'isolating.' Well, if we did not, they did not." Along with the lines of soldiers and police, the crowd had swept up the official greeters.

James does not explain why the reception committee would want to prevent reporters from reaching Lindbergh, but someone had to be blamed for his failure to carry out the "isolating" order from New York. When James learned that the one responsible was the American ambassador, he did not dare expose him, not to mention embarrass Lindbergh, who had become a world acclaimed hero overnight. None of the correspondents, in fact, ever suggested that Herrick was involved in the flier's disappearance from the field after he landed. To have done so would have made them look ludicrous, and since they were able to see the flier before dawn anyway, the correspondents could be forgiving.

James and his crew were crawling back empty-handed in heavy traffic to Paris when one of them, Carlisle MacDonald, asked him, "Say, James, do you think we will get fired for this?" Thanks to Herrick's concern about his good relations with the press, and Lindbergh's insistence on fulfilling his contract with the paper, nobody was. James, "a tough, hard-bitten character," ended his long newspaper career as the managing editor of *The New York Times*.

Once back at the office, James recalled how they went to work "getting the story together. Then we remembered we had not got Captain Lindbergh. . . . 'Ambassador Herrick is a good fellow,' someone said, 'he will tell.' Off Mac went and found Captain Lindbergh sitting on the edge of the bed in the Embassy drinking a glass of milk." Unless Herrick did tell, locating Lindbergh could hardly have been so easy. As MacDonald himself conceded, the ambassador's son, Parmely, cordially let him in at the embassy as if he had been expected all along. "'Come on in, Mac. He's upstairs talking to Father.' There were no other reporters in the Embassy."

Herrick had lingered behind at Le Bourget to throw the press off the scent, and give Lindbergh and his escort time to reach the embassy. On returning there, the ambassador found his guest was upset because he had not met the *Times* reporters at the airport as he had expected. The flight to Paris was only the first stop on what Lindbergh hoped would be a trip around the world, and for that he needed money. Aside from a few testimonials he had given before leaving New York, he had no ready source of income other than what the *Times* would pay him. Although he had won the $25,000 Orteig prize for making the flight, he fully expected his St. Louis backers would claim most of it to pay for the plane.

Herrick insisted he should rest and wait until the next day to talk with the *Times* men, but once determined to have his way, Lindbergh was not easily swayed even by an ambassador nearly three times his age. Herrick finally yielded and telephoned James as to where he could find the most sought man in all of Paris. At the embassy, MacDonald was ushered up to the flier's room, finding him "wide-awake, coherent and most cooperative" during a half-hour interview.

Herrick was later accused of working hand in glove with the *Times* in his handling of Lindbergh. Back home, press czar William Randolph Hearst sent a protesting telegram to Secretary of State Frank Kellogg on being advised that "the Ambassador and his family were keeping all the newspapermen away from Lindbergh except *The New York Times*." The flier, replied Kellogg, was Herrick's "personal guest," and the government "has nothing whatever to do with Mr. Lindbergh's affairs."

Herrick, understandably sensitive to the charge of favoritism, later sought to explain himself to his biographer. As newsmen gathered outside the embassy, he said he suggested to the flier, "if he was not worn out, he let them all in for a minute," but he declined, citing his "exclusive contract" with the *Times*. Herrick added he realized "this thing seemed too big an affair to be made the exclusive news of any one paper." Since MacDonald was still at the embassy, Herrick sent his son downstairs to discuss the situation with him.

According to the reporter, he took it upon himself, evidently without consulting James, to release Lindbergh from his contract "in deference to the world importance of the story. . . . I never regretted it. Through all the giddy weeks afterward . . . he remained true to the *Times*." Herrick apparently was much relieved to be off the hook. MacDonald, he praised, "showed himself the high-class man he is . . . and all the journalists came up to hear what Lindbergh would tell them."

The truth be told, that is not precisely how the flier got to meet the press early that Sunday morning. Herrick had no intentions of allowing him to talk to other newsmen after his interview with MacDonald, who undoubtedly was of the same mind. Lindbergh was tucked in and told to get some sleep. Not long afterward, a band of reporters led by Ralph Barnes of the *Paris Herald* arrived in taxies outside the embassy gate. Convinced Lindbergh was inside, Barnes asked to see the ambassador. Herrick met the reporters in a small reception room, and admitted the flier was upstairs sleeping. Pleading that his guest was too exhausted to be disturbed, the ambassador insisted there would be no interviews until he awoke and was alert enough to talk with them.

In the group was Jay Allen, whom Wales had sent out to follow up on what had happened to Lindbergh. He called his office and reported the impasse to Shirer, who answered. Angrily snatching the phone, Wales bellowed, "Listen, Jay. Tell Herrick you fellows have got to see him. . . . And if that doesn't work, barge up to the bedroom yourself. We got to talk to him."

Still awake, Lindbergh overheard the commotion when the reporters arrived at the embassy. Herrick's son came downstairs and announced that the flier "did not care to go to sleep just yet and would be glad to see the newspaper men for a few minutes." While barnstorming, Lindbergh had learned that advance billing and publicity were important to get the townspeople out to the fair-grounds for the air show. Flying the ocean alone had been like stunting over an empty grandstand, and now he was more than anxious to tell his story. The correspondents let out a whoop, and swept the ambassador out of their way as they dashed up the staircase.

When they entered the room, Lindbergh jumped up from his bed and asked, "Is *The New York Times* man here?" Only after MacDonald stepped forward was he ready to talk. "Questions were fired at him from all sides," observed the *Times* reporter. Charming the correspondents with his boyish smile and seeming humility, Lindbergh became more expansive and dramatic as he recounted his flight. Although he had traveled through "sleet and snow for over 1,000 miles, he refused to take seriously the problem of flying the Atlantic." He said he could not get over at "how short a time it took to cross the ocean," calculating he could have gone on for another five hundred miles, if not a thousand. "I didn't get at all sleepy," he boasted.

As the questions shifted from the flight to his arrival at Le Bourget, Herrick became very uneasy. The ambassador abruptly ended the interview after only seven or eight minutes, explaining it was "too much strain on the flier to submit him to further questioning." As Lindbergh himself recalled, "Paris clocks marked 4:15 in the morning before I went to bed. It was sixty-three hours since I had slept."

It remained for Herrick to end the momentous day with a transatlantic cable that would tug at the heartstrings of mothers all over America. Addressed to Evangeline Lindbergh in Detroit, it appeared in the *Times* Sunday editions after MacDonald received a copy before he left the embassy. It read:

> WARMEST CONGRATULATIONS. YOUR INCOMPARABLE SON HAS
> HONORED ME BY BECOMING MY GUEST. HE IS IN FINE CONDITION
> AND SLEEPING SWEETLY UNDER UNCLE SAM'S ROOF.
> MYRON HERRICK.

The ambassador later maintained he had not "realized the magnitude of this event . . . until the next morning, when I saw the newspapers. . . . Then the thought came to me of the significance of it all, also of my act of taking him to the Embassy, which placed the United States Government behind him."

For political reasons, Herrick had acted, even before Lindbergh landed safely Le Bourget, to create the impression that his flight had the endorsement of Washington. The ambassador wanted to impress upon French authorities at the highest level that the American pilot merited being well-received and honored by their country, while at the same time assuaging their own sense of loss and resentment over the disappearance of Nungesser and Coli. Undoubtedly, the French Foreign Office was provided with an advance copy of a congratulatory message that was to be handed to Lindbergh *immediately on his arrival.* [Emphasis added.]

Cabled from Washington, the message recommended, if not drafted, by Herrick read in part: THE AMERICAN PEOPLE REJOICE WITH ME AT THE BRILLIANT TERMINATION OF YOUR HEROIC FLIGHT. Told that his feat CROWNS THE RECORD OF AMERICAN AVIATION, the flier was reminded that he was BRINGING THE GREETINGS OF THE AMERICAN PEOPLE TO FRANCE. The cable further charged him with carrying THE ASSURANCE OF OUR ADMIRATION OF THOSE INTREPID FRENCHMEN, NUNGESSER AND COLI, WHOSE BOLD SPIRITS FIRST VENTURED ON YOUR EXPLOIT, AND LIKEWISE A MESSAGE OF OUR CONTINUED ANXIETY CONCERNING THEIR FATE. The communication was signed, CALVIN COOLIDGE.

After putting his "guest" to bed, one of the first things Herrick did was to acknowledge the "worthy tribute" from Washington. FOR THE PRESIDENT, began the ambassador's cable that was transmitted through Secretary of State Kellogg.

ALL FRANCE IS DEEP IN JOY AT CHARLES LINDBERGH'S BRAVE FLIGHT. . . . IF WE HAD DELIBERATELY SOUGHT A TYPE TO REPRESENT THE YOUTH, THE INTREPID ADVENTURE OF AMERICA AND THE IMMORTAL BRAVERY OF NUNGESSER AND COLI, WE COULD NOT HAVE FARED AS WELL AS IN THIS BOY OF DIVINE GENIUS AND SIMPLE COURAGE.

Lindbergh had arrived with only the clothes he wore—his full-length flying suit over a pair of breeches, shirt and tie, and his long-sleeved sweater—the outfit in which he had posed for countless pictures in New York. After he got up about noon, he dressed in a borrowed, double-breasted dark blue suit. Someone said he looked "the picture of a typical American farmer boy."

Ambassador Herrick and his embassy staff had to improvise because the "hero of the hour" could not be kept hidden much longer. By early afternoon, a large crowd had gathered outside the front gate, chanting, "We Want Lindbergh!" In response, Herrick led the flier out onto a balcony overlooking the street. The throng cheered on seeing the elderly ambassador and the tall, fresh-faced youth standing side by side with their arms entwined, smiling broadly down on them. A French flag was brought out, and together they let it "unfurl in the breeze." The loud cheering continued until an embarrassed Lindbergh left the balcony "with a final wave and another of his engaging smiles."

Once he was back inside, it was high time to appease the reporters besieging the embassy. Earlier, the flier had chatted leisurely with James and MacDonald as he ate a hearty breakfast. Finally, he walked down the grand staircase locked arm-in-arm with Herrick on his right and a man on his left who very likely was the ambassador's son. In depicting the scene, Waverley Root mistakenly identifies him as Benjamin F. Mahoney, the builder of the *Spirit of St. Louis*. He had followed the flier from San Diego to New York by train and then sailed for Europe, but had yet to arrive in Paris.

Writing decades later, Root was still deeply resentful of having been kept downstairs with the other reporters while the *Times* men were upstairs with the flier. Since he outlived practically everyone there, including Lindbergh, Root could also be very candid. As he came down for his first formal press appearance, Root recalls, "Lindbergh looked as if he were being led to the electric chair between two husky guards."

The flier's opening statement obviously had been written for him with the cable from President Coolidge in mind. "I brought with me, gentlemen, the great sorrow of the American people for Nungesser and Coli," he said somberly. "The French attempt was in the heart of the whole nation, and we grieve with France over their noble failure." Not surprisingly, the first question asked was what did Lindbergh think of French women. "I haven't seen any yet," he curtly replied. According to Root, this was "his last contribution to the conversation except for the syllable 'Uh'. . . . If a question opened an opportunity to make political capital, Herrick answered for Lindbergh before he could get his mouth open. If it were technical, the Ryan man pounced on it. Between these answers, Lindbergh was helpless."

On his first full day in Paris he had only one other engagement, a late afternoon call on "la Maman du Capitaine Nungesser." Although the visit was said to have been "unknown to anyone except the immediate household of the Ambassador," it turned out to be a badly kept secret. By the time Herrick and his party arrived, thousands of people crowded the street and the police were already there in force to clear the way. The visitors had to climb six flights of creaky stairs to reach a small apartment where Mme. Nungesser herself admitted them. On

seeing the youthful American who had survived the Atlantic, the griev-
ing woman embraced him and wept.

"She was in a pitiful state of emotion over the loss of her son,"
Herrick sympathized, "and begged Lindbergh to find him for her." He
supposedly told her that the search was continuing and that her son
would likely be found in the wilds of Canada. "This graceful gesture,"
observed the *Times*, "has earned for the bashful, fair-haired boy from
the West the undying affection of the whole French nation." Lindbergh later denied that he had given "Mme. Nungesser any hope for
the return of her son, as there was practically none." In all fairness, he
was as much a pawn as Mme. Nungesser in their emotional meeting
which Ambassador Herrick had carefully arranged.

The following day the flier spoke publicly for the first time at a
luncheon hosted by the Aero Club of France. He limited his remarks
to Nungesser and Coli, stating that those "brave airmen attempted a
greater thing in taking off from Paris to New York than I have done in
accomplishing the trip from New York to Paris. Their difficulties were
far greater than mine. . . ." Lindbergh's response, after other speakers
had hailed his own flight as "the greatest thing ever done in the history
of aviation," struck everyone for its modesty. As one American resident
in Paris remarked, "It was as if the spirit of their own aviators had returned. The French accepted him as one of their own."

David Lawrence, a syndicated columnist, reported from Washington that Herrick "has taken charge of the young hero. . . . The Government here is pleased, indeed exuberant. Diplomacy knows what it
means to get a whole nation speaking in praise of an American." Some
months later, Henry Wales elaborated on the political fallout of the
flight. "Flag-waving, nationalism, and politics played their part in the
drama afterward," he wrote. "Washington discovered the value of this
'ambassador without portfolio,' and cabled Herrick in secret code to
exploit the hero to the utmost in order to link up more firmly America's
diplomatic relations with France weakened since the war."

Herrick himself testified as to the effort made to comply with that
directive. "For more than a week," he said, "the ambassador to France
and almost his entire staff were busy night and day attending to nothing except matters which concerned a young American who a few days
before had never been heard of. It was not a question of whether we
wanted to do it . . . it had to be done. . . . There was no escape. Of
course, nobody wanted to escape; we were all charmed with him and
delighted that things turned out as they did."

The ambassador effectively became the architect of the flier's celebrafication both official and personal. "Shy, Nordic Lindbergh was just what the clever diplomat needed," commented *Time* magazine. "He rushed to Le Bourget waving French and U.S. flags; seized 'Lucky Lindy' with avidity; put him to bed in his own diplomatic pajamas; wrapped him in the tricolor; had him photographed, interviewed, dined and decorated; and caused the greatest enthusiasm for things U.S."

At noon on Monday, Herrick escorted Lindbergh to the Elysée Palace, the official residence of the French President. MacDonald, in his *Times* dispatch, reported that "within five minutes after arriving—a speed which would give American efficiency methods cause for thought— President Gaston Doumergue had pinned the Cross of the Legion of Honor upon the lapel of his blue suit—the one lent to him by Ambassador Herrick's son. In so doing France's Chief Executive set a new precedent, for never before has he personally conferred this distinctive decoration on an American." The act of a chief of state bestowing a high decoration on Lindbergh was also a precedent invariably followed in all of the other countries he later visited with the *Spirit of St. Louis*.

Before the day was over, the flier met the French Premier, Raymond Poincaré, who shook his hand and congratulated him on his "belle exploit." Summarizing "Capt. Lindbergh's first day of being lionized," the Associated Press concluded he had been "showered with such honors as France in all her history has never spontaneously bestowed on another private citizen."

Later that week, Herrick arranged for the young hero to have lunch with the Minister of War, Paul Painlevé, as well as the Foreign Minister, Aristide Briand, at the Quai d'Orsay. "The days that followed were carbon copies of the first," Root elaborates. "We followed Lindbergh through a succession of presentations of awards, official receptions, banquets, and laudatory speeches, reporting word after banal word. . . . Lindbergh was moved through his labyrinth of ceremony like a puppet, wearing a perpetual expression of bewilderment."

After his arrival in Paris, the flier had barely caught up on his sleep before he was showered with invitations to visit other European cities. Herrick did all he could to dissuade him from going, particularly to Berlin. To do so, he told the flier with some heat, would be an affront to the French after they had honored him with the Legion of Honor. Although the ambassador wanted him to return home directly with a message of friendship and goodwill from the French people, Lindbergh was easily persuaded by a British delegation from England to fly to London with a stop in Brussels enroute.

Herrick vainly counseled against the flight, "if explaining a situation a man does not understand, is giving advice." After all he had done, he was much concerned about losing all control over Lindbergh. He telephoned the American ambassador in London, Alanson B. Houghton, and urged him to put the flier up in his own embassy, so as "to protect him and give his visit official recognition."

Lindbergh left Paris with his plane exactly one week after his tumultuous arrival at Le Bourget. After seeing him off, Herrick cabled Secretary of State Kellogg, stating in part:

> LINDBERGH HAS JUST DEPARTED. THROUGHOUT THE WEEK IN PARIS NOT ONE UNTOWARD THING HAS HAPPENED. HE HAS CAPTURED EVERYONE BY HIS COURAGE, MODESTY AND INHERITED GOOD SENSE. . . . AN EXPRESSION OF APPRECIATION BY THE PRESIDENT AND BY YOU WOULD BE GREATLY APPRECIATED AND WOULD CONSOLIDATE THE GOOD THAT HAS BEEN EFFECTED. . . . ALTHOUGH HE CAME UNOFFICIALLY . . . [LINDBERGH] HAS BECOME A REAL AMBASSADOR TO FRANCE. . . .

The flier never went beyond London. Aside from the pressure from Herrick, his St. Louis backers were agitating for his return with the plane they felt belonged to them. They appealed to Secretary of War Dwight Davis who, being from St. Louis, was also anxious to have the city reap its share of the glory. After some discussion, Ambassador Houghton advised the reluctant flier in the strongest possible terms to comply with "the wish of Washington and those who have your best interest at heart." Lindbergh later stated he only agreed to go back because "it was an order from the President of the United States." Sorrowfully, he gave up his plane for dismantling and crating in England, and returned to Paris in a borrowed military aircraft.

Since Lindbergh had first landed there, Herrick insisted it was only fitting and proper he should depart from France. Houghton expedited arrangements for his return on an American warship, while Herrick worked with the French to have the flier sail from Cherbourg where the local chamber of commerce organized an elaborate farewell. Lindbergh had fallen into the hands of two skillful ambassadors who managed to subordinate his wishes to what they believed were "our best national interests."

Until the moment he sailed, Herrick used the flier with uncanny shrewdness to improve Franco-American relations, a stratagem for which he made no apologies. "From the moment I decided to take him to my house," he elucidated, "all the rest followed inevitably. Providence had interposed in the shape of this boy, and if I did not seize the occasion offered I was not worth my salt. I did not make the opportunity; I only took advantage of it. Lindbergh made it."

Without Ambassador Herrick, it is highly questionable whether Lindbergh would have become an American icon with the status of near royalty, the closest thing the country ever had to a Prince of Wales. Even so, Lindbergh, without Herrick, would surely be as well remembered as Amelia Earhart, the first person after him to fly the Atlantic alone, and who received many of the same honors, including the French Legion of Honor. But, then, her legend lives on not because of that solo flight but for the mystery of her later disappearance without a trace over the Pacific. The irony is that if Lindbergh had suffered a similar fate in 1927, he would be no better known today than the other fliers who set out like him to fly the Atlantic and never made it. In the making of heroes, much depends on time, place and circumstances.

A Story Told But Unrevealed: Sleuthing the Sources

While Charles Lindbergh has the unique distinction of being the first to fly solo across the Atlantic, he did not do so in a vacuum, as international political, economic, and sociological forces converged to make him one of the brightest "superstars" in aviation history. The process began even before his landing and unceremonious reception at Le Bourget, a story which, if revealed, would have acutely embarrassed Ambassador Herrick, not to mention Lindbergh himself.

Herrick, in his "autobiographical biography," (Mott, T. Bentley, *Myron T. Herrick: Friend of France*. Garden City, N.Y. Doubleday, Doran, 1929, pp. 340–55), devotes an entire chapter on Lindbergh in Paris, explaining what he does not openly acknowledge, i.e., that his youthful guest was effectively detained on his arrival until he, the ambassador, assumed custody and had him taken to the American embassy. The messages between Herrick and Washington concerning Lindbergh appear in full text in *The Flight of Captain Charles A. Lindbergh From New York to Paris, May 20–21, 1927*. As Compiled from the Official Records of the Department of State. Washington: Government Printing Office, 1927.

Lindbergh, in his two books about the flight, makes the best of the situation he found himself in on landing at Le Bourget. In the first, (*We*. New York: G.P. Putnam's Sons, 1927), he states very simply that, after the attention of the crowd was diverted from him, "I managed to get inside one of the hangars." (p. 226.) After a lapse of a quarter-century before his second book was published (*The Spirit of St. Louis*. New York: Charles Scribner's Sons, 1953), Lindbergh was more expansive in a brief afterword. (pp. 495–501.) He wrote it on the advice of his editors who felt that ending the book with the crowd rushing toward his plane at Le Bourget was too abrupt.

Henry Wales, the correspondent who was on close terms with Herrick, lived to read the book. Lindbergh, he tellingly complains in a review (*Chicago Sunday Tribune*, September 13, 1953), "chokes off his successful arrival in Paris in ten pages, says practically nothing of the tremendous reception that awaited him, and remains mute on the intrigue and political passion afterward." Another well-informed reader was Willy Coppens, the Belgian air attaché in Paris in 1927. "Lindbergh himself," he notes parenthetically in his own account, "has not reported exactly the vicissitudes of his arrival, not comprehending what was happening to him. . . ."

Lindbergh's confident narrative of his "rescue" from the crowd and peripatetic journey which eventually ended at the American Embassy prevails in all of the biographies and other books about him. Their authors evidently were of the same mind as Brendan Gill, the first among them to publish a work with full access to Lindbergh's papers. The best authority on his subject, Gill professed, was Lindbergh himself. In his brief book, (*Lindbergh Alone*. New York: Harcourt Brace Jovanovich, 1977), Gill describes the tumultuous scene at Le Bourget by quoting verbatim, with attribution, five consecutive paragraphs from *We*. (pp. 146–47.)

In his writings, Lindbergh never mentions his contractual arrangements with the *New York Times*, but they are reported in detail in an early history of the paper. (Berger, Meyer. *The Story of the New York Times, 1851–1951*. New York: Simon and Schuster, 1951, pp. 291–305.) Also included is the full text of a lengthy, follow-up dispatch from Edwin James in which he attempts to explain what happened after Lindbergh landed.

Many other American correspondents also wrote retrospective accounts of that momentous night (see, Koyen, Kenneth. "Desperately Seeking Lindy." *Air & Space*, Vol. 5, No. 1, April/May 1990, pp. 44–49), but they add little to the story beyond their anguish at having to meet deadlines without having seen, much less interviewed, Lindbergh.

One of them was William L. Shirer who likely knew more than he wrote in his book. (*20th Century Journey, The Start 1904–1930.* Simon and Schuster, 1976, pp. 323–44.) Shirer worked for Wales who had advance information on the reception planned for Lindbergh. Wales himself provides many revealing details in two magazine articles written ten years apart. ("Lindy and the French Fans." *Liberty*, September 10, 1927, pp. 71–74, and "Formidable." *Atlantic Monthly*. June 1937, pp. 669–80.)

Another correspondent, Waverley Root, reflects somewhat cynically on the intrigue involving Wales and Herrick, as well as the ambassador's press-agentry, in a partial autobiography published after his death. (*The Paris Edition*. San Francisco: 1987, pp. 28–37.) Root devotes an entire chapter to "The Flying Fool."

Since the press was excluded, the best eyewitness report, at least by an American, of what occurred on the upper level of the terminal building where Herrick's plan for welcoming Lindbergh went awry is a letter John P.V. Heinmuller, chief timer of the National Aeronautic Association wrote home to his wife shortly after. The text was later published in his book about notable airmen, including Lindbergh. (*Man's Fight to Fly*. New York: Funk and Wagnalls, 1944. pp. 68–85.)

Without French sources, no account of Lindbergh's arrival at Le Bourget can be complete as well as reasonably accurate. Major Weiss's story, which does not mention Herrick at all, was published in English as a news article on the first anniversary of the event. (*New York Herald Tribune*, May 20, 1928.) Two years later, Jean Claude d'Ahetze, the stand-in who felt slighted because he was not the one carried to the airport terminal to be welcomed by Herrick, wrote a long letter replete with inconsistencies to the *New York Times*. It was published on July 13, 1930 under the heading, "One of Lindbergh's Doubles Tells How It All Happened."

Although in French, other personal recollections saw print on the occasion of the fiftieth anniversary of Lindbergh's flight when *Icare*, a solid French aeronautical review, put out a commemorative issue featuring transatlantic flying. (No. 81, Summer 1977.) A long piece by Willy Coppens ("La véridique histoire de l'arrivé de Charles Lindbergh au Bourget," pp. 65–75.) affords the reader a comprehensive picture of the dramatic event, beginning that Saturday morning with a much preoccupied Major Weiss issuing "precise orders" to his men in case the American pilot reached Paris. Although Coppens claims that "only the commandant and myself are able to relate the true story," he does not place Weiss at the scene of the landing melee, as others testify in their accounts.

While much briefer, the story of Chief Mechanic Fernand Sar-razin ("J'ai accueilli Lindbergh," pp. 77–82) is no less significant. He recalls "officers belonging to the 34th Aviation Regiment based at Le Bourget," arriving at Lindbergh's plane before the crowd, and only seconds after he, being first, did so.

Commenting on Sarrazin's story, *Icare* editor Jean Lasserre recalls d'Ahetze's own version which he had published ten years before (No. 42), on the fortieth anniversary of the flight. In it, d'Ahetze claims he greeted Lindbergh before anyone else as he landed. Lasserre tactfully concedes both may have been there "at the same moment, on opposite sides of the machine. We will probably never know. . . ." Perhaps with a closer reading, even a little research, the editor might have credited Commandant Weiss and Sergeant Detroyat with being first, a distinction they never claimed for themselves. Over a lifetime, one remained loyal to Ambassador Herrick, the other to Charles Lindbergh.

Sarrazin's account in *Icare* was actually written in 1927. Still living on the fiftieth anniversary, he was interviewed by a reporter on his encounter with Lindbergh at Le Bourget. The retired mechanic told much the same story, but with one major alteration. He said nothing about the soldiers driving up in cars with blinding headlights, and yanking Lindbergh out of his cockpit. All he remembered was the wave of people dashing across the field toward the plane.

"The crowd almost kidnapped Lindbergh, and it began to tear souvenirs from the fabric covering the fuselage," Sarrazin told the reporter. Changing his story fifty years later, he had perhaps read Lindbergh's book by then, and decided not to contradict it. After all, who would take his word against that of aviation's greatest hero?

JOSEPH ROBERT WHITE

✯ ✯ ✯ ✯ ✯ ✯ ✯ ✯

"Even in Auschwitz . . . Humanity Could Prevail": British POWs and Jewish Concentration-Camp Inmates at IG Auschwitz, 1943–1945

Through the memory of British POWs held in forced labor at IG Farben's Auschwitz plant, this article provides unique, even "privileged," insight into an important aspect of the Holocaust. It relies upon Nuremberg statements, recently accessible German documents, international Red Cross materials, and questionnaire responses. Confronted with palpable evidence of Nazi criminality, the British extended a helping hand to the Jewish inmates at the Auschwitz-Monowitz concentration camp, sounded the alarm about their ongoing mass murder to the international Red Cross and to the British Government, and challenged the Nazi racial hierarchy imposed at IG Auschwitz. Although themselves not immune to an anemic form of antisemitism, their behavior stood in marked contrast to that of German bystanders.

O n a cold and blustery morning at IG Farben's Auschwitz plant in winter 1944, an argument erupted between a German supervisor and three British prisoners of war. In reply to the demand to attach cable on top of a slippery girder, the POWs adamantly refused, for want of proper equipment. The scene attracted the unwelcome attention of a German Army sergeant. *Unteroffizier* Benno F. bellowed orders for Corporal Reynolds to climb the girder, but, convinced that the tirade was all bluff, Reynolds walked away in protest. The German NCO thereupon shot and killed him, *pour un example aux autres*. On another occasion, when Private Campbell disobeyed regulations by helping a young Polish woman lug food to the job site, the same sergeant replied with a literal stab-in-the-back. Campbell fortunately survived the assault. Excluding some clubbings with rifle butts and occasional fights, the Reynolds and Campbell incidents were the only two known atrocities committed against British POWs at IG Auschwitz.[1]

Confined to E715, a work detachment of Stalag VIII B, the largest prisoner-of-war camp in Germany, and under Wehrmacht guard, the British received legal protection under the Geneva Convention of 1929. Calling themselves "kriegies," slang for *Kriegsgefangenen* (prisoners of war), the British stood in an unusual position relative to everyone else at the plant, thanks to their protected status and to Red Cross parcels. Their food, treatment, morale, clothing, and free time were the envy of the other laborers. Yet they faced two grim realities: one was the dim prospect for successful escape from eastern Upper Silesia; the other was the fact that a Nazi concentration camp stood a literal stone's throw away. The POWs' response was to help Hitler's ideological "enemies," the concentration-camp inmates. Offering them food, cigarettes, the latest war news, and treatment as men, not racial inferiors, the kriegies extended a lifeline to the drowning.[2]

The British experience supplies valuable insights about the Nazi racial hierarchy at IG Auschwitz, the extent of moral autonomy under the Nazis, and the degree to which the secret of Jewish extermination had emerged into the open. Apropos of the present discussion is what German sociologist Rainer Baum has termed "caring concern." Learning about the gas chambers during their first days at the plant, the POWs sought to inform themselves and, to the degree possible, to understand the Nazi killing machine, refusing to be bribed by the relative privilege Nazi racial hierarchy accorded them in the camp world. Later, some served as witnesses in war crimes trials and in a civil suit brought by former inmate Norbert Wollheim against IG Farben in-Liquidation *(in-Abwicklung)*. After sketching some salient features of IG Auschwitz, this essay examines the Holocaust through the memories of British POWs at E715.[3]

Intended to manufacture Buna (synthetic rubber), synthetic oil, methanol (wood alcohol), and other chemicals, IG Auschwitz was a product of Nazi dirigism, ideology, and corporate interest. At a cost of RM 776 million, IG Farben, the parent corporation of IG Auschwitz, erected what turned out to be a white elephant—reminiscent of the Reichswerke Hermann Göring plant at Salzgitter, or the Soviet steel colossus at Magnitogorsk, two troubled manufacturing centers built by command economy—producing neither oil nor rubber before the Soviet Vistula-Oder Offensive in January 1945 led to its abandonment. Although the long-held assertion that IG Farben had selected the Auschwitz site to benefit from the supply of cheap slave labor does not withstand careful scrutiny, the firm did placate importunate governmental invitations and pursue its own long-term corporate interests by becoming a participant in forced population resettlement, slave labor, spoliation, and mass murder.[4]

IG Auschwitz fielded a workforce of twenty-nine thousand by December 1944. That figure included seven thousand concentration-camp inmates, thirteen thousand foreign workers, eight thousand Germans, six hundred British POWs, and a few dozen Italian military internees. The multinational workforce represented a cross-section of Europe; the POWs came from nearly every Commonwealth country, even South Africa. When the Auschwitz-Monowitz concentration camp became operational in October and November 1942, Jews from almost every European nation passed through its gates, along with German, French, Slavic, and other Gentiles. Such a "Tower of Babel," as Primo Levi characterized it, had practical effects quite apart from the plant racial hierarchy: on the building site, signs had to be posted in at least four, and sometimes more, languages.[5]

The "racial" hierarchy found palpable expression in destructive labor, what the Nazis termed *"Vernichtung durch Arbeit."* Those at the bottom labored under conditions intended to demoralize, weaken, and kill them. In a careful analysis of Jewish work camps in Poland, Christopher Browning has observed that "destruction *through* labor" often gave way to the "destruction *of* labor" [emphasis original], since Heinrich Himmler overruled pragmatic considerations in favor of extermination, e.g., during the notorious 1943 killing orgy Operation *Erntefest* (Harvest Festival). But as if to underscore Browning's emphasis upon situating the contexts of Jewish forced labor, the situation at IG Auschwitz was profoundly dissimilar from those at Lublin or Starachowice, the camps he has examined, because of Himmler's personal commitment to completion of the IG Auschwitz plant. The first concentration-camp inmates—non-Jewish Poles and German kapos— arrived at the new building site on 21 April 1941. Though the prisoners were supposed to be under the firm's control at the work site, the SS guards who brought them continued to abuse them by forcing them to work at a murderous pace and setting them to "sport" (physical exercises designed to kill or injure), in addition to an exhausting five-kilometer hike to and from work. Initial managerial complaints about the deleterious effect such brutality had for productivity eventually gave way to apathy and even identification with SS methods. Managers had become more accepting of brutality by the time Jewish inmates started arriving in early July 1942. Toward the end of the month the latter were quarantined as a result of typhus and typhoid outbreaks; by the time they re-entered the general workforce in November, German overseers were regularly stimulating productivity through violence, with some threatening consignment to the gas chambers as punishment for laggard performance. Even after the erection of a plant fence placed more distance between inmates and SS guards, and management undertook half-hearted measures to augment the laborers' diet, inmate working conditions evinced little improvement before late 1943. By that time plant construction (and a growing labor shortage) had advanced to the point that skilled inmate labor became a valuable commodity, while Auschwitz underwent a command shake-up that brought war-economic priorities to the fore.[6]

By 1944, the incremental barbarization of IG Auschwitz had long passed the point of no return. Some idea of how plant leaders internalized SS values is evident in the "temporary-duty column" (zbV-Kolonne) established in March of that year. The Gestapo had been assigning the plant's recalcitrant foreign workers to a work discipline camp (Arbeitserziehungslager, or AEL), first in the Auschwitz I main camp and then in Monowitz. Management registered its dissatisfaction with high AEL attrition rates by establishing the "column" as an alternative exclusively under its own direction. Emulating the SS's form of destructive labor, the assignees performed menial and backbreaking tasks at a furious pace. But unlike the AELs, management limited sentences to two weeks' duration.[7]

Managerial complicity in Nazi crimes extended far beyond destructive labor, to include trade with the SS and decisions abetting mass murder. The plant obtained clothing from the Auschwitz facility called "Canada" as early as autumn 1942, in a barter agreement involving SS-Obergruppenführer (lieutenant general) Oswald Pohl and IG Farben director Otto Ambros. In exchange for garments, IG Auschwitz furnished the SS with luxury items obtained on the Belgian black market by IG representatives. At the Nuremberg trials it emerged that the trade originally involved only a few thousand garments; no figures were given for later years, but the fact that the trade continued until the close of 1944 suggests a significantly greater scale. In summer 1942, IG Auschwitz began construction of an Auschwitz subcamp, under the banal appellation of Lager IV, near the former Polish hamlet of Monowice. The inmates had many names for the camp, including "Buna," "Buna-Monowitz," and "Auschwitz-Monowitz." Located adjacent to the plant's southern fence, Monowitz became operational in October and November 1942, exploiting primarily Jewish inmates. The Gestapo located an AEL within its confines in summer 1943, over management's vociferous objections. In November 1943, the incoming Auschwitz commandant, SS-*Obersturmbannführer* (lieutenant colonel) Arthur Liebehenschel, consolidated Rudolf Höss's unwieldy domain by reorganizing nearly all forty sub-camps as Auschwitz III, under the command of SS-*Hauptsturmführer* (captain) Heinrich Schwarz at Monowitz. In November 1944, the Monowitz concentration camp emerged as a separate camp, with Schwarz as commandant. IG Auschwitz financed the construction of Monowitz, but obstinately refused to permit barracks and hospital-ward construction to keep pace with the influx of new inmates. Such indifference lent the SS the convenient excuse of selecting Jewish inmates for murder to limit overcrowding. While their involvement in "selections" was more complex than presented at Nuremberg, where former victims alleged that IG Auschwitz, not the SS, set selection criteria, plant leaders knew enough about the killing process to look the other way, rather than to connect the SS's insatiable demand for fresh labor with the chimneys that billowed smoke some seven kilometers away at Birkenau. The most reliable estimates put the number of Monowitz dead by exhaustion, disease, shooting, hanging, and selection for gassing at between 23,000 and 25,000 lives.[8]

Into this context, 1,400 British POWs arrived in autumn 1943 and winter 1944 to form subcamp E715. When Italy capitulated to the Allies in September, the German Army had illegally transferred almost 51,000 British POWs from Italy to the Reich, principally to the colossal main camp at Lamsdorf, called Stalag VIII B. A member of the Swiss Legation in Berlin, Gabriel Naville, inspected Lamsdorf between 7 and 8 October 1943 in his capacity as Protecting Power Representative for the United Kingdom and the United States. Describing it as "shockingly overcrowded," he found that base camp population had risen from 7,890 to 12,973 in the months immediately preceding. At first, Stalag VIII B coped with the problem by transferring POWs to work detachments throughout eastern Upper Silesia, including E715.

But after numerous complaints, the Germans subdivided the original main camp in November 1943. Lamsdorf became Stalag 344, and a new Stalag VIII B formed at Teschen, along the former Polish-Czechoslovak border. Throughout its existence, E715 remained under the administration of Stalag VIII B.[9]

E715 consisted principally of veterans of North Africa, although a few had been in the "bag" (kriegie slang for captivity) since Dunkirk. Most had spent one or two years in Italian confinement before transfer to Germany. The Italians imposed hardships different from those later imposed under the Germans; the former distributed Red Cross parcels less regularly than the latter. POWs who had subsisted upon macaroni and bread for months or years, and under dreadful sanitation, found better living conditions in German custody. But the Germans were more insistent than their southern ally that the British POWs contribute to the Axis war effort.[10]

Despite spurious German claims to the contrary, the use of POW labor at IG Auschwitz violated the Geneva Convention of 1929 in spirit, if not letter. The Convention permitted compulsory labor for enlisted POWs, so long as such work was neither war-related nor dangerous. Officers could not be compelled to work, while noncommissioned officers could be compelled only to supervise their charges; both groups retained the prerogative of volunteering for "suitable" work. Constructing synthetic oil and methanol installations certainly contributed to the German war effort, even if the POWs did not engage in the "final assembly" of weapons and munitions, the German Army's narrow construction of Convention protocols. (A 1949 Geneva Convention specific proscription of POW labor in a detaining power's chemical industry underscored deficiencies in the 1929 treaty and recognized belatedly that any work in a nation's chemical industry contributed to its war economy.) When British prisoners complained about the war-related nature of work at IG Auschwitz, their guards responded with cajolery, lies, and intimidation. As kriegie Eric Doyle paraphrased the point made by a German guard: "at the threat of a gun, there was no choice."[11]

The original E715 camp was Lager VIII, then from mid-1944 Lager VI. The numeration caused confusion in postwar testimony, because the plant leadership and the Wehrmacht employed separate systems to designate labor camps. Management assigned a Roman numeral to every labor camp at IG Auschwitz; the Wehrmacht employed a letter and Arabic-numeral system for work detachments. POWs generally knew their camp by Wehrmacht, not management, designation, so

"E715" referred to two sequentially-occupied locations. In design, the E715 section of Lager VIII displayed standard POW camp architecture, except there were no guard towers and the prisoners lacked a mess hall. But the camp departed from the conventional in another sense: the British shared space with German and foreign civilians, each of whom occupied different sections. It was immediately due south of Lager III, which meant POWs marched four blocks to arrive at the plant perimeter, while the distance to the huge construction site where they were employed required a much longer hike. The months spent in Lager VIII witnessed the greatest fluctuations in prisoner strength. After population peaked in January 1944 at 1,400, 800 POWs were transferred to IG Farben plants at Blechhammer and Heydebreck later that winter. A Red Cross report in June 1944 placed camp strength after the move to Lager VI at 643 POWs, and population stabilized thereafter at around 600 until the final evacuation took place on 21 January 1945.[12]

In mid-1944, E715 was moved to Lager VI, directly adjacent to the plant. The reason behind the move is unclear. Security considerations were a likely possibility, because the arrangements in Lager VIII violated German Army protocols by facilitating contact with civilians. The air campaign was another, because the timing coincided with Allied attacks on oil targets, and suggested that management may have placed POWs near the plant as a deterrent. Cutting marching time is a further possibility, since the Geneva Convention stipulated that travel to and from work counted in POW wage calculations. A final possibility is that the German workers housed in Lager VI, envious of Lager VIII's spaciousness and cleanliness, demanded the exchange. Whatever the case, the decision proved momentous. Lager VI was only two blocks away from Auschwitz-Monowitz. The two camps were in plain sight of each other, so a prisoner could look beyond his own fence and glimpse activity inside the other unobstructed. For six or seven months, the kriegies marched past Monowitz on the way to work, affording the British a stark look inside a Nazi concentration camp, which made a horrible and lasting impression.[13]

At first most POWs worked as a cable gang, laying the foundation for the plant power grid. Once that task was completed, probably in November 1943, they were assigned to various kommandos, a number of which included concentration-camp inmates and foreign workers. A few assisted skilled workers, such as electricians and locksmiths; some may have become low-grade foremen. Other jobs included pipe-laying, trench-digging, and painting. Troublemakers, particularly those suspected of sabotage, performed menial assignments, like portering oxyacetylene gas bottles for welders. Together with eighteen others, John Green and Reginald Hartland hoisted sizable fittings up to the top of eighty-foot filtration towers at the methanol plant. It was no accident that sappers like Hartland and Green worked at IG Auschwitz: the Wehrmacht cross-indexed available skills with labor deployment needs. Working hours were long, usually twelve per day, but some kriegies found easier jobs than others. Ronald Redman's supervisor took a laissez-faire approach, allowing his charges the run of the plant, which afforded them "great opportunities" for mischief. A fortunate few were able to work inside and learn new skills. Alfred Stow was in the electrical shop: "I took the opportunity to learn much more about workshop practice and the use of tools and metals[,] something that has been useful . . . ever since." According to Douglas Tilbrook Frost, the Germans "assigned [him] to swamp work gathering reeds" before his transfer inside IG Auschwitz. A few also assisted plant administration. The POWs made a generally positive impression on plant managers, though security (not surprisingly) kept them under a watchful eye. In November 1944, the British Red Cross Society rather blandly described E715 as performing "constructional work for a local firm[!]." Despite this, in postwar statements the veterans devoted little attention to their own labor. Typical was Charles Hill's understatement: "I worked for the IG Farben factory, first on the cable gang and later doing general labor."[14]

If the labor the British had been forced to perform did not prompt much postwar reflection, the treatment of concentration-camp inmates seared their memories. A shocking sight greeted the British POWs on their very first day at the job site. Wearing thin striped uniforms that afforded no protection against the elements, emaciated Monowitz inmates, predominantly Jewish, toiled under kapos and meisters who beat them to extract as much work as possible before their deaths. The British saw fallen inmates, their eyes lifeless, strewn about the plant. On one day alone they counted no fewer than thirty dead and dying. The inmates' physical dilapidation made every step a struggle and labor a torture, something exacerbated by management's insatiable demand for performance. "Once [the inmates] were assigned . . . they became the slave of each respective Meister," said Leonard Dales. Owing to their blue-gray striped clothing, some kriegies called them the "stripees." Still others preferred the stark expression "working corpses." Cliff Shepherd recalled yet another, ironic moniker: "The Jews . . . were known as the 'Healthy Life Boys,' because in the Red Cross parcels from Stirling in Scotland there were tins of biscuits [with striped packaging called]

'Healthy Life Biscuits.'" So weak were the stripees that "[a] dozen of them would struggle to pick up a pipe that three to four of our boys could pick up without too much trouble," as Horace Charters observed. Many kriegies echoed Frederick Davison's description of the consequence for stragglers unable to keep pace: the kapos would "beat the inmates with sticks or iron bars or punch them with their fists and kick them." Cruelty extended to the laboring process, even when economic rationality dictated otherwise. Charles Hill remembered that while "we were placed one man to each foot of cable . . . the inmates were placed one man to the yard." George Longden saw a stripee fall from a great height: "the Germans forcibly prevented any of his mates from helping him out or picking him up." Frederick Wellard succinctly summarized the lot of Jews in the racial hierarchy at IG Auschwitz: "All treatment of Jews was mistreatment."[15]

The casual brutality witnessed at the plant was just the beginning. Once relocated to Lager VI, the British heard shootings and screams from Monowitz at night. They also saw hanging victims dangling beside the camp gate. In G. J. Duffree's words, "From our compound we could see the hanging rail, where they often strung up their victims and left them. . . ."[16]

So pervasive was Nazi racial barbarism that it assaulted practically every sense. The British saw the beatings; they heard the meisters say the Jews were just getting what they deserved; they tasted the Buna soup, the inmates' midday ration; and they inhaled the acrid smoke that regularly wafted over IG Auschwitz from Birkenau. The deathly odor was the first clue that the British lived near the *anus mundi*. Some recalled the smell from the very first day in camp, though not everyone initially understood its significance. "Our new huts [in Lager VII] were comfortable and clean, but we could not get away from that awful smell," said Duffree. From the meisters, foreign workers, and stripees came the answer. "We did learn about the [F]inal [S]olution, especially on burning days when the wind was in the right direction," recalled Douglas Bond. Their sources were secondhand, but the ubiquitous rumors, what sociologist Tamotsu Shibutani once labeled "improvised news," were largely the same. The POWs discovered that the Jewish inmates lived on borrowed time, as the SS selected for gassing those who had exhausted their productive utility. Stripees recounted the danger of staying longer than two weeks in the Monowitz hospital, which they correlated with selection for gassing. That was why, Frederick Wooley explained, Jewish inmates worked to the breaking point: "When these poor fellows fell down you could be pretty sure that it was impossible for them to keep standing because they all were familiar with the slogan 'not fit to work, not fit to live.'" The POWs heeded their sensory perceptions and, unlike others at IG Auschwitz, began to ask questions about what Winston Churchill aptly described in 1941 as the "crime without a name."[17]

When assigned to the same kommandos, kriegies and stripees quickly formed friendships. Many Jewish inmates spoke English and the POWs communicated with others through hand gestures. Inquiries about missing stripees lent immediacy to gassing rumors, as Ronald Redman remembered: "When familiar faces were missed we were informed that they [had been] deemed unfit for work at the morning check and sent to the 'showers.'" Cyril Quartermaine reported similarly: "We could talk to the slave labourers a[nd] if we missed one after some days we questioned others [about] where he was, [and] the answer would be 'Smoke up chimney,' so we had a good idea what was happening." Eric Doyle had the unsettling experience of seeing someone he recognized from peacetime in striped uniform:

> a lightweight fighter whom I had seen fight in 1938. In 1943 I saw him as an inmate in Auschwitz. He was on the same working party as myself. I never saw a bigger wreck of any kind. I should say he had both arms broken, his shoulders were bowed like an old man, and he looked to be about 50 years old. I would not have recognized him if I had not known it was he. He disappeared and I don't know what happened to him. There were quite a lot of cases of disappearance like that.

From "a Dutch Jew," Leonard Dales gained a detailed description of the Birkenau killing center. The stripee admonished him to "tell the rest of the world what had happened."[18]

Norbert Wollheim, a Monowitz inmate from March 1943, volunteered to work on the building site as a welder in order to contact the kriegies. He had learned English in school and just before World War II had assisted the immigration of German-Jewish children to Great Britain. Upon hearing about E715, he used connections inside Monowitz to join a kommando that worked alongside POWs. "I [gave] them as much information as possible [telling] them time and again, 'You'll probably be able to . . . survive because you're under the protection of the . . . Red Cross.'" Wollheim became especially close to Reginald Hartland, with whom he worked in Workshop 797. He passed along war news from Nazi newspapers discarded at the building site, while Hartland reciprocated in kind with news from the BBC, obtained from a secret radio in E715. So close did they become that Hartland informed Wollheim's family in the United States as to his whereabouts. Their friendship survived the war: they had reunions at the IG Farben Trial, and during a 1962 BBC *This Is Your Life* episode that honored Charles Joseph Coward, the camp spokesman of E715. Hartland and Wollheim continued to correspond for decades.[19]

The German meisters were well-informed about the extermination campaign, and the POWs discovered that the murders met with their general approval. A few exceptions were the meisters Alfred Stow encountered in the electrical shop. While antisemitic, these men professed to deplore Nazi treatment of the Jews. One with whom Stow was particularly close expressed contempt for the Nazis. But many others clearly identified with the regime and employed stock rationalizations to justify racial barbarism before British interlocutors. When Cliff Shepherd first saw concentration-camp inmates after his transfer to E715 in January 1944, he naturally assumed they were "convicts." A meister disabused him:

> When I first arrived I asked one of the Germans who the men were in these striped uniforms. He said they were Jews, the "Parasites" as he called them. . . . I said, "What have they done wrong?" He says [sic], "They're Jews." I said, "Why are they working in forced labor?" He said, "Because they're rotten. . . . They're the dregs of the earth. . . . They've bled Germany dry. . . . They've got to be gassed when they can't work any more." I said, "How do they gas them?" He said, "They put them in a chamber, like a tank, and seal it." It distressed me a lot. It still does.

The explanation Robert Ferris received for anti-Jewish persecution revealed the same stark barbarism: "The German foreman of my work detail used to say that until Hitler came the Germans worked for the Jews and now the Jews were working for the Germans." The supervisor added that Jews worked "until they got so they can't work and then they put them in the crematorium and the gas chambers." But before concluding that the meisters had always harbored an "eliminationist antisemitism," it is important to recall that their barbarization began well before the first Jews arrived at the building site. By the time the British encountered them, the supervisors had had over two years to learn from the SS's example.[20]

Without engaging in a formal, planned effort to wage war against the "Final Solution," the kriegies gave the stripees what help they could. In the process they demonstrated that some groups could maintain their moral autonomy, even under conditions of forced labor, although their ability to exercise that autonomy was necessarily circumscribed. Almost every veteran to testify, whether immediately after the war or fifty years later, recalled the British giving food and other goods to inmates. The British usually refused to eat their own German rations, which were marginally better than the inmates' Buna soup, and left that food in strategic locations for the taking. The procedure was dangerous for the inmates, because if caught their kapos or meisters beat them to a pulp. It was not particularly dangerous for the POWs, but upon discovery the guards or meisters issued a verbal dressing down and overturned the bowls. Such help underlined the importance of the Red Cross, because the influx of high-quality food from Allied and neutral countries rendered the British largely independent of German rations. So desperate were stripees for food that a charitable act sometimes sparked a melee, as G. J. Duffree discovered: "we fed them as much as we could spare, but I've seen the poor barstards [sic] fight to the death for a potato."[21]

For a kriegie a cigarette could be either a consumable item or currency in the Stalag economy, because such luxuries were more common in the POW camp; but for a concentration-camp inmate it equated to a day's rations on the plant's black market. Stripees bartered Red Cross cigarettes for bread or other food as part of what they called their "organizing" activities. With an antisemitic undertone W. N. Davis observed: "The most amazing part of the trading in the factory was the fact that although the Jew[ish] 'Stripees' were the worst off in the place, they were the ones who did nearly all the deals." He added, "Most of us British POWs would try to slip the 'Stripees' a drop of soup, a few cigarettes, or a bit of chocolate and usually one of our gang would keep watch whilst this went on because it meant real trouble if we got caught." Since there were seventeen times as many Monowitz inmates as British POWs by late 1944, the kriegies could not help everyone. Ronald Redman echoed the frustration of many by stating:

> Gradually as one got accustomed to them in their prolific numbers one hardened as it was not possible to provide all of them with a cigarette, piece of underclothing, food, or unwanted soup. Despite this they seemed to regard us as having unlimited means, knowledge of the war, even to sheep-like following during an air-raid as "we knew where the bombs were going to fall"??!!²²

Those who had nothing naturally looked upon the British as a privileged group. Primo Levi described a kriegie he encountered in a plant lavatory: the captive soldier wore a smart uniform, displayed a military bearing, and appeared to be the picture of health. The POW, in his estimation, inhabited another world. Levi went on to observe that some concentration-camp inmates "cultivated" the POWs, raising panhandling to high art form. Young Henri, one of the most memorable persons in his testimony, employed guile and "pity" to obtain food and other valuables from many on the job site, especially POWs. Thanks to "wealthy" benefactors, Henri was able to eat well by Monowitz standards. He "was once seen in the act of eating a real hard-boiled egg," a prize that might well have circuitously derived from British barter with Polish workers. "Manna" was how Norbert Wollheim described British generosity and encouragement, adding that: "England can be very[,] very proud of these men, . . . who really proved that even in Auschwitz . . . humanity could prevail." He encountered British largesse immediately upon joining the welding kommando, as "they were throwing cigarette packages at us, and chocolate packages at us, and . . . said, 'Don't worry, you'll be home by Christmas.'" In his words, the British "extended the . . . hand of solidarity of man" to Monowitz inmates.[23]

But British succor sometimes had ironic, even tragic, consequences. One POW who accidentally incurred SS wrath and brought disaster on an inmate was Frank Harris. "I myself have two scars on my face, i.e. chin and left eyebrow, for giving a young Jewish [inmate], 13 yrs. old, a hand to get to his feet after falling down through weakness. The SS guard shot him and rifle-butted me in the face." Abraham Fuks received ten cane strokes for panhandling among the British when he should have been working. Paul Steinberg received the same in August 1944 as "he talked on his place of work . . . with English prisoners of war . . . and received food and smoking material from them." In June 1944, Pepo Pitson "fetched a container with food from the plant kitchen. He claimed to have acted upon an order from English prisoners of war." The SS gave him twenty-five lashes. For talking with the British and ignoring his duties as inmate foreman, Israel Majzlik received dire penalties on 28 February 1944: fifteen lashes, "demotion," and deployment to the mines, the latter euphemistically termed "underground work" by the SS. One stripee severely injured his leg while reaching for a Red Cross cigarette. As Leonard Dales remembered, "He didn't seem so much hurt as scared when he said, 'I guess this is the end. It means the gas chamber for me.'"[24]

The kriegies attempted still bolder forms of aid. The British camp spokesman (Man of Confidence, or *Vertrauensmann*), Battery Sergeant-Major Charles Coward, complained about inmate privation to IG Auschwitz management and offered to establish a clothing drive inside E715 for distribution in Monowitz. "My suggestion was turned down flatly with the answer that it would look bad if Farben could not supply the necessities." As Wollheim attested, the British persisted in giving away old clothing, if only on an individual basis. Aside from the Hartland-Wollheim case, other POWs also informed inmates' relatives overseas about their loved ones inside Monowitz. Ronald Redman wrote to inform the father of two inmates:

> I managed to convey a message to the Jewish Austrian ambassador in London via a friend of mine in one of my allowed letter cards of his two sons in Auschwitz—name of Linder—later on he acknowledged me in England but sadly stated his sons were dead in Belsen.[25]

The kriegies also complained to international authorities about the extermination campaign. The Swiss visited E715 twice in summer 1944, during which occasions Coward complained about Jewish maltreatment, but the inspectors appeared uncomfortable with the subject. As he described it at Nuremberg, "They took one or two notes, but it seemed to me as if they were actually, I am sorry to say it, actually helpless to alter any conditions whatever in Auschwitz." Although direct evidence has yet to come to light, an International Red Cross report of September pointed to E715 as a source for rumors of gassing at Stalag VIII B.[26]

Dr. Rossel of the International Red Cross secured permission to visit the Auschwitz main camp, in order to ascertain whether the SS had actually distributed Red Cross parcels to their rightful recipients. Sending relief parcels to concentration-camp inmates was a recent innovation that saved some prisoners from starvation. The Commandant, SS-*Sturmbannführer* (major) Richard Bär, gave him a Potemkin-Village tour. To some degree, Rossel recognized that the SS put on a rather elaborate show for his benefit: "Every word is well-calculated and you are conscious of the dread of letting slip the least piece of information." But before he and his assistants visited Auschwitz, they stopped at Stalag VIII B, Teschen, to gather information. The camp spokesman, Regimental Sergeant-Major Lowe, passed along what he had heard, as Rossel recounted:

Indeed, a Kommando of British POWs work in a mine [sic] at Auschwitz in contact with these people. We have requested the principal Man of Confidence of Teschen to do all he can for obtaining all useful information from the Man of Confidence of the Kommando of Auschwitz.

Spontaneously, the principal British Man of Confidence of Teschen asked us if we were well-informed about the "shower room." Indeed the rumor runs that in the KZ a very modern shower room exists where the detainees will be gassed in series. The British Man of Confidence has, through the intermediary of his Kommando of Auschwitz, tried to obtain confirmation of this act. This was impossible to prove. The detainees themselves did not talk about it.[27]

The report confirmed two points. First, the senior camp spokesman at Teschen, some fifty miles distant, had heard rumors of gassing at Auschwitz. Second, the rumor spread from the work detachments to the parent camp. There were other, smaller British detachments in the Auschwitz area, notably E711a at Heydebreck, but none had E715's breadth of contacts with concentration-camp inmates and German civilians. Charles Coward had already tried other means to inform the Swiss of the gassing, and, as discussed below, he warned the British Government as well. As camp spokesman, he had the ability to travel to Teschen and to speak with Lowe privately. But who attempted verification of the rumors: the kriegies, to whom stripees were eager to talk, or Rossel, surrounded by intimidating SS officers? In abbreviated and ambiguous form, Rossel probably referred to his own muddled attempt to confirm gassing rumors. The POWs inferred Auschwitz-Birkenau's existence from the nauseating evidence that wafted under their noses. Perhaps Rossel, who spent at most one day at the Auschwitz main camp, where a functioning gas chamber and crematorium no longer existed, chalked up Birkenau's cremation odor to "normal" inmate mortality, if he smelled anything at all. But the kriegies inhaled the noxious odor so often, for so long, and in such pungency, as to gain some sense of scale.[28]

In extremis, Coward exemplified the British challenge to the Nazi racial hierarchy, as well as the foibles of memory. Various postwar investigations accepted his testimony into evidence; he also garnered accolades from British intelligence and the State of Israel. His story became public in the 1950s and 1960s with the release of his biography and a Metro-Goldwyn-Mayer film, both entitled *The Password Is*

Courage. The latter starred Dirk Bogarde as Charles Coward. Some of his claims, such as to having gathered explosives used in the October 1944 Sonderkommando Uprising, were too flimsy to withstand criticism. Moreover, several E715 veterans regarded Coward less as Man of Confidence than confidence man, due to his gift of gab and his spotty relations with other kriegies. Yet sufficient evidence has emerged to demonstrate that he waged a personal campaign against the mass murder of Jews while at E715. His principal activities included warning the British War Office about Nazi atrocities at Auschwitz; passing a terrifying night inside Monowitz to search for a former British Jewish POW; and finally, helping a few Jewish inmates to escape.[29]

Writing to his deceased father in care of "William Orange"—i.e., War Office—Coward listed recent Jewish transports, described killing techniques, and recounted military matters. "I wrote giving the particular dates on which I had witnessed thousands arriving and marched to the concentration camp [at Monowitz]." Coward posted some five to six letters per week in that manner to his home address, where his wife passed them along to the War Office (once she figured out the significance). MI 9, the British intelligence agency in charge of escape and evasion work, later honored the effort with a commendatory letter. (Whether the commendation was for matters military or humanitarian is unclear. Perhaps the effort should be recognized with those of Eduard Schulte, Jan Karski, Rudolf Vrba, and others, but since the letters have yet to come to light or perhaps to be declassified, we cannot evaluate their content.) According to M. R. D. Foot and J. N. Langley, early code users (CUs) in German POW camps employed prearranged signals with loved ones to pass letters to the War Office, where MI 9 evaluated them. The agency maintained formal and informal connections with British POWs throughout the war, thereby gaining valuable information about escape needs, conditions in Germany, and POW treatment. Coward himself had been a POW since Dunkirk in 1940, and had tried out his informal code technique with his wife as early as 1943.[30]

The illicit night at Monowitz was more dangerous. During the IG Farben Trial in 1947 Coward recounted the terrifying experience. By way of an intermediary, Coward had earlier received a note from a "British ship's doctor" held there. The physician described himself as a Jewish naval officer whom the Germans had sent to the concentration camp, and asked for someone to contact his family. Coward bribed a kapo with cigarettes to allow him to exchange uniforms with another inmate, then joined the kommando upon its nightly return to Monowitz with the aim of contacting the physician. The fortunate inmate with whom he exchanged clothes spent a blissful night at E715, where he ate Red Cross rations while Coward witnessed with his own eyes the terror that held the stripees in thrall. He passed a sleepless night in a grossly overcrowded barrack and sweated out morning roll call with the interminable head count. Managing to come through the ordeal without mishap thanks to the stripees around him, he nevertheless failed to find the naval doctor. Whether he acted upon the original request to contact the latter's family members, is unclear but probable.[31]

The story appeared incredible: why would anyone sneak into a Nazi concentration camp, when so much could go wrong, and especially when the price for discovery would be so great? Coward had made several unsuccessful escape attempts in the past, before his stint at IG Auschwitz, so he understood something of the risks. Moreover, the POWs in E715 had already practiced a uniform-swapping ruse in league with foreign workers. To maintain a proper count inside E715, the kriegies smuggled foreign workers into camp, where they enjoyed British rations and wore military uniform, while the escapees enjoyed a few days in the company of local women. German guards with greasy palms assured a safe pass, out of fear of blackmail for past breaches, if not simple greed. The modus operandi thus followed techniques long in use. Coward ably parried attempts to impugn his credibility at Nuremberg and further amplified how he had eluded discovery during his nocturnal visit. Reginald Hartland and Ronald Redman confirmed hearing rumors in camp about his exchanging places with a stripee.[32]

Inside Monowitz, a British naval doctor did work in the inmate hospital *(Häftlingskrankenbau)*. Karel Sperber, inmate number 85512, was a POW captured in late 1942 after the Germans torpedoed and sank his ship. A Czech-Jewish physician who had immigrated to Britain before the war, he served as a medical officer in the Royal Navy and resided in Sunderland, England. He was in Monowitz, and not a POW camp, because the Germans had succeeded in isolating him from the other British captives on account of his "race." The Germans usually treated Jewish POWs from the United Kingdom and the United States under the guidelines of the Geneva Convention, but only after considerable pressure. A Senior Allied Officer, or Man of Confidence, had to remind them to respect the Convention and to threaten recourse to the Swiss if they persisted. Ambiguity concerning his citizenship enabled the Germans to transfer Sperber to Auschwitz shortly after his arrival at an officers' camp (Oflag), although the fact that he was technically a foreign national and not a British citizen in no way compromised his rights under the Geneva Convention.[33]

By the time E715 was established, Sperber had been in Monowitz for nine months, from January to September 1943. The dates of his message and Coward's response are not firmly established, but doubtless Sperber had to make several attempts to contact the POWs. Sperber had little choice but to fall back upon indirect methods of communication, because he worked in the hospital kommando: unlike Wollheim, he was not in a position to volunteer for work at the plant. The SS kept him inside in part because he was a British officer, while British soldiers remained just beyond the wire. Why did Coward not find him in Monowitz? The probable culprit was a communications mix-up, because they relied upon an intermediary and Sperber probably never expected anyone to attempt to sneak into Monowitz. Fortunately, Sperber survived. He received the Honorary Order of the British Empire in 1946 and served as a medical officer in the British Colonial Medical Service in Ceylon (Sri Lanka). He died in 1957.[34]

The other means by which Coward sought to save Jews was by aiding escapes. He set out to purchase dead bodies found at the building site, these from a German whose task was to collect them for disposal. Buying two or three bodies for cigarettes and explaining that they were part of a "joke," Coward and his comrade, Yitzhak Persky, a Palestinian-Jewish POW living under an assumed identity, placed the bodies where the inmate columns passed, after securing the help of a Hungarian-Jewish inmate who prepared the escapees. Coward intended to exchange the dead for the living. In one version of the escape account, the kriegies operated at the IG Auschwitz entrance gate as the inmates left for the night. The escapees fell out at a prescribed time and received some supplies for the journey ahead. When SS guards or kapos searched for the missing they found the dead bodies and reconciled the count. In a second version, Coward and company initiated the escapes on the road from Monowitz to Birkenau in order to save inmates who had been selected for the gas chambers. Such means allegedly allowed four hundred to eight hundred Jews to escape, although the actual number of survivors is far from clear. For his effort, Yad Vashem awarded Coward the Righteous Among the Nations medal in 1962. He was the first Briton so honored.[35]

Two kriegies came forward after the war to confirm his role in aiding Jews to escape. One was Yitzhak Persky, known later as Gershon Peres, the father of Shimon Peres, future foreign minister and prime minister of Israel. Before captivity, Persky had served in the Royal Engineers in Greece in 1941. Erroneously, he claimed to have met Coward while the two hid in occupied Greece, although the latter became a POW in France in 1940 and no other source has ever placed him in the Balkans. Whatever the case, Persky and Coward became friends; Coward swore other POWs to silence about Persky's Jewishness to shield him from the Nazis. Persky assumed the identity of a deceased Gentile POW and the two ended up in E715, where they hatched the plot to save Jews from extermination. Another POW, although not a witness, substantiated Coward and Persky's accounts. G. J. Duffree recalled hearing rumors about the escapes while inside E715.[36]

Coward testified to Yad Vashem researchers in 1962. But the former Man of Confidence was down on his luck financially and apparently eager to tell what he thought the audience wanted to hear. Crediting the Poles with help, he offered a few details about escapee identities and fates: "It is not known exactly [sic] how many of these people regained their freedom, because some people went different ways and to different countries." He added: "And naturally no records were kept of them because once they arrived in their new country, special papers were given to them and perhaps different names, etc." Inexplicably absent was any mention of the visit to Monowitz or of the MI 9 correspondence, though earlier he had described both as intended to help Jews. Interviewer Ella Mahler later depicted him as "a true Christian . . . who helped Jews out of his innate kindness and feeling of brotherhood of all men." Without extensive corroboration, Yad Vashem honored him as one of the Righteous Among the Nations. Could politics have factored in the decision? Shimon Peres then served as defense minister. Israeli interpretations of the Jewish catastrophe may have played a role. Coward's visit came shortly after the Eichmann Trial, which had brought into the open generational and cultural differences over issues such as survival, resistance, and victimization under the Nazis. Young Sabras and Zionists asked why European Jews had permitted themselves to die like sacrificial lambs during the Shoah. The image of British soldiers—among them a member of the Yishuv—cheating the hangmen resonated with many.[37]

But when considered in the light of varied evidence, Coward's escape account revealed grave inconsistencies. First, standard procedure called for the dead to be returned to the concentration camp along with the living, and for the latter to be repeatedly counted. Coward's visit to Monowitz had established those two facts: "We had been counted when we marched out of the factory but were also counted when we came into the camp. When the inmates were counted, the other chaps would hold up the dead for counting purposes." If cumbrous, the procedure ensured that absences were soon discovered. Second, Monowitz recorded only thirty-three escapes between 1942 and 1945, not hundreds. The claim of saving 400 to 800 lives seems spurious. Third, the escapees' identities are as yet unknown. While it is possible that all were recaptured and killed, enough Jewish inmates managed to get away from other camps to make their total absence as witnesses in this case a troubling lacuna, especially because Coward himself believed that some survived the war.[38]

The more dramatic rendition, which had escapes taking place on the road to Birkenau, falls apart on additional grounds. First, the SS transported Jews slated for destruction by truck, not foot. Robert Ferris observed, "We often saw big open-top trucks come out of the camp [at Monowitz] filled with standing inmates and headed out toward Auschwitz. We understood they were going to the gas chambers." Second, those to be gassed were *Muselmänner*, inmates who were in no physical condition to escape. Coward's trade in dead bodies probably involved deceased foreign workers, a much less common commodity than deceased Jews at the building site: not hundreds, or tens, but two or three Jews could have gotten away thanks to this man, which comports better with the known statistical record. Lest anyone dismiss his memories out of hand as empty braggadocio, Persky and Duffree insisted that an escape plot took place under Coward's leadership. Yet it seems to me that he embellished the details over the years and retrospectively attributed more calculation in memory than was the case in 1944.[39]

Coward personified what Norbert Wollheim observed about E715 in general, the fact that "even in Auschwitz . . . humanity could prevail." But what sentiments lay behind his and the other kriegies' deeds? Before the Israelis in the early 1960s, Coward represented himself as a philosemite, but other POWs openly harbored "benign" antisemitic attitudes in camp and afterward. Some referred to having "Jew friends" or to Monowitz as the "Jew camp," while others accepted the notion that Jews were too powerful in the economy. At E715, Eric Lindsay produced a version of Lord Dunsany's one-act play, [A] *Night at an Inn*, that included a Shylock-type character, "The Hunchback Saul," who was not part of the original. The POWs were products of a "diffuse cultural antisemitism," in the apt phrase of Nechama Tec. During World War II, British antisemites saw Jews as money-grubbers, black-marketeers, and draft dodgers. POWs in E715 were working-class young men who grew up during a rare period of anti-Jewish incidents in their nation's recent past, particularly in London's East End.[40]

As in the case of the Polish rescuers Tec studied, the E715 case suggests that mild antisemitism presented no significant obstacle to aiding Jews during the Holocaust. Help was largely "spontaneous," to borrow Tec's description, as kriegies reacted in horror to what they saw, without systematic planning or calculation. However, differences still exist between her cases and E715. The British were not at liberty and, through little choice of their own, watched the Holocaust unfold every day. On the one hand, Poles could more easily ignore the crimes committed around them. On the other hand, these British worked alongside those whom the Nazis defined as *Untermenschen.* They could not help but see what the Nazis were perpetrating. The British had less choice than Tec's rescuers. But in captivity they exercised what freedom they had in a manner running counter to some of their own parochial attitudes. Recognizing Jews at Monowitz by the Star of David formed by two triangles on their uniforms, the British tended to equate the category of concentration-camp inmate with Jewishness. In other words, when helping inmates they understood they were helping Jews. Tony Kushner has argued that British liberals deemed the Jews responsible for antisemitism, because the latter obstinately preferred difference to assimilation. Such an attitude was alien to E715, even among mild antisemites. The POWs witnessed defenseless human beings beaten, starved, throttled, punched, kicked, whipped, murdered outright, selected for gassing, and worked to death, all because the Nazis defined them as racial enemies. None left IG Auschwitz with any doubt as to who perpetrated the Holocaust, or against whom.[41]

What prompted British succor were two sentiments alien to National Socialism: pity and shame. Pity was the heartstring the young Henri tugged when cultivating British POWs. As John Adkin put it: "We felt sorry for them and would gladly have helped them." The kriegies had seen the horrors of combat, but IG Auschwitz appalled them. Shame stemmed from the degradation attendant to witnessing acts of barbarism. Before the Wehrmacht, Coward complained that the brutalization of Jews "was upsetting the morale of the British prisoners of war." Although his words fell upon deaf ears, they were more than just pretense, because E715 veterans would have to live with those images for the rest of their lives.[42]

In both the near and long term, assimilating what they witnessed at IG Auschwitz proved difficult. While in captivity, the POWs passed some time with entertainment and diversions as a means to relieve boredom and stress. Such activities included football (soccer) matches, occasional variety shows, and discussion of war news. G. J. Duffree observed that their mental health would have suffered without such pastimes, adding, "One or two did go religious in a bad way and one or two slung themselves onto the wire to a certain death." The latter recollection awaits confirmation. Save those who testified at Nuremberg, the veterans had few opportunities to place their experiences in perspective. Most aging veterans kept silent until British filmmaker Maurice Hatton produced in the 1990s a documentary about their experience, *Satan at His Best*.[43]

The months leading up to liberation compounded the stress of bearing witness by giving kriegies a taste of what deprivation the stripees had suffered for years. The Monowitz concentration camp disbanded on 18 January 1945, but E715 remained at work for a further three days. Even with the Soviets closing in, the Nazis continued to enforce their racial order, shooting racial "inferiors" unable to keep pace, while protecting those they deemed "Aryan," such as the British. Treading snowy paths the stripees had taken days before, the kriegies saw bloody corpses lining the roads. Staggering to Gleiwitz in order to entrain for camps in the "Old Reich," Monowitz inmates embarked on a death march; POWs in E715 experienced a hunger march: the latter suffered much want, but the guards did not shoot them for physical weakness and obtained medical care for those in need of it. When Red Cross trucks nick-named the "white ladies" finally located their column after a month, the Germans permitted the POWs to receive relief.[44]

Difficulties for E715 had begun in the month prior to evacuation, and were to continue until American forces liberated them at Stalag VII A, in Moosburg, in April 1945. Allied bombing of German transportation in the autumn had prevented Red Cross parcels from arriving during December 1944, which left the POWs dependent upon inadequate German rations. An aimless three-month journey ensued, the guards having little idea of where to go except far away from the advancing Red Army. The column zigzagged from western Poland through the present-day Czech Republic to Bavaria. Privation, sleeping in barns, and frostbite took a toll on mental and physical health. American psychological studies after the war established that prolonged malnourishment tends to exacerbate the incidence of post-traumatic stress disorder (PTSD), misleadingly labeled "combat fatigue" during World War II. For E715 the sickening sights at IG Auschwitz combined with hunger to intensify the unremitting anxiety.[45]

But after World War II the British Government paid scant attention to the mental health of demobilized, or "demobbed," soldiers. Little empathy and less interest greeted veterans of E715, because their testimonies were fundamentally at variance with British experience. Eric Doyle expressed their frustration to a Nuremberg investigator: "Their [the inmates'] condition and treatment was [sic] so bad that it is impossible to explain it to people in England. . . ." Upon demobilization, the British Government implored veterans to get on with their lives and to forget the past, something they took as an order. While avoidance worked well in the short run, problems surfaced for many at retirement age, when work and rearing families no longer occupied their time. One veteran who died (of a brain tumor) in 1992 spent his last days in anguish over E715, Auschwitz, and the evacuation march of 1945.[46]

The British challenged the Nazi racial hierarchy at IG Auschwitz by treating the Jews from Monowitz as men, not *Untermenschen*. They demonstrated that however slight the framework for individual agency, workers at IG Auschwitz—and by extension elsewhere in the Third Reich—had the ability to make moral decisions, despite the dangers posed by the security apparatus, and that individuals could combat the Nazi regime if they employed some intelligence and discretion. What agents elected to do with that admittedly limited autonomy separated the helpers and the rescuers from the compliant and the bystanders. British testimony demonstrated that Churchill's "crime without a name" had been plainly evident in Upper Silesia. The POWs gathered relevant details from variegated sources, smelled the acrid smoke, and observed destructive labor. That imprisoned English-speakers could acquire so much knowledge about Nazi killing operations in so short a time casts a damning shadow upon German bystanders who later claimed they had known nothing.

WILLIAM J. HOURIHAN, PH.D.

★ ★ ★ ★ ★ ★ ★ ★

U.S. Army Chaplain Ministry to German War Criminals at Nuremberg, 1945–1946

W e had two of the finest chaplains a prison commandant could have been given,"[1] wrote Colonel Burton C. Andrus, the tough Commandant of the Nuremberg Prison, which housed high-ranking German war criminals during their trial for war crimes after World War II. The two chaplains he praised so highly were Henry F. Gerecke and Sixtus R. O'Connor, both part of one of the most singular ministries ever undertaken by U.S. Army chaplains; a ministry to the surviving leadership of the Third Reich who were tried for war crimes at Nuremberg.

While the historical record of the Chaplaincy shows that Army chaplains ministered to enemy prisoners of war (POWs) in the past, this was not done in an organized way and was generally carried out by individual chaplains on an temporary, non-official basis.

In the aftermath of World War I, for example, elements of the U.S. Army were engaged in protecting parts of the Trans-Siberian railroad system. The 27th Infantry Regiment found itself at one point guarding and protecting some 2,000 German and Austrian prisoners in the Lake Baikel region deep in central Siberia.

Chaplain Joseph S. Loughran, who was attached to the 27th, found himself not only conducting services for the prisoners, but also acting as the liaison officer between the captives and American military authorities.[2]

All this changed in World War II when large numbers of Axis prisoners of war were sent to camps in North Africa, in liberated Europe, and in the United States. Fort Slocum, New York, for example, the home of the Chaplain School from 1951 to 1962, served as an Army-run installation for German and Italian POWs during the war.[3]

After the war, Army Chaplain Norman Adams headed an organization based in Paris, France, which supplied religious coverage to approximately 130 German POW camps with responsibility for about half a million men.[4] With the total defeat of Germany, Italy and Japan, the question of how to treat the leadership of these nations, which had plunged the world into this terrible conflict, also had to be addressed.

The issue of how to treat the high-ranking leadership of a defeated state was one that had arisen in the United States only once before, and that was in the wake of the Civil War. At that time, there had been serious consideration given to bringing to trial certain individuals in the Confederate hierarchy. While Jefferson Davis, the Confederate president, was imprisoned for a time at Fort Monroe, Virginia, and Alexander Stephens, the vice president, incarcerated at Fort Warren in Boston harbor, no Confederate leader was ever tried for treason or war crimes.

After World War I there was an effort to bring Kaiser Wilhelm II to an international court of justice, but he fled to the Netherlands (neutral during World War I) and was granted asylum.

In fact, there had been only one trial and execution in United States history prior to World War II for what conceivably might be defined as a war crime in today's parlance; i.e., Confederate Army Captain Henry Wirz, the commandant of the Andersonville prison camp.[5]

The unimaginable horrors perpetrated during WW II by Germany and Japan however, made their political and military leadership particularly open to legal retribution. At the end on the Yalta Conference on 12 February 1945, the Allied leaders declared: "It is our inflexible purpose to destroy German militarism and Nazism and to . . . bring all war criminals to just and swift punishment."[6]

After President Roosevelt's death on 12 April 1945, the new president, Harry Truman:

> accepted the wisdom of a trial, based on a model proposed by the War Department, and he convinced the British, the Russians, and

the French, who were brought into the discussions. Following agreements in principle at the United Nations founding Conference in San Francisco, experts from the four occupying Powers met in London in June to work out the details. On 8 August 1945, the representatives reached agreement on a charter establishing an International Military Tribunal [IMT] 'for the just and prompt trial and punishment of major war criminals of the European Axis.'[7]

This tribunal was made up of one member and an alternate chosen by each of the four signatory powers. The first session took place in Berlin on 18 October 1945. Beginning on 20 November 1945, the tribunal sessions were held at the Palace of Justice in Nuremberg. This city was chosen as the venue because of its close association with the Nazi party. Originally there were 24 members of the Nazi leadership charged with the perpetration of war crimes. One defendant, Robert Ley, committed suicide on 23 October; a second defendant, Gustav Krupp von Bohlen und Halbach, was judged incapable of being tried because of his mental and physical condition. A third, Martin Bormann, would be tried and condemned to death in absentia.[8]

Security for the remaining 21 prisoners was provided by the Army's 6850th Internal Security Detachment, under the direction of the commandant of Nuremberg Prison, Colonel Andrus. Initially Chaplain Carl R. Eggers, 1st Battalion, 26th Infantry, was assigned to work with the prisoners. Chaplain Eggers, who spoke fluent German and was a Lutheran (Missouri Synod), held this position briefly. On 12 November 1945, as the trial moved from Berlin to Nuremberg, he turned over his duties to Chaplain Henry F. Gerecke, another Lutheran (Missouri Synod). A second Army chaplain was chosen to be his Roman Catholic counterpart, Chaplain Sixtus R. O'Connor. These two chaplains, along with the prison Army psychologist, Dr. G.M. Gilbert, were the only American officers on the prison staff who could speak German.[9]

As a result of the Reformation and the ensuing religious wars of the 16th and 17th centuries, German society was sharply divided between Protestantism (mainly Lutheran), and Roman Catholicism. Nazi leadership mirrored this split. Adolf Hitler and Josef Goebbels, for example, were born, baptized and raised in the Roman Catholic faith.

Of the 21 on trial at Nuremberg, the 13 Protestants would be ministered to by Chaplain Gerecke. They were: Herman Goering (Reichmarschall and Luftwaffe-Chief); Joachim von Ribbentrop (Foreign Minister); Field Marshal Wilhelm Keitel (Chief of Staff of the High

Command of the Wehrmacht); Hans Frick (Governor-General of Poland); Walter Funk (Minister of Economics); Hjalmar Schacht (Reichbank President and former Minister of Economics); Admiral Karl Doenitz (Grand Admiral of the German Navy); Admiral Erich Raeder (Grand Admiral of the German Navy); Baldur von Schirach (Hitler Youth Leader and Gauleiter of Vienna); Fritz Sauckel (Chief of slave labor recruitment); Albert Speer (Reich minister of Armaments and Munitions); Baron Konstantin von Neurath (former Foreign Minister and later Protector of Bohemia and Moravia); and Hans Fritzsche (Radio Propaganda Chief).[10]

Chaplain O'Connor would serve the four professed Catholic prisoners: Ernst Kaltenbrunner (Chief of SS Security HQ); Franz von Papen (Ambassador to Austria and Turkey); Hans Frank (Governor General of Poland); and Artur Seyss-Inquart (Austrian Chancellor and later Reich Commissioner for the Netherlands).

Four of the prisoners refused to align themselves with either chaplain. They were: Rudolf Hess; Alfred Rosenberg (Chief Nazi philosopher and Reich minister for the Eastern Occupied Territories); Julius Streicher (Gauleiter of Franconia); and General Alfred Jodl (Chief of Operations for the High Command).[11]

The ministry of these two chaplains is mainly seen through the eyes of Chaplain Gerecke. While both he and Chaplain O'Connor worked closely together, only Gerecke has left us a detailed written record of the experience. This was not without controversy. Initially, Chaplain Gerecke's request to publish an account of his ministry was denied by the Office of the Chief of Chaplains.

The objection was based on the ground that the manuscript revealed intimate confidences which were deserving of the secrecy of the confessional. The War Department discourages anything that would possibly suggest to men that chaplains did not zealously guard intimate knowledge and confidence.[12]

When Gerecke did publish his experiences he introduced his story by saying:

> Remember, friends, this report is unofficial and has no connection with any report that may come from the War Department. These are my personal observations and feelings about the men on trial at Nuremberg.[13]

Maintaining his silence, Chaplain O'Connor wrote nothing for publication.

Chaplain O'Connor was a former parish priest from Loudonville, New York, who had entered the Army in 1943. Chaplain Gerecke was a 53-year-old pastor from Missouri, who had also entered the Army in 1943. A hospital chaplain, he was serving in Munich with the 98th General Hospital Unit, when he was ordered to report to the 6850th Internal Security Detachment at Nuremberg. He had not seen his wife in two-and-a-half years, and two of his sons had been severely wounded in the war, one during the Battle of the Bulge.

Prior to coming to Munich, he had spent "15 melancholy months in English hospitals, sitting at the bedsides of the wounded and dying." Chaplain Gerecke had many doubts about this new assignment. The Office of the Chief of Chaplains told him that the decision to accept or reject it was up to him.[14] Colonel Andrus wrote that Gerecke told him: "How can a humble preacher from a Missouri farm make any impression on the disciples of Adolph Hitler?"[15] Despite his doubts, Gerecke accepted the assignment.

From November 1945 to October 1946, Chaplains Gerecke and O'Connor ministered to their charges on a daily basis. Gerecke's first communicant was Fritz Saukel. He regularly prayed with the chaplain, often ending his prayers with: "God be merciful to me, a sinner." Fritzche, von Schirach, and Speer, were regular takers of Communion. Field Marshal Keitel asked Gerecke, "to convey his thanks to the Christian people of America for sending a chaplain to them." At one point Keitel told him: "You have helped me more than you know. May Christ, my Saviour, stand by me all the way. I shall need him so much."[16]

On the Catholic side, Hans Frank told Dr. Gilbert, the Army psychologist, in December 1945:

> I am glad that you and Pater Sixtus, at least, still come to talk to me. You know, Pater Sixtus is such a wonderful man. If you could say 'virgin' about a man you would say it about him—so delicate, so sympathetic, so maidenly—you know what I mean. And religion is such a comfort—my only comfort now. I look forward to Christmas now like a little child.[17]

The prisoners who refused to see either chaplain were adamant in their stance.

Hess, of course, was mentally disturbed, and probably, like Krupp, should not have been on trial. Streicher's response to some religious leaflets left by the chaplain was that: "I don't put any stock in that stuff . . . All that stuff about Christ—the Jew who was the Son of God—I don't know. It sounds like propaganda."[18]

Rosenberg, the party theoretician, treated Gerecke with a cool disdain. He told him that he had no need of his services, but he thought it was nice that someone could be so simple as to actually accept the story of Christ as Gerecke had done.[19]

Hermann Goering, the highest-ranking Nazi on trial, was for Gerecke the most interesting and the most troubling. When Gerecke held services in the little prison chapel, Goering was always the first to arrive, sat in the front, and sang the loudest. His rationale for this was somewhat disconcerting, since he told Gerecke that with his position as the highest-ranking member of the prisoners, it was his duty to set an example. "If I attend," he maintained, "the others will follow suit."[20]

The depth of his faith was questionable. Once, ending a session with the prison psychologist, Dr. Gilbert, he said that he must get to chapel. When Gilbert said that prayer was beneficial, Goering replied: "Prayers, hell! It's just a chance to get out of this damn cell for a half hour."[21] He told Chaplain Gerecke at one point that he was not an atheist, but rejected Lutheranism. He believed in a higher power, but not in Christianity.[22]

By the spring of 1946, both chaplains had established strong bonds with the prisoners. When a rumor spread that Gerecke wanted to leave, all 21 defendants signed a letter to Mrs. Gerecke in St. Louis telling her how much they had benefited from his ministry and how much they needed him.[23]

After 216 court sessions, on 1 October 1946, the verdict was handed down. Twelve of the defendants (including the absent Bormann) were sentenced to death by hanging. Seven were given prison sentences—Hess, Funk, and Raeder for life. Three—Schacht, von Papen, and Fritzsche—were acquitted. The time for the executions was set for midnight, 15 October 1946.[24]

As the final hour approached, Colonel Andrus reported that "Father O'Connor and Chaplain Gerecke were untiringly moving from condemned cell to condemned cell. Prayers were now taking on a new meaning, a new urgency."[25]

At 2030 hours Gerecke saw Goering. He requested communion but refused to make a confession of Christian faith. Chaplain Gerecke in turn refused to give Communion, basing his decision on denominational grounds. Two hours later Gerecke was hurriedly summoned and found that Goering had committed suicide and cheated the hangman by taking a cyanide capsule.[26]

The chaplain was later criticized for this refusal of the sacrament, and Gerecke himself had struggled with his decision. "If I blundered in my approach to reach this man's heart and soul with the meaning of the Cross of Jesus," he wrote later, "then I'm very sorry and I hope a Christian world will forgive me."[27]

As the ten remaining condemned prisoners walked the "last mile" that night the chaplains went with them. "I put my trust in Christ," von Ribbentrop confided to Gerecke.[28] As the hood was pulled over his head he turned to him and said: "I'll see you again."[29] Field Marshall Keitel said: "I thank you and those who sent you, with all my heart."[30]

The place of execution was located in the gymnasium of the prison. Brightly lit, the room contained three wooden scaffolds painted black. Thirteen steps led up to the platforms on which the gallows were erected. The lower part of the gallows was draped with a curtain. Hands tied behind their backs, a black hood pulled over their heads, one by one each man went to his death. Master Sergeant John C. Woods of San Antonio, Texas, and his two assistants conducted the executions. By 2:45 a.m. it was over.[31]

Kingsbury Smith of the International News Service, who attended the executions as a representative of the American press, remembered that "most of them tried to show courage. None of them broke down."[32]

At four o'clock in the morning two Army trucks arrived at the prison. Eleven coffins were loaded and the trucks, protected by vehicles equipped with machine guns, drove off in the direction of Furth, followed by a procession of newspapermen in automobiles. At Erlangen the press contingent was prevented from proceeding any further and the two trucks containing the bodies drove off into the early morning mist. Taken to Munich on a roundabout route, the remains were reduced to ashes in the crematorium of the East Cemetery. These ashes were then scattered in the river Isar.[33]

Chaplains Gerecke and O'Connor were soon reassigned, returning to their normal duties as U.S. Army chaplains. Yet, for a year they had played an intimate part in one of the most historically significant episodes of the 20th century special ministry.

LIEUTENANT COLONEL REX R. KIZIAH, USAF

The Emerging Biocruise Threat

The simultaneous proliferation of cruise missile delivery systems and BTW [biological and toxin warfare] production capabilities may pose a serious strategic threat in the future.

— JONATHAN B. TUCKER
"The Future of Biological Warfare"

The United States clearly demonstrated the strategic and operational effectiveness of cruise missiles to the world between 16 January and 2 February 1991, when US Navy surface ships and submarines in the Persian Gulf, Red Sea, and Eastern Mediterranean launched 288 Tomahawk land-attack missiles (TLAM) and the US Air Force expended 39 conventional air-launched cruise missiles (CALCM) against "strategic" targets in Iraq. These attacks targeted command and control headquarters, power-generation complexes, weapons of mass destruction (WMD) facilities, and oil-production and refining factories.[1] Although Department of Defense (DOD) sources and outside analysts disagree regarding the degree of success of these land-attack cruise missile (LACM) strikes, the consensus is that LACMs proved to be very effective weapon systems. As stated in DOD's *Conduct of the Per-*

This article is based upon the author's essay "Assessment of the Emerging Biocruise Threat," in *The Gathering Biological Warfare Storm*, 2d ed., ed. Col (Dr.) Jim A. Davis and Dr. Barry Schneider (Maxwell AFB, Ala.: USAF Counterproliferation Center, April 2002), 193–251, on-line, Internet, 21 January 2003, available from http://www.au.af.mil/au/awc/awcgate/cpc-pubs/biostorm/kiziah.doc.

sian Gulf Conflict: Final Report to Congress, "The cruise missile concept—incorporating an unmanned, low-observable platform able to strike accurately at long distances—was validated as a significant new instrument for future conflicts."[2]

Since Operation Desert Storm, LACMs have become a centerpiece of US military strike operations. Our leaders value LACMs for their ability to penetrate enemy air defenses, strike at long ranges (over 1,000 miles from the launch platform for the TLAM), and, most importantly, to do so without endangering the lives of US personnel. Increasingly, operational war fighters view LACMs as the ultimate "smart weapons." The rest of the world has also observed and learned. Given nearly a decade of prominent, successful, and escalating use of these weapon systems—along with the proliferation of enabling technologies such as precision navigation and guidance, compact and efficient turbojet and turbofan engines, and composite and low-observable materials—it should come as no surprise that countries around the world desire and actively pursue cruise missile technologies, especially land-attack versions.[3]

Nations value LACMs not only for their long-range, precision-strike capabilities and their conventional, high-explosive warheads, but also for their potential to deliver payloads of chemical and biological warfare (CBW) agents. Advances in dual-use technologies such as satellite navigation (the US Global Positioning System [GPS] and the Russian Global Navigation Satellite System [GLONASS]) and highly efficient, small turbofan engines used in aircraft allow Western nations to improve their long-range, precision-strike weaponry. However, they also allow lesser-developed countries to close the technology gap and begin inserting comparable weaponry into their arsenals relatively "on the cheap" by historical standards, compared to other weapon systems such as modern aircraft and ballistic missiles. Additionally, with years of determined efforts that have recently intensified, the United States has pursued theater missile and air defense systems to counter potential adversaries' aircraft and increasingly sophisticated ballistic missiles. Consequently, competitors seek to acquire and develop hard-to-detect-and-engage LACMs to maintain, and possibly to enhance, their capabilities to deter and confront the United States and its allies.

These developments have clearly captured the attention of government officials, defense planners, and intelligence analysts. Dr. Ramesh Thakur, vice rector of United Nations University in Tokyo and author of numerous proliferation and arms-control articles, argues that "for developing and rogue countries, the balance in cost, accessibility, lethality, complexity, and operational requirements is shifting from ballistic to cruise missiles."[4] More specifically, in an address to the National Defense University Foundation in April 1999, Donald Rumsfeld, now the secretary of defense, stated that "the United States must expect such states as Iran, Iraq, and North Korea to acquire or develop cruise missiles over the next few years."[5] The National Intelligence Council's unclassified report *Foreign Missile Developments and the Ballistic Missile Threat to the United States through 2015* (September 1999) echoes this assessment: "We expect to see acquisition of LACMs by many countries to meet regional military requirements."[6] Thus, trends indicate that cruise missiles may represent a greater long-term threat to US interests and global stability than do ballistic missiles.

Land-Attack Cruise Missiles: The Basics

A comprehensive description of a cruise missile includes the following characteristics: an unmanned aircraft configured as an antisurface weapon intended to impact upon or detonate over a preselected surface (land or sea) target; an integral means of sustained self-propulsion and a precision-guidance system (usually autonomous but possibly requiring limited external input from a human operator); aerodynamic surfaces that generate lift to sustain the missile's flight; and autonomous achievement of a sustained cruise phase of flight at a predetermined level, relative to overflown terrain or water.[7] Thus, cruise missiles represent a subset of armed, unmanned aerial vehicles (UAV) or standoff weapons.

Typically, cruise missiles are categorized according to the intended mission and launch mode instead of their maximum range, which is the classification scheme for ballistic missiles. The two broadest categories are antiship cruise missiles (ASCM) and LACMs.[8] On the one hand, ASCMs—currently in the military arsenals of 73 countries—are the most widely deployed cruise missiles[9] and represent the most important naval weapons possessed by many of these countries: "The punch provided by ASCMs has made it possible for Third World countries to maintain relatively powerful naval forces that rely on comparatively inexpensive missile-armed patrol boats or small corvettes."[10] ASCMs are designed to strike small targets such as ships at sea at relatively long ranges (up to approximately 500 kilometers [km]) and thus are terminally guided to ships with high accuracy. The terminal-guidance systems include active or semiactive radar, radar homing, infrared (IR), television, or home-on-jam.[11]

On the other hand, LACMs are designed to attack ground-based targets, either mobile or fixed. Basic components include the airframe, propulsion system, navigation and guidance system, and warhead. Basically, the LACM airframe is an elongated, cylindrical missile/aircraft structure constructed from metals and composite materials, with short wings and rudders. The propulsion system (rocket or air-breathing engine) is located in the rear; the navigation and guidance system is located in the front; and the fuel and warhead are typically located in the midbody.[12] LACM guidance occurs in three phases: launch, midcourse, and terminal. During launch, the missile receives initial guidance information from its onboard inertial navigation system (INS). In the midcourse phase, a radar-based terrain contour matching (TERCOM) system and/or satellite navigation system such as GPS or GLONASS correct for the inherent inaccuracies of the INS.[13] Upon entering the target area, the terminal-guidance system (one or a combination of the following: GPS/GLONASS, TERCOM with more accurate terrain-contour digital maps, Digital Scene Matching Correlator [DSMAC] or a terminal seeker [optical- or radar-based sensor]) controls the missile to the desired impact point.[14] The mission ranges of LACMs currently in military arsenals around the world vary from 50 to more than 3,000 km, and most of the missiles fly at high subsonic speeds.

Proliferating Cruise Missile Technologies

The elimination of substantial technological barriers that prevented Third World countries from producing accurate LACMs coincided with the "eye-opening" performance of US TLAMs during the Persian Gulf War of 1991. Until the late 1980s, accurate LACMs required sophisticated guidance and navigation technologies—stand-alone, accurate, and complex INS, TERCOM, and DSMAC—controlled through Missile Technology Control Regime auspices and thus available to only a few countries such as the United States, United Kingdom, Soviet Union, and France.[15] In the 1990s, critical enabling technologies became commercially available, thus allowing states to begin pursuing viable LACM procurement programs. Such technologies included precision navigation and guidance technologies; high-resolution satellite imagery and sophisticated Geographical Information Systems (GIS); high-efficiency, reduced-volume, air-breathing engines; more efficient fuels; and composite and low-observable materials.

The commercial availability of accurate satellite navigation information has allowed Third World countries to bypass approximately 15 years of research and development for long-range, fairly accurate LACMs. Low-cost GPS receivers can augment relatively inaccurate and widely available INS systems to achieve the navigational accuracies of stand-alone, fairly accurate, expensive INS systems formerly produced only for Western commercial aircraft.[16] GPS, Differential GPS (DGPS), and GLONASS receivers can be incorporated into all guidance phases of LACM flight. Used in combination, these technologies allow nations seeking to compete militarily in the international arena to develop relatively inexpensive LACMs that can deliver payloads to within a few meters of the intended target. Commercial DGPS systems are available worldwide that can improve the accuracy of GPS coarse/acquisition (the GPS signal available to all users and providing accuracies around 30 meters [m]) guidance by an order of magnitude.[17] Additionally, GLONASS, used in conjunction with GPS, improves the robustness and accuracy of guidance systems.

GPS, DGPS, and GLONASS guidance technologies provide sufficient LACM accuracies for delivery of both conventional and nuclear, biological, and chemical (NBC) payloads without the need for TERCOM- or DSMAC-like systems that require extensive digital maps. However, developing countries may want to develop a LACM that flies at very low altitudes while maximizing terrain masking in order to increase survivability and penetration of air defenses. Such low-altitude flight profiles require accurate digital-mapping capabilities that, until recently, were too expensive for most developing nations. Now such capabilities are commercially available within affordable ranges. Potential adversaries can purchase one-meter-resolution satellite imagery, add accurate GPS/DGPS position information with GIS, and produce very accurate three-dimensional digital maps.[18]

Increasingly efficient fuels as well as turbojet and turbofan engines available on the international market provide poorer countries the ability to field cruise missiles with ranges of at least 1,000 km.[19] Additionally, commercially available radar-absorbing structures, materials, and coatings, along with IR-suppression techniques, can greatly reduce the signatures of cruise missiles. Potential competitors who combine these technologies with LACMs significantly complicate regional air defense scenarios for the United States and its allies.

Besides accessibility to the technologies described above, many advantageous characteristics of LACMs as weapon systems motivate lesser-developed countries with limited fiscal resources to acquire or develop them as part of a balanced military strike force that includes combat aircraft, ballistic missiles, and cruise missiles. One particularly desirable feature is their small size compared to aircraft and ballistic missiles. LACMs are easily deployable on a wide variety of platforms— ships, submarines, and aircraft, as well as small, fixed, or mobile land-based launchers. This flexibility translates into increased survivability before launch. Unlike combat aircraft, LACMs are not restricted to operating from vulnerable airfields susceptible to preemptive attacks. Also, the fact that, on land, LACMs are much easier to hide from op-posing forces and are more mobile than ballistic missiles further en-hances an enemy state's ability to conduct "shoot and scoot" launches, such as those the Iraqis executed with great success during the Persian Gulf War in spite of intensive "Scud hunt" operations by coalition forces.

By 2005–10, modestly equipped states could produce LACMs with a range of 500 to 700 km (8.5 m in length, an .8 m body diameter, and a 2.4 m wingspan) that could fit into a standard 12 m shipping con-tainer along with a small erector constructed for launching the LACM directly from the container.[20] A range of 500 to 700 km allows an ad-versary deploying such ship-based LACMs to strike most key popula-tion and industrial centers in Europe and North America yet remain outside the 200-mile territorial-waters limit. Such a threat poses diffi-cult monitoring challenges for both the intelligence and defense com-munities. Dennis Gormley writes that "the non-governmental 'Gates Panel,' in reviewing NIE [National Intelligence Estimate] 95-19 . . . concluded that not nearly enough attention was being devoted to the possibility that land-attack cruise missiles could be launched from ships within several hundred kilometres of U.S. territory."[21] Perhaps in response to this criticism, the intelligence community's unclassified na-tional intelligence estimate of September 1999 on the ballistic missile threat to the United States through the year 2015 stated that "a com-mercial surface vessel, covertly equipped to launch cruise missiles, would be a plausible alternative for a forward-based launch platform. This method would provide a large and potentially inconspicuous plat-form to launch a cruise missile while providing at least some cover for launch deniability."[22]

Because of its small size, a LACM has inherently low visual, IR, and radar signatures—characteristics that translate into increased sur-vivability. The reduced radar observability, referred to as a reduced radar cross section (RCS), makes the missile difficult for air defense radars to detect, identify, track, and engage, especially compared to the conventional combat aircraft in a rogue state's arsenal. Complicating the air defense problem, the application of low-observable materials can make a LACM even more difficult to detect. The simplest approach would be to apply radar-absorbing coatings to the airframe surface and to incorporate an IR reduction cone around the engine. The airframe could also be constructed with radar-absorbing polymers and non-metallic composites that would only minimally reflect radar energy. Finally, engineers could design the LACM's shape, structure, composition, and integration of subcomponents to be inherently stealthy. Clearly, this option would require the most technical skill.

The impact of lowered observability can be dramatic because it reduces the maximum detection range from missile defenses, resulting in minimal time for intercept. For example, a conventional fighter aircraft such as an F-4 has an RCS of about six square meters (m^2), and the much larger but low-observable B-2 bomber, which incorporates advanced stealth technologies into its design, has an RCS of only approximately 0.75 m^2.[23] A typical cruise missile with UAV-like characteristics has an RCS in the range of 1 m^2; the Tomahawk ALCM, designed in the 1970s and utilizing the fairly simple low-observable technologies then available, has an RCS of less than 0.05 m^2. The US airborne warning and control system (AWACS) radar system was designed to detect aircraft with an RCS of 7 m^2 at a range of at least 370 km and typical nonstealthy cruise missiles at a range of at least 227 km; stealthy cruise missiles, however, could approach air defenses to within 108 km before being detected. If such missiles traveled at a speed of 805 km per hour (500 miles per hour), air defenses would have only eight minutes to engage and destroy the stealthy missile and 17 minutes for the nonstealthy missile. Furthermore, a low-observable LACM can be difficult to engage and destroy, even if detected. According to Seth Carus, a Soviet analyst, cruise missiles with an RCS of 0.1 m^2 or smaller are difficult for surface-to-air missile (SAM) fire-control radars to track.[24] Consequently, even if a SAM battery detects the missile, it may not acquire a sufficient lock on the target to complete the intercept. Even IR tracking devices may not detect low-observable LACMs, and IR-seeking SAMs may not home in on the missile. To further thwart engagement, a LACM could employ relatively simple countermeasures such as chaff and decoys.

A LACM can also avoid detection by following programmed flight paths on which the missile approaches the target at extremely low altitudes, blending with the ground clutter while simultaneously taking advantage of terrain masking. Technologies that enable "terrain hug-ging" flight—such as radar altimetry; precision guidance and satellite navigation, computerized flight control, high-resolution satellite im-agery, and digitized terrain mapping via sophisticated GIS—are be-coming increasingly available from commercial sources at affordable costs. These technologies allow longer-range LACMs to fly lengthy and circuitous routes to the target, thus minimizing or eliminating their exposure to air defense systems.

Another approach to defeat air defenses afforded by the opera-tional flexibility of the LACM entails launching multiple missiles against a target simultaneously from various directions, thereby overwhelming air defenses at their weakest points. Adversaries could also launch both theater ballistic and cruise missiles to arrive simultaneously at the desig-nated target. The different characteristics of these two approaching missiles—the high-altitude, super-sonic ballistic trajectory of the ballis-tic missiles and the low-altitude, subsonic flight of the cruise missiles—could overwhelm the capabilities of even the most sophisticated air defense systems. A Joint Chiefs of Staff official interviewed by an *Avi-ation Week and Space Technology* reporter commented that "a sophisti-cated foe might be able to fire 20 or 30 [Scud-type] battlefield ballistic missiles, followed by aircraft that pop up to launch waves of cruise mis-siles. The resulting problem for U.S. defenders would be staggering in complexity."[25] Similarly, a former senior planner for Desert Storm noted that "during Desert Storm, if the Iraqis could have fired even one cruise missile a day—with a two-city block [accuracy]—into the headquarters complex in Riyadh [Saudi Arabia], we would have been out of commission about half the time."[26] To further complicate the defender's situation, the attacker could time LACM strikes to coincide with the return of the defender's aircraft. As stated by a senior official at the Pentagon's Joint Theater Air and Missile Defense Office, "The challenge with ballistic missiles is hitting them. . . . With cruise mis-siles, it's figuring out whether it's friendly or not."[27]

Enabled by the increasing commercial availability of advances in key technologies for all components of a LACM—airframe, propul-sion, guidance and navigation, and warhead—the combined accuracy and range attributes of LACMs now exceed those of ballistic missile systems at far less cost per weapon system. For example, LACMs can be developed with warheads and ranges similar to those of substantially more complex ballistic missiles but at less than half the cost and with at least 10 times the warhead-delivery accuracy (10–100 m circular error probable [CEP] compared to 1,000–2,000 m CEP).[28] By carrying differ-ent warheads, a LACM provides competitor states more cost-effective options for a deep strike of heavily defended targets such as airfields; ports; staging areas; troop concentrations; amphibious landing areas; logistics centers; and command, control, communications, and intelli-gence nodes. Because the accuracy of the LACM is significantly better than that of a similar-ranged ballistic missile, the probability of destroy-ing or damaging the target is much higher. Furthermore, the range of a LACM is extended by the range of its launch platform, thus giving it the potential to attack targets well beyond the range of comparable ballistic missile systems.

The characteristics discussed above make LACMs ideally suited for disseminating biological warfare (BW) agents. As would be the case for aircraft dissemination, a subsonic LACM, using an aerosol sprayer embedded in its wings and built-in meteorological sensors coupled to the guidance-and-control computer, could alter its flight profile and release a line source of BW agent tailored to the local topography, mi-crometeorological conditions, and shape of the target, thus maximiz-ing the resultant lethal area of the BW payload. The advantage of employing a LACM for the delivery of BW agents as opposed to an aircraft is that it involves no risk to the pilot; the disadvantage is forfei-ture of pilot improvisation.

Gormley argues that "the lethal areas for a given quantity of CBW, and this is a very, very conservative calculation, are at least ten times that of a ballistic missile delivery program. This judgment reflects the results of extensive modeling and simulation."[29] In Gormley's simulation, an op-timal pattern of distribution of CBW agents using submunitions was as-sumed for ballistic missile delivery. For LACM delivery, both worst-case and best-case distributions were averaged for the comparison. The in-creased lethality area for a LACM-delivered CBW payload is primarily attributable to the aerodynamic stability of the LACM and the capability of distributing the CBW agent payload as a line source. It is interesting to note that the United States investigated using the Snark cruise missile for delivery of BW and chemical warfare (CW) agent payloads as early as 1952 and funded projects for developing dissemination systems for cruise missiles and drones through the early 1960s.[30]

In addition to achieving significantly more effective dissemination of BW agents, subsonic LACM delivery is less challenging technically than supersonic ballistic missile delivery. There are considerable tech-nical difficulties with packaging BW agents within a ballistic missile warhead and ensuring that the agent survives and is disseminated as an aerosol at the correct height above the ground.[31] The reentry speed is so high during the descent phase of the ballistic missile's trajectory that it is difficult to distribute the agent in a diffuse cloud or with the precision to ensure dissemination within the inversion layer of the atmosphere. Also, the high thermal and mechanical stresses generated during launch, reentry, and agent release may degrade the quality of the BW agent. US tests have shown that, without appropriate agent packaging, less than 5 percent of a BW agent payload is viable after flight and dissemination from a ballistic missile.

A few other operational features may make LACMs economically and militarily appealing to developing nations intent on building strike capabilities with very limited defense resources. Compared to aircraft and ballistic missiles, LACMs require less support infrastructure and have lower costs for operations and maintenance. The fact that they can reside in canisters makes them significantly easier to maintain and operate in harsh environments. Furthermore, the fact that they are unmanned eliminates the need for expensive pilot and crew training.

Potential adversaries have numerous reasons for pursuing WMDs and their means of delivery. The most compelling motivation may be that WMDs are the only viable levers of strategic power in the post–Cold War world for many nations. They are often the most realistic means for carrying out the three actions adversaries desire to accomplish—deter, constrain, and harm the United States—but cannot with the conventional military forces at their disposal. During the Persian Gulf War, the United States demonstrated to the world that it had developed overwhelming superiority in conventional military force against any other nation. Although since that war, the US defense budget has decreased significantly, so have the budgets of most other countries, and no country appears to be narrowing the US superiority gap. Currently, the US defense budget is more than triple that of any potentially hostile nation and more than the combined military spending of Russia, China, Iran, Iraq, North Korea, and Cuba.[32] As Richard Betts, director of national security studies at the Council on Foreign Relations, further notes, "There is no evidence that those countries' level of military professionalism is rising at a rate that would make them competitive even if they were to spend far more on their forces."[33] Hostile states and potential competitors simply cannot currently—or for the foreseeable future—confront the United States successfully on conventional military terms. Many countries are fully aware of this situation and see WMDs and their delivery vehicles as an effective means of asymmetrically challenging the overwhelming conventional military power of the United States. In essence, WMDs can be a weaker country's equalizer to the larger and more advanced conventional forces of the United States and its allies.

WMDs, combined with standoff delivery systems, provide lesser-developed countries far less expensive yet qualitatively superior military and political options for deterring, constraining, and harming the United States, compared to strategies that rely on advanced conventional forces, whose price tag is prohibitive. In other words, WMDs and long-range delivery systems allow countries to achieve regional and strategic objectives "on the cheap." Rogue nations see WMDs as an inexpensive means of coercing neighbors, deterring outside intervention, deterring other WMD threats and aggression against their interests, and—if necessary—directly attacking the United States and its allies.

The widespread proliferation of enabling technologies and the weapon systems themselves, along with ineffective post–Cold War barriers to such proliferation, is allowing rogue nations to acquire cost-effective WMDs and associated delivery systems. In the nuclear arena, India and Pakistan are prime examples of how determined states will pursue and obtain WMDs regardless of the international treaties, agreements, and sanctions imposed to prevent their acquisition. Similarly, Iraq surprised the international community with the expansiveness of its programs in all areas of WMDs—NBC weapons and delivery systems such as ballistic missiles, aircraft, and UAVs. These programs continued in spite of pre-Persian Gulf War proliferation barriers, concentrated attacks during that war, comprehensive international sanctions, and unprecedented intrusiveness of the UN Special Commission (UNSCOM) on Iraq, all directed at destroying Iraq's WMD capabilities. The abundance of countries willing to provide assistance—by offering WMDs and delivery systems for direct purchase and providing components and technologies for in-country production—further exacerbates the proliferation problem. The most notorious are China, North Korea, and Russia, all of whom actively assist the proliferator nations in their efforts to develop WMD arsenals.

Eroding inhibitions on WMD use further encourage developing states to acquire WMDs and various delivery systems. Iraq, in particular, has clearly demonstrated its willingness to use WMDs on the battlefield. Throughout the Iraq-Iran War of 1980–83, Iraq employed CW agents against Iranian troops. In 1983 Iraq fired at least 33 Scud missiles at Iranian targets and is believed to have employed mustard gas on some of the missile launches against Iranian forces. During the last year of the war, in March–April 1988, Iraq attacked Tehran with 200 Scud missiles, causing approximately one-quarter to one-half of the city's residents to flee, fearing that some of the Scuds were armed with poison-gas warheads.[34] These Iraqi WMD attacks and others left a lasting impression on Iranian leaders and on their views of the effectiveness and international acceptability of WMDs.

WMDs also figured prominently in the Persian Gulf War when Iraq deployed modified Scuds armed with CW and BW payloads, along with other large quantities of CW agents. Some 25 Scuds were armed with BW agents, including 10 with anthrax.[35] The Iraqi regime also kept a dedicated aircraft in a hardened shelter equipped with spray tanks for dispersing BW agents. Had the Iraqis employed this weapon on the first day of the ground war, analysts at the Office of the Secretary of Defense estimate that over 76,000 of the 320,000 coalition troops southeast of Kuwait City would have died if they had not been vaccinated against anthrax. Apparently, US and Israeli threats of nuclear retaliation deterred the Iraqis from launching WMD attacks against coalition forces.

But the credibility of the United States's historically successful, punitive deterrence of WMDs by threatening nuclear retaliation may be declining. Betts offers a brief answer to a very relevant and interesting question: "Would the United States follow through and use nuclear weapons against a country or group that had killed several thousand Americans with deadly chemicals? It is hard to imagine breaking the post-Nagasaki taboo in that situation."[36] What if Iraq had used BW agents to kill 76,000 troops at the beginning of the Persian Gulf War? Further addressing the credibility of the US nuclear deterrent, Gormley and Scott McMahon, experts in the area of the proliferation of WMDs and delivery systems, note that

> this seems to have convinced Saddam Hussein not to use his chemical or biological weapons in 1991. But there are reasons to believe that future threats of nuclear retaliation will neither deter NBC strikes nor reassure regional allies enough that they would permit Western use of their bases while under the threat of NBC attack. Senior U.S. military officers, for example, have declared that they would not condone nuclear retaliation under any circumstances, even if NBC weapons were used against the United States. Although such comments are unofficial, when they are combined with a termination of nuclear testing and the virtual

elimination of nuclear planning, it becomes apparent that nuclear deterrence is fast becoming an existential rather than practical option.[37]

Another issue with exercising deterrence to prevent the use of WMDs is that deterrence relies on retaliation, and retaliation requires knowledge of who has launched the attack. Combining a WMD such as a BW agent, which inherently creates difficulties in identifying the source of the resulting disease, with a delivery system such as a long-range LACM, which can be programmed to fly circuitous routes to the target, may provide an adversary with a nonattributable method of attack, thus eliminating any attempt at retaliation.

National prestige also influences a country to acquire WMDs and associated delivery systems. Robert Gates, former director of Central Intelligence, observes that "these weapons represent symbols of technical sophistication and military prowess—and acquiring powerful weapons has become the hallmark of acceptance as a world power."[38] Similarly, referring specifically to the WMD means of delivery, Willis Stanley and Keith Payne comment that "some regimes in the developing world see a missile force as a talisman which imparts international respect and ushers them into the company of the great powers."[39] For this symbolic effect, countries like China, India, Pakistan, and others have concentrated on acquiring ballistic missiles. The demonstrated effectiveness of US TLAMs during the Persian Gulf War has perhaps elevated the prestige of LACMs to that of ballistic missiles. As Richard Speier, a consultant for the Carnegie Non-Proliferation Project, notes, "In the Gulf War the U.S. used three times as many cruise missiles as the Iraqis used ballistic missiles, and our cruise missiles had a very telling military effect."[40]

A growing community of experts has come to view the proliferation of biological weapons with increasing concern. One of the main reasons for this trend can be expressed with a slight modification to a popular phrase: biological weapons provide "more bang for the buck and effort." As Betts observes, biological weapons combine maximum lethality with ease of availability. Nuclear weapons wreak massive destruction but are extremely difficult and costly to acquire; chemical weapons are fairly easy to acquire but possess limited killing capacity; and biological weapons possess the "best" qualities of both (table 1).[41] (One should note that biological weapons most closely resemble a special category of nuclear weapons called "neutron bombs." They harm people, not property, with lethal effects against living organisms.)

TABLE 1
COMPARISON OF NBC WEAPONS

Type	Technology	Cost	Signature	EFFECTIVENESS			
				Protected Personnel		Unprotected Personnel	
				Tactical	Strategic	Tactical	Strategic
Biological	+	–	–	–	–	+	++
Chemical	+	+	+	–	–	++	+
Nuclear	++	++	++	++	++	++	++

++ Very High   + High   – Lower

Source: Lester C. Caudle, "The Biological Warfare Threat," in *Medical Aspects of Chemical and Biological Warfare*, ed. Frederick R. Sidell, Ernest T. Takafuj, and David R. Franz (Washington, D.C.: Office of the Surgeon General at TMM Publications, 1997), 459.

A number of pathogens (bacteria and viruses) and toxins are generally considered to be effective BW agents (table 2). Edward Eitzen, a researcher at the US Army Medical Research Institute of Infectious Diseases, notes that under suitable weather conditions, cruise missiles equipped to deliver anthrax could cover an area comparable to that of the lethal fallout from a ground-burst nuclear weapon.[42] More rigorously, the Congressional Office of Technology Assessment conducted a study in 1993 that investigated the airplane dissemination of 100 kilograms (kg) of anthrax as an aerosol cloud over Washington, D.C., on a clear and calm night. The study showed that between one and three million deaths could result—300 times the number of fatalities that could occur from a similar release of 10 times the amount of sarin gas.[43] A study by the World Health Organization in 1970 concluded that a BW attack on a large city (five million people) in an economically developed country such as the United States, using 50 kg of anthrax disseminated from a single airplane under favorable conditions, could travel downwind in excess of 20 km with the potential to kill upwards of 100,000 people while incapacitating an additional 250,000.[44] Additionally, US military scientists verified the order-of-magnitude effects of the release of BW agents against urban populations estimated by these studies by conducting combat-effects investigations at Dugway Proving Ground, Utah.[45] Thus, after comparing the killing power of WMDs on a weight-for-weight basis, one finds that BW agents are inherently more lethal than CW nerve agents and that biological weapon

TABLE 2
CANDIDATE BW AGENTS FOR WEAPONIZATION

Disease	Causative Agent	Incubation Time (Days)	Fatalities (Percent)
Anthrax	*Bacillus anthracis*	one to five	80
Plague	*Yersinia pestis*	one to five	90
Tularemia	*Francisella tularensis*	10 to 14	five to 20
Cholera	*Vibrio cholerae*	two to five	25 to 50
Venezuelan equine encephalitis	*VEE virus*	two to five	< one
Q fever	*Coxiella burnetti*	12 to 21	< one
Botulism	*Clostridium botulinum toxin*	three	30
Staphylococcal enterotoxemia	*Staphylococcus enterotoxin type B*	one to six	< one
Multiple organ toxicity	*Trichothecene mycotoxin*	Dose Dependent	

Source: *The Biological and Chemical Warfare Threat* (Washington, D.C.: US Government Printing Office, 1999), 2.

systems can potentially provide broader coverage per pound of payload than can CW weapons.[46]

In addition to being extremely lethal and offering feasible alternatives to nuclear weapons as a strategic arsenal, biological weapons are economically and technically attractive, or, as Betts describes, easily available compared to nuclear and chemical weapons. The costs to launch a BW program are much lower than those for comparable nuclear- and chemical-weapons programs: estimates are $2 to $10 billion for a nuclear-weapons program, 10s of millions for a chemical program, and less than $10 million for a BW program.[47] Adding to the appeal of biological weapons, almost all the materials, technology, and equipment required for a modest BW-agent program are dual use, obtainable off the shelf from a variety of legitimate enterprises, and widely available. Moreover, the technical skills required to initiate and conduct an offensive BW-agent production program are commensurate with those of graduate-level microbiologists, thousands of whom received advanced training in some of the best Western universities and who are now available worldwide.[48]

The most significant technical hurdle to overcome in obtaining biological weapons involves weaponizing the BW agents. Primary weaponization concerns include (1) effectively disseminating the BW agent for maximum effect (area coverage and lethality or incapacitation); (2) maintaining the viability and virulence of the agent; and (3) selecting the appropriate delivery system and conditions.[49] BW agents should be disseminated as an aerosol cloud for maximum infectivity via inhalation through the lungs and for maximum geographic dispersal over the target population. Obtaining the right aerosol particle size is extremely important. Carus, a world-renowned expert and prolific writer on proliferation issues, notes that aerosolized BW agents of the wrong size can render a BW attack completely ineffective.[50] The ideal particle size ranges from one to five microns in diameter. An aerosol formed from particles in this size range is stable and can be carried downwind over long distances without significant fallout of the BW-agent particles. Also, one to five microns is the ideal range of particle sizes for retention in the lungs—particles less than one micron are readily exhaled, and those greater than five microns are filtered out by the upper respiratory passages, unable to reach the lowest level of the lungs.

BW agents can be produced and aerosolized in either liquid or dry-powder form. The liquid form is easier to produce but has a relatively short shelf life (most liquid BW agents can be stored for only three to six months under refrigeration) and can be difficult to aerosolize. Commercial sprayers can be modified for disseminating liquid BW agents, but one encounters nontrivial issues associated with the clogging of the sprayer nozzles and with destroying the agent during the spraying process.[51] Both the shelf life and spraying limitations can be overcome by producing BW agents in dry form through using lyophilization (rapid freezing and subsequent dehydration under high vacuum) and milling the appropriate particle sizes into a powder. Anthrax spores produced in this fashion can be stored for several years.[52] However, producing dry BW agents is extremely hazardous and requires more specialized equipment and greater technical capabilities.

Whether the BW agents are in liquid or dry form, individuals who seek to weaponize them must overcome environmental conditions that kill or reduce the virulence of the agents. The rate of biological decay depends upon several factors, including ultraviolet radiation, temperature, humidity, and air pollution.[53] The optimal atmospheric conditions for a BW attack would occur on a cold, clear night with relative humidity greater than 70 percent. The inversion layer (the stable blanket of cool air above the cool ground) would prevent vertical mixing of the aerosol cloud, thus keeping the BW agent near the ground for inhalation. Weaponization of BW agents presents many challenges. Nonetheless, from a proliferation viewpoint, it is important to note that more than 40 years ago the US Army Chemical Corps overcame these challenges and successfully demonstrated and conducted tests of large areas and effective dissemination of biological agents.[54]

Because of the low costs associated with initiating and conducting biological-weapons programs and the dual-use nature of BW research and equipment, a BW program can flourish clandestinely under the guise of legitimate research. This unique feature of biological-weapons programs may make them particularly attractive to rogue nations. No unambiguous signatures readily discriminate a program focused on conducting legitimate biomedical research on highly contagious diseases from one that researches and produces BW agents for offensive military purposes. The absence of verification provisions in the Biological and Toxin Weapons Convention adds to the difficulty of detecting and countering clandestine BW programs. As the Iraqi situation illustrates, detecting and understanding the extent of a clandestine BW program is extremely difficult. In January 1999, UNSCOM officials provided a report to the UN Security Council summarizing eight years of extensive investigations and destruction of Iraq's chemical and biological weapons programs. Even with these intensive and powerful inspections, UNSCOM officials now believe that Iraq, through well-coordinated concealment and deception efforts, may have produced another, as yet unidentified, BW agent in an unreported and unlocated production facility.[55]

From an aggressor's perspective, another advantage of biological weapons over chemical or nuclear weapons is that, currently, no reliable detection devices exist to provide advanced warning of a BW attack, thus allowing a greater probability of large numbers of casualties per weapon. Additionally, coupled with the delayed onset of symptoms from a BW attack and the fact that these symptoms could easily be attributed to a natural outbreak of disease, biological weapons potentially provide the country employing them plausible deniability. Thus, an aggressor may use biological weapons as a precursor to a conventional military attack to wreak havoc and weaken the target forces of a conventionally superior foe with a reduced risk of retaliation and condemnation from the attacked country and international community. It would be possible to identify a large outbreak of anthrax, for example, as an almost certain BW attack since such episodes occur rarely, if at all, in nature. However, the outbreak of a common disease regularly found in a given region of the world would possibly be seen at first as a natural occurrence.

Conclusion

From the perspective of a competitor facing the formidable conventional military power of the United States and its allies, a LACM equipped with a BW-agent payload could represent a politically attractive, cost-effective, and militarily useful weapon system. Politically, the mere threat of using a system with a payload of 120 kg of anthrax against a major US or allied city could deter the United States from becoming involved in an adversary's aggression against a neighbor or bid for regional hegemony. Militarily, such a delivery system, especially if it is equipped with low-observable technologies and simple endgame countermeasures such as chaff and decoys, would have a high probability of penetrating air defenses and accurately delivering its payload, thus causing large numbers of casualties. Such weapon systems are cost-effective, especially compared to similarly ranged ballistic missiles and conventional combat aircraft. As such, lesser-developed states with limited defense resources could purchase relatively large numbers of LACMs and use them to complicate the air defense problem for the United States and its allies.

With the emergence of commercially available enabling technologies for precise navigation and guidance; sophisticated mission planning; low-weight, high-efficiency propulsion; and air defense penetration, the development of biocruise weapon systems is now within the reach of many potential adversaries. States such as Iran, Iraq, and North Korea have persistently demonstrated the will to acquire weapon systems that will provide them with strategic leverage against the United States and its allies. Such nations pursue multiple-acquisition strategies that have the potential to provide them with highly capable LACMs. These strategies include direct purchase of advanced LACMs from various countries, including France, Russia, and China; indigenous development, with or without outside assistance; and development of a highly capable LACM via the relatively low-cost and technically straightforward conversion of an ASCM such as the Chinese HY-4 Sadsack. Given these proliferation conditions, which clearly favor adversary states, the probability is quite high that by 2005 one or more such competitors will possess a biocruise weapon system with a range of 500 to 1,000 km, capable of effective BW-agent delivery against US and allied military operations in regional conflicts around the world or against military and civilian targets within the United States and allied countries.

Just as disturbing, these capabilities will likely emerge with little if any warning. The National Intelligence Council's 1999 report *Foreign Missile Developments and the Ballistic Missile Threat to the United States through 2015* states that

> a concept similar to a sea-based ballistic missile launch system would be to launch cruise missiles from forward-based platforms. This method would enable a country to use cruise missiles acquired for regional purposes to attack targets in the United States. . . . We also judge that we may not be able to provide much, if any, warning of a forward-based ballistic missile or . . . LACM threat to the United States. Moreover, LACM development can draw upon dual-use technologies.[56]

Assessing, predicting, and tracking the proliferation of strategically significant LACMs is difficult for the intelligence community. George Tenet, director of the Central Intelligence Agency, testified before the Senate Select Committee on Intelligence that the US intelligence services might be incapable of monitoring the proliferation of NBC expertise and technologies. He also stated that, now more than ever, "we risk substantial surprise."[57] By adding to these sobering assessments the disturbing knowledge that some states have clearly demonstrated that they will use WMDs and that the United States and its allies are not likely to deter such use, one can appreciate the need to develop strategic, operational, and tactical structures to counter the emerging biocruise threat.

COLONEL (DR.) JIM A. DAVIS, USAF

The Looming Biological Warfare Storm: Misconceptions and Probable Scenarios

Yet, this is still a dangerous world, a less certain, a less predictable one. . . . Many have chemical and biological weapons. Most troubling of all, the list of these countries includes some of the world's least-responsible states.

—President George W. Bush
National Defense University, 1 May 2001

The likelihood that biological weapons will be used against our nation continues to rise. Many in the recent past have considered the talk of such horrific weapons as only hype to justify funding for certain programs for DOD, other governmental agencies, or government contractors. The stark reality of 11 September 2001—when hijacked airliners were used as missiles, and anthrax attacks followed—has changed that perception for many. However, since we have not yet suffered a mass-casualty biological warfare (BW) event, there are others that still dismiss the scenario as highly unlikely.

If this view is persuasive to US decision makers, it will impede

This article is based upon the author's essay "A Biological Warfare Wake-Up Call: Prevalent Myths and Likely Scenarios," published as chapter 10 in *The Gathering Biological Warfare Storm*, 2d ed., ed. Col (Dr.) Jim A. Davis and Dr. Barry Schneider (Maxwell AFB, Ala.: USAF Counterproliferation Center, April 2002), 289–307, on-line, Internet, 21 January 2003, available from http://www.au.af.mil/au/awc/awcgate/cpc.pubs/biostorm/davis.doc.

the nation's ability to prepare for or prevent such an event. Until very recently, the lack of focus on this subject had resulted in a lack of appropriate funding and accountability. There are six important myths that have caused some senior civilian and military government leaders to develop an inappropriate view of this threat.

It would be valuable to those who recognize the nation's vulnerability to BW to know the most likely scenarios we should expect to encounter. Such informed speculations and visualization allow us to prepare before the event or possibly even to prevent it. This article describes six common myths about BW and three of the most likely future BW scenarios we may face.

Why Postulate?

Thomas C. Schelling observes that "the tendency in our planning is to confuse the unfamiliar with the improbable. The contingency we have not considered seriously looks strange; what looks strange is thought improbable; what is improbable need not be considered seriously."[1]

The United States has limited funds to spend on social and military programs. The military budget is currently 3 percent of the US gross national product (GNP) as compared to 6 percent of the GNP during the late 1980s.[2] The most devastating terrorist attack ever perpetrated against the United States occurred on 11 September 2001 and not only cost many lives, but the associated economic impact exceeded hundreds of billions of dollars in direct replacement costs, lost revenues, and costly response efforts. Yet, the human impact and economic impact of 11 September 2001 will be dwarfed if adversaries are able to effectively deploy mass-casualty biological weapons against the United States. Unless we focus appropriate dollars and develop a coherent national plan to prepare for and prevent such actions, the United States will likely suffer an enormous economic loss that could even lead to our demise as a superpower.

Will There Really Be an Attack?

A belief in one or more of at least six false assumptions or myths helps explain why individuals, including senior civilian and military leaders, do not believe that a mass-casualty BW attack will occur.

MYTH ONE: THERE NEVER REALLY HAS BEEN A SIGNIFICANT BW ATTACK

This contention is counter to historical fact. Even before the fall 2001 anthrax terrorism in the United States, incidents of BW and bioterrorism have occurred on multiple occasions. Today, more countries have active BW programs than at any other time in history, which increases the likelihood that BW will be used again in the future.

Military organizations have used biological weapons many times. One BW event occurred in 1346 when the Mongols used plague (*Yersinia pestis*) at the Battle of Kaffa. More recently, during the French and Indian War, the British used smallpox (*Variola*) against the Delaware Indians and also are alleged to have used smallpox against Gen. George Washington's forces during the Revolutionary War.[3] The Germans used anthrax (*Bacillus anthracis*) and glanders (*Pseudomonas mallei*) against the horses and mules of the US Army and its Allies in World War I. The Japanese used typhoid (*Salmonella typhi*) in World War II in direct attacks on approaching Russian forces.[4] They also used over 16 different BW agents (plague, anthrax, etc.) on Chinese forces and citizens, US prisoners of war, British detainees, and others. Ken Alibek, former head of the civilian branch of the Soviet offensive biological program, has unearthed information that leads him to believe that the Soviet army may have used tularemia (*Francisella tularensis*) to halt the oncoming German army in World War II.[5] The *Textbook for Military Medicine*, published in 1997, states that an estimated 10,923 deaths resulted from the Soviet use of chemical and biological warfare (CBW) agents in Afghanistan, Laos, and Kampuchea (Cambodia).[6] In 2001, the US Senate and other US government offices were attacked through the mail system by letters filled with lethal anthrax spores milled to the 1–5 micron size, which can inflict death from inhalation. BW, it must be concluded, has been an accepted practice for a number of states for a long time.

MYTH TWO: THE UNITED STATES HAS NEVER BEEN ATTACKED BY A BW AGENT

Counting the 2001 anthrax attacks, there are at least six known instances where BW has been used against US citizens or resources. The British were alleged to have used smallpox in the Revolutionary War. The Germans used glanders against US horses and mules during World War I. The Japanese used multiple biological agents against their foes during World War II. The Aum Shinrikyo cult failed in 1990 in its botulinum toxin attack on the two US naval bases located at Yokosuka and Yokohama.[7] In 1984, the Bhagwan Shree Rajneesh cult contaminated 10 restaurant salad bars in Oregon with salmonella and infected at least 750 local citizens.[8] This BW attack, like the naval base attacks, was not discovered until several years after the event. Proliferation experts, such as the National Defense University's Seth Carus, agree that these examples lend credence to the possibility that the United States may have unknowingly fallen victim to still other BW attacks in the past.[9]

MYTH THREE: YOU HAVE TO BE EXTREMELY INTELLIGENT, HIGHLY EDUCATED, AND WELL FUNDED TO GROW, WEAPONIZE, AND DEPLOY A BW AGENT

Financial status or brilliance is no longer a major roadblock for an individual or group to acquire a significant BW capability. Dr. Tara O'Toole, deputy director for the Center for Civilian Biodefense Studies at Johns Hopkins University, believes we have probably crossed over the threshold from "too difficult" to accomplish to "doable by a determined individual or group."[10] It is true that there are certain technical hurdles, but there are many thousands of highly educated microbiologists or other health science professionals worldwide that are capable of growing, weaponizing, and employing a BW agent. Much of the technical information is readily available on the Internet, in libraries, and through mail order channels that provide "how-to" manuals. For example, Steve Priesler, who has a degree in chemistry, wrote such a manual and made it available on the Internet for only $18.[11] This manual, titled *Silent Death* by "Uncle Fester," tells the reader where to find, grow, and weaponize agents such as *Bacillus anthracis* and *Clostridium botulinum;* it also instructs the reader on how to employ the agents to kill small or large numbers of people.

MYTH FOUR: BIOLOGICAL WARFARE MUST BE TOO DIFFICULT BECAUSE IT HAS FAILED WHEN IT HAS BEEN TRIED

Most of the BW attempts mentioned in this article resulted in deaths or casualties. However, not all attempts in the past have been successful. For example, it was not known until 1995 (when several of its incarcerated leaders confessed) that in 1990 the Aum Shinrikyo cult had sprayed two US naval bases in Japan. It is not known why their attack failed, but there were thousands of US sailors and dependants who were one breath away from dying had the Aum Shinrikyo cult been a bit more skilled. While this cult may have failed to master the technological hurdles, several nations had learned a great deal about how to make and effectively use these weapons over half a century earlier. The Japanese began their BW program in the early 1930s and used it against their opponents in World War II. The United States, Great Britain, and the Soviet Union also started BW programs during the 1930s and 1940s. Basic BW technology has been around for 60 years, and all of these countries were to develop large and potent BW programs. This was long before the era of genetic engineering and the mapping of genomes. Although some of the BW program secrets were probably not available to the Aum Shinrikyo cult, the 1990s brought a proliferation of information and biotechnological advances.[12] In light of all the previously successful attacks, it is a weak argument to say that BW "has not been successful," based only on the Aum Shinrikyo's inability to kill Americans with botulinum toxin or its failed attempts to kill Japanese with anthrax.[13] In the twenty-first century, technological barriers are no longer as formidable as they once were, and some experts believe that a determined individual or group can independently develop BW mass-casualty weapons.[14]

MYTH FIVE: THERE ARE MORAL RESTRAINTS THAT HAVE KEPT AND WILL KEEP BW AGENTS FROM BEING USED

Most states in the twentieth century have generally avoided the use of BW agents. For example, the United States had an offensive BW program from 1942 to 1969, but it never used BW agents. The Soviets had enough BW agents weaponized to kill the world several times over and yet exhibited restraint. It may be that the various political, military, and moral constraints against BW use have thus far prevented BW on a mass scale, but it appears that we are now entering a new era. Jessica Stern, in *The Ultimate Terrorists*, outlines four techniques of "moral disengagement" that individuals and groups have used to justify their use of mass-casualty weapons.[15]

The following examples illustrate the lack of moral inhibition by various types of terrorism. On 26 February 1993, terrorist Ramzi Yousef and several other Muslim terrorists exploded a bomb intended to topple the World Trade Center twin towers and kill at least 250,000 people.[16] The blast, although not completely successful, killed six, injured more than 1,000, and inflicted costs in excess of $600,000,000.[17] On 19 April 1995, Timothy McVeigh committed the worst act of domestic terrorism by an American citizen when he bombed the Alfred P. Murrah Federal Building in Oklahoma City.[18] More than 550 people were targeted, and the resulting tragedy left 168 dead and hundreds of others wounded.[19] On 11 September 2001, international terrorists destroyed the twin towers of the World Trade Center, ruined over 20 adjacent buildings, and significantly damaged the Pentagon by hijacking and crashing US commercial airliners into these icons of American society. In less than two short hours, these brutal acts of terror killed approximately 3,000 innocent civilians and military personnel while injuring many thousands more and bringing US air travel to a temporary and very costly halt.[20]

We can look to the emergence of organizations such as al Qaida, Osama bin Laden's group, and see that any previous moral constraints to inflicting massive civilian deaths are no longer applicable. They have launched a "holy war" against the United States and are not reticent to inflict heavy casualties on US citizens—even if it entails the loss of their own lives. In fact, according to the holy war paradigm propagated by Bin Laden, great honor is supposed to accrue to those who die killing many "infidels." Thus, "morality" can be marshaled as a reason both to limit BW use and to advocate mass killings—depending on the decision maker's values and perspectives.

MYTH SIX: THE LONG INCUBATION PERIOD REQUIRED FOR BW AGENTS BEFORE ONSET OF SYMPTOMS MAKES BW USELESS TO USERS

There have already been multiple BW attacks, and to a savvy biological weaponeer, the incubation period can be used as an advantage rather than a disadvantage. The two following scenarios illustrate that advantage. In the first scenario, an anthrax attack is made on an adversary's military installation. That attack could render the installation nonfunctional within 72 hours. The first clinical cases of anthrax would probably manifest themselves in around 24 hours, with the number of subsequent cases increasing rapidly. A follow-on conventional military attack that was timed to occur three to four days after the BW attack would likely find the installation defenders laid low by the disease and therefore would be more likely to succeed. Moreover, because of the nature of the *Bacillus anthracis* organism, the attackers would not have to be overly concerned about significant secondary infections from their infected adversaries or by large amounts of residual spores in the environment.

The second scenario involves an attack on an adversary's population or military installation with Q fever (*Coxiella burnetti*). With Q fever's two- to 10-day incubation period, the attacker and his followers would have days to escape before their adversary would recognize that there had been an attack. Between the fifth and 10th day after the attack, the attackers could announce that a nonlethal weapon had been used as a "show of force and resolve" and demand whatever concessions they were after. The attackers would have little concern of being exposed to secondary infection because Q fever is not communicable. Likewise, the low fatality rate would take away the adversary's justification for a massive retaliation but at the same time leave the adversary's population with a heightened sense of fear because of their proven vulnerability.

What Would Motivate a BW Attack on the United States?

There are two primary motivations that might drive an adversary to attack the United States with a BW agent. Either one is enough to cause a nation, organization, or individual to act against the United States, but concerns should be particularly heightened when both of these motivations intersect.

The first motivation is to gradually "erode US influence" as a world superpower. Adversaries such as Iraq, Iran, or the al Qaida organization desire more influence in their region. They are infuriated that American infidels have increased their presence in the Middle East from three ships in 1949 to over 200,000 US military personnel in 2001.[21]

Likewise, there are other emerging economic powers in the world that see the United States in a love/hate relationship. They realize the United States is helping them to become economically sound, but they would ultimately like to take a piece of the economic action from the United States. These nations might also want to inflict damage to the US economy, and in their mind, level the playing field in a way that would minimize damage to their own economy. The far-right wing of groups with this motivation include religious terrorist groups such as Osama bin Laden's al Qaida who declare that they have a religious obligation to destroy the "evil race" in the name of "Allah."

The second motivation is categorized as "revenge or hate." At a time when the United States is an integral part of stimulating the global economy and thereby improving the standard of living for millions in the world, the so-called transparency of the United States inflames envy, which often leads to hatred, in millions around the world. The United States has 5 percent of the world's population yet uses 24 percent of the global energy.[22] The extravagance of the United States is seen by some as the reason for a worldwide moral decay. Often these same individuals may want to inflict revenge because of what they perceive the United States or its "puppet nations" have done to them individually, their family, or their group. Many of these individuals have been taught from childhood to hate the United States. This prejudice often grows as they see images on television that portray the United States as a drunken, immoral, gluttonous, and violent society.

There is synergism when a nation, group, or individual desires to erode US influence as a world superpower and is also full of revenge and hate. This effect would amplify their desire and ability to enlist support financially and deliver an effective BW attack. They then have a cause where emotion reinforces or even overrides the logic or illogic of such an attack.

Possible Future BW Scenarios

This author believes that there are three most likely BW scenarios the United States and its allies might face in the future:

- An agroterrorist event against the United States,
- A BW attack on United States and allied troops in the Middle East, and/or
- A bioterrorist attack against a large population center in the United States or an allied state.

Scenario One: An Agroterrorist Event

Anne Kohnen states that "agricultural targets are 'soft targets,' or ones that maintain such a low level of security that a terrorist could carry out an attack unobserved. Biological agents are small, inexpensive, and nearly impossible to detect. A terrorist may choose to use BW against agriculture simply because it is the easiest and cheapest way to cause large-scale damage."[23]

As was articulated by Mark Wheelis, a senior microbiologist at the University of California, Davis, many of the moral constraints that might inhibit an adversary can be overcome by using agroterrorism.[24] The US economy could be made chaotic by inflicting damage to the US agricultural industry with three to five BW agents over a few years. For example, the United Kingdom suffered a severe disruption in day-to-day life in 2001 when foot-and-mouth disease broke out, forcing the slaughter of hundreds of thousands of livestock. Estimated cleanup and economic loss is assumed to have reached $30 to $60 billion.[25] Belgium suffered an apparent agroterrorist event when dioxin was discovered in chicken feed.[26] This resulted in boycotts across Europe and Asia of Belgian meat products that cost their economy nearly $1 billion.[27] Such an incident in the United States could potentially jeopardize $140 billion in yearly pork, beef, and poultry exports.[28] Table 1 was developed to show the status of some of the offensive agricultural BW capabilities developed or maintained by certain nations.

This type of attack has an added benefit for the adversary: unless he desires otherwise, he may never be identified. Since the goal is not to achieve attention, but to promote the demise of and inflict pain on the United States, the perpetrators could maintain a safe distance and enjoy the daily news of turmoil in the United States. They could watch the successful completion of their plan as the contagious nature of their weapon operated on its own—the gift that keeps on giving. Perpetrators willing to use this style of BW attack(s) would have to recognize that it might take years to achieve their objective. Some world terrorists may be willing to wait and see their strategic plans carried out over this longer period of time.

SCENARIO TWO: A BW ATTACK ON FORCES IN THE MIDDLE EAST

This attack's goal is to have the United States withdraw its military forces from the region and possibly reduce its aid to allies like Israel. The Middle East contains more states with biological weapons than any other region of the world. According to the Center for Nonproliferation Studies at the Monterey Institute of International Studies, there are 11 states with suspected or confirmed offensive biological programs. Of these, six reside in the Middle East.[29] Additionally, more weapons of mass destruction (WMD) attacks have occurred in the Middle East than in any other region. Although most of the examples in table 2 are chemical warfare (CW) and not CBW, use clearly indicates that this region of the world has an entirely different view about the use of weapons considered taboo by much of the rest of the world. Table 2 shows some regional highlights.

So how would a BW attack be carried out in the Middle East?

Table 1
States with Past and Present Agricultural BW Capabilities

State	Status	Dates	Disease	Comments
Canada	Former	1941–60s	Anthrax, Rinderpest	Exact date of project termination unclear.
Egypt	Probable	1972–present	Anthrax, Brucellosis, Glanders, Psittacosis, Eastern Equine Encephalitis	(none)
France	Former	1939–72	Potato Beetle, Rinderpest	Exact date of project termination unclear.
Germany	Former	1915–17, 1942–45	Anthrax, Foot-and-Mouth Disease, Glanders, Potato Beetle, Wheat Fungus	In World War II experimented with Turnip Weevils, Antler Moths, Potato Stalk Rot/Tuber Decay, and misc. anticrop weeds.
Iraq	Known	1980s–present	Aflatoxin, Anthrax, Camelpox, Foot-and-Mouth Disease, Wheat Stem Rust (Camelpox may have been surrogate for Smallpox)	Believed to retain program elements despite UN disarmament efforts.
Japan	Former	1937–45	Anthrax, Glanders	During World War II experimented with misc. anticrop fungi, bacteria, nematodes.
North Korea	Probable	?–present	Anthrax	(none)
Rhodesia (Zimbabwe)	Uncertain/ Former	1978–80	Anthrax	Suspicious epidemic of cattle anthrax resulted in 182 human deaths. Some scientists believe government forces infected livestock to impoverish rural blacks during last phase of civil war.
South Africa	Former	1980s–93	Anthrax	(none)

TABLE 1 (CONT.)

State	Status	Dates	Disease	Comments
United Kingdom	Former	1937–60s	Anthrax	Exact date of project termination unclear.
United States	Former	1943–69	Anthrax, Brucellosis, Eastern and Western Equine Encephalitis, Foot-and-Mouth Disease, Fowl Plague, Glanders, Late Blight of Potato, Newcastle Disease, Psittacosis, Rice Blast, Rice Brown Spot Disease, Rinderpest, Venezuelan Equine Encephalitis, Wheat Blast Fungus, Wheat Stem Rust	(none)
USSR (Russia, Kazakhstan, Uzbekistan)	Formerly active; current status unclear	1935–92	African Swine Fever, Anthrax, Avian Influenza, Brown Grass Mosaic, Brucellosis, Contagious Bovine Pleuropneumonia, Contagious Ecthyma (sheep), Foot-and-Mouth Disease, Glanders, Mazie Rust, Newcastle Disease, Potato Virus, Psittacosis, Rice Blast, Rinderpest, Rye Blast, Tobacco Mosaic, Venezuelan Equine Encephalitis, Vesicular Stomatitis, Wheat and Barley Mosaic Streak, Wheat Stem Rust, parasitic insects, and insect attractants	(none)

Source: Monterey Institute of International Studies, Center for Nonproliferation Studies, *Agro-terrorism: Agriculture Biowarfare: State Programs to Develop Offensive Capabilities,* created October 2000, on-line, Internet, 25 January 2003, available from http://cns.miis.edu/research/cbw/agprogs.htm. (Chart edited for space considerations; see complete chart and extensive footnotes on Web page.)

There are multiple options an adversary might choose to pressure the United States to withdraw from the region. The three options discussed below are illustrative of the variety of problems those attacks could create.

An adversary might choose to use a nonlethal BW agent, perhaps VEE (Venezuelan Equine Encephalitis), on a US installation. Such an attack would make personnel sick and incapacitated, but would not kill them. It could be used to demonstrate an adversary's capability, resolve, and even compassion. The adversary could allow time to ensure that the attack was effective, that deaths were minimal, that people were recovering, and then announce why and what he had done. If the BW attack failed, then the adversary would not make an announcement or lose credibility. Likewise, if the attack caused many unexpected deaths, he could merely remain quiet and potentially avoid US retaliation.

With a successful attack, the adversary's announcement of responsibility could include a stated abhorrence to killing. He could announce that while he has lethal BW agents, he had elected not to kill the sons and daughters of the United States, because he only wants the US forces out of the region—killing would only be used as a last resort.

This approach would likely trigger great debates in Washington, D.C., and Middle Eastern countries, and might even cause the US Congress to pressure the president to withdraw US forces. If the United States then elected to stay in the region and a lethal attack did occur, local populations around US bases would die along with the targeted Americans. Thereafter, local governments would be under enormous pressure and might choose to ask the United States to withdraw rather than suffer additional BW attacks on their populations.

Another options an adversary might choose would be to release a lethal agent just outside a US base so that the wind would carry it away from the base. A desirable effect could be achieved by even a small attack aimed at killing as few as 20 to 50 of the local population. The downwind casualties would be blamed on the Americans, creating a local mistrust of the American government. The responsible group would never claim credit but would inform the media and others that the deaths were caused by US BW agents (even though the United States does not have any offensive BW agents). It's likely that the regional media would have a "heyday," which would lead to a groundswell of anger against the United States. Another similar attack could be launched after several months if the United States had not elected to significantly downsize its presence in the region. Again, the United States would be blamed, and locals might evacuate areas close to US installations. A

TABLE 2
EXAMPLES OF CBW USES IN THE MIDDLE EAST

Date	Country	Specific CB Agent	Description
1917	Iraq	glanders	In 1917, German agents infected over 4,500 British pack animals in Mesopotamia.
1920–30	Morocco	mustard	Spain employed mustard shells and bombs against the Riff tribes.
1930	Libya	mustard	Italy dropped 24 mustard gas bombs on an oasis fighting Libyan rebels.
1935–36	Ethiopia	mustard, tear gas, various other agents	Benito Mussolini authorized the use of chemical weapons on 16 Dec 1935, with the first attack on 23 Dec, when Italian air force planes sprayed mustard gas and dropped bombs filled with mustard agent on Ethiopian soldiers and civilians. Italian forces repeatedly attacked Ethiopian soldiers and civilians with mustard gas and used tear gas, sneezing gas, and various asphyxiating agents. A letter from the Ethiopian delegate to the League of Nations, dated 13 Apr 1936, alleges Italy made 20 "poison gas attacks," with mustard gas being used frequently.
1930s	Kurdistan	lung irritants	Soviet Union was accused of using lung irritants against Kurdistan tribesmen.
1944	Israel/ Palestine	unknown	Plot by the grand mufti of Jerusalem and Germans to poison wells in Tel Aviv. Ten containers were discovered with enough poison to kill 10,000 people.
1957	Oman	BW	Britain was accused of using biological warfare agents in Oman.
1963–67	Yemen	mustard, phosgene, tear gas, possibly nerve gas	Egypt employed chemical weapons against royalist forces in the Yemen civil war. Egypt used Soviet-built aerial bombs to deliver phosgene and aerial bombs as well as artillery shells abandoned by British forces after World War I to deliver mustard gas. According to chemical weapons expert Milton Leitenberg, some of the nerve agent reportedly used by Egyptian forces may actually have

TABLE 2 (CONT.)

Date	Country	Specific CB Agent	Description
			consisted of hand grenades fitted with containers of organophosphate pesticides. This incident is sometimes referred to as the first use of nerve gases, but according to some reports, this is unsubstantiated.
1965	Iraq	unknown	In May 1965 at a press conference in London, a spokesman for the Kurdish Democratic Party stated that on at least two occasions during the pervious six weeks the Iraqi army had used gas against Kurdish forces.
1984–88	Iran/Iraq	sarin, tabun, sulfur, mustard	During the 1980s Iran-Iraq War, Iraq repeatedly attacked Iranian troops with chemical warfare agents. The first allegation of Iraqi CW attacks was in Nov 1980. In Nov 1983, Iran made its first official complaint to the UN regarding Iraqi CW attacks. Iraq was confirmed to have used mustard/nerve agents against Iranian forces from 1983 to 1988. Iran is believed to have conducted initial CW attacks by firing captured Iraqi CW munitions at Iraqi forces in 1984 or 1985. By the end of the war, Iran reportedly employed domestically produced CW munitions against Iraqi soldiers. First-ever use of tabun (nerve agent) on the battlefield was by Iraq in 1984.
1987	Chad	unknown	Libya reportedly used Iranian-supplied chemical weapons against Chad troops.
1988	Iraq	hydrogen cyanide, mustard, sarin, tabun	Iraqi warplanes attacked the Kurdish city of Halabja, Iraq, with mustard and nerve agents, killing up to 5,000 people, mostly civilians. (Following Iraqi mustard gas attacks on Halabja, fleeing Kurds may have been mistaken for Iraqi troops and bombarded with hydrogen cyanide [AC] artillery shells by Iranian forces.)
1990	Sudan	mustard	President Omar al-Bashir's Sudanese government had been accused of

TABLE 2 (CONT.)

Date	Country	Specific CB Agent	Description
			producing CW with Iranian and/or Iraqi assistance. The government was accused of initiating several mustard gas attacks on civilians and Sudanese People's Liberation Army forces in the Nuba mountain region. The allegations were not independently confirmed.
1997	Jordan	toxic gas	Israeli agents used toxic gas in assassination attempt on a Hamas official in Amman.

Source: Unclassified research at the USAF Counterproliferation Center, Maxwell AFB, Ala., 2001.

continued US presence in the region could become politically impossible to maintain. Such small-scale attacks could be repeated over and over with lethal or nonlethal BW agents.

An adversary could also use a lethal agent directly against a US installation in the region. The adversary would never claim credit for this attack option, but might release a small dose of BW agent like anthrax or tularemia to try to kill two to 10 Americans. These deaths could raise fear of future lethal attacks and cause US officials and members of Congress to debate the merit of a continued US presence in the Middle East. In a response similar to the last option, the host government might become uncomfortable with a US presence if a few of its local citizens also died. A single attack might not cause the United States to "tuck tail and run," but if repeated often enough, the United States might reconsider and remove its forces from harm's way.

SCENARIO THREE: A BIOTERRORIST ATTACK ON A LARGE US OR ALLIED POPULATION CENTER

The American public learned to fear anthrax after letters containing the substance had been sent via the US Postal Service to senators and various new agencies shortly after the 11 September 2001 terrorist attacks. The resultant deaths and the discovery that some al Qaida terrorists had explored renting crop dusters caused the US government to temporarily ground these important agricultural aircraft. The news media, in turn, informed the public that biological attacks were possible.

Similar to the 11 September attacks, a BW attack might be a coordinated attack and take place in several major US cities. Anthrax would probably be the agent of choice in a mass-casualty attempt since it is not contagious and the perpetrators would not have to worry about the disease getting back to their country. Five 100-pound bags of anthrax could easily be smuggled into the United States using one of the many shipments of grain that arrive at US ports every day. These bags could be made to blend in with the shipment and lined with plastic so that no powder would be prematurely released. Three to five major cities, on the order of Houston or Los Angeles, could be targeted and would require only a 100-pound bag each. An appropriate aerosolizing device, easily procured in the United States, could be mounted on an automobile, airplane, or boat. The terrorists that perpetrate this attack would not have to die because they could be vaccinated and treated with antibiotics prior to delivering the agents, which would protect them even if they were exposed. They could also easily depart the country before the first symptoms appeared and defeat the ability of federal authorities to respond and arrest them.

Hundreds of thousands of American citizens could potentially become infected and die if the agent were correctly manufactured and employed and if optimal climatic conditions were present during the attack. Such a mass-casualty attack would overwhelm the US medical system and a human, economic, and political catastrophe would result.

Summary

Many of our national leaders still do not believe that a mass-casualty BW event will happen in the next 10 years—in spite of our experience with the anthrax attacks that followed the 11 September 2001 attacks. This view is based on their belief in one of the several myths discussed in this article. Such myths continue to inhibit the adequate funding of US and allied biodefense.

US national security leaders must appreciate the urgency to refocus programs and develop appropriate budgets to support a concerted biodefense effort to counter BW possibilities. The counteragroterrorism effort is woefully underfunded. This program is of extreme importance, and it needs billions of additional dollars to upgrade the protection of our agricultural industry.

United States military forces in the Middle East must be well prepared for a BW attack, but all countries in the region have a long way to go before their biodefense equipment and tactics are adequate for the threat. US Central Command and the Office of the Secretary of Defense have an aggressive cooperative defense initiative (CDI) with allies and friends in the region designed to overcome the threat of WMD. Huge steps forward have already been made in preparation for a BW attack, but there is still much work ahead. While detection capabilities in the region have improved, lab results still require several hours, and these are limited to just a few of the possible BW agents. Only US installations have detection capabilities in place, and there are none in the local areas. Although there is a correct emphasis on ballistic missiles within the CDI, the biocruise missiles threat, described by Kiziah in his *Assessment of the Emerging Biocruise Threat*, may be an even more likely threat and should be addressed with an equal effort.[30]

One of the most horrifying possibilities would be a coordinated and simultaneous BW attack against several major cities in the United States and in allied countries. Those attacks could occur today, and we might not become aware of them for days. A series of major exercises have documented the likely and frightening results; many hundreds of thousands could die, and US and allied societies could be thrown into chaos and panic.

Myths to the contrary, the biological warfare and bioterrorist threats are real and require the full commitment of the United States and its allies to have a well-funded biodefense effort to produce an effective defense. The United States must take up the yoke of preventing such attacks and prepare for consequence management—managing the aftermath of such attacks—with the same vigor our nation used during the cold war. Otherwise, our national security stands in jeopardy.

PHILIP HANDLEMAN

Winged Cowboys:
The Story Behind
Air Mobility Command's
Latest Biennial Rodeo

Standard for the Lifeline

A day after the election of 2000, in which Americans went to the polls
in what was tantamount to a referendum on a sometimes surreal presi-
dency, a Vietnam-era Air Force sergeant, unknown to the public, quietly succumbed to the ravages of cancer at his home in Connecticut. In
the election's chaotic aftermath, the passing of the sergeant, his heroic
deeds, and his sweeping influence on the Air Force went virtually unnoticed.

Thirty-one years earlier, aboard an obsolete military aircraft drawing enemy ground fire on a night mission northeast of Saigon, John L.
Levitow, the aircraft's loadmaster, performed acts of incredible bravery, securing his place in the pantheon of Air Force icons. The AC-47,
a slow moving World War II-vintage cargo plane converted into an
aerial gunship, was a veritable sitting duck, a manifestation of America's ill-preparedness for a guerilla war. In theory, the gunship, orbiting
overhead, would lay down a concentrated salvo from rapid-firing side-
mounted weapons, incapacitating clusters of enemy troops. But, in the

darkened sky, a mortar shell tore into the starboard wing of Levitow's aircraft, blasting away a three-foot section. Shards flew in every direction, swarming the airframe, ripping into it with a multitude of perforations.

A high-intensity flare, about to be thrown from the side hatch of the gunship as part of normal procedure to illuminate the jungle canopy below, was jarred loose from the hands of a crewman. It fell onto the floor of the mid-cabin where it began to wobble near thousands of rounds of live ammunition as the pilot of the now seriously damaged plane strained to regain control. Since the fuse, with a built-in delay of a few seconds, had been armed, it was critical for the flare, a kind of ticking time bomb, to be expelled before setting off a catastrophic explosion.

Five crewmen, including Levitow, were wounded from the flying debris of the mortar shell. Levitow's body had been slashed in 40 places, causing him to bleed profusely. Despite the severity of his injuries, he retrieved a disabled compatriot who was in jeopardy of falling out of the plane's open hatch. Levitow then turned his attention to the potentially cataclysmic flare, trying to grab it, but its 27-pound weight coupled with the aircraft's steep angle of bank made that futile. Refusing to give up, the loadmaster then threw himself over the flare, hoping that its fuse had been disturbed from the jostling, but knowing that its encased magnesium might ignite at any moment.

Nearing unconsciousness, Levitow crawled towards the open hatch with the treacherous flare under his belly, streaks of blood delineating his path across the cabin's floor. He pushed the flare out of the crippled plane in the nick of time for it detonated the moment it left the cabin. Having saved seven crewmates, Levitow then passed out.

The gunship staggered back to base that night, concluding a new chapter in the history of Air Force heroism. Amazingly, following hospitalization in Japan, the 23 year-old Levitow returned to Vietnam and flew another 20 combat missions bringing his total to 200. He was summoned to the White House 15 months after his life-saving achievement where he was awarded his country's highest military decoration for valor under fire, the Medal of Honor. Serving at the rank of airman first class at the time of his harrowing mission meant that Levitow became the most junior Air Force recipient of the nation's highest honor.

For the crews flying and maintaining Air Force heavies today, Levitow's legacy lives on in a tangible way. Taking its cue from the naval tradition of naming capital ships after the sea service's heroes, the Air Force fittingly selected a leviathan of the air, sometimes deployed on humanitarian missions to remote corners of the world, to commemorate its courageous sergeant. In 1998, one of the aircraft in Air Mobility Command's fleet of new cargo planes, a mammoth C-17 Globemaster III, was christened *The Spirit of Sgt. John L. Levitow.*

This plane, with the name of an Air Force legend painted on its nose, cruises higher, faster, and farther than the antiquated AC-47 gunship ever could. Yet, Air Force leaders would assert that certain foundational principles transcend technological superiority, and that these values, gallantry among them, underlie any mission success. On a continuum of flights spanning the globe, the *Levitow* is a powerful reminder of the lofty expectations for the men and women of Air Mobility Command (AMC), the tanker and transport lifeline of the American military.

Converging on Fort Bragg

By the first Sunday in May of the new millennium, more than 100 teams in over 80 aircraft from around the world descended on Pope Air Force Base, the main air terminus servicing historic Fort Bragg in rural North Carolina, for a week of competitions known as Air Mobility Rodeo. Started in 1962, the biennial event features competitions in such mobility related operations as aerial refueling, aeromedical evacuation, and personnel airdrops. Aimed at honing the skills of a wide array of AMC's professionals, the biennial exercise must have as its nexus a facility like Pope for it adjoins a major Army post, which offers the necessary support elements from paratroopers to firing ranges.

Fort Bragg, a sprawling reservation that dwarfs the local town of Fayetteville, is famous in its own right as the home of the XVIII Airborne Corps, the 82nd Airborne Division, and the Special Warfare School of the elite Army Rangers. The history of the home-stationed units is reflected in street names like Ardennes, Normandy, and Desert Storm. The rows of vintage brick buildings and wide-open parade grounds contribute to a sense of place, the evocation of the warrior spirit. Young men and women, many yet to outgrow their teens, stand guard at various locations on the post, attired in berets whose colors signify their affiliation. When, at the end of the day, trumpets blare retreat over loudspeakers, these soldiers turn to the flag nearest them and snap to attention in a ritual that lets any observer know America is in good hands.

The air base and the fort are inescapably intertwined. Members of the 82nd Airborne Division, known as the "All-American Division," often boast that they are ready to deploy on a moment's notice, sort of like a worldwide 911 force. When the President hits an impasse in his dealings with an obstreperous foreign ruler and needs to display the national will, the denizens here are fond of saying that their Commander-in Chief's first call will be to Fort Bragg. What makes rapid troop deployment possible—part of the Air Force concept of global reach—is the nearby airlift capacity at Pope. For their part, the Air Force folks at Pope assert that they put the "air" in "airborne."

Examples of the two installations meshing to get men and equipment overseas in a hurry include the actions in Grenada (1983), Honduras (1988), Panama (1989), and the Persian Gulf (1990–1991). Pope, which traces its establishment to the days immediately following World War I, finds itself oddly confined to a main runway that is about 7,500 feet in length. Surrounding terrain and surface roads have the base hemmed in. When temperatures and humidity rise to oppressive levels at midday, impeding aircraft performance, commanders aboard the older heavies have been known to privately wish for an extra 1,500 feet of runway.

The expanse of land adjacent to the runway is, however, rich in breadth. In fact, the air base is awash in a sea of concrete ramp space, a welcome feature when it comes to accommodating the scores of transient aircraft participating in Rodeo. Just to be sure there would be enough room, most of the permanently-based A-10 close air support fighters of the 23rd Fighter Group, which sport shark's teeth symbolizing the unit's lineage to the legendary "Flying Tigers," had been flown to other locations in advance of Rodeo.

Upon landing at Pope preparatory to the official start of Rodeo, the teams were processed in a sweltering hall on the edge of the tarmac. Enlisted personnel behind counters labored to fill out the inevitable forms for the mass of humanity flooding into the building. Lines grew longer and longer, but the arriving crews, accustomed to the military's ubiquitous bureaucracy, took it in stride.

The magnitude of the logistics—providing lodging, meals, ground transportation, fuel, spare parts, etc. for the hordes of participating airmen and their aircraft - challenged the host organization, mirroring the real-world scenario of a sizable force buildup. The hangar-like structure, referred to during the week of Rodeo as the "Bunkhouse," filled with the sounds and smells of thousands of perspiring flight-suited personnel alternately taking swigs from complimentary water bottles and greeting friends with high-fives. Following a spine-tingling Sunday afternoon of pomp and ceremony, the teams would be able to collect their thoughts one last time before the start of the competitions early the next morning.

STICKING TOGETHER AND PRESSING ON

Every AMC wing represented at Rodeo sends its most outstanding crew in each competition category. Reservedly and absent bluster, participants refer to the assembled teams as the best of the best. Air Mobility Rodeo is a kind of Olympics for the people in the business of tankers and transports. The Air Force invites U.S. allies to "play" in these "games," and at Rodeo 2000 teams came from Belgium, Brazil, Canada, Egypt, France, South Korea, Turkey, and the United Kingdom. Encouraging international participation allows the Air Force to gauge its proficiency and at the same time permits the foreign teams to strive towards compatibility with the air arm of the world's remaining superpower.

For 11½ hours in each of the next four days, starting at 5:00 A.M., an inexorable line of aircraft thundered down the runway, usually to the northeast given the prevailing winds, on an average of one every 10 minutes. Even though the heat and humidity conspired to produce stifling conditions, the tankers and transports lifted easily from the scorched pavement as they were loaded lightly. The skies over rural North Carolina came alive with crisscrossing military planes finished mostly in the now standard colors of low-visibility gray and camouflage green.

Tankers, including an ancient E model KC-135 from a Reserve unit, had to arrive at their rendezvous points at the designated time. Venerable C-130s, the most numerous of the aircraft types at Rodeo, were graded on the precision with which they performed personnel airdrops. In a remote section of Fort Bragg, new C-17s showed their worth kicking up clouds of dust at a short, unimproved airstrip during stimulated assault landings. At every juncture, umpires were on hand, keeping track of the participants (maybe contestants would be a more apt term), scoring each aspect of an aircrew's performance.

Ground crews came in for their share of scrutiny as well. The Air Force's most senior maintainers and crew chiefs, wearing hats or armbands to convey their status as umpires, watched mechanics and loadmasters from a distance so as not to interfere with the engine inspection of a C-141 or the on/off loading of a C-5. Often the umpires came to the ramp armed with clipboards, which they used for keeping tally.

Points were deducted from a team's score when, for example, the loadmaster forgot to comply with the regulation mandating human remains be loaded with the head facing to the forward of the aircraft. This simple measure of respect, though not life threatening if unfulfilled, was on the umpires' checklist. The heart-wrenching images in recent years of AMC transports returning from distant lands and off loading coffins serve as a reminder that proper handling in this category is not merely academic.

On the teeming concrete, which on some days during Rodeo 2000 radiated palpable waves of heat that prompted some observers to remark that they might be able to fry eggs on the surface, it was easy to become distracted. The situation was exacerbated by tight operating tolerances and bulky materials, which, in the absence of solid training and a dedication to the mission, could have led to a debilitating frustration. Moreover, loadmasters were given time constraints in which the task had to be accomplished, as though the aircraft were subject to enemy attack if they stayed stationary too long. Handling cargo under these non-conducive conditions, crews had to strain to keep their focus. Concentration was key to success.

Life-threatening mistakes result in proportionately more points being taken away. This happened, for example, when an aircrew member performing a post-flight inspection forgot to install a locking pin in his aircraft's nose wheel door mechanism before poking his head up into the wheel well, creating a scenario whereby the doors could come crashing down on him. Importantly, though, the embarrassment that flows from such a procedural lapse, when penalized by the peripatetic umpires, virtually guarantees that the offending crew member will never repeat that mistake.

The unvarnished grading by umpires was a humbling experience for most teams, fostering renewed attention to detail. Every crew learned something on the flightline or in the air during the week of Rodeo. Perhaps by holding airmen accountable before their peers, with potentially lifesaving after effects, Rodeo makes its greatest system-wide contribution. The lessons of Rodeo would be carried back to home bases and shared with squadron mates.

Each team member knew that his or her performance would affect the overall grade, so every participant within sight on the massive ramp demonstrated a perceptible commitment. A leading example was a certain wing's operations group commander, one of the highest time tanker pilots at Rodeo, who one night during the week consumed some exotic concoction offered by the French team. Although suffering the next morning from, shall we say, an inability to keep things down, he came to the ramp and stood by his aircraft as his ground crew competed. Looking like death warmed over and turning to the side every so often for nature to do its work, be stayed until ordered to bed.

Nowhere was the spirit of teamwork and the ethic of loyalty more apparent than when one of the big jets spooled up its engines and began taxiing out. Invariably, on each such occasion during the week of Rodeo, its ground crew formed up line abreast to one side of the aircraft just beyond the reach of its wingtip, facing the flight deck. Then the behemoth started to move. The senior airman called his colleagues to attention and then, in perfect unison as if practiced many times but with the enthusiasm of a first try, they raised their hands in a mass salute, inside the cockpit, the gesture of respect, the noblest of military honors, was snappily returned. The ground crew members held their salute until their plane started to turn. Then all hands swung down in a coordinated arcing motion. It was the ground crew's way of saying: "Have a good flight, sirs, and we are with you all the way."

Meanwhile, in the densely wooded thickets on the sprawling grounds of Fort Bragg, amid the intermittent booms of distant artillery, competing teams of security forces scrambled through the demanding gauntlet of an obstacle course that surely would leave even the likes of a James Bond panting. After running a winding path and vaulting over assorted shoulder-high barricades, the men confronted a large diameter rope that had been moistened by splashes from a muddy pond directly underneath.

Although the competition manual calls for the use of gloves in this part of the event, most participants refused, preferring the better grip of bare hands. Eschewing band protection, which assures deep and painful rope burns, also evinces a raw machismo, an unwritten but important requisite for acceptance into the brotherhood of Air Force security forces. Most participants do not make it all the way up the daunting rope and fall unceremoniously into the pond, becoming drenched in brown murk for the rest of the competition. After a second attempt at the rope climb, competitors were waved on by the ever-present umpires.

The finale for competing security forces came later in the week at the ominous "Combat Tactics Event" where teams in full combat gear were brought to a make-believe Third World village, constructed like a Hollywood set and located in a desolate corner of the Fort Bragg reservation. A 150-pound dummy, outfitted in battle dress uniform and nicknamed Sergeant Lucky, represented a wounded American hostage awaiting rescue. As soon as the security forces team entered the perimeter, its members were surrounded by shabbily garbed and boisterous "villagers" who in reality are off-duty military personnel volunteering for a line of work not described in any recruiting brochure.

In the post-Cold War era, U.S. military leaders believe the likeliest form of combat for ground forces, including those of the Air Force, is urban warfare—close-in fighting along village streets, flushing out hidden adversaries building by building. Searching for Sergeant Lucky, the security teams fall under sniper fire and quickly start shooting back, all weapons having been muted with specially-designed lasers instead activating sensors which sound alarms if participants are "shot." At times, the scene took on the appearance of a modern version of a classic shootout in a frontier town of the Old West.

On a typically blistering afternoon under the unforgiving North Carolina sun, a security forces team made remarkable progress in extracting the dummy from a church on the village square. But snipers popped up, and the team members' alarms started to whale. Only one team member was left unscathed. With his adrenaline pumping copiously, he darted out into the field of fire, miraculously dodged the bullets (laser beams), and dragged Sergeant Lucky to a parked HUMVEE. With the half-hour time limit for rescue almost expired, the team member struggled to lift Sergeant Lucky into the vehicle, ending up shoving and kicking the dummy into compliance.

Racing the vehicle down a side road to an outer perimeter about a half-mile away, which constituted the finish line, the team member exceeded the time limit by only a matter of seconds. It was a valiant effort that left everyone watching from the luxury of a rooftop vantage point both exhausted and awed. Within minutes, the wing commander, who had been observing his security forces team, joined the team in the shade of a stand of trees and began to tell his men, one by one, how proud he was of their performance.

The team member who hauled out Sergeant Lucky was overcome with emotion for earlier in the week he had let down his teammates on the firing range by improperly loading his sidearm, causing it to jam at a critical moment. Redeemed, he now held back tears and embraced his wing commander.

Dodge City

By custom, the Rodeo experience includes an outdoor shindig for all teams following the completion of the competitions. By late afternoon of the fourth day, the only official business remaining was the next day's closing ceremony at which awards would be presented to Rodeo's winners. Given the conclusion of the graded events, the participants were noticeably relaxed as they came together in this traditional second-to-the-last-day celebration.

"Pizza Night" as it was billed occurred atop a modest plateau, referred to as "Dodge City" for the week in keeping with Rodeo's theme. Practically all of Rodeo's 2,500 participants filtered into the fenced off plateau, an ordinarily abandoned perch which rises to one side of the air base's central infrastructure. They passed through a guarded checkpoint in cars brimming with their teammates, ready to party and burn off the vestiges of the receding tension. A constant bewailing of rock music, albeit a tame variety courtesy of an Air Force jazz band, satiated the air as those in attendance strolled with a pizza slice in one hand and a can of beer in the other. Conversing with squadron buddies required shouting over the pervasive background noise.

Circulating among his troops on Pizza Night was the popular and effective AMC Commander at that time, General Charles T. "Tony" Robertson, Jr. Against the backdrop of an escalating operations tempo (even before Operation Enduring Freedom) coupled with service-wide budget cuts until recently, AMC, like the Air Force as a whole, has had its hands full meeting its obligations. The situation has been compounded by aging hardware. In some cases the airframes in use are older than the flight crews who operate them. Procurement of upgrades like engine retrofits for KC-135 tankers and of new aircraft like C-17 transports seems to move at a glacial pace.

Under the circumstances, holding together the patchwork fleet and maintaining a sense of purpose down the chain of command deserve note and praise. Robertson, who projected a high profile at Rodeo 2000 IV made improved infrastructure and caring for the troops high priorities on the premises that a military force, especially one as important as the aerial lifeline, must have adequate resources and an unwavering faith in the leadership. He would know about such things for, like the sergeant whose heroic deeds are memorialized on the nose of one of the cargo planes then under his command, Robertson received his baptism of fire aboard a gunship in Vietnam.

Now commanded by General John W. Handy, himself a Vietnam veteran with more than 300 combat hours flying the C-130, AMC has been stretched even thinner by its intense operational tempo in support of the global war on terrorism. The experiences of Rodeo 2000 are being applied in real-world scenarios, including the airlifting of troops and materiel to the far corners of the world with commensurate aerial refueling. Also, no less than 2.4 million humanitarian food rations have been delivered in the Afghani theater.

Because of the demands of the new war on terrorism, AMC announced in early 2002 that its biennial exercise originally scheduled for spring 2002, would be postponed until June 2003. The Rodeo cycle, though delayed, will resume, and when that time comes there will be many AMC aircrew and maintainers with new lessons to pass on.

At Rodeo on that spring evening in 2000, with the sun sinking behind the horizon and casting a magnificent glow, the North Carolina countryside became enveloped in an all-encompassing aquamarine firmament showcasing wispy clouds enlivened by reddish-orange tints. It was at once a tranquil and inviting sky, the special province of the proud men and women of Air Mobility Command.

ROBERT J. BUNKER, PH.D.

★ ★ ★ ★ ★ ★ ★ ★

Defending Against the Non-State (Criminal) Soldier: Toward a Domestic Response Network

Increasingly, national security scholars recognize that the world in which we were born is passing away and, with it, many of the premises, conventions and structures of modern civilization. Research suggests that the transition into the post-modern era will usher in scientific, economic, social, political and military changes of a magnitude never before experienced in American history. Equivalent in scale to the European Renaissance and the Dark Ages, this revolution in political and military affairs, offers both great potentials and dangers for the American public. One of the more fundamental challenges we will face concerns the protection of our citizens. Traditional methods of public policing will become increasingly inadequate as the nature of war changes and assumptions concerning "the rule of law" come into question. Ultimately, the development of a domestic response network will be required if our public institutions are to fulfill the basic security needs of a democratic society.

The Non-State (Criminal) Soldier

One of the more significant attributes of epochal change is the emergence of the non-state (criminal) soldier. Research suggests that this development stems from the failure of the dominant state to remain relevant to the requirements of new forms of civilization, energy sources and developing technologies. As the transition to the post-modern epoch proceeds, the failed-state phenomenon will become an increasingly global issue. Within these former nation-states, war and crime has fully blurred. Conflict has become an intra-state rather than an inter-state activity, with the focus on tribal and ethnic divisions and fragmented social structures based on "haves" and "have nots." The combatants no longer represent the public institutions of the state, but rather non-state entities such as terrorist and guerrilla groups, private armies and security firms, militias, narco-cartels and other criminally based organizations.

Domestically, we must be concerned about the metamorphosis of disenfranchised citizens into non-state soldiers within the United States in the decades to come. In his November 1997 *Crime & Justice International* article, "Third-Generation Street Gangs: Turf, Cartels and Net-Warriors," law enforcement professional and analyst John Sullivan discusses the likely rise of a mercenary-type street gang based on power or financial acquisition goals, with fully evolved political aims. An analysis of linkages between San Diego and Chicago street gangs and the Arellano-Felix cartel in Mexico and the Libyan government, respectively, portray the growing internationalization of some of these criminal groups. If only 1 percent of the estimated 650,000 to 1 million street gang members were to develop into Net-Warriors (a "cyber" form of post-modern soldier), there would be a considerable insurgent force with which to contend within the continental United States.

Segments of other disenfranchised groups within American society must also be considered for their potential to evolve into non-state soldiers. The anti-government Patriot or Militia movement of recent years is also of concern. The Southern Poverty Law Center estimated that 858 active Patriot groups existed in the United States in 1996, and that they were attempting to create a national militia intelligence network. Motorcycle gang members tied into criminal enterprise networks, violent anti-abortionists such as Phineas Priests, malicious hackers allied to various cyber-tribes, and body armor-clad, assault gun-toting criminals are among the growing list of those who may pose security issues because of their propensity for acts of domestic terrorism.

Nation-State Capability Gap

The public institutions of the nation-state were never designed to counter such an unconventional threat. Law enforcement is meant to contend with a minimal level of crime within a relatively peaceful society. The armed forces address *external* threats to such a society by confronting the armed forces of other nation-states. Non-state forces disrupt the natural order of the international system because of the gray area between crime and war within which they exist. Further, the command and control structures of these groups are becoming increasingly sophisticated. Communications via the Internet provide criminal-soldiers with quicker reaction cycles than traditional, hierarchical police and military forces.

Law enforcement is often outclassed when faced with proto-criminal soldiers who employ secondary devices to kill first responders, religious fanatics who use nerve agents in transit systems, or drug posse members who use hand grenades or assault-type weapons. Similarly, Western military forces have tremendous difficulty operating in failed-state environments against local militiamen who use mobs of women and children as human shields and strike at weak points such as troop barracks with truck bombs.

As a result of this capability gap, police and military functions have a tendency to blur toward each other. Domestically, this can be seen with the rise of Tactical Operations Units (TOUs)—also known as Special Weapons and Tactics (SWAT) teams—which are meant to contend with high-risk situations. In their March 1997 *Police Chief* article, "Tactical Operations Units: A National Study," Dr. Peter Kraska and Larry Gaines reported that 89 percent of non-federal U.S. law enforcement agencies with at least 100 sworn officers and populations of more than 50,000 had TOUs. Used far more frequently than ever before, these units are regularly armed with tactical headsets (77 percent), night vision equipment (76 percent) and military-style weaponry such as HK MP5s (83 percent) and M-16s (61 percent).

On the flip side, U.S. armed forces that are deployed for stability and support operations in failed states now recognize the value of military-police units, various forms of less-lethal weaponry and public relations with the media. This is because American soldiers are increasingly being held accountable for the well-being of the non-combatant citizens in their area of operations. Rather than assuming the traditional role of occupation forces of a vanquished nation-state, American troops increasingly operate more like a global police against a different enemy—the spread of chaos and anarchy.

Private Security Forces and Mercenaries

Periods of epochal change are also marked by the proliferation of private security forces and mercenaries. Because of both real and perceived vulnerability to lawlessness and criminality, these private armies contract out to individuals, businesses and even governments to provide security services.

Domestically, private security guards far outnumber public police officers, with this trend intensifying. In Dallas, private security guards now outnumber local law enforcement officers by about seven to one. In other areas of the country, such as South Florida, the firm Critical Intervention Services (CIS) is being used to patrol failed communities represented by low-income housing tracts. With their bullet-resistant vests and .357 magnums, these security forces dress to intimidate.

In regions across the country, private gated communities and complexes are mushrooming, as many citizens decide to withdraw from public areas and wall themselves and their families off from the dangers around them. Firms such as Pinkerton's, Inc., and Kroll Associates, Inc., are expanding their influence as top corporate clients seek to better protect their business operations and personnel. Since 1997, Pinkerton's has been offering businesses around-the-clock Suspicious Package Evaluation Teams to quickly scan suspicious parcels on site.

This trend toward the privatization of "public defense" is also evident in foreign stability and support operations where calls for "mercenary peacekeepers" have become increasingly frequent. Besieged underdeveloped countries, the United States and even the United Nations are now involved in varying degrees with the hiring of private security forces and mercenaries for operations in failed or failing states.

Why a Domestic Response Network?

The very real danger is that the public institutions of the nation-state may not be able to respond in a "not war-not crime" operational environment. If our people are unable to live, work and raise their families in relative peace, then the state has failed to provide for the common defense. There is also a real concern that private security firms may begin to usurp the position of public law enforcement agencies in protecting our people. Basic protection would then become a commodity sold to the highest bidder, rather than a public good guaranteed by the constitution.

This strategic-level domestic security dilemma has not yet been fully recognized by the government, which has been focused on the more immediate danger of the non-state soldier threat—the eventual employment of weapons of mass destruction (WMDs) by international or domestic terrorists. While a centralized federal approach is fine for dealing with conventional threats to national security, it is less effective in addressing the new threats developing from the post-modern security environment.

Ultimately, what will be required in support of federal directed efforts is a state, county, and municipal level public, and probably private, integrated network to emerge in support of the qualitatively different domestic security requirements of the 21st century. Rather than a centralized approach to crisis and consequence management, this would be a "webbed" structure based upon a nodal organizational scheme.

Such "semi-leaderless and leaderless networks" can provide many benefits in support of traditional public law enforcement agencies and other first responders. First, they increase the information flow among agencies as data and knowledge are shared outside of traditional hierarchies and bureaucratic fiefdoms. This helps to eliminate informational seams—a key vulnerability within the emerging "cyber" battlespace.

Second, these networks allow a joint approach to identifying and solving (or neutralizing) problems. Trends, incidents and events are analyzed in parallel to each other simultaneously across the network. A physical, phone or virtual query can be analyzed by the rest of the network. Over time, this allows the network to develop a shared image of the state it is attempting to achieve.

Third, networks possess reaction cycles far superior to those of hierarchical structures. In an ever-changing environment, such as during a WMD incident, the crisis management team's ability to be proactive, rather than reactive, is critical.

Fourth, virtual reachback and support capabilities emerge where none existed before. A TOU member with a computer link and direct camera-feed to HAZMAT or bomb disposal personnel has a significant advantage in making immediate life-and-death decisions.

Early Domestic Response Networks

The benefits of a networked approach to countering street gangs, domestic terrorism, drug trafficking and other emergent domestic security concerns have increasingly been recognized by a dynamic group of entrepreneurial law enforcement, emergency responder, military and national security professionals. Three of these networks are institutionally sanctioned; the fourth is a private, free-standing, open-source intelligence group. All can be considered both "informational bridges" between traditional hierarchical agencies and new proto-entities themselves. Because most of these networks are experimental in nature, they tend to represent a trial-and-error process of inter-agency and even inter-sector (government, academia and industry) cooperation. Being so new, they are also typically underfunded, and rely heavily on participants' donations of additional time, effort and funds to keep them viable in their early stages of development.

Early networks appear to be of two types. The first is physically based, bringing together professionals from across agency jurisdictions to meet each month in a centralized location. In crisis situations, the network can be activated by means of pagers or fax lines. The second type is virtual-based, operating as a closed, unclassified information-sharing group using either an electronic mailing list and/or a secure Web site location. Hybrid networks are dual-dimensional in nature, combining both physical and virtual characteristics.

Most of these networks seem to be emerging first in the extended Los Angeles and San Diego metropolitan regions, which were early centers of street gang and cross-border drug cartel activity respectively.

In Los Angeles, county sheriff's department members have used this network approach first to combat street gangs and now to address domestic terrorism. The Southern California Gang Investigators' Association, originally established in 1977, has not only spread throughout California but replicated itself in network associations across the United States. This mature network of primarily law enforcement, probation, parole and prosecution agencies has been tracking gang members via the Gang Reporting, Evaluation and Tracking (GREAT) system since the mid-to late 1980s. Today, a second-generation system known as CAL/GANG, which is a Web-based application, is further extending this network by allowing for better cross-departmental cooperation.

Inaugurated in April 1996, the Los Angeles County Terrorism Early Warning Group (TEW), based at the County Emergency Operations Center, has emerged as an integral component of the Los Angeles Operational Terrorism Response & Management Plan, providing the link between existing crisis and threat warning capabilities and the local emergency response community. This experimental physical network is even more comprehensive than the more mature one directed toward street gangs. Its membership and linkages include city, county and federal law enforcement and emergency services, infrastructure and support, national laboratories, private industry, the military and academia both within and outside of Los Angeles County. As this network begins to generate national interest, similar networks are being established in such major urban centers as San Francisco, San Diego and Las Vegas.

Closer to San Diego, there are the physically based Imperial Valley Drug Coalition (IVDC) in Imperial County and Get-The-Word-Out Intelligence (G2i), which is headquartered in San Diego, but operates exclusively on the Internet.

Conceptually linked to the TEW, the IVDC is deliberately organized much like the drug trafficking organizations against which it is directed. According to its coordinator, its strengths include "unobstructed communication across traditional bureaucratic lines, redundant information paths and rapid mini-task force implementation to exploit short-term tactical situations." The mission of this network is to coordinate the assets of 21 participating law enforcement and governmental agencies in support of the U.S. Attorney, San Diego Specialized Drug Enforcement Operations. These counter-drug operations focus on deterring, detecting and interdicting the flow of illegal drugs in and around Imperial County. As the coordinating element for the IVDC, the Law Enforcement Coordination Center facilitates the planning, coordination, operations and intelligence process.

Formed in September 1996, G2i provides assistance to Defense Department intelligence and counterintelligence personnel by providing open-source intelligence (OSINT) useful to their missions. Selected members of civilian law enforcement, private OSINT professionals and academics with specialized, national security-related expertise are also allowed membership in this listserver. Members can be found globally, depending on duty stations and force deployments, but the majority tend to be spread throughout the continental United States.

G2i generates many e-mail messages based on posting guidelines daily, along with numerous queries about specific intelligence and point-of-contact membership needs.

While all four of these networks have come in contact with each other, the three newer networks have developed more open-channel linkages and, as a result, may have begun to generate a limited synergy. This can be better understood by examining a ground-breaking incident that took place in January 1998.

The L.A. County TEW:
A Cooperative Intelligence and Warning Framework for Combating Terrorism

The mission of the Terrorism Early Warning (TEW) group is to monitor trends that could result in terrorist threats or attacks in Los Angeles (L.A.) County. The group evaluates open-source intelligence (OSINT) and research information about threats in order to guide the training and planning efforts of the interagency Terrorism Working Group (TWG). These early warning efforts also support fire service and other emergency response efforts. The TEW works to identify precursor events, with an eye toward prevention and mitigation.

Monitoring Trends and Potentials

Since its inaugural meeting in April 1996, the TEW has been a vehicle for analysis of the strategic and operational information needed to combat terrorism and protect critical infrastructure. Special emphasis is placed on early detection of emerging threats, including weapons of mass destruction, such as nuclear, biological or chemical (NBC) agents, and information warfare (or cyber-terrorism). The TEW supports the County Emergency Operations Center, the interagency TWG and the L.A. County Metropolitan Medical Strike Team. The TEW is coordinated by the Sheriff's Emergency Operations Bureau, which serves as the group's permanent secretariat.

The TEW will join with criminal intelligence groups (such as the L.A. Task Force on Terrorism) to provide the "unified command" at a terrorist incident with a net assessment of response capabilities and the projected "event horizon." To develop the skills necessary to assess trends and potentials and conduct a net assessment, the TEW group conducts regular briefings on such topics as

- chemical and biological terrorism
- advanced terrorism concepts and the non-state soldier
- future war and terrorism (terrorism in a strategic context)
- cross-border potentials
- recent trends (gangs, mercenaries and drugs)
- chlorine attacks and railway bombings in New South Wales
- critical infrastructure protection—telecom
- water system vulnerability

- airbase defense for civil aviation
- counter-terrorism technology issues
- OSINT analysis
- electromagnetic (EM) terrorism potentials
- advanced less-lethal weaponry
- improvised EMP devices
- RF weapons
- Chemical, Biological Incident Response Force (CBIRF) operations and medical capabilities
- the Henderson, NV, "anthrax" incident
- Skinheads and White Supremacists
- Phineas Priests
- problem-solving with biological agents
- nuclear detection issues
- anti- and counter-terrorist technology, including medical technology for mitigating NBC agents and technology for countering cyber-terrorism

Presenters, Participants and Guests

The guest presenters and lecturers at the briefings—all of them experts in their fields—include members of TEW, practitioners and distinguished scientists and policy analysts from throughout the United States. The following agencies and organizations have all been represented: the Emergency Response Research Institute, the FBI, G2i, GTE, the Imperial Valley Law Enforcement Coordination Center, the Lawrence Livermore National Laboratory, the Los Alamos National Laboratory, the L.A. County Department of Health Services-EMS Agency and Disease Control Programs, the L.A. police and sheriff's departments, the Metropolitan Water District, the National Security Studies Program at California State University-San Bernardino, the RAND Corporation, Sandia National Laboratories, Scientific Applications Research Associates (SARA Labs), The Simon Weisentahl Center and the U.S. Marine Corps' CBIRF.

Participating agencies are classified as either core or cooperating. The core agencies are the L.A. police and sheriff's departments, the city fire department, the county fire and health services departments, and the L.A. division of the FBI.

The cooperating agencies include the California Office of Emergency Services-Law Enforcement Branch; Federal Aviation Administration Security; the Long Beach police, fire and health departments; Long Beach Emergency Management; the L.A. Department of Airports; the L.A. County District Attorney's Office; the Metropolitan Transportation Authority; the

National Security Studies Program at California State University-San Bernardino; the RAND Corp., and U.S. Customs.

Guests at TEW briefings have included representatives from ATF's L.A. field office, the California Department of Justice, the California National Guard, the California Office of Emergency Services-Fire Branch, the San Francisco and San Diego field offices of the FBI, G2i, GTE/BBN, the Imperial Valley Law Enforcement Coordination Center, the Lawrence Livermore National Laboratory, the Los Alamos National Laboratory, the National Law Enforcement and Corrections Technology Center-Western Region, Sandia National Laboratories, SARA Labs, the San Bernardino and San Diego sheriff's departments, and the U.S. Marine Corps.

TEW Reports

In addition to monthly OSINT reports, the TEW has produced the following information papers: "Domestic Terrorism: Army of God," "Domestic Terrorism: Phineas Priests" and "A Bio-Conspirator? Larry Wayne Harris: An Open-Source Profile" (public safety-sensitive). Created for the internal use of the TEW, these documents are designed to educate participants about current issues and build participants' analytical skills.

The Ricin Alert Incident

On January 6, 1998, a San Diego television station aired a news report concerning a "rumor" that drug traffickers were using a chemical warfare agent to booby-trap loads of methamphetamine. Reportedly, this substance would produce a toxic gas, with effects similar to Mustard Gas, that would be harmful or fatal to law enforcement or military personnel conducting a presumptive drug test. This report apparently originated with an Officer Safety Bulletin from a San Diego law enforcement agency, whose origins can be traced back to a narcotics group bulletin from Kansas.

The news report was seen by a law enforcement officer, who related it during a briefing attended by members of a drug interdiction team on January 7. One of those officers sent a private e-mail message to the G2i moderator, who forwarded it immediately to the chief analyst of the virtual-based Emergency Net News Service (ENN) headquartered at the private Emergency Response & Research Institute in Chicago. On January 8, a request for information was posted on the G2i network on behalf of this law enforcement officer, while ENN simultaneously conducted its own investigation. Early research conducted by a G2i member seemed to rule out Mustard Gas, but because this was only a general perception, further verification was requested. Shortly after that posting, an emergency management professional in Texas tracked down a U.S. Border Patrol Intelligence Safety Bulletin that identified the CW-type agent as Ricin, a deadly toxin. That bulletin is believed to have been derived from the same bulletin that was generated by the narcotics group in Kansas.

Because of the potentially deadly implications of these postings, they immediately generated intense G2i activity in the general listserver, as well as in private e-mails, faxes and phone conversations not only within G2i but also involving agencies and groups with nodes in this virtual network. Queries were made into the validity of the safety bulletin and the inconsistency concerning the production of Mustard Gas as a byproduct of analyzing suspected narcotics with a field testing kit.

Segments of L.A.'s TEW group and the IVDC networks quickly obtained conflicting reports concerning the accuracy of the bulletin in question. By comparing their information and sources, they were able to jointly confirm that the bulletin was invalid—no known or suspected use of Ricin by drug traffickers had taken place. Within six hours of the original G2i posting, a member associated with one of these networks posted a non-law enforcement attribution message stating that the original safety bulletin was inaccurate and that no chemical or biological warfare agent was involved. Those individuals with a vital need to know were placed in contact with the law enforcement personnel and/or agencies who had verified that the alert was inaccurate. Over the course of the next day, concerns over the bulletin subsided as more information came in on the general listserver and G2i members with technical expertise verified that it was chemically impossible for Ricin to produce Mustard Gas.

The incident entered its second phase on January 13, 1998, when a new posting on G2i concerning a Ricin alert came in from a public safety professional in New York. It turned out that the original safety bulletin had been widely disseminated and then rebroadcast by a major California agency as another variation of the original alert. Because of the non-linear nature of this incident, ENN was also sent an e-mail that same day from another California agency about this new bulletin. Luckily, the East Coast professional who posted his message on G2i had remembered the earlier discussion on this topic and simply sought confirmation of its inaccuracy. Within a couple of hours, two postings from members of the Los Angeles County TEW network stated that the alert was erroneous. The next day, ENN agreed that the alert was inaccurate and began widespread distribution to subscriber police, fire and emergency medical services agencies in order to help spread the word that the new bulletin concerning this incident was false.

As late as January 16, 1998, reports were still coming into G2i determining that the Ricin alert was bogus, but by then the issue was considered dead and the dreaded Ricin scare was over. Nonetheless, over the course of the next three months, ENN and various law enforcement groups were queried about some sort of Ricin alert. The incident had now become something of an "urban legend," with its suspected origins traced back to a November 17, 1996, *U.S. News & World Report* article on chemical warfare.

The analysis phase of this incident, which occurred from approximately the 14th to the 22nd of January, produced numerous e-mail messages about lessons learned and resulted in a week-long "virtual capture session" concerning what had taken place. Eric Nelson, the G2i moderator, notes the following aspects of the "non-linear, non-hierarchical" joint operation:

- no inter-agency territorialism
- instant linkage of remotely located parties
- constant sharing of information

- joint effort
- rankless and non-linear medium

What can be learned and applied from the Ricin experience on G2i? Nelson observes:

> It is no small event we have just witnessed. When in the history of the United States has this great a collection of military organizations, civilian law enforcement and academics jointly worked on an important issue from remote locations until it was resolved?
>
> This is no mere information distribution network. We are a laboratory that is experimenting with the future: joint operations between military and civilian forces. We are also experimenting with non-linear interconnectivity and non-hierarchical joint efforts.
>
> This entire phenomenon bears great thought. It has worked so well that we were days ahead of non-connected agencies, many of whom are still passing bad information.
>
> Let's tear this thing apart and figure out how we can do it again.

Some of these lessons, as well as other Ricin-related news items obtained from information sources outside of G2i, were summarized in an ENN synopsis of the event published on January 18 primarily for general law enforcement and first responder audiences not included in the G2i listserver membership.

It should be noted that just three days prior to that final ENN synopsis, the San Diego Union-Tribune was still reporting that an officer safety alert concerning a toxic poison known as Ricin was being broadcast across the county by a major counter-drug agency and was in turn being picked up by local law enforcement agencies. Fortunately, those progressive law enforcement and governmental organizations that were "webbed" into the experimental domestic response network were already aware that the alert was erroneous.

Conclusions

In order to respond to the challenges facing law enforcement as a result of the rise of the non-state soldier, a domestic response network will be a needed addition to the traditional top-down federal approach to domestic defense. Such a network would represent a natural evolutionary step for the more than 17,000 independent public law enforcement entities found throughout the United States, and would greatly support the federal government in its endeavors to provide for the common defense. Ultimately, such a network would allow those agencies and allied organizations the ability to share information and decrease response times for crisis and consequence management.

As one member of the L.A. County Sheriff's Department notes with respect to the Ricin incident:

> I think we have demonstrated the value of intelligence support to both crisis and consequence management of emerging threats. . . . [A]n expanded recognition of the utility of virtual OSINT networks by decision- and policy-makers (not to mention field commanders) is essential to future success.

Policy makers must begin to fuse open-source information about street and motorcycle gangs, terrorist groups, militias, extremist and hate groups, drug cartel activities (both along the border and internally) and private security forces to obtain a baseline strategic picture of our current domestic security environment. These areas of concern are not unrelated and discrete trends; linked together, they can provide us with important insights into the health of our society.

We must ask ourselves—while we still have the time to prepare—whether we are going to place our trust in private security forces and gated communities, or take the responsibility for ensuring that our public law enforcement institutions will be up to the challenges of the future. If it is to be the latter—as indeed it must be if we are to preserve our constitutional rights and liberties—then a domestic response network will be essential.

COMMANDER STEPHEN
E. FLYNN, USCG

Homeland Security Is a
Coast Guard Mission

Homeland defense and homeland security have become the lat-est rage in commissions and think tanks around Washington. Over the past year, eight major studies and reports have rolled off the presses, sharing a remarkable degree of consensus. They agree that there is a real and imminent threat of a catastrophic attack on the American people and the critical infrastructure that is the backbone of our power-ful society, and that the U.S. government is unprepared and possesses no adequate organizational structure to prevent or respond to such an at-tack. The Bush administration seems to be taking these findings to heart. In early May, Vice President Dick Cheney was tasked with overseeing the development of a coordinated national effort for protecting the na-tion against the use of weapons of mass destruction. At the Pentagon, a recent study prepared for the Secretary of Defense incorporates defense of the U.S. homeland into U.S. military strategy guidelines for the first time in decades.

The idea that we need to protect our homeland from attack does not sit well with most Americans. Ever since we won our national indepen-dence, we have enjoyed relative freedom from direct military threat, with the exception of some pesky Redcoats during the War of 1812 and Pancho Villa's incursions along the Southwest border at the start of the last century. But it not just that our 21st-century adversaries may prefer to bring their battles to U.S. soil that makes us queasy. It also is a concern that the cure might be worse than the disease. Americans have never been enthusiastic about standing armies. In the post-World War II era, we accommodated ourselves to the need for a large national security establishment by clearly demarcating where its writ would run—overseas. We were willing to make an unparalleled investment to contain the Soviet Union and to deal with conflicts "over there." But the quid pro quo was supposed to be that civilians could enjoy their full freedoms here at home.

For many with memories of World War II, the surge in interest in homeland security undoubtedly conjures up images of enforced blackouts and armed beach and port security patrols. Those who lived through the first decades of the Cold War are likely to have flashbacks of air raid drills and backyard bomb shelters. For contemporary planners in the Pentagon, struggling to match paltry resources to growing missions, the increase in interest undoubtedly generates new anxieties that this will become an additional mandate that will distract them from their other important work.

The homeland security issue may generate uneasiness in many quarters, but it should not make the U.S. Coast Guard uneasy. Indeed, it would be a mistake for senior Coast Guard leaders to remain mute as this national debate unfolds. By stepping out smartly, the Coast Guard can both advance the service's interests and serve the American people.

The Terrorist Threat

As the world's predominant military, economic, and cultural power, the United States is "Public Enemy No. 1" for any group or nation that resents its global dominance. But terrorists, radical religious or ethnic sects, and rogue states who want to give form to their pique over the United States' unequaled global reach can hold few illusions about winning direct contests with U.S. military forces. Instead, the targets of tomorrow increasingly will lie in the civil realm, where the economic and cultural components of national power are vulnerable. The disturbing trends toward unconventional weapons proliferation—including nuclear, chemical, and biological weapons of mass destruction—portend that terrorists likely will have access to the means for conducting a catastrophic attack.

In the largely unprotected ports, waterways, and coastal regions, there is ample opportunity to harm Americans, gain access to critical national infrastructure, and disrupt the nation's vital transportation lifelines.

The Bush administration appears poised to spend up to $100 billion to construct a national ballistic missile defense system, but officers and inspectors charged with policing the vessels and cargo moving to, from, and through U.S. ports and waterways know that it is not only the nation's aerospace that is wide open but its maritime space as well. Despite their best efforts over more than two decades, these inspectors have been able to interdict only a fraction of the illicit narcotics destined for our shores. Most ports have no security except that provided by minimum-pay private security guards hired by commercial tenants. The volume and velocity of people, cargo, and commercial and recreational traffic that move on the water far exceed the resources available for ensuring that these cross-border flows are complying with U.S. laws.

If an adversary wanted a weapon of mass destruction to reach the United States, he likely would consider the merits of transporting it on board a vessel or within a maritime container. When launched, a ballistic missile has a very pronounced signature, and the United States is capable of conducting a devastating retaliatory strike. So why would not an Osama bin Laden or some rogue state choose an alternative scenario, such as loading a chemical weapon into a container originating from a front company in Karachi, Pakistan, and ultimately destined for Newark, New Jersey? A terrorist might use a Pakistani exporter with an established record of trade in the United States. The container could have a global positioning system (GPS) device so it could be tracked as it moved through Singapore or Hong Kong to mingle with the more than half a million containers handled by each of these ports every month. It could arrive in the United States via Long Beach or Los Angeles and be loaded directly on a railcar for the transcontinental trip. Current regulations do not require an importer to file a cargo manifest with the U.S. Customs Service until the cargo reaches its "entry" port—in this case, Newark, 2,800 miles of U.S. territory away from where it first entered the country—and the importer is permitted 30 days' transit time to make the trip to the East Coast. When the container reaches the rail yard outside Chicago—which is one of the most important rail hubs in the United States—the weapon could be set off, long before its contents were even identified as having entered the country.

Most Americans and their defense planners are oblivious to just how open U.S. maritime borders are. If they were not, they likely would reconsider plans to spend so much on some rather fanciful technology against what most respected observers see as a very low-probability threat, and instead—or at least concurrently—would invest in lower-cost homeland security measures designed to prevent and protect against an attack by unconventional means.

The "weapon-in-a-container" scenario frames what is the essential challenge of homeland security. We must strike the optimal balance between permitting the free movements of legitimate travelers, cargo, and information, and advancing the capacity to identify and intercept illegitimate people and goods that would cause Americans harm. Pursuing the latter without being mindful of the former is not an option. Measures that would sacrifice freedom for the sake of security essentially are un-American, and sustaining U.S. economic competitiveness in a world where 95% of the consumers and much of the raw materials lie outside the United States requires that the barriers associated with conducting global business be kept to a minimum.

Anomaly Detection

Because striving for a failsafe system to protect the U.S. homeland is both unrealistic and likely to be counterproductive, does this mean that the only alternative is to standby for globalization's heavy rolls? No. The best way to balance the imperatives of openness and control is to embrace a risk management approach. Risk management involves developing the means to identify transnational activities and actors that pose little or no risk to the United States so that limited regulatory, enforcement, and security resources can be targeted at those that present a high risk.

With so much of the world's trade moving by sea, and with so many vessels engaged in both work and play transiting along U.S. maritime frontiers, managing risk within the nation's largely open maritime space is no simple task. In 2000, 5.8 million 40-foot maritime containers and 211,000 commercial vessels entered U.S. ports, most registered under foreign flags. On the Great Lakes alone there are more than 4 million U.S.-registered small boats. How is it possible to filter the bad from the good given such numbers? The answer lies in anomaly detection, a relatively new concept being promoted by cyber-security experts that most seasoned Coast Guard boarding officers and Customs inspectors have been practicing for a long time.

In the computer industry, anomaly detection is the most promising means for detecting hackers intent on stealing data or transmitting computer viruses. The process involves monitoring the flows of computer traffic with an eye toward discerning normal traffic that moves by way of the most technologically rational route. Once this baseline is established, software is written to detect aberrant traffic. A good computer hacker will try to look as much as possible like a legitimate user. But because he is not legitimate, he inevitably must do some things differently. Good cyber-security software will detect that variation and deny access. For those hackers who manage to get through, their breach is identified and shared so that this abnormal behavior can be removed from the guidance of what is normal and acceptable.

In much the same way, the overwhelming majority of the vessels, people, and cargo that move in and out of our waters—particularly those originating in overseas ports—move in predictable patterns. If we have the means to track these flows, we will have the means to detect aberrant behavior. This is what happens when a Coast Guard boarding officer climbs on board a fishing vessel and discovers that it has the wrong kind of gear for the fishery in which the captain claims he is working. Anomaly detection within the maritime space is possible if the regulatory and enforcement agencies whose daily tasks place them in that space are given access to intelligence about real or suspected threats or are provided the means to gather, share, and mine data that provide a comprehensive picture of normal maritime traffic to enhance their odds of detecting threats when they materialize. Coast Guard Commandant Admiral James Loy calls this "maritime domain awareness." Around Washington, he has been making the case that the nation needs this kind of capability. Through his advocacy, he also has been demonstrating that the Coast Guard is well positioned to play a leadership role in developing it.

Of course, possessing the means to detect a threat within the maritime domain is only the first step. The nation must also have the means to intercept that threat and exercise law enforcement action. A busy waterfront pier in Los Angeles or Seattle is hardly an optimal place to find and defuse a bomb. A better approach would be to intercept the vessel carrying the weapon offshore. If a shoreside evolution is required, the vessel could be escorted to a less vulnerable locale. For this kind of mission, the country would want a fleet of modern, swift, and capable cutters that can safely operate on the high seas, in all types of weather, deploying helicopters and small boats to transport boarding teams, night or day, while communicating securely with the National Command Authorities.

Around the clock, 365 days a year, the Coast Guard is patrolling our nation's waterways, coastal regions, and exclusive economic zones, and operating far from our shores when the missions require. But increasingly the service performs its missions with platforms that are well past their useful service lives and kept operational only by constant repairs, thereby robbing an already austere operating budget. The service's Deepwater acquisition properly aims to rectify this unsustainable situation so that the United States will have the kind of maritime interception and law enforcement capabilities it needs to stop threats to the homeland before they arrive.

Because a terrorist still may succeed at evading good intelligence, detection, and interception assets, the final pieces to the homeland security mission are protection of critical infrastructure and the management of the consequences of an attack. The extent to which ports are critical infrastructure is highlighted by the dependency of California on a single pier in the Port of Long Beach for the offloading of 45% of all the maritime crude shipments (408,000 barrels per day) or roughly 25% of all the crude oil consumed by the state. Because California's gasoline refineries are all operating at full capacity, at any given time there is only enough oil stored in the region to supply them for two days. Accordingly, if the kind of terrorist attack that was conducted in Yemen against the USS *Cole* (DD-67) took place against a tanker tied up to that one pier, the economy of Southern California—which is bigger than the economies of most of the world's nations—would grind to a halt within a matter of days. Given such an attractive and almost completely unprotected target, a terrorist might prefer to attack that pier at Long Beach rather than a Navy frigate tied up at the San Diego Naval Base.

Coast Guard captains of the port will have an increasingly important role to play in gathering data to support intelligence collection efforts, conducting vulnerability assessments, raising awareness about those vulnerabilities, and leading local, state, and federal efforts designed to make ports more secure. These protective measures should help reduce the consequences of a terrorist incident within a U.S. port, but there would be consequences nonetheless. Coast Guard shoreside and afloat assets will play the role of first responder, as well as help manage the aftermath as the on-scene federal incident coordinator.

A Coast Guard Opportunity

The homeland security mission presents a historic opportunity for the U.S. Coast Guard to highlight the critical role it plays in the nation's defense. The nature of that mission goes well beyond the warfighting potential of the service's port security units and larger cutters, drawing on the entire tapestry of Coast Guard missions and capabilities. The most astute eyes and ears within the maritime domain belong to Coast Guard men and women doing their day-to-day missions. Whether conducting boating safety, marine and harbor safety, and fisheries patrols, or monitoring and working within our nation's waterways on a buoy tender or in a vessel traffic system, these personnel are positioned to detect aberrant activities that can pinpoint a terrorist threat. The service's work in support of migrant and drug interdiction provides it with many of the means to share information in the interagency process. Its long-standing relationships with the Navy and the Department of Defense make it an ideal go-between among the national security, law enforcement, and regulatory worlds. The work of Coast Guard marine safety offices provides an entree to the maritime industry, port authorities, and local and state officials, which is essential for advancing critical infrastructure protection and consequence management within our nation's seaports. And the Coast Guard's superb international reputation can support necessary overseas efforts to improve security and information sharing arrangements that can reduce the risk that the world's maritime transportation system will be exploited by terrorists to hurt Americans at home. No matter how large an investment is made to reinvent the U.S. national intelligence and defense establishment for the post-Cold War world, it will be unable to duplicate the kinds of capabilities that the Coast Guard brings to the table.

The appeal of the Coast Guard's low-cost, multimission platforms coupled with its unique civil-military attributes make capitalizing on the Coast Guard as a lead agency for the homeland security mission an idea whose time has arrived. These attributes have the potential for real political resonance as the national missile defense and homeland defense debates unfold. There are many inside the D.C. beltway who have misgivings about the huge investment, the abandonment of the Anti-Ballistic Missile Treaty, and the consequence for U.S. relations with Russia, China, and our European allies that missile defense entails. There also are those who have understandable reservations about assigning the U.S. military and national intelligence establishment a prominent role in domestic security. Collectively, these politicians and commentators are in search of alternatives that address their concerns without allowing their critics to portray them as weak on defense. A compelling alternative is a homeland security strategy that emphasizes a risk and consequence management approach enlisting the unique capabilities of the U.S. Coast Guard and other agencies with border-management responsibilities.

ADAM J. HEBERT

Homeland Defense

All previous American wars of the modern era—two World Wars, plus conflicts in Korea, Vietnam, and the Persian Gulf—had at least one important feature in common: They took place somewhere else.

Each of these conflicts was fought "over there," far from American soil. The Japanese attack on Pearl Harbor brought war to US territory, true, but thousands of miles of Pacific Ocean stood between the battle and the mainland. Even the Cold War with the Soviet Union focused largely on Europe.

Protected for nearly two centuries by broad oceans and docile neighbors, the United States simply has not had to face a significant military threat "over here."

All of that changed utterly on Sept. 11. In the aftermath of the devastating September terrorist attacks on the World Trade Center towers in New York and the Pentagon in Washington, D.C., the national homeland is now squarely on the front lines.

The attacks, which killed thousands of American civilians, not only brought a war to US soil but instantly vaulted homeland security issues from a series of warnings in studies to a top national priority.

Declaring a war on terrorism, top leaders across the government said that those who support terror will be hunted and killed or punished, and radical changes in the way the United States defends its territory, citizens, and assets are being investigated.

There is much at stake. As President Bush noted in the aftermath of the attacks that left thousands dead, "This is a fight for freedom. This is a fight to say to the freedom-loving people of the world we will not allow ourselves to be terrorized by somebody who thinks they can hit and hide in some cave somewhere. It's going to require a new thought process. And I'm proud to report our military . . . understands it's a new type of war, it's going to take a long time to win this war."

Despite doom and gloom in many quarters, that was not the attitude of Air Force Maj. Gen. John L. Barry, director of strategic planning at USAF headquarters in the Pentagon, in an interview conducted before Sept. 11. Barry said the nation already has significant homeland security capabilities in place—though they exist at this time somewhat by default through capabilities provided for their primary missions.

Warnings

A series of high-profile studies have concluded that the American homeland had become increasingly vulnerable to threats from crude nuclear weapons, cruise missiles, cyber-war, biological agents, and other "asymmetric" types of attack. As September's outrages demonstrated, it did not take an actual invasion of the United States to kill thousands and rock the national business, political, and military establishments.

According to members of the Defense Science Board in a report "Protecting the Homeland" (which was released before the attacks), the nation faces not only new vulnerability as a result of advances in the means of attack but also difficulty in even responding to the threat. The Pentagon has to overcome bureaucratic lethargy, find the money for new investment, and rethink the whole concept of open borders, it said.

The Defense Department is expected to play a key role in future homeland security missions, these experts said, because the department (and the Air Force in particular) already has many of the resources and capabilities needed to prevent or respond to an attack on US society.

Still, much work needs to be done to protect the US, and evolving the Defense Department to better meet the threat will be an expensive and time-consuming process—a point top officials freely admit.

The Threat

US military dominance in areas such as fighter aircraft, tanks, and submarines means adversaries are highly unlikely to challenge the nation head-on. This makes America a target for asymmetric attack, as were the September attacks on the twin towers and the Pentagon, presumably engineered by exiled Saudi extremist Osama bin Laden.

By taking advantage of failures in aviation security, hijacking US airlines from domestic airports, and turning them into guided missiles to strike targets elsewhere in the United States, terrorists were able to bypass existing security and defense measures.

Even NORAD at the time was outward-looking, focused on tracking aircraft entering US airspace. NORAD did not respond to the developing terrorist incident until notified of the hijackings by the Federal Aviation Administration.

Complicating the matter, there is no shortage of other options adversaries may use to bypass US strengths to strike the homeland directly. "Biological, chemical, and information technologies are very inexpensive and widely available," said the DSB's report. "The trend is toward lower cost, higher performance, and even wider availability."

The report presented a lengthy outline of the homeland security challenge, describing parts of the threat as "grim" for the United States. Outlining the "gravity of the problem," the DSB determined the threat is real and growing.

The report concluded that "unconventional" nuclear weapon attacks, those not coming via peer ballistic missiles, present the largest single asymmetric risk to the United States—but are also the most preventable.

Still, according to the DSB task force, "the ability to protect against an [unconventional nuclear] attack is sorely lacking. This point is increasingly disconcerting given the magnitude and timescale of devastation associated with a successful attack."

Most homeland defense advocates find missile defenses to be a critical element, needed to defend against the threat from expanding and proliferating cruise and ballistic missile technology. When these missiles can be nuclear-armed, the threat to the United States is magnified.

At the time of the September Massacre, Congress and the Administration were bracing for a showdown over Bush's plans for a robust and expensive national missile defense system. Some critics such as Sen. Carl Levin (D-Mich.), chairman of the Senate Armed Services

Committee, immediately called for the debate to be set aside while a plan is formulated to respond to the attacks. But Levin also noted that the attacks confirmed his belief that the nation should be focusing more resources on the types of attacks the US is more likely to see. One requirement is for more human intelligence and better processing capability for the information that is collected, he said in September.

Although the threat of nuclear ballistic missile attack from a so-called rogue nation such as North Korea received the most attention in homeland security circles prior to this fall, other, less publicized nuclear threats remain important, the DSB determined.

The report stated the greatest nuclear threat comes from state actors, not roaming terror organizations, and the threat continues to grow because "more than 1,500 tons of weapon-grade materials in Russia [are] under loose control," while smaller nuclear weapons could be carried and concealed in a backpack or truck.

Transportability creates a major problem when viewed in conjunction with our nation's open borders. Keeping backpack-sized nuclear weapons or chemical and biological agents out of the United States will always require good intelligence, because random checks are unlikely to do the job.

Retired Air Force Gen. Charles G. Boyd, executive director of the US Commission on National Security/21st Century, said that US borders are the most porous in the world and will probably remain that way.

"You can stand on the Ambassador Bridge [between the US and Windsor, Canada] and observe eight lanes of traffic coming into Detroit. There's no way you can examine more than a half of one percent of the traffic coming in," he said, adding "more than 1.3 million people cross our borders a day." Little can be done about that aspect of the homeland threat, Boyd noted.

There is talk in the aftermath of the recent attacks to better control the constant influx of people into the United States, possibly through controversial measures such as the profiling of potential terrorists.

Porous borders also contribute to the emergence of threats from chemical or biological weapons. If spread effectively, they could, in many cases, be as devastating as a successful nuclear attack upon the United States. As horrific as the Sept. 11 attacks were, experts have cautioned that the devastation could have been exponentially worse if the terrorists had used chemical or biological weapons in conjunction with the hijacked airliners.

In 1995, a Japanese cult released Sarin nerve gas into Tokyo's crowded subway system. The crime turned out to be relatively unsuccessful. However, it demonstrated the challenge posed by chemical weapons. As Charles Cragin, who was then acting Pentagon reserve affairs chief, noted in 1998, "The Tokyo first-responders didn't have a clue for the first three hours on what they were dealing with, so people exposed to sarin gas wandered into hospitals, potentially contaminating them."

Considered even more deadly is the threat from biological weapons such as anthrax. Defense Department preparations for the biological warfare threat are not sufficiently advanced, the DSB found. Russia has created enough anthrax to "kill the world's population four times over," and the US health care system's ability to deal with mass casualties is suspect.

"This nation does not have an effective, early capability to assess the BW [bioweapon] threat, and as a consequence, cannot prevent such a crisis," the report stated. "The task force paints a grim picture of the effectiveness of biological warfare. For example, an attack on a city with 100 kilograms [220 pounds] of bio-agent would kill one to three million people." Further, it is much more difficult for the United States to monitor bioweapon development than it is to track nuclear weapons programs.

Recently thrust into the spotlight is the cyber-threat, typified by the sudden emergence of a series of computer worms and viruses. According to Army Maj. Gen. J. David Bryan, commander of DOD's Joint Task Force for Computer Network Operations under US Space Command, there has been "significant growth" in the tempo, complexity, and destructiveness of computer threats over the past two years.

Commonly known viruses and worms such as Melissa, I Love You, Anna Kournikova, and Code Red (as well as many less well-known ones) have all affected the Defense Department to varying degrees. These broad threats and other outright attacks directed at DOD represent an ever-growing challenge, Bryan said.

Meanwhile, at least 20 nations are "developing tools to attack computer-based infrastructure," while at their disposal is an Internet that "actually provides a superb command-and-control system, which was part of its original intent," the Defense Science Board noted.

In the immediate aftermath of the twin towers and Pentagon attacks, it was widely suggested that the terrorists were able to prevent their planning from being detected by the US Intelligence Community by communicating via Internet rather than telephone.

Lawmakers are already calling for revisions in the rules counterterrorism units must follow when tracking threats. For example, one proposal would give police agencies permission to connect eavesdropping to a person instead of an individual telephone number—in recognition of the fact that mobile phone proliferation allows a single terrorist to use many different phones.

Phone and Internet service can also be a liability for DOD in other ways. Heavy reliance upon the commercial world for telecommunications and Internet access also poses a challenge to the Defense Department, the Defense Science Board found, as the department "leases the vast majority of those services from private industry, which for economic reasons tend to use the most cost-effective option rather than the most secure."

With all these threats still emerging, defense experts assert that the nation can no longer effectively address national security by concentrating on forward perimeter defenses in Europe, the Middle East, and Asia—the approach taken throughout the Cold War. The September attacks show that perimeter defenses can be bypassed, bringing the conflict directly to America.

Not Helpless

Barry, USAF's top strategic planner, said these high-profile reviews detailing homeland security shortcomings do serve a purpose. He noted that the studies "identify the areas where we are not strong," a critical first step in correcting shortcomings. Barry also noted that, although the list of homeland security shortcomings is likely to be immense at first, identification will help the Air Force prioritize its investments.

In the meantime, homeland security capabilities already in place mean the Air Force is not starting from a "clean sheet of paper" when facing the problem.

The Air Force's ability to respond to homeland threats encompasses well-developed capabilities—although some areas of the homeland defense mission certainly need improvement, Barry said.

"I don't want to paint a rosy picture here that we've got this thing licked, because there is a lot of work to do," said Barry. "There are concepts, organization, there are technological elements that have to be resolved—and we have to get better at it. So, we've got a long way to go."

The Air Force also needs to "take credit for what is already out there," said Barry. "NORAD, with US Space Command, certainly has a role" in defending the homeland against missile and electronic attacks, for starters. NORAD is able to provide early warning notification that missiles or hostile aircraft are approaching US airspace.

Now, it looks like NORAD will have a new dimension to its operations—surveillance of internal airspace. In the September attacks, terrorists were able to sidestep NORAD observation by commandeering airplanes already operating within US airspace. According to command officials, NORAD did not begin tracking and responding to the hijacked airliners until it was notified of the developing crisis by the FAA.

Barry also called attention to the role of existing air and space-borne Air Force intelligence, surveillance, and reconnaissance capabilities in homeland security, assets that are expected to play critical roles in responding to the attacks militarily.

These observational capabilities "can be brought to the table" to deter potential threats to the homeland before they ever occur—or to help respond to attacks after the fact, he said. Systems such as the E-8 Joint STARS ground surveillance and E-3 AWACS airborne warning and control aircraft "are not exclusive capabilities," he said. "Whether we are working the front end of the problem before we get hit, or consequence management after we get hit, there are some common elements on both ends of that spectrum."

Although the aftermath of a homeland attack is often perceived as a civil matter to be dealt with by the FBI and Federal Emergency Management Agency, Barry noted the Air Force also has much to offer when recovering from an attack.

"We can do retaliation," he observed. "We clearly would focus on that capability where we would go after the culprits . . . to destroy their capability."

DOD's National Guard and Reserve components are expected to have a significant role in dealing with homeland attacks. Current reserve affairs chief Craig Duehring said in August that the department is continuing to expand the number of civil support teams designed to respond to attacks with weapons of mass destruction. Ten of 32 planned emergency response teams, designed to respond to attacks anywhere in the United States within four hours, are in place now. Each is staffed with 22 Air and Army National Guard responders.

Meanwhile, the Air National Guard stepped into action as the September attacks unfolded, scrambling fighters based at Otis ANGB, Mass., and Langley AFB, Va., to defend New York and Washington.

Days after the attacks, Vice President Dick Cheney revealed in an interview with Tim Russert of NBC's "Meet the Press" that Bush had authorized the pilots of the Air Guard aircraft to shoot down any civilian airliners that appeared to be threatening a city. They have continued to perform their Combat Air Patrol missions in the days and weeks since the September attacks.

"It doesn't do any good to put up a Combat Air Patrol if you don't give them instructions to act," Cheney said. "If the plane would not divert, if they wouldn't pay any attention to instructions to move away from the city, as a last resort our pilots were authorized to take them out."

Shortly after the attacks, Air Force F-15 and F-16 fighters with supporting tankers and AWACS aircraft were flying CAP over about 30 American cities. Defense officials have declined to be specific about how many fighters will continue to remain airborne and over what locations, but they said aircraft are on "strip alert," ready to fly within 10 to 15 minutes, at 26 bases.

Who's in Charge?

Cheney, in his role as vice president, had been named as a possible homeland security czar, a position that could be established in response to the mismatch of civil and military agencies expected to pitch in to prevent and respond to homeland threats.

Before the attacks, the US Commission on National Security/21st Century (known informally as the Hart-Rudman Commission) recommended establishment of a Cabinet-level homeland security agency and czar. Under the proposal, FEMA and related organizations, including the Customs Service and Coast Guard, would be combined into a new National Homeland Security Agency.

The Hart-Rudman Commission also suggested that a new assistant secretary of defense for homeland security be created to oversee the military side of the equation. Currently US Space Command at Peterson AFB, Colo., and US Joint Forces Command at Norfolk, Va., are just two of the commands playing key roles in the homeland security mission.

The DSB report also suggested creation of a high-level office to assume responsibility for the homeland defense mission, without suggesting who should take the lead. The DSB took notice of a "mismatch between those formally in charge and those that actually have capability."

Barry noted that a clear chain of command up to a unified leader does not exist for military homeland security, although Air Force Gen.

Ralph E. Eberhart—Commander in Chief of NORAD and US Space Command—comes close.

Asked if Eberhart, as CINCSPACE, is therefore a logical choice to assume a mission of homeland security CINC, Barry said such decisions must come from the President.

President Bush did announce Sept. 20 in his address to the nation that he was creating "a Cabinet-level position reporting directly to me, the Office of Homeland Security." Pennsylvania Governor Tom Ridge will lead the office. His role will be to coordinate the efforts of all the agencies involved, including DOD.

Defense Department activity definitely is on the rise. Even before the attacks, however, Barry felt that much work still had to be done. "We do clearly have to do better on this organization, as several commands all have a piece of the puzzle," he said.

Uncomfortable Challenge

American traditions of freedom of speech and movement, restrictions against unreasonable search-and-seizure, and open borders all make homeland security especially challenging. As analysts have noted, the relationship between the nation's law enforcement and military communities is an uneasy one, but the consensus is that more cooperation will be needed.

"Homeland security encompasses all aspects of the government," said Barry. "These kinds of attacks affect not just the military; they can affect the whole country."

Other changes suggested by the review groups may not be popular with the Pentagon, further complicating the establishment of new homeland security capabilities. Boyd, who retired in 1995 as deputy commander of US European Command, warned that implementing the recommendations advanced by the Hart-Rudman Commission will be a long-term challenge.

The Pentagon bureaucracy will challenge homeland defense initiatives, he said. "How do you stop the services, for example, from doing all the things they know how to do—and that they like to do?" Boyd asked. "They've got to do some things that they're not so interested in," such as deal with "the asymmetrical threats that have us worried."

The DSB also forecasted a difficult institutional road to homeland security. In a telling passage from the homeland report's executive summary, the authors wrote:

"It has been observed, 'Here is the Defense Science Board again making recommendations to spend money, and there is just no money.' The DSB believes that this situation must be regarded as something quite different. This is not a case of 'yet another aircraft to go along with the many aircraft we now have.' These threats are different, and the DSB sees a more fundamental need for the DOD and the Intelligence Community to restructure their investment balance."

Perhaps one small bright spot emerging from this September's attacks is that the homeland security mission and requirements can no longer be given simple lip service.

Effective homeland security requires layered, nontraditional protection—and the DSB report said homeland defense funding should be increased. For example, DOD has not prioritized information defenses properly, the DSB task force contended. "Too much money and time is being spent on the lower-level threats to the nation's networks (e.g., hackers) and not enough on figuring out how to protect information systems from state and terrorist warriors who understand how to exploit compromised data," the report read.

After the attacks, analysts suggested that the US had focused too much on the high and low extremes of homeland threats—at the top, ballistic missile attacks and, at the bottom, car bombs. Consequently, the government missed the midlevel threat that became a horrifying reality.

Intelligence, Considered Broadly

The DSB suggested that DOD and the Intelligence Community rethink their investment balance "which is always hard in a large bureaucracy." The board noted that in the Fiscal 2001 budget, roughly $264 billion was devoted to "deterring regional conflicts to protect allies, friends, and American interests," while only $3 billion was allocated to protecting the "homeland against biological, chemical, information, and unconventional nuclear attacks."

This is not likely to be an issue in the future. Just the very first bills to recover from the Sept. 11 attacks and to begin planning for a way forward came to $40 billion. Much more cost and planning are expected.

Reprioritization is needed, experts say, because homeland defense is not a mission that should simply be dropped on top of existing DOD responsibilities.

Traditionally, homeland threats "are equated in peoples' minds with 'terrorism,' and 'terrorism' is viewed more as an irritating, annoying mosquito bite than as a true threat to the homeland," the DSB noted. "This is not the case"—not that anyone in the US will ever overlook terrorism again.

The problem is larger, and the solution must be more comprehensive, the DSB said. For example, good intelligence can not only deter potential adversaries by creating better attribution but can also be a key factor in heading off and responding to almost every type of possible homeland attack.

Critics such as Levin said there was apparently a complete intelligence failure before the attacks. Analysts had warned for years about the threat of a "space Pearl Harbor" or a "cyber-Pearl Harbor" but seemingly ignored was the likelihood of a Pearl Harbor-style terror attack using domestic airliners.

Barry agreed that more is needed. "It's a bigger issue than intelligence. . . . We are all looking at how to improve [Intelligence, Surveillance, and Reconnaissance] and what forks in the road we need to work to get the most ISR and the optimum ISR complex," he said. "That ISR challenge is going to be a big part" in the future, he said, and the service's leadership is cognizant of the need.

Air Force Secretary James Roche "has said this is probably the biggest intellectual challenge we have for the future," Barry observed. "This is a major point for this new Administration," he said, and the service is attempting to determine "what is the role that United States Air Force aerospace power can provide for homeland security?"

The ultimate goal is to "go to a global perspective where we can find, fix, assess, track, target, and engage any target. That brings home how valuable ISR is," he said.

An Attention Getter

The attention heaped upon the homeland security mission began to catch DOD's attention even before Sept. 11. When Deputy Defense Secretary Paul Wolfowitz announced five principles that would guide the Quadrennial Defense Review and military transformation earlier this summer, four of the priorities had a clear homeland security perspective when the resources needed to sustain operations have to be protected.

"Protecting our bases of operation and being able to defeat nuclear/biological/chemical weapons and ballistic missile attack" is a top planning priority, Wolfowitz said.

The other key points in the planning guidance are to "project and sustain US forces in distant anti-access or area-denial environments. . . . Be able to deny enemy sanctuary through various means, particularly long-range precision strike of different kinds. . . . Be able to conduct space operations. And . . . to ensure joint and combined interoperability integration of long-range strike and deep maneuver forces."

With a much smaller "garrison force" than in the past—requiring operations based and controlled in the United States—homeland security has become more than a simple protection issue. It is now a national priority.

DR. MILAN VEGO

What Can We Learn from Enduring Freedom?

Operation Enduring Freedom was highly successful, accomplishing most of the stated U.S. strategic objectives. The fundamentalist Taliban regime collapsed in a matter of weeks, and the Afghani people enjoy far more freedom now than at any time during the past 20 years. The al Qaeda international terrorist network and its supporting structure in Afghanistan have been seriously, if not fatally, disrupted. Thousands of Taliban and al Qaeda fighters were killed or captured. The U.S.-led victory was relatively quick and achieved at the cost to the United States of only 31 killed and fewer than 100 injured. Yet despite these successes, some serious political and security problems remain in Afghanistan.

Operation Enduring Freedom confirmed that the relationship between policy and strategy remains the most critical factor in conducting a war. Policy always dominates strategy, and clear, militarily achievable political objectives are critical for ultimate success in any conflict. Determining a desired end state is the first and most important step before the use of military sources of national or coalition power. Mistakes made in policy are hard to overcome by strategy and operational art.

The operation showed a high degree of professionalism and dedication by all service members. U.S. air power was undoubtedly the key factor—although not the only one—in the U.S.-led victory. Smart munitions, unmanned aerial vehicles (UAVs), satellite communications, and advanced information technologies were used extensively and successfully during the conflict. The operation, however, revealed some potentially serious problems in the application of operational warfare. Moreover, the U.S. military is in real danger of learning some false strategic and operational lessons from the conflict.

Desired End State and Strategic Objectives

Any military action with a strategic objective and intended to end hostilities requires the determination of a desired end state by the highest national leadership. Such guidance should state in clear terms what political, diplomatic, military, economic, informational, and other conditions should exist in a theater after the end of the hostilities. Only afterward can strategic objectives be determined.

The broader the desired end state, the greater one's flexibility to determine strategic objectives and to modify, refine, or alter them in the course of a conflict. Also, by articulating a militarily achievable desired end state, the highest national leadership would be in a much better situation to measure the progress of a campaign or major operation.

The United States had two courses open in determining the desired conditions at the conclusion of Enduring Freedom: the establishment of a commonly accepted central government in Kabul or a country fragmented along ethnic lines. The establishment of a central government would lead to the end of civil war, free elections, and the start of economic reconstruction and recovery. Such a situation, while highly desirable for both political and military reasons, is extremely difficult to create given the country's recent history. A fragmented Afghanistan perhaps is a more realistic ultimate outcome. Yet such a situation most likely would lead to greater instability in the region as the neighboring powers support their proxies and try to carve up spheres of influence in the country. Ironically, a fragmented state would reduce the possibility of the emergence of another radical Islamicist regime that could provide safe haven for international terrorist networks such as al Qaeda. Also, a fragmented Afghanistan would be too weak to pose a serious threat to any of its neighbors, although it would not serve as a buffer between competing powers. Other aspects of the desired end state could include the creation of conditions for the country's economic reconstruction, significantly reducing the production of opium, and the appeal and influence of militant Islam on the Afghani population.

The U.S. national strategic objectives in the war against international terrorism include the destruction of all components of the al Quada network worldwide and other radical groups dedicated to attacking the United States and denying the terrorists safe havens and other forms of support. The ultimate objective of these efforts should be to reduce drastically the ability of international terrorist groups to inflict political, economic, psychological, and other damages on the United States and its allies.

The task of Commander in Chief, U.S. Central Command (CinC-Cent), was to translate these national strategic objectives into strategic objectives for the theater. On 7 October 2001, President George W. Bush announced that the U.S. military action was designed to disrupt the use of Afghanistan as a terrorist base of operations, to attack the military capability of the Taliban regime, to bring bin Laden and other al Qaeda leaders to justice, and to prevent al Qaeda's network from posing a continuous terrorist threat.

Method of Combat Force Employment

Even in an undeveloped theater such as Afghanistan, strategic objectives usually cannot be accomplished in one fell swoop. Therefore, the planners work backward to derive intermediate operational objectives. In a conventional war, the accomplishment of each operational objective would require planning and the conduct of a major operation. The ultimate strategic objective was accomplished through a single major offensive air operation and series of major tactical actions aimed at seizing the northern, eastern, southern, and western parts of Afghanistan. The unique feature of the operation was that each of the four operational objectives on the ground was accomplished through a major tactical action rather than a major operation. Enduring Freedom can be considered a counterterrorist campaign, the first such in history.

Critical Factors and Center of Gravity

In any conflict, the optimal use of one's military and nonmilitary sources of power is achieved by focusing on defeating or neutralizing an enemy's center of gravity (COG). For any military objective, there is a corresponding center of gravity. The higher the level of war, the smaller the number of COGs because there are fewer—although larger—objectives to be accomplished. At the strategic level, there is a single COG, while at the operational and tactical levels normally multiple COGs exist.

A COG always is found among an enemy's critical strengths, never among his critical weaknesses. It cannot be identified in isolation from a specific military objective to be accomplished. Both the objective and its corresponding COG are related closely. Whenever the objective changes, the enemy's critical strengths and weaknesses must be reevaluated as well. This, in turn, would require modification or refinement of the existing COG, or in case of a drastic change in the scope and the content of an objective, identification of a new COG.

For U.S. planners, the enemy's strategic center of gravity was the leadership of al Qaeda and the Taliban—and their will to fight. Because the Taliban regime was largely dependent on al Qaeda for its own survival, bin Laden and his inner circle represented the most important part of the enemy's strategic center of gravity. In many cases, an enemy's will to fight can be degraded seriously by inflicting on him a series of defeats in the field. This is hard to achieve when fighting fanatics such as hard-core Talibans or al Qaeda fighters. The only way to accomplish one's objective is by physically eradicating or capturing the leadership. Reportedly, of the 20 to 25 close associates of bin Laden, so far only one-third have been eliminated or captured. At least 15 top aides of bin Laden are in flight. Most of the 550 al Qaeda members held in Kandahar or Guantanamo are foot soldiers.[1] As long as the leadership is at large, the ultimate strategic objective in Afghanistan will be difficult to consolidate.

In planning and executing a campaign against terrorists, one's efforts should be focused against an enemy's strategic COG. In contrast to a conventional war, an international terrorist network's leadership must be physically eradicated or at least captured. Otherwise, it is difficult to consolidate and exploit one's strategic success.

In Afghanistan, for each of the operational objectives there was a corresponding COG. Initially, the Taliban fighter aircraft and surface-to-air missiles were operational COGs. Subsequently, the Taliban and al Qaeda forces defending the northern, eastern, southern, and western parts of the country also were considered operational COGs.

The conflict in Afghanistan reconfirmed the enduring value of favorable military positions in planning, preparing, and executing major operations or campaigns. The U.S. maritime forces, land-based aircraft, and ground forces and their logistical supplies had to be moved from staging areas—in some instances a dozen of thousands miles away.

In the initial phase of the operation, the U.S. military lacked adequate host-nation support to insert its ground forces and tactical land-based aircraft into the area adjacent to Afghanistan. Hence, the U.S. Navy's carrier battle groups deployed in the Arabian Sea played a critical role in the initial phase of the operation. They made subsequent successes possible by carrying out the major part of the initial sorties. Without their contribution, the collapse of the Taliban regime would have taken longer. A combination of long distances and the short effective range of the aircraft, however, limited carrier aircraft to an average of 100 attack sorties per day.[2] In addition, they needed a large number of tanker sorties to reach their targets.[3] The carrier-based aircraft flew some 500 miles each way. Similarly, the B-1s and B-52s that flew from Diego Garcia and the B-2s from the United States required heavy use of in-flight refueling and significant diplomatic efforts in securing basing and overflight rights.[4] The B-1s and B-52s had to fly a total distance of some 5,500 miles and each of their trips lasted 12 to 15 hours.

The conflict in Afghanistan confirmed some old lessons, such as the importance of geographical positions and distances on the outcome of a major operation. While information has an ever-increasing effect on the factor of space, one's forces still have to be moved at a relatively low speed and over large space. They also must be supplied and sustained to overcome the factor of space and time. Hence, it is preposterous to claim that the geography and distances are somehow devalued. The United States was able to project its power over many thousands of miles from home bases and sustain that power for a long time. Even the ability of the United States to project power was limited, however, because of lack of support from host nations and restrictions imposed on its forces based on land. As in the past, the sea continues to provide the easiest access to many parts of the world's land mass. The conflict in Afghanistan was perhaps the first in which carrier-based air power created conditions for subsequent success in the employment of land-based tactical aircraft.

Operational Command and Control

Sound command organization is one of the most critical prerequisites for the successful employment of forces at any level, but especially at the operational and higher levels. During the operation, CinCCent remained in Tampa, Florida. It was explained that the advances in communications and teleconferencing allow theater commanders to control his forces regardless of long distances involved. Also, it was argued that a modern commander does not need to be physically in the area of operations to exercise effective command and control, or to lead and motivate his subordinate forces. Relocating CinCCent's headquarters to Saudi Arabia would have resulted in a symbolically larger U.S. presence in the region that could potentially lead to more political complications and also increase security risks.[5]

Some experts assert that what matters is whether the commander can be where he needs to be to influence the conduct of the battle.[6] This view, however, misses a key point in modern command and control at the operational level. A theater-strategic commander should remain at his main headquarters so that he can most effectively monitor and control the events in his entire area of responsibility, not just the part of his theater where combat takes place. CinCCent is concerned not only with the conflict in Afghanistan, but also has to be involved in planning and preparation for possible contingencies in other parts of his area of responsibility. Ideally, he should maintain undivided attention to the strategic aspects of the situation. The ability to use advanced communications and information technologies should not be used as a justification for not establishing an intermediate level of command. Distance and time still matter, and the need for a commander to lead and motivate his forces remains one of the tenets of successful operational leadership.

One solution would have been the establishment of a theater of operations (perhaps called the Southwest Asia Theater of Operations). Such a theater command could have been led by a three-star flag officer directly subordinate to CinCCent and headquartered close to Afghanistan. The boundaries of such a theater would have encompassed Afghanistan and adjacent land areas used for basing of U.S. and other coalition forces, the Arabian Gulf, the Gulf of Oman, the Arabian Sea, and parts of the Indian Ocean. There would be significant improvement in control of subordinate forces deployed in the theater, and a great reduction in the amount of information passing on to CinCCent headquarters.

One of the principal tenets of U.S. command and control is centralized direction and decentralized execution. Decentralization of the decision-making process is a prerequisite for giving subordinates sufficient freedom of action. In contrast, a centralized execution leads to lack of initiative on the part of subordinates and forces the higher commander to take over part of their responsibilities in combat. This is not only bad for morale, but distracts the theater commander. The conflicts in Kosovo and Afghanistan reinforced the trend toward further central-ization of command and control in U.S. military. Rather than reinforce decentralized command, advances in information technologies have led in the opposite direction.

Perhaps the most serious problem in the U.S. military today is the continued deterioration of the previously successful and well-proven method of centralized direction and decentralized execution of planning military actions at all levels. Advances in information technologies and communications should lead to further decentralization. The theater-strategic commander should focus on his responsibilities in the entire area of operations and leave the planning and execution of a major oper-ation or campaign to a subordinate theater commander. This not only would preclude the theater-strategic commander from interfering with subordinate commanders, but would prevent his being bogged down in tactical details. The U.S. joint doctrine regarding operational com-mand and control is sound and has proven its value. The problem is that it is poorly applied or is not applied at all. This is a potentially fa-tal flaw that could cost us dearly in a conflict with much stronger and smarter opponent.

Role of Air Power

The use of U.S. airpower was the principal factor in the speedy col-lapse of the Taliban regime. In the initial phase of the operation, U.S. heavy bombers and carrier-based attack aircraft destroyed the Taliban's air defenses, communications, and military installations. It was not un-til the fourth week of the offensive, however, that air power shifted to the support of the proxies on the ground. The end of the Taliban regime then came rather quickly because of the combination of the punishing air strikes and the offensive of Afghani allies on the ground. The key to success was the availability of Special Forces on the ground to identify and designate targets for the aircraft. Reportedly, in many cases the response time was less than 20 minutes from the moment a target was spotted to its destruction. Fewer aircraft and fewer sorties were required to destroy targets than in the past. Some missions re-portedly involved only a pair of bombers or attack aircraft.[7]

The role of Navy carriers as a platform of choice was reconfirmed. There should be no discussion of whether we need carriers or land-based air. We need both because their capabilities are complementary. Without carriers in the area, it is difficult to see how success would be achieved.

Operation Enduring Freedom demonstrated that the effectiveness of air power against enemy forces on the ground was much higher than in other conflicts because of the extensive use of smart munitions and much more accurate targeting information provided by the Special Forces on the ground. This led to a smaller number of air sorties with much higher effectiveness per sortie. Simply because these tactics proved highly successful in Afghanistan, however, does not mean that they could be repeated with the same results in some other conflict against a much stronger and resourceful enemy. Also, inserting Special Forces on the ground to provide timely targeting information would be much more difficult and riskier in the urbanized environment or territory under tight control of the enemy forces. In short, the use of air power in combination with the Special Forces on the ground can be expected to be successful in some counterterrorist operation or campaign in the future, but not in major regional contingencies.

The greatest danger of the lessons from Afghanistan is that U.S. policymakers will rely predominantly on land-based aircraft in resolving the next crisis. Air power should be used in combination with forces on the ground and at sea to achieve the best results.

Targeting

The target selection followed a similar pattern to NATO's Allied Force (Kosovo), where the targets were selected and attacked regardless of whether and to what degree they contributed to the accomplishment of a given military objective.[8] Among other things, focusing on targeting makes it much harder to determine whether and when a certain objective is accomplished and leads to a considerable waste of one's time and resources. As Kosovo showed, such an approach to warfare almost invariably leads to a war of attrition at the operational and strategic levels. This might not be important in operations like Enduring Freedom where victory is assured, but it is a different matter in fighting a much stronger opponent.

Another problem in the use of U.S. air power in Afghanistan was a clear overemphasis on avoiding collateral damages. Reportedly, virtually every strike or attack was approved by CinCCent in Tampa.[9] Lawyers were heavily involved in approving the list of targets to be attacked, at all command echelons. The lawyers participated in determining whether a specific target was used for military purposes, evaluating the propriety of using certain type of munitions, and deciding whether a successful attack on such a target was outweighed by civilian losses.[10] Although the commander made a final decision, this process was unnecessarily complicated, cumbersome, and time consuming. Reportedly, on too many occasions excellent intelligence and great advances in shortening the time for carrying out a strike were severely degraded because of the unduly long time for getting approval from the higher commanders. In some instances, the planners were forced to remove some targets from the list because of legal objections, although they were considered important for military reasons.[11] While concern for avoiding collateral damage is critical for maintaining and sustaining public support for war, a better balance should be found so that legal issues are not allowed to adversely affect the success of a given military action.

Objectives and tasks—not targets—should dominate the planning process at any level of command. A targeteering approach is inherently attritional, and thus leads to a waste of time and effort because targets are selected and attacked without regard to their relationship to tasks and objectives. More seriously, such an approach to warfare, especially at the operational and higher level, cannot but lead to the loss of the broader perspective on the situation on the part of the operational commanders and their staffs. Enduring Freedom reinforced this negative trend toward overreliance on technology and tactics of platforms and weapons over combined arms tactics and operational warfare. Target selection and approval is becoming increasingly complex and time-consuming. The resultant loss of military effectiveness cannot be justified by using specious political and legal arguments.

In Afghanistan, proxies on the ground proved to be the key for the speedy collapse of the Taliban regime. The Northern Alliance and Eastern Alliance troops forced the Taliban and al Qaeda forces to concentrate, thereby becoming an easy target for devastating U.S. air strikes. The United States was faced with a choice of either relying on the Northern Alliance and other Afghani proxy forces or introducing a larger U.S. ground force. An advantage of relying on Afghani proxies was a significant reduction of political complications and greater chance for success in the post-hostilities phase. A disadvantage was that the Afghani proxies often had different objectives than the United States. In contrast to the U.S. way of warfare, which seeks clear-cut victories, the Afghanis generally prefer negotiated surrenders and switching sides rather than utterly defeating their domestic opponents.

The fighting at Tora Bora in December 2001 and Shahi Kot in February 2002 was less conclusive for the United States and its proxies than official statements might otherwise suggest. In both operations, a major part of the Taliban and al Qaeda fighters apparently survived and escaped to fight another day. Reportedly, during the fighting in Tora Bora, several hundred al Qaeda fighters escaped over the White Mountains into the poorly controlled north-western frontier area of Pakistan.[12] Many experts believe that if the United States had committed larger numbers of ground troops during the fighting, bin Laden and his top aides would have been captured.[13] The consequences of the failure to capture the top leadership of al Qaeda are still to be seen.

The lack of sizable U.S. presence on the ground almost certainly avoided protracted and costly conflict with the majority of the Afghani population because the United States was not perceived as a foreign occupier. At the same time, a high price was paid for using Northern Alliance and other Afghan surrogates instead of sending in sizable U.S. ground forces.

Role of Technology

Many experts have asserted that the success in Afghanistan proved the value of the "revolution in military affairs." While many new technologies successfully passed the test, it must be remembered that U.S. forces possessed overwhelming power and faced a weak opponent. The enemy never had a chance to challenge air power. The victory in Afghanistan was easy and cheap because Afghanistan had few economic centers and poor infrastructure. The Taliban air defenses were virtually nonexistent and that accounts for the fact that the United States obtained air superiority within hours. The Taliban had few, if any, antiaircraft weapons with the reliability, range, and guidance systems to pose a credible threat against high-flying aircraft equipped with the most advanced sensors.[14] The UAVs were used against almost nonexistent opposition, and Special Forces were allowed to roam freely in the countryside.[15] At sea, the U.S. and coalition forces faced no opposition at all. Nor did the Taliban possess any capability to interfere with or attack U.S. computer networks.

Network-centric warfare enthusiasts assert that their ideas have been proven in Afghanistan because targeting information from sensor to shooter was obtained almost instantly. Critical advances in computer networking and broadband satellite communications enabled intelligence from UAVs and other sources, such as the radars on board the E-8 Joint Surveillance Target Attack Radar System (J-STARS) aircraft, to be combined with signals intelligence and satellite images. But the conflict in Afghanistan only proves that netting of diverse platforms technically works in a nonhostile or low-threat environment. It does not tell us whether U.S. systems are robust enough to operate smoothly in the face of a determined physical and electronic attack by a resourceful and skillful enemy.

Too much emphasis on technology is unsound because the human element of warfare is being dismissed as irrelevant to our modern age. Technological advances have steadily reduced uncertainties in the situation on the battlefield, but they cannot eliminate the Clausewitzian "fog of war" and "friction."

The emphasis on technology and tactics of weapons and platforms already has some serious and negative repercussions. This trend must be reversed soon. Otherwise the United States might find itself outthought and outfought by a relatively weaker but a more agile opponent who pays attention not only to tactics, but also to operational art and strategy and therefore better snatches ends, means, and ways to achieve victory.

COLONEL DARREL
WHITCOMB, USAF (RET.)

Combat Search and Rescue:
A Longer Look

As the recent events in Serbia indicate, combat search and rescue (CSAR) is still with us. The successful rescues of the pilot of an F-117—known as Vega 31—and of Hammer 34, the pilot of an F-16, make for exciting stories, but little has appeared in print on these two operations. No doubt, this is prudent because operations continue in-theater. But when the stories are eventually told, readers will find much in common with SARs or CSARs from earlier conflicts. These accounts will take their place in the rich lore of rescue operations, which go back to the beginning of manned flight and honor the men who go in harm's way so "that others may live."

From a historical perspective, these rescues seem to fit into long-term patterns from which we can draw lessons to apply to future operations. Winston Churchill, a great student of history, once said, "The farther backward you can look, the farther forward you can see."[1] Aviation history abounds with stories of rescue. Perhaps some of that history would prove useful to stimulate discussion or debate to help us take a longer look at the subject. The reason we do this seems obvious. After all, those are our troops out there, and we will try to get them out if they go down. But perhaps the answer is not quite that simple—perhaps there is quite a bit more to this complex issue.

In any military operation, we must be prepared for CSAR for any crew, group, or team that may be isolated behind enemy lines. This means being able to rescue people from a single-seat fighter, an airborne warning and control system aircraft, a special forces team, or myriad other sources. (The three US soldiers not rescued from Serbia during the recent Balkans conflicts were on a routine ground patrol.)

The first and perhaps main point is that *CSARing is war fighting*—pure and simple. We cannot think of it separately. CSARing is just another form of battle. In that vein, the principles of war do apply. There will be a time and place for mass or economy of force and perhaps deception operations, depending on the situation. Unity of command will be essential to focus the effort. Security will be critical because of the need for timely, focused action and the realization that the enemy will try to counter our actions. We must carefully guard critical information and intelligence.

In a theater of operations in which many actions, battles, and perhaps campaigns take place, CSARs will add to the fog and chaos of war. As opposed to other types of operations whose objectives are not clear or easily understood, however, a CSAR's objective is clear, understood by all, and easily measurable. Furthermore, it appeals to us on a human level—perhaps a dangerous trait because it can detract from other efforts. That is, we find it easy to divert resources meant for other battles to a CSAR effort. Are we willing to rescue somebody regardless of the cost? Seemingly, the mantra today is that "the war will stop for CSAR." Is this prudent?

It goes without saying that CSAR demands absolute precision. In a larger theater of operations with so many other things going on, we literally have to reach into realms of organized chaos to pluck a specific person or persons out.

Experience shows that when an aircrew is down, time works against us. Our enemies realize that we will make the effort and will try to rescue our personnel. We must assume that they know of our efforts and probably have some knowledge of our specific techniques. A recent test at Nellis AFB, Nevada, suggested that after two hours on the ground, the odds begin to turn against a successful rescue.[2]

CSARing seems to involve two paths of knowledge. For lack of better terms, the labels *logos* or logic and *pathos* or emotion will suffice. Both have a role in this business.

Logos

Looking at all this historically, the accomplishment of five things dramatically increases the chances of a successful rescue. Of course, no one can guarantee success because, after all, we are operating in the realm of conflict and chance.

First is the matter of *position*—we have to find the survivor(s). This sounds very basic, but that is the point. It is absolutely fundamental to the whole process. As a recent CSAR report stated, "Accurate coordinates are critical" to recovery[3] (remember that the S in CSAR stands for *search*). In the old days of Southeast Asia, we used to send in a pack of A-1s to sweep the area to find the survivor(s). Today, with sophisticated radars, guns, and missiles, this is becoming harder to do. We should be prepared to use all available assets, both theater and national, to locate the survivor(s). This is critical because we cannot begin to properly marshal our forces for a recovery until we know their whereabouts. We should also emphasize that we must prevent the enemy from discovering the location of the survivor(s).

Position appears to have value on four levels:

1. *Strategically.* The location of the survivor in relation to national boundaries can have a substantial impact on the relationship of nations, rules of engagement, and such matters as the need for overflight privileges. In Southeast Asia, we had different operation rules for South Vietnam, North Vietnam, Laos, and Cambodia. We launched no rescue operations for crews lost over China.
2. *Operationally.* We must determine whether the location of the survivor(s) will affect anything else going on in the larger conflict. Will a focused CSAR operation in a particular time and place interfere with some other operation, or can we conceivably use some aspect of that operation to aid the recovery effort?
3. *Tactically.* What do we have to do to get into the immediate area of the survivor(s) to effect the recovery? This requires classic intelligence preparation to understand what we must do to counter enemy attempts to defeat the CSAR effort.
4. *Precision.* What do we have to do to facilitate the actual linkup of the survivor and his recovery vehicle—the most critical event in the entire process? Once we commit the recovery vehicle, it must expeditiously maneuver to and link up with the survivor(s) and then depart the area.

Second, we must establish *communication* with the survivor(s) and those agencies necessary to plan, coordinate, command, and execute the rescue. The Korean War showed us that we needed to equip our downed crews with survival radios.[4] Preplanning can prove very effective here in determining how disparate units and elements can come together to execute a short-notice CSAR. The air tasking order and special instructions can be very useful in this regard, as well as common terms understood by all. Conversely, code words understood by one element of the CSAR effort but not by others can sow confusion at absolutely the wrong moment. Do we all agree on the meaning of *bingo*? How many fighter guys know what a *spider route* is? How many helicopter drivers know what *magnum* means? Moreover, during the intensity of a CSAR event, we must exclude those who cannot contribute. Useless information or chatter is just communication jamming.

Third, we have to have a recovery vehicle. They do not just happen. We always think of the big rescue helicopters—we call them *Jolly Greens*—as the vehicles, but we must think beyond that. Naval vehicles, ground vehicles, or maybe even a ground team can do the job. It does not matter what patch that vehicle wears. The vehicle is not important—the recovery is.

Fourth, we need to have *smart survivors*. As a recent CSAR report states, "Survivor actions are an integral part of the success or failure of any rescue operation."[5] The history of successful rescues resounds with this theme.

Fifth, we must be able to establish around that survivor the necessary level of situational superiority so that we can control events long enough to effect the recovery. One of the lessons learned from the Korean War was that air superiority is critical to the successful operation of a recovery task force.[6] But the necessary superiority is really three dimensional, for some of the most serious threats today are ground based. This makes CSARs unique, separating them from SARs. The first four points actually apply to just about any rescue operation. But again, in combat the enemy will oppose our actions. We must impose our will. We must control events long enough in the survivor's area to allow the recovery vehicle to make the recovery and depart. This is battle. This is war fighting. We now turn to several historical examples from which we can learn.

World War II

In February 1944, a carrier task force attacked the Japanese forces at Truk Atoll. During the battle, a Grumman F-6F from the USS *Essex* was shot down. The pilot ditched his aircraft in the lagoon surrounding the islands. The flight leader watched him go down, fixed his position, and saw that he was alive and in his raft. He then called back to the *Essex*, requesting air-sea rescue. Another ship in the task force, the USS *Baltimore*, launched an OS2U-3 Kingfisher amphibious aircraft to recover the pilot. Before the aircraft could arrive, however, the flight leader spotted a Japanese destroyer entering the lagoon, apparently to capture the pilot. He led repeated attacks on the ship, driving it away and maintaining enough situational superiority around the survivor to facilitate his rescue.[7] This procedure repeated itself two months later but with a twist. As the task force once again pounded Truk, more Navy aircraft went down. In one incident, another Kingfisher, this time from the battleship *North Carolina*, recovered 10 downed airmen. Too heavy to take off with survivors literally camped out on the wing, once again Navy fighters covered the Kingfisher as it taxied out to open water and transferred survivors to a waiting submarine, the USS *Tang*.[8]

KOREAN WAR

In June 1951, a pilot ditched his flak-damaged Mustang fighter in the Taedong River, 50 miles northeast of Pyongyang. His flight mates saw him swimming in the river and called for a rescue aircraft. An SA-16 Albatross flown by 1st Lt John Najarian responded and flew to their position. The covering Mustangs, joined by other flights, suppressed the enemy guns along both shores as Najarian landed in the cold waters and picked up the pilot. But the sun had gone down, and the current swept the Albatross toward high-power lines across the river. To help Najarian see the wires, the Mustang pilots turned on their landing lights and flew just above him as he made his takeoff under the wires.[9]

VIETNAM WAR

A number of stories about Southeast Asia deserve telling, one of them being Oyster 01 Bravo. In May 1972, an F-4 was shot down northwest of Hanoi. The weapon system operator (WSO), 1st Lt Roger Locher, evaded the enemy for 23 days before he established communication with friendly forces, who positively located him. Rescue forces in the theater responded, but enemy forces initially drove them off. Gen John Vogt, commander of Seventh Air Force, directed that the entire next day's effort be dedicated to establishing enough local superiority to support the rescue operation. Those efforts proved successful.[10]

Bat 21 Bravo/Nail 38 Bravo, a huge SAR, the largest of the war, took place in April 1972. Our forces established communications with the survivors and easily located them. Although we had rescue forces available, we could not establish local superiority so that a rescue helicopter could recover them. Indeed, the enemy shot down several in the effort. A small ground team, using stealth and very precise fire support, recovered the two men.[11]

An unsuccessful recovery, Owl 14 Bravo, is nevertheless instructive. Another F-4 went down over North Vietnam in May 1972, just north of the demilitarized zone. Only one survivor (Capt Ray Bean, the WSO) made radio contact with covering forces, who located him. Rescue assets were available, but thick enemy antiaircraft forces covered the area. Before we could suppress them enough for a helicopter to enter the area, the enemy captured Bean, releasing him from Hanoi a year later. Captain Bean said that the enemy forces were so heavy that they would have destroyed any helicopter entering the area.[12]

GULF WAR

On 21 January 1991, an Iraqi missile downed Slate 46, an F-14. We established intermittent radio contact with the pilot but had only general knowledge of his position. The enemy captured the radio-intercept officer. An MH-53 piloted by Capt Tom Trask proceeded deep into Iraq. In the general vicinity of the survivor, a flight of two A-10s joined the helicopter. They managed to locate the survivor and vector the helicopter crew to him. But enemy troops were in the area, including some trucks obviously homing in on the pilot's radio transmissions. Capt Paul Johnson, the lead A-10 pilot, attacked the enemy forces and vehicles—only 150 meters away from the Navy pilot—and facilitated his recovery.[13]

BALKANS WAR

Also useful is knowledge of the failed recovery of Ebro 33, a French Mirage crew shot down in late August of 1995 during the North Atlantic Treaty Organization's (NATO) Operation Deliberate Force. We never established radio contact with the survivors and never determined their location. Although we had rescue forces available and possibly had sufficient force to establish enough local superiority, we never recovered them; in fact, friendly forces were injured in the search efforts.[14]

Pathos

We now turn to pathos, the emotional "why" of all this. Again, the answer seems obvious. The survivor is one of ours, and we never leave our people behind.

But don't combat aviators accept the risk of loss and death in battle? Don't they get extra flight pay to accept the risk? As one US Air Force general said in 1972, at the height of the Bat 21 Bravo SAR, "As airmen or soldiers or sailors, we should expect that there are times when as one person, we must be sacrificed for the overall [mission]."[15]

Yes, we do accept the risk but have never easily accepted the view that our people are easily expendable—especially in a war we do not seem intent on winning. So, why so much for one man? Several reasons come to mind.

First is *human nature*. Rescue stories are some of our most heroic. People always come forward to help those in distress. The fact that the enemy contests CSARs only causes us to redouble our efforts.[16]

Second is the fact that *we can*. We have developed the hardware to recover anybody from just about anywhere. Additionally, we do not hesitate to use any technology if it benefits the process. We have also learned how to organize our forces to achieve the necessary level of situational superiority for our rescue forces to operate.[17] For *Joint Vision 2010* junkies, we call that dominant maneuver and precision engagement.

Third, rescue operations involve a *morale factor* for our troops, something Gen Hap Arnold noted in World War II. He directed the initial establishment of rescue forces to recover downed airmen, as had the British and Germans.[18] Part of his thinking was, in fact, pragmatic, for it takes an incredible number of resources to produce trained crew members.[19] This is not to say that in humanistic terms, they are more valuable than other Americans—just that they are harder to replace. Gen Hugh Shelton, chairman of the Joint Chiefs of Staff, addressed this recently when he said, "By pledging to put every effort into recovering our highly trained [personnel], we send a powerful signal about their importance and help sustain their spirit under the stress of combat."[20]

Fourth, rescuing our people denies the enemy a valuable resource. Intelligence and propaganda value are the obvious issues here. Consider Mogadishu or the shootdown of Capt Scott O'Grady by the Bosnian Serbs.[21] During the Gulf War, Saddam Hussein tried to exploit captured aircrews. No doubt, he will do so again if we lose any personnel in Operation Northern or Southern Watch.

Finally, a covenant or bond binds the brotherhood of airmen.

Again, General Arnold noted that aircrews performed their missions more efficiently with the expectation that if they went down, we would make every effort to rescue them.[22]

Ground warriors call this bond unit cohesion, noting that, over time, soldiers must believe in what they do and must believe that the cause they fight for is worth the sacrifice. If not, they will fight for each other. Stephen Ambrose has eloquently documented this phenomenon among American fighting men in World War II.[23]

Our covenant is not so much unit specific as it is specific to the breed—the breed of airmen. It is the common thread stretching from the beginning of flight to the recent rescues in Serbia. What is that bond? It is simple: if at all possible, we will not leave our downed fellows behind without making an attempt to get them out.

This does not mean that we are unrealistic about war. Airmen understand, accept, and expect that we will take losses. But we do not give up those losses lightly. We expect that whatever we are asked to do is worth the sacrifice—that we will not be wasted for some specious task or mission and that our troops "shall not have died in vain," as President Lincoln said at Gettysburg.

But I would suggest that our propensity to prosecute CSAR missions exists on a sliding scale inversely proportional to the level of effort we are willing to expend in any conflict. In other words, in a total conflict in which national existence is at stake, we will pay any price. I clearly remember as an A-10 pilot in the 1980s listening to a NATO general telling us that he would "litter the west bank of the Elbe River with A-10s to keep the Warsaw Pact forces from crossing." I was horrified by his pronouncement until I thought through what that statement meant. Such an event would have been a total conflict, and the survival of our nation would have been at stake. The intensity of operations would have forced such sacrifices upon us. Our nation has accepted such losses in time of crisis, such as the Civil War or World War II. But in limited conflicts, we will be prepared to pay only a limited price. Why?

I am reminded of the old saw that military forces do not fight wars—nations do. And they fight for political objectives. Carl von Clausewitz explained all this many years ago when he said, "The political object is a goal, war is a means of reaching it, and means can never be considered in isolation of the purpose."[24] But that goal or objective determines the war's value, against which the public assesses the costs of the war in determining its support for the war. The public measures these costs in terms of taxes and, more importantly, risks to the lives of its sons and daughters. Again, Clausewitz explained this by saying,

"Once the expenditure of effort exceeds the political object, the object must be renounced."[25]

In a total conflict, then, CSARs will be limited—but not so in limited engagements, in which we prepare ourselves to pay only a limited price to achieve a limited objective. Today, it seems that airpower is the weapon of choice for doing so. Indeed, our political leaders evidently feel—based on what they hear from their constituents—that the public has little tolerance for loss. The fact that aircrews are now about the only ones put at risk puts a real premium on CSAR, accentuating the covenant. I saw this happen firsthand as a young lieutenant in Southeast Asia.

About 1969, my nation had begun to turn against the war. The object, whatever it was, was not worth the price. America wanted to withdraw. President Nixon called it "peace with honor." But I clearly remember hearing my squadron commander say to us, "There is nothing over here worth an American life—except another American."[26] That gave us cause for reflection, considering the fact that we were fighting alongside our allies.

By 1972, after eight years of war, we were still fighting there without any real dedication to a cause—except withdrawal. Like warriors from earlier wars, we fought for each other. We kept that article of faith that if we went down, the Jolly would come for us. In fact, the rescue helicopter became the symbol of that bond or covenant. To the rescue crews, it was a call sign. To the rest of us, it was a prayer. To many, it was salvation. It was the bond.

Now, we airmen have not been too good about recording these feelings. But consider the words of a US Navy PT boat sailor who explored this subject in a different way. When discussing a failed attempt to recover buddies lost in a night battle, he said, "The gain in going back is in the message it sends. Even if you're seen to disappear in a ball of flame, your friends will come back looking for you."[27]

Again, General Shelton recently accentuated this determination when he said, "This bond among warriors promises not to leave a comrade behind on the battlefield, a promise that extends to a shipmate at sea or a wingman who gets hit deep behind enemy lines."[28]

But there is danger here. We must not do this at the expense of our ground forces. We must perform rescue operations as part of the larger battle and must do so in proportion. Where does the line break? I don't know. Again, Churchill gives us a useful vector. In 1940 the German armies overran the countries of Western Europe, driving the British army back into an enclave at the French port of Dunkerque. The Royal Navy and individual British seamen in their private boats rallied to bring a large portion of that force safely back to Great Britain—without equipment or organization. After a spring of constant bad news and humiliation, the British people celebrated this event as a major victory. But Churchill stood in Parliament to remind them that "we must be very careful not to assign to this deliverance the attributes of victory. Wars are not won by evacuations."[29] One can also argue that they are not won by CSARs. But the ability and propensity to execute CSARs are key to the aircrew morale, *especially* if they are the only ones at risk. General Vogt understood this when he sent that large task force up near Hanoi to rescue Roger Locher in 1972.

We must never rescue our people at the expense of our allies. In coalition warfare, the relationship between allies is a center of gravity that a skillful enemy can exploit. Hitler tried to do this to the grand coalition in World War II. The North Vietnamese were very skillful in driving a wedge between us Americans and our South Vietnamese allies. We must make sure that we are willing to do CSAR for all our allies—as we did for Ebro 33.

So that is the pathos. These are powerful forces, and we are occasionally reminded of them in small but very significant ways. In November 1997, several hundred of us gathered at Arlington National Cemetery to bury the crew of Jolly Green 67, the men lost in the Bat 21 Bravo rescue effort in 1972. It was a beautiful, memorable day. One could not help noticing all the veterans of that era who gathered to welcome home the crew. Indeed, the blue suits of the highly decorated vets covered the site and part of an adjoining hill. Two MH-53 helicopters, descendents of the Jolly Greens, made a magnificent flyby. Lt Gen Dave Vesely, representing the chief of staff of the Air Force, said, "All of us who have flown in harm's way know what a difference it makes to believe that every effort will be made to rescue us if we are down. . . . Today while we count the high cost, we should also count ourselves fortunate to be the beneficiaries of these, the best of men—men who gave their lives so 'that others may live.' "[30]

As the ceremony ended, many of the now aged veterans of those times, missions, and battles went up to the coffin. Some laid their maroon berets on it or placed roses or stickers. Some saluted or just touched it. In all of that there was a message. Those still proud veterans had come for the Jolly because they remembered a time when, if necessary, the Jolly would have come for them.

That is the covenant, the bond that binds this brotherhood of airmen. It is palpable, and, as we saw again in Serbia, it is timeless.

Pearl Harbor

W ar was coming to the ocean called "Pacific." Imperial Japan, in need of oil to feed its growing ambition, squirmed under the stricture of an American embargo (implemented because of Japan's aggression toward China). Japan would not be denied its self-proclaimed destiny, so Tokyo's warlords cast covetous eyes southward to the petroleum-rich Dutch East Indies, ripe for the plucking. The Pacific was to be "their" ocean, and the only major obstacle was the U.S. Pacific Fleet based in Hawaii. The focus of the two-year-old war in Europe was about to swing dramatically to what would soon be the world's largest theater of operations.

Pearl Harbor

To U.S. servicemen in 1941, Hawaii was a tropical paradise and a "dream" duty station. Army air and ground forces enjoyed a pleasant tour of duty; after all, the only potential enemy was 3,400 miles to the west. In 1940, the Pacific Fleet had moved to Pearl Harbor from San

Diego despite the objections of Adm. J.O. Richardson, "CinCPac," who felt that basing the fleet in Hawaii was no more a deterrent to Japanese aggression than leaving it by the mainland; furthermore, it made a tempting target. His objections were overridden by President Franklin D. Roosevelt, who replaced him with Adm. Husband E. Kimmel. His Army counterpart, Gen. Walter Short, had no more influence than Kimmel on Roosevelt's decision.

Meanwhile, the Army, Navy and Marine airmen on Oahu basked in the joy of flying in a pleasant climate, even amid growing concern about Tokyo's actions in China. Many of the fliers at Hickam, Pearl and Ewa ("Evva") would later clash with Axis aircraft in other sorties around the globe. Lt. Francis S. Gabreski, currently America's highest-scoring living ace, remembered duty in Hawaii as "wonderful." He said, "Unless you had the duty that day, you flew from eight a.m. to noon or so, maybe did some paperwork then had the rest of the day for surfing, fishing, or chasing girls." "Gabby" Gabreski met his future wife in Hawaii, eventually trading his P-36s and P-40s for P-47s in England.

Status of Forces

On the morning of December 7, 1941, the U.S. Army Air Force had about 230 aircraft in Hawaii; the Navy and Marines had about 170, plus 70 to 80 each on the aircraft carriers USS *Lexington* (CV-2) and *Enterprise* (CV-6). *Lex* was delivering Marine scout-bombers to Midway, 1,100 miles northwest of Honolulu. "The Big E" was en route home to Pearl Harbor, having delivered Marine fighters to Wake Island.

The Army had 45 bombers in Hawaii, though 33 were obsolete Douglas B-18s, barely capable of 200 mph. A dozen B-17D Flying Fortresses represented the USAAF's best striking arm, with excellent range and payload and a 25,000-foot capability. At that early time, however, it had not yet been realized how ineffective high-altitude bombers would be against moving ships. More promising were 13 Douglas A-20 attack bombers, later demonstrably effective in the Southwest Pacific.

Defending Hawaiian skies were 152 "pursuit ships" of various numbers and performance. The largest contingent was 99 Curtiss P-40B and C Tomahawks, with decent armament and speeds approaching 350 mph. First delivered early in 1941, they were the most modern fighters available.

Dating from 1938 was the Curtiss company's earlier entry, the radial-engine P-36A. Though claiming a 310 mph top speed, the 39 fighters with Pratt & Whitney R-1830s lacked the altitude performance of the -40s and packed a less lethal punch. Owing to export contracts for Britain, France and other nations, however, Curtiss was unable to deliver enough P-40s to its own country, so the second-line -36 soldiered on. Some squadrons flew both types interchangeably.

The P-36 may have been lacking in speed and firepower, but it was two-and-a-half laps ahead of the petite Boeing P-26. Fourteen of the fixed-gear, braced monoplane fighters remained in Hawaiian squadrons, and though the "Peashooters" had been considered hot ships in 1934, they were now more than 100 mph slower than the opposition—fit only for proficiency flying. The other USAAF aircraft on hand represented a variety of obsolete observation and liaison types.

By far the most significant naval aircraft in Hawaii was Consolidated's long-lived PBY flying boat. Newly named "Catalina," the big twin-engine patrol plane equipped two air wings with a total of 69 aircraft. They were based at Kaneohe Naval Air Station on the east coast of Oahu and were largely responsible for long-range patrol of Hawaiian waters. However, the Pacific Fleet commander, Adm. Kimmel, realized that he had too few PBYs to provide adequate coverage of all the approaches to the Hawaiian Islands. America was heavily committed to the ill-named "Neutrality Patrol" covering the Atlantic, where American-flown PBYs had been involved in destroying the German battleship *Bismarck* seven months before.

The Navy service wing at Kaneohe owned nearly 40 utility and scout-observation Grumman, Beech and Sikorsky types. There was also a small fleet-aircraft pool with 21 replacement fighters and dive bombers.

Marine Air Group Two, based at Ewa, comprised two scout-bomber squadrons with 29 Douglas SBDs and Vought SB2Us, a fighter squadron with 11 Grumman F4Fs and a utility squadron with eight "cats and dogs."

Naval aviation's offensive arm was built around its three aircraft carriers. As noted, *Lexington* and *Enterprise* were ferrying Marine planes to Midway and Wake, while the *Saratoga* (CV-3) was loading more leatherneck fighters in San Diego. Each flattop had nearly identical air groups, nominally flying 36 SBDs, 18 fighters (*Saratoga* had Brewster F2As) and 18 Douglas TBD torpedo planes. One of the luckiest breaks in American history was that all three PacFleet carriers were out of port on December 7. Because so many battleships were destroyed or damaged during the attack, and because submarines were largely irrelevant owing to the scandalous failure of their torpedoes (a problem that persisted for nearly two years), carrier aviation became America's only way to conduct a war in the Pacific.

Japan's Sunday Punch

In contrast to the rather anemic American forces, the Japanese Navy committed itself wholeheartedly to the Hawaii operation: all six fleet carriers, embarking 427 aircraft plus cruiser-based floatplanes for reconnaissance. The carrier air groups owned 144 Nakajima B5N torpedo planes, 138 Aichi D3A dive bombers and 138 Mitsubishi A6M fighters, arguably flown by the most experienced naval aviators on earth. Certainly, they had a high degree of competence, having trained relentlessly over the previous several months.

The effort that went into the aerial torpedoes alone was significant. Pearl Harbor was shallow—only 40 feet deep in places—and the challenge was to get torpedoes to level off before they plunged into the muddy bottom. After the British Navy's air attack on Taranto Harbor in November 1940, the Japanese naval attaché examined the damage done to Italian battleships (U.S. intelligence was aware of this) and concluded that it was possible to make torpedoes run shallow enough. Fitting large wooden fins to the torpedoes' aft ends proved to be workable; otherwise, Operation *Hawaii* probably would not have been executed.

The Japanese navy's standard torpedo plane was the Nakajima B5N, which entered service in 1937—the same year as America's ill-fated Douglas TBD. Reasonably fast and armed with the world's finest aerial torpedo, the Type 97 Carrier Attack Aircraft (later called "Kate" by the allies) represented a lethal threat against enemy ships. It also proved effective as a high-level bomber and performed well in both roles on December 7.

The counterpart of the Douglas Dauntless was the Aichi D3A, the Type 99 carrier bomber (aka "Val"). Despite its spatted, fixed landing gear, the Aichi demonstrated excellent stability and, therefore, accuracy in addition to a decent top speed—nearly 250 mph. The crews assigned to Operation *Hawaii* drilled incessantly before deploying, both against stationary and moving targets. Toward the end, they frequently recorded hit rates upward of 50 percent on maneuvering ships.

The Japanese Imperial Navy possessed an air-superiority design unlike any other in the world in the Mitsubishi A6M Type 0 fighter. Fast, long-range, agile and well-armed with cannon and machine guns, it was flown by competent, aggressive pilots, including combat veterans with kills over China. All three Japanese carrier planes became first to last warriors, flying from 1941 through 1945. In contrast, most of their American rivals were largely replaced by newer, more capable planes before 1945. The notable exceptions were the Flying Fortress, Catalina and Wildcat.

Japan's newly created First Air Fleet was easily the most powerful naval aviation force in existence. Six fast carriers were specially trained and equipped for the Hawaii operation, with adequate escorts and tankers to support a prolonged sweep of the largest ocean on Earth. Organized into three divisions with two flattops each, the Carrier Striking Force (Kido Butai) was led by Vice Adm. Chuichi Nagumo, an experienced surface officer. He commanded *Akagi, Kaga, Soryu, Hiryu, Shokaku* and *Zuikaku.* His lack of aviation expertise was more than off-set by his excellent staff, including two of Japan's ablest airmen and planners: Cmdrs. Minoru Genda and Mitsuo Fuchida. The latter would lead the first of two waves against Hawaii with a total of more than 300 planes.

Kido Butai departed Japanese waters on November 26, steaming the northerly route where weather was thick and shipping rare. Though U.S. intelligence picked up radio signals indicating that the carriers were out and headed east, the information was never used; nor did the decrypts of Japanese diplomatic codes clearly show that only Pearl Harbor had been divided into targeting grids.

Arriving at his launch point some 200 miles north of Oahu, Nagumo ensured that his aircrews were carefully briefed to recognize specific targets. At 0600 on December 7, the first 183 planes were launched in only 15 minutes—an accomplishment in itself—and de-ployed off the northern tip of Oahu at 0740. Ten minutes later, the fighters and dive bombers turned inland and aimed at Army air bases at Hickam and Wheeler fields plus the Naval air stations at Ford Island in Pearl Harbor and beautiful Kaneohe Bay on the east coast. Bellows Field, the Army facility south of Kaneohe, was mostly ignored, as it was known to be the home of an observation squadron.

Meanwhile, the Nakajima level and torpedo bombers skirted the southwest coast, arriving above the harbor at 0755. They overflew the Marine Corps base at Ewa, which Zeros strafed with eerie efficiency. By then, of course, the surprise was complete, despite the fact that a destroyer had sunk a midget submarine an hour previously and because of the fact that the huge formation detected by radar north of Oahu was deemed to be a dozen B-17s arriving from California.

"Don't Shoot!"

Vice Adm. William F. Halsey, commanding the *Enterprise* task force, had placed his ships on a war footing in November. Taking no chances, he had launched 18 Dauntlesses southwest of Kaula Island toward Pearl Harbor that morning. The SBDs found nothing remarkable between their carrier and the shore, but they flew directly into the Sunday surprise. The first "the Big E" knew of Pearl's peril was a frantic radio call from a young Dauntless pilot: "This is an American plane! Don't shoot!"

Over the next half hour or so, Japanese planes shot down five SBDs while American gunners downed a sixth. Three pilots and two radiomen were killed, and three more fliers were wounded.

It only got worse. After the carrier launched a futile search-strike that evening, the Wildcat escorts were diverted to Ford Island. In yet another snafu, gunners on the ground assumed that any airborne planes were hostile. Three F4F pilots were killed by "friendly fire." The Big E's revenge would be deferred for six months, but the debt was repaid with compound interest at Midway.

Nowhere was the efficiency of Japanese bombing and strafing more evident than Kaneohe. Of the 36 Catalina flying boats based there, 27 were destroyed, and six were damaged. Only three escaped enemy attention; they were on scheduled patrol missions.

Some of the best flying of the entire attack was by the Nakajima B5Ns that skimmed the waters of Pearl Harbor to deliver their Type 95 aerial torpedoes against "Battleship Row." The pilots had only seconds to descend to drop altitude, pick their aim points, release and pull out. The outboard ships took a succession of hits from the powerfully efficient torpedoes: *West Virginia* (BB-48) and *Oklahoma* (BB-37) were sunk at their moorings. *Arizona* (BB-39) took an armor-piercing bomb that detonated a magazine and exploded, taking more than 1,100 men with her—half the American fatalities on that day. The two inboard battlewagons—*Maryland* (BB-46) and *Tennessee* (BB-43)—sustained relatively light damage and were under way again in weeks. *Nevada* (BB-36), the only battleship to work up steam, became an immediate target as she headed for the harbor mouth. Bombers and torpedo planes jumped her as she pushed along at 10 knots, and her captain wisely beached the behemoth off Hospital Point rather than risk its sinking and blocking the channel.

Two other battlewagons were also hit: *California* (BB-44), moored alone off Ford Island, was sunk but eventually refloated; *Pennsylvania* (BB-39) was damaged in dry dock. The old *Utah* (AV-16) was destroyed

DAUNTLESS PILOT MEMOIRS

In 1941, Lt. Clarence E. Dickinson was a Douglas Dauntless pilot aboard USS *Enterprise* (CV-6). With the rest of Scouting Squadron Six, he flew into Pearl Harbor from a launch point about 200 miles southwest of Oahu that Sunday morning, expecting to end a period of several months of exercises and training. Instead, he flew into the beginning of the Pacific war. Attacked by Mitsubishi Zeros, his plane on fire and the gunner dead in the rear cockpit, Dickinson was out of options.

"I yelled at Miller, but got no reply. Then I started to get out, and although it was the first time I had ever jumped, I found myself behaving as if I were using a checklist. I was responding to indoctrination and training. I unbuckled my belt, pulled my feet underneath me, put my hands on the sides of the cockpit, leaned out into the right side and, as I shoved clear, the rush of wind peeled my goggles off.

"I had shoved out on the right side because that was the inside of the spin. I was facing the revolving ground because the plane was close to being vertical, spinning around its nose. I was in the air tumbling over and over, grabbing and feeling for the ripcord's handle. Pulling it, I flung my arm wide.

"There was a savage jerk. From where I dangled, my eyes followed the shroud lines up to what I felt was the most beautiful sight I had ever seen: the stiff-bellied shape of my white silk parachute. I heard a tremendous thud; my plane had struck the ground nose first and exploded. Then I struck the ground feet first, seat next and head last. My feet were in the air, and the wind had been jarred out of me. Fortunately, I had jumped so low that neither the Japs overhead nor the Marines defending Ewa Field had time to get a shot at me."

—*from "The Flying Guns" by Clarence E. Dickinson, Scribner's, New York, 1943.*

on the opposite side of Ford Island, but fortuitously, she absorbed Japanese ordnance that would have been better expended elsewhere: she was the Pacific Fleet's training target vessel.

Antiaircraft Efforts

Legends arose from the smoke and twisted wreckage in the harbor and onshore that day. Popular music contributed to the mood with the jaunty tune, "Praise the Lord and Pass the Ammunition," a statement attributed to the chaplain of one ship as he encouraged the antiaircraft gunners blasting away at enemy aircraft.

Ashore, the mood was decidedly less festive. Under peacetime regulations, live ammunition could not be issued without written authorization from a commissioned officer. At Army posts such as Fort Shafter and Schofield Barracks, soldiers clamored for machine-gun and antiaircraft ammunition that remained locked in storage. Career noncoms—the "lifers" often disliked by rookies and draftees—reportedly declined to issue ammo, even with bombing and strafing in progress. Yet common sense more often ruled, and Japanese aircrews remarked on the speed and ferocity of AA fire. The Pacific Fleet report stated that some ships opened fire within two minutes of the attack; most did so within seven minutes. The Navy alone fired 4,620 three- to five-inch shells and 276,000 rounds from automatic weapons.

The most common antiaircraft weapon was the three-inch gun, firing a shell with a fuse that detonated a bursting charge. Sixteen were in place to defend the harbor, plus those aboard ship, and photos show the sky pockmarked with black flak bursts. A few Japanese planes were downed by heavy flak, but a confidential report later admitted that many of the 68 civilian deaths were caused by falling shell splinters.

A variety of automatic weapons was employed both afloat and ashore. Probably the most effective was the Browning .50-caliber machine gun—a 1918 design with a cooling water jacket around the barrel. Mounted on a pedestal with sights high over the bore, the .50s put out a sustained rate of fire that could knock down a single-engine aircraft. One of 15 Navy Medals of Honor that day went to a .50-caliber gunner, Chief John Finn of Kaneohe Naval Air Station, who remained at his gun despite multiple wounds. Another Navy machine gunner was Mess Attendant Doris "Dorsey" Miller, the *West Virginia's* heavyweight boxing champ. Though not trained in gunnery, he proved his fighting spirit aboard a sinking ship as well as in the ring. Elsewhere,

THE ONLY SURVIVING AIRCRAFT

Nearly lost in the ordered ranks of Japanese aircraft and the pitifully few U.S. fighters was another American airplane. Approaching John Rodgers Airport was a 65hp Aeronca 65C flown by Ray Vitousek with his 17-year-old son Martin in the back seat. Sunday mornings were usually a good time to fly over Oahu because the Army and Navy seldom operated on weekends. But not this Sunday! Ray Vitousek looked down from 2,000 feet and saw numerous strange airplanes passing beneath him, headed for Pearl Harbor. Realizing his peril, he circled for 30 minutes or so, seeking a way to get down without drawing unwelcome attention.

Eventually, the odds caught up with the flying Vitouseks. Two Nakajima torpedo planes passed close by, and one of the gunners opened fire. Ray and Martin evaded them, returning NC 33768 to Gambo Flying Service with at least two 7.7mm bullets in the airframe. Today, the restored Aeronca is displayed at Honolulu's Pacific Aerospace Museum; it is the only surviving aircraft of those involved in the Pearl Harbor attack.

infantry weapons such as .30-caliber tripod-mounted machine guns and automatic rifles also came into play.

Interceptors Aloft

Few USAAF fighters got off the ground that morning: 14 P-36 and 11 P-40 sorties were logged, mostly from the 46th and 47th Pursuit Squadrons. The P-40 pilots claimed six shootdowns; the P-36s four more. At least one P-36 fell to U.S. gunfire over Schofield Barracks.

Two second lieutenants from the 47th Pursuit became famous for their efforts. Kenneth M. Taylor and George S. Welch had barely returned from an all-night poker game and were badly in need of rest when the Japanese arrived. Still partly dressed in civilian clothes, they drove to the alert strip at Haleiwa, scrambled into their P-40s and took off. In a 30-minute fight, they intercepted enemy aircraft near Ewa and shot down four. They claimed to have hit dive bombers, but they probably bagged level bombers. Low on ammunition, they landed to rearm and were back in the air in barely 15 minutes. Later, over the north shore, they chased more bandits; Taylor was wounded, while Welch claimed a fighter and a dive bomber.

Legend has it that "Wheaties" Welch and Ken Taylor were nominated for the Medal of Honor but were awarded Distinguished Service Crosses because they had taken off without authorization. True or not, no Army men were given the MOH for that day, although 15 Navy officers, noncoms and sailors were recognized with the nation's highest award.

The Second Wave

One hour behind the first wave were 168 more planes from Kido Butai. By now, there was no need for stealth: they crossed the coast heading directly for Pearl, though more fighters turned to port to keep the pressure on Kaneohe and starboard to "cap" Wheeler. Other Zeros pressed southward for Hickam and Ford Island. The dive bombers attacked Pearl Harbor from the northeast while the level bombers overflew the southeast of Oahu, passing south of Honolulu and turning west for Hickam and Ford and east for Kaneohe.

EDWARD L. BYRNES

Mortal Sting: How the USS *Hornet* Cured the Imperial Japanese Navy of Its "Victory Disease"

"Two large bogey groups headed your way, angels twelve." With this ominous warning from USS *Hornet's* (CV-8) outbound attack group, the bridge of *Hornet* immediately sounded general quarters. The date was 26 October 1942, and Japanese transmissions intercepted by U.S. intelligence had indicated that the destruction of *Hornet* had become the primary objective of the Imperial Japanese fleet. Unfortunately for the Japanese, it was too late to even the score, for *Hornet* and her air group had already inflicted irreparable damage from which they would never recover.

A mere six days earlier, *Hornet's* crew had celebrated the ship's first birthday. Her existence came as a result of the Naval Expansion Act passed by Congress in May 1939, and she was the last carrier to be commissioned—on 20 October 1941—prior to the United States' entry into World War II. Under the command of Captain Marc A. Mitscher, a portion of *Hornet's* place in history would be quickly established in the form of 16 Army Air Forces B-25 *Mitchells* that launched from her deck in the early morning of 18 April 1942. Led by Lieutenant Colonel James "Jimmy" Doolittle and known as "Doolittle's Raiders," 80

courageous men flew their planes straight to Tokyo, Nagoya, Yoka-
hama and Kobe, each loaded with three 500-pound bombs and one
500-pound incendiary, to carry out the single most bold and daring
mission made against the Japanese in the entire war, and perhaps in
naval history.

Although the mission was portrayed as a tactical failure by the
Japanese for the relatively light damage the bombings actually pro-
duced, it was in fact an overwhelming success for the United States.
From the pitching and rolling wooden flight deck of *Hornet*, a tremen-
dous morale boost for the nation had been created and a much-needed
impetus for the war effort had taken root. For the sake of secrecy—and
perhaps to confound the Japanese even further—President Franklin D.
Roosevelt announced to the world that the planes had launched from
"Shangri-La," the fictitious, mysterious Tibetan city found only in
James Hilton's novel *Lost Horizon*.

Doolittle's Raiders had sent a firm and unsettling message to the
Japanese, but *Hornet*'s contributions, whether measured in actual combat success or in the covert deception of the enemy, were far from complete. And for her part, she would also experience her share of tragedy.

Hornet returned to Pearl Harbor on 25 April, where she spent only
five days before scurrying out to sea again, joined by USS *Enterprise* (cv-
6), to stop the Japanese push toward Port Moresby. The carriers missed
the ensuing Battle of the Coral Sea on 8 May, in which planes from USS
Lexington (cv-2) and USS *Yorktown* (cv-5) sank the Japanese carrier
Shoho, severely damaged *Shokaku* and decimated *Zuikaku*'s air group. In
this fierce battle, *Lexington* was sunk and *Yorktown* was forced to return
to Pearl Harbor for repairs. In lieu of combat, *Hornet* ferried 12 Marine F4Fs to sea to be flown off to Espiritu Santo, then returned to
Hawaii. Only a few days later she would be called back into harm's way.

On 28 May 1942, *Hornet* departed Pearl Harbor with *Enterprise*
upon reports that elements of the Imperial Japanese Navy were steaming toward Midway Atoll. United States' forces based at Midway
amounted to 38 Naval aircraft, 54 Marine planes and 23 Army bombers,
in addition to 19 submarines in the battle area. However, the Japanese, in
four separate groups, brought six carriers, three seaplane carriers, 11 battleships, 14 cruisers, 46 destroyers, 16 submarines and several support
ships to the arena. Taking into account the addition of the Japanese invasion force, the odds seemed decidedly grave.

In the early morning hours of 4 June, as *Hornet* and *Enterprise*, now
joined by *Yorktown*, moved westward approximately 325 miles northeast of Midway, they received a contact report from a Midway-based

PBY *Catalina* search plane—a Japanese carrier force had been sighted. *Hornet* launched 35 dive bombers and 15 torpedo bombers with a number of F4F fighters for escort. *Enterprise* also launched TBDS and SBDS, and *Yorktown* followed suit after recovering her morning search aircraft about an hour later. Though the Japanese fleet changed course and was not sighted by *Hornet*'s SBDS, Torpedo 8, led by Lieutenant Commander John Waldron, turned northward and soon fell upon the enemy. Japanese Mitsubishi A6M (Type 0) fighters (an aircraft soon to acquire the Allied codename *"Zero"*) quickly pounced upon the American fliers, and the ships' anti-aircraft gunners did their best to add to the immense hail of fire. The undaunted Americans boldly pressed home their attack, but one by one they began falling into the sea until all 15 TBDS were shot down. The TBDS from *Enterprise* and *Yorktown* met similar fates. After more than 30 minutes of enormously successful defense—no American planes scored hits, while 35 of 41 planes were shot down—the Japanese fleet's anti-aircraft gunners continued to search the horizon for low-flying torpedo planes. The Japanese fighters, having been brought down to low altitude to engage the torpedo bombers, remained at that level and did not return to an adequate defensive position above the fleet.

What they failed to detect, consequently, were *Yorktown* and *Enterprise*'s squadrons of dive bombers arriving simultaneously over the fleet. The ensuing attack in which the American planes fatally damaged three Japanese carriers (a fourth Japanese carrier was sunk later that same day) proved to be a miraculous turning point in the Pacific War.

While 4 June 1942 was a cause for celebration throughout most of the U.S. Pacific fleet as a result of the "Miracle at Midway," it wasn't an equally joyous occasion in the hearts and minds of the men aboard *Hornet*. Torpedo 8 was virtually annihilated, only three men (including two from the Midway-based detachment) survived their missions and no planes scored a hit; Bombing 8 had completely missed the enemy fleet; and most of Fighting 8, after getting separated from the bombers, was forced land on Midway or ditch in the ocean after running low on fuel. To add insult to injury, five men aboard *Hornet* were killed and another 20 injured when a wounded VF-5 pilot crash-landed his crippled F4F *Wildcat* on *Hornet*'s flight deck. Battle damage had caused the aircraft's machine guns to remain live, even though the pilot had turned the master switch to the "off" position. As the plane impacted the deck and caught an arresting wire, the pilot inadvertently sent a short but lethal two-second burst of gunfire into the crewmen as they stood watching the flight operations.

Despite *Hornet's* several misfortunes that day, the men of Torpedo 8 managed to provide a powerful example for the United States' fighting forces to follow throughout the remainder of the war. Lieutenant Commander Waldron and his squadron had faced the enemy head-on. They were outnumbered, unprotected and outgunned; yet they remained resolute and completely undeterred from the mission at hand. With unsurpassed selflessness, 42 men of Torpedo 8 made the ultimate sacrifice. Through their determination, they diverted the Japanese fighters and anti-aircraft gunners and allowed their brothers in arms to deliver the first defeat of the Imperial Japanese Fleet at sea, consequently turning the tide of World War II.

To offer some light consolation for having not hit the enemy fleet the day before, planes from *Hornet*, with assistance from planes from *Enterprise*, sank the Japanese cruiser *Mikuma* and severely damaged the cruiser *Mogami* on 6 June before heading back to Pearl Harbor.

Months of naval dominance had fostered in the Japanese navy leadership an enormous confidence. In the course of three short months however, a most humiliating sea-borne attack on their homeland had taken place, and their mighty fleet had suffered its worst defeat in history. Still, this now unwarranted confidence persisted. They would soon be cured of what they themselves later came to call the "victory disease."

Hornet steamed into Pearl Harbor on 13 June, and two days later Captain Charles P. Mason assumed command of the ship. Although *Hornet* had been steaming hard throughout the Pacific most of the past three months, she required no repairs, but did receive the installation of a new CXAM radar, thought to be a vast improvement over the unreliable SC unit that would now be relegated to secondary status. The CXAM radar may have been new to *Hornet*, but it was not new to service. It was previously installed on the battleship uss *California* (bb-44), but after that ship was heavily damaged in the attack on Pearl Harbor, the equipment was salvaged from the ship and utilized by an Army unit on Oahu. Once the threat of Japanese attacks dissipated in Hawaii and Midway, the Army returned the unit to the Navy, and it was installed on *Hornet* in early July. To improve her anti-aircraft capability, *Hornet* was fitted with a new 1.1-inch 75-caliber anti-aircraft gun as well.

Hornet participated in three days of training exercises around the Hawaiian Islands in mid-July, returned to port, then went out again for a short stint of tactical exercises, gunnery practice and other training, including the carrier qualification of a number of Marine pilots. By this time, *Hornet's* own air group had been completely overhauled. Among the many changes, vt-6 came aboard as *Hornet's* new torpedo squadron, while vf-72 relieved vf-8, which was then disestablished in late August. This relative down time was also used to give the ship's company some well-deserved and necessary liberty. Although American forces in the Pacific had delivered some significant blows to the enemy, the men of *Hornet* would need their rest and the chance to blow off some steam. Unbeknownst to them, they would soon be operating the only U.S. carrier left to hold the line in the Pacific.

In the meantime, on 7 August, 17,000 Marines began pouring into Guadalcanal to occupy the strategically vital island. Japanese determination to retake this crucial area was evidenced in several subsequent bombardments of the newly constructed Marine airstrip known as Henderson Field. Still, the Americans were able to trickle in replacements and supplies to the embattled Marines to stave off the Japanese. The U.S. command anticipated an inevitable major assault on the stranded Marine encampment, and sent *Hornet* to join uss *Wasp* (cv-7) and uss *Saratoga* (cv-3) and their respective task forces in covering the embattled sea approaches to Guadalcanal. *Hornet* steamed out of Pearl Harbor bound for the Solomons on 17 August with what would be her first and only flag officer aboard, Rear Admiral George D. Murray. While en route, the ship received word on 24 August that the carriers *Saratoga* and *Enterprise* were engaged with enemy forces in the Eastern Solomons. In that battle, *Enterprise* would receive bomb damage that would send her back to Pearl Harbor for repairs.

On the 29th, *Hornet* joined up with *Saratoga* and *Wasp* to patrol the waters from Guadalcanal and Tulagi to New Caledonia and the New Hebrides. On the morning of the 31st, a Japanese submarine put a torpedo into *Saratoga*, and the ship retreated to Pearl Harbor to join *Enterprise* at the repair facility. The encounter had sent the entire task force into twisting and turning evasive maneuvers, and it would be much of the same for *Wasp* and *Hornet* in the ensuing weeks. After several submarine contacts and a few close calls, the law of averages finally caught up with the task force. On 15 September, as *Hornet* and *Wasp* supported transports carrying reinforcements headed for Guadalcanal, *Wasp* suffered three quick and successive torpedo hits. The resultant damage set off massive internal explosions that spelled doom for the ship. Moments later, torpedoes meant for the *Hornet* slammed into the battleship uss *North Carolina* (bb-55) and destroyer uss *O'Brien* (dd-415), both of which eventually left the battle area under their own power. As U.S. destroyers chased and depth-charged the enemy subs, *Hornet* continued on unscathed, but alone, as the only U.S. large-deck fleet carrier operating in the Pacific.

Her supplies nearing exhaustion, *Hornet* retired to New Caledonia for resupply on 26 September. Back out to sea on 2 October, she would be the sole provider of air cover in the Solomons for the next two weeks. *Hornet's* air group conducted several raids against enemy airfields on Bougainville and enemy anchorages at Faisi and the Shortland Islands, sinking several barges and float planes. They also made many strafing runs on enemy installations, hangars, ships, and personnel. Though many of these raids experienced varying degrees of success as a result of low visibility over the targets, they did serve to disrupt the flow of Japanese shipping in the area. On 15 October, *Hornet* was rejoined by the newly repaired *Enterprise* to once again take up the task of covering the sea approaches to Guadalcanal.

As the ships and their respective task forces conducted a counter-clockwise sweep around the Santa Cruz Islands, the anticipation of a large-scale Japanese push for Guadalcanal was reaching a fever pitch. With Vice Admiral William F. "Bull" Halsey's 18 October appointment as Commander-in-Chief, South Pacific, came his unhesitant and characteristic declaration, "Attack! Repeat, attack!" Accordingly, when the Japanese fleet was sighted 300 miles out just before nightfall on 25 October, Rear Admiral Murray turned the task force to intercept the enemy. It was an evening *Hornet* CO Captain Mason would describe as "like the night before a big game."

At 0832 the next morning, with the Japanese fleet only 220 miles away and closing from the northwest, *Hornet* began launching her two strikes of 24 dive bombers, 15 torpedo planes and 15 fighters. *Enterprise* also launched a wave of 19 planes. At the same time, two search planes from *Enterprise*, acting on earlier contact reports, sought out the enemy fleet and found the light carrier *Zuiho*. At 0840 the two planes rendered the Japanese ship's flight deck inoperative with two 500-pound bomb hits. Sixty miles out, *Hornet's* air group radioed back to the carrier, "Two large bogey groups headed your way, angels twelve." The Japanese and American attack groups passed each other with only a handful of planes breaking off into dogfights.

Shortly after 1000, *Hornet's* combat air patrol began tangling with the incoming Japanese attack group. At 1010, with *Enterprise* obscured by cloud cover, the Japanese attack group pounced on *Hornet* with the full brunt of its power. Several dive bombers that had evaded the *Wildcats* now bore in from port, through heavy anti-aircraft fire from *Hornet* and her screen. Many were shot down before they could release their bombs. One that made it through immediately scored a devastating bomb hit to *Hornet's* forward flight deck, while others scored two near misses. The pilot of the lead Aichi D3A1 dive bomber (later code-named *Val*), his plane crippled by anti-aircraft fire, decided to head straight for the stack of *Hornet*. With his three bombs still attached, he plunged his plane straight into the signal bridge. One bomb exploded on impact, killing seven men. The second bomb exploded as it hit the flight deck, and the third penetrated to the gallery deck but proved, fortunately, to be a dud.

Only seconds later, a torpedo plane attack came quickly from starboard, and two torpedoes struck *Hornet* in her engine rooms. A lone Japanese Nakajima B5N2 (Type 97) torpedo bomber (later codenamed *Kate*), already aflame, flew into *Hornet*'s port bow. This highly concentrated and coordinated attack lasted only 10 minutes, but left *Hornet* dead in the water.

As *Hornet* burned, her attack group was busy making life miserable for the Japanese carrier *Shokaku* and the cruiser *Chikuma*, both of which suffered extensive damage. *Shokaku* received four 1,000-pound bomb hits from *Hornet*'s first wave. The second wave failed to find the carriers, but did pounce on *Chikuma*, which had become separated from the main force. Two hits and two near misses caused major flooding, inflicted massive casualties and slowed the ship.

Throughout the day, *Hornet*'s crew fought the numerous fires and worked hard to save the ship, despite sporadic attacks from *Zuikaku*'s air group. The ship received an additional bomb and torpedo hit, and at 1650 she took her final bomb hit from a high-level bomber. At 1727 the order was given to abandon ship. After all the survivors and wounded had been taken off the ship and plucked from the sea, the remainder of the task force, except the U.S. destroyers USS *Mustin* (DD-413) and USS *Anderson* (DD-411), retreated south at high speed. *Mustin* and *Anderson* were given the undesirable task of scuttling *Hornet* before she fell into enemy hands. The destroyers fired a total of 16 torpedoes—of which only nine detonated—into *Hornet*, but she refused to go down. Having exhausted their torpedoes, the ships fired 350 rounds of 5-inch ammunition at the ship in an attempt to ignite the gasoline system. Several large fires did result, yet she still refused to sink. The American ships were forced to leave the area as Japanese destroyers and cruisers, two of each, closed in. Destroyers *Makigumo* and *Akigumo* arrived on scene and fired four more torpedoes at the abandoned, burning *Hornet*. At 0135 on 27 October 1942, she reluctantly slipped beneath the waves.

For 371 days, *Hornet* had haunted the Japanese throughout the Pacific. She launched Doolittle's Raiders, she fought at the decisive Battle of Midway, she held the line in the battle of attrition known as Guadalcanal, and for two long weeks she patrolled the sub-infested waters of the South Pacific alone. At the same time, her air group bombed and strafed a powerful and confident enemy into humility and prepared him for his eventual defeat. She fought valiantly to the end; as she was taking blows, she was delivering them as well. Her work ensured that she would be the last large carrier the U.S. would lose in the war. The ship earned four World War II battle stars, and the men of her torpedo squadron earned the Presidential Unit Citation and Navy Crosses "for extraordinary heroism and distinguished service beyond the call of duty" in the Battle of Midway. *Hornet* and her crew would not be forgotten. On 29 November 1943, the eighth USS *Hornet* (CV-12) was commissioned; and less than a year later, on 15 September 1944, USS *Shangri-La* (CV-38) was born. The legacy of CV-8 would live on.

No Gun Ri Revisited: Historical Lessons for Today's Army

A number of colleagues have asked for my "take" on two recent but contrary accounts of an alleged American massacre of Korean War refugees: *No Gun Ri: A Military History of the Korean War Incident* by Robert L. Bateman (Mechanicsburg, Pa.: Stackpole Books, 2002) and *The Bridge at No Gun Ri* by Charles J. Hanley, Sang-Hun Choe, and Martha Mendoza (New York: Henry Holt, 2001). These queries have come to me and my associates not only because of the Center of Military History's responsibility for preserving and interpreting the history of the United States Army, but also because of our early and continuing involvement in research relevant to the incident, which ultimately became a cause célèbre pitting Pulitzer Prize–winning journalists against outraged Korean War veterans and their supporters. The episode's notoriety began in September 1999 with the publication of an explosive Associated Press article entitled "The Bridge at No Gun Ri," and it did not quite end with the release of the Department of the Army inspector general's investigation of the subject sixteen months later. In my view the several examinations of this episode, collectively considered, have led to a more thorough understanding not only of the Korean War but also of military responsibilities toward non-combatants. They have also demonstrated that the best remedy for the damage inflicted by a free press is, in fact, a free press.

The Center of Military History's direct involvement with No Gun Ri predates the publication of the Pulitzer Prize–winning article. We write the Army's official history, so we were, of course, no strangers to accounts of confusion and tumult during the desperate fighting in Korea during the summer of 1950. In December 1998 we were given several weeks to determine whether anything in our official records supported an allegation forwarded by the Reverend Dong-Wan Kim of the National Council of Churches in Korea that American soldiers had perpetrated a deliberate massacre of Korean civilians near the village of No Gun Ri. In our research we benefited from a sizable packet of translated Korean accounts and had at our disposal unofficial American accounts and eyewitness testimony as well. We found little in the American materials that could be linked with confidence to actions at No Gun Ri itself, and certainly nothing to suggest a deliberate massacre. However, the testimony of Koreans who alleged that they had been fired upon by American troops seemed plausible enough, and it corresponded in nature to accounts we did have of Korean civilians becoming the unintended victims of American firepower. In the early months of the Korean War, desperate and outnumbered American defenders experienced the customary problems of green troops in distinguishing friend from foe when coordinating fire and movement. Their challenges were greatly aggravated by their woefully deficient state of training and by their conviction, often supported by fact, that Communist infiltrators were mingling with refugees in order to penetrate American lines. The Center's report of 18 February 1999 concluded that "doubtless unintended civilian casualties were caused by . . . U.S. . . . units in the confusion of battle" at No Gun Ri.

Seven months later the article "The Bridge at No Gun Ri" made headlines around the world. It alleged that American troops had perpetrated a massacre under orders and then had sustained the secret for fifty years. Indignant, the Center of Military History promptly drafted a rebuttal for possible use by the Army's Public Affairs Office. In it we complimented the article's authors for the breadth and depth of their research, the extent to which they captured the horrors and confusion of the war's opening months, and the vividness of their reconstruction. We took issue, however, with the way they had extrapolated from rather slender data to characterize the killings as a deliberate massacre, the numbers they had cited, and the suggestion that the Army had engaged in a fifty-year cover-up to hide its involvement. The case for a deliberate American massacre seemed to boil down to the testimony of three veterans—Edward Daily, Delos Flint, and Eugene Hesselman—supported by severe interpretations of battlefield documents that could be otherwise explained. Four hundred or so victims seemed high for the incident as we had tentatively reconstructed it and implausible for an event that had attracted so little notice. The Army had not denied possible involvement in such an incident but had simply asserted it was not liable for damages. In our twentieth century wars we have in the course of combat operations inadvertently killed thousands of French, Belgian, Italian, Filipino, Korean, and Vietnamese civilians, as well as those from other countries. As dreadful as these unintended casualties were and as extensive as was the physical devastation of war, it was not practical to assume financial liability for property destroyed or civilians inadvertently maimed or killed by soldiers who were conducting operations in accordance with the laws of war. That is probably why the letter from the Reverend Kim had been careful to allege that "the U.S. Army soldiers did kill innocent civilians deliberately, under non-combat circumstances," actions not countenanced by the laws of war. We also noted that the article's authors ignored the humanitarian instincts that the Eighth Army did display. Its refugee evacuation plan represented a major effort to integrate compassion into the maneuver scheme, and its medical regimen for the refugees remains a case study in assuming responsibility for an endangered civilian population. The fact that these efforts fell short does not denigrate the good intentions involved.

Our proposed rebuttal never left the Department of the Army. The Associated Press article had created a firestorm, and within days top officials in the governments of both South Korea and the United States, including our secretary of defense, the secretary of the Army, and the Department of the Army inspector general, committed themselves to an exhaustive review at considerable cost to determine "the full scope of the facts surrounding these press reports."

Because such an investigation was under way, external Army correspondence with respect to No Gun Ri, including ours, ceased. The Center of Military History fully supported the inspector general's review, from early in-briefings to participation in the drafting of the final report. There was a bit of political theater in the choreography of the inspector general's review, but its essence was painstaking research of a very high caliber. The review team examined over a million official documents; interviewed 200 American and 75 Korean witnesses; reviewed press reports, aerial imagery, and forensic evidence; and visited the incident site several times. In the end the researchers developed extraordinary detail, but their conclusions had about the same thrust as CMH's earlier report: American soldiers probably inflicted the casualties, no orders to kill refugees had been given, aerial imagery and forensic evidence did not support a claim of hundreds of deaths, and no war crime had been covered up. Aerial imagery supported the possibility that the refugees had been strafed but not that they had been bombed, and prohibitions against refugees crossing "battle lines" (i.e., positions in or imminently expecting contact with the enemy) did not preclude safely evacuating refugees through "friendly lines." This last point seems to have accounted for some of the confusion regarding the Associated Press article's assertion that the Army had issued standing orders to kill refugees.

During the Army's sixteen months of self-imposed official silence while it investigated No Gun Ri, the Associated Press and other news media were not similarly uncommunicative. One purported exposé after another appeared in print, expanding on the original No Gun Ri article by "discovering" further incidents in which American troops had killed Korean civilians. Television inevitably became involved, culminating in an extraordinary bit of soap opera when Tom Brokaw showcased a tearful episode of reunion, remembrance, and forgiveness involving alleged assailant Edward Daily and a handful of his purported erstwhile victims. Korean War veterans reacted to this cascade of calumny with indignation, first at the Associated Press and others for perpetrating it and then at the Department of the Army for allowing it to roll along uncontested. Ultimately recognizing that the Army was for a period incommunicado, these veterans and their friends took up their own defense. Many contributed, but Joseph Galloway of *We Were Soldiers Once and Young* fame[1] and Edward Offley of Stripes.com led the charge. They were greatly assisted in this counterattack by the insights of Maj. Robert L. Bateman, an associate professor of history at the U.S. Military Academy who had known Daily for some years and now began to research this high-profile incident.

No Gun Ri: A Military History of the Korean War Incident should be appreciated in part as an effort by Bateman to make for the Army the case that he perceived the Army was failing to make for itself. It is fine work. Its first half is classic military history as historians should hope to write it. In lucid prose Bateman recounts the experiences of the 2d Battalion, 7th Cavalry, a unit of which he was a recent veteran, from constabulary duty in Japan through the incident at No Gun Ri and beyond. His account is thoughtful, superbly documented, and well supported by maps. He does benefit from the product of the Army inspector general's investigative team, but his research is independent of theirs. He concludes that the number of slain refugees was about twenty-five and persuasively argues that the words the Associated Press construed as instructions to massacre take on a less malignant tone when fully understood and placed in context. Perhaps most significant, he makes the case that among the slain refugees there were Communist guerrillas who had fired on the Americans and that the U.S. soldiers had killed these guerrillas and seized their weapons. Moreover, he asserted that forensic evidence, eyewitness testimony, and extant records documented the use of these weapons and their evacuation through American logistical channels. If he is right about all this, the civilians slain at No Gun Ri represent neither a massacre nor a case of mistaken identity, but rather a group of noncombatants unfortunate enough to have remained in the vicinity of a legitimate military target.

For the most authoritative single account of the incident at No Gun Ri, I would recommend the first 130 pages of Major Bateman's book. In the second half of *No Gun Ri*, Bateman shifts his attention from the historical incident itself to the circumstances and the journalistic processes that led to the publication of the Associated Press article. His analysis is thoughtful, insightful, and entertaining, but ultimately overdrawn. He firmly establishes that Edward Daily was never present at No Gun Ri and makes a persuasive case that Delos Flint and Eugene Hesselman were not present at the time of the incident either. These stunning revelations virtually gut the allegations of massacre from American sources; only these men had unequivocally asserted that they had received orders to kill refugees.

Bateman follows up on his advantage to give us a brief history of American journalism and its methods, which helps explain the media's fervor for a story that he believes misconstrued the events at No Gun Ri. In this effort he borrows heavily from insights presented by B. G. Burkett and Glenna Whitley in *Stolen Valor: How the Vietnam Generation Was Robbed of Its Heroes and History* (Dallas, 1998). Burkett and Whitley exposed dozens of fraudulent Vietnam veterans, outlining the techniques they used to paint themselves into the memory of actual veterans while participating in reunions and the like. Oral history is always risky, and is particularly so when contaminated by the passage of time, fading or jumbled memories, the published accounts of others, or a species of "group think" in which participants—or alleged participants—collectively work themselves into a consensus over time. Truth can become even more imperiled if those taking the oral testimony already have a version of the facts in mind that they are trying to induce their witnesses to support. Reading Bateman, however, one might go so far as to believe that the Associated Press journalists nefariously manipulated confused old men into disgraceful confessions, that the dozen or so American witnesses corroborating aspects of the Associated Press story were delusional, and that the testimony of the Korean witnesses was altogether dominated by the $400 million they hoped to collect in damages. As satisfying as it is to see the Fourth Estate take its just lumps, we should consider the possibility that the journalists may have been biased but nevertheless attempted to get the story straight, that the American veterans still have most of their mental faculties intact, and that the Koreans who pursued redress when even their own government was hostile to such efforts were probably sincere in doing so.

The book *The Bridge at No Gun Ri*, much improved in coverage and tone over the article for which the book's authors had won a Pulitzer Prize, inclines one toward this more favorable view. The authors clearly benefited from the criticism their article had provoked. Daily disappears from the narrative, the Army inspector general's investigation is addressed, and far more is done to establish a context. It is true that the authors do not simply confess their previous sins and try, with endearing persistence, to salvage their conspiracy theory from the discrediting of Daily and the others; that they emphasize the ugly-American aspects of the GIs over their more benevolent side; and that they manage the incredible feat of working an account of Wounded Knee into a book on the Korean War, but one can nevertheless look through this bias to see that they are attempting to balance their account. In their discussion of the incident itself, for example, we find them crediting the 7th Cavalrymen for providing succor and safe passage to some refugees even as they are shooting others. We also find the Korean victims knowledgeable enough about the possibility of mistaken identity to attempt to convince the Americans that they were not Communist infiltrators, and we learn of refugees and soldiers in another battalion working together to extricate American vehicles over a narrow mountain trail. The book produces enough evidence of the soldiers' confusion and inconsistency to be broadly compatible with the inspector general's findings of tragic mistake rather than calculated massacre.

As a historical account per se, I would recommend *No Gun Ri: A Military History of the Korean War Incident* over *The Bridge at No Gun Ri*. With thirty-five pages of endnotes, numerous maps, and direct attention to discrepancies among accounts, Bateman's history is clearly more in line with contemporary expectations of scholarship. The Associated Press journalists make a different contribution. Their flyleaf advertises the book's presentation of "the untold human story behind the killing of Korean civilians by American soldiers in the early days of the Korean War." This characterization is accurate. In their pages we get to know many of the individuals whose lives came together so tragically during July 1950. We meet the Koreans and their families and learn of their prewar lives. We follow their prolonged efforts to reconstruct those lives and achieve closure with respect to lives cut short. We also get to know a number of the American soldiers involved. For the most part they were militarily ill-prepared young men who proved courageous and capable at later times and in different places, but who had to live with the fact that in their first great wartime paroxysm of firepower they had killed women and children for the most part. It is not necessarily a bad thing for historical tragedy to have a human face.

A number of my military colleagues have opined that the Associated Press reporters have done us a disservice. I respond that intellectual discourse puts at a disadvantage only those who do not participate in it. The journalists' original article was far more flawed and inaccurate than an article on the same subject written today would be. This is as it should be. The Army knew of numerous incidents in which Korean civilians became the victims of American firepower, yet we had never quite forced ourselves to do a detailed case study of any of them. Indeed, the Army did a far better immediate postmortem of the incident at Wounded Knee in the 1890s than we did of any comparable tragedy in Korea in the 1950s. Now we have several detailed analyses of a single Korean War incident supported by dozens of maps and photos, scores of documents, and hundreds of eyewitness accounts. It would not be hard to use this knowledge of No Gun Ri to improve our efforts to avoid similar tragedies. This is a useful aspect of history. The first step in such a reevaluation would be to reflect upon the horrible consequences of sending ill-prepared units into battle. All accounts of No Gun Ri agree that the poor state of soldier training, the hasty integration of individual replacements, and the uncertain leadership of American soldiers contributed significantly to the ultimate results. These conclusions accord with the views of Roy E. Appleman, T. R. Fehrenbach, Gordon R. Sullivan, and a host of others who have elevated the Korean War intervention into the premier example of the price paid for military unpreparedness. They also expand the circle of the victims of our unpreparedness to encompass our intended beneficiaries as well as ourselves.

We didn't fault the Associated Press reporters for merely bringing up an unpleasant subject, of course. Rather we faulted them for inflating the casualties, inaccurately alleging deliberateness, and accusing the Army of engaging in a cover-up. It does seem that those killed numbered in the dozens rather than in the hundreds, but that does not much alter the horrific character of the event for those involved. Both Bateman and the inspector general's review argue persuasively that there were no deliberate orders to kill refugees, but all accounts admit to considerable confusion in that regard in the foxhole. The inspector general, for example, found a number of soldiers who considered themselves authorized to use deadly force on civilians who did not comply with instructions. Today we attempt to avoid such confusion by thinking through the possibilities in advance and issuing comprehensive rules of engagement to all echelons. Military lawyers have progressed from awaiting reports of transgressions to becoming active participants in decisions on engagement policies and prospective targets. We have learned through hard experience that it takes thoughtful preparation to minimize unintended casualties. The accounts of No Gun Ri underscore the importance of such efforts. Over the years the Army may have neglected the events that unfolded at No Gun Ri, but it does not seem to have consciously suppressed information about them.

The Associated Press reporters do not have to apologize much for seizing on an unpleasant topic, researching it in some haste, and delivering it in a manner calculated to emphasize drama and excite controversy. They are, after all, journalists. We should not be surprised that historians and investigators following up on their lead found much to improve upon in their account, and we should be gratified that the same free press that aired the Associated Press version of events was receptive to contrary views as well. The consequent give-and-take has enriched our understanding of the No Gun Ri incident, the Korean War, military responsibilities toward noncombatants, and the interplay between journalistic and historical processes.

I would recommend both *No Gun Ri: A Military History of the Korean War* and *The Bridge at No Gun Ri* to all officers and noncommissioned officers responsible for preparing soldiers to cope with the confusion of the battlefield. Read collectively and in tandem with the inspector general's review, available at *http://www.army.mil/nogunri*, they provide a gripping case study from which to draw lessons learned. Indeed, they should be required reading for all military lawyers, and the case study should become an important feature of judge advocate education. I can think of no better testimony to the value that sensible rules of engagement and adequate discipline can bring to the fight.

NOTE

1. Galloway was co-author with Harold G. Moore of *We Were Soldiers Once and Young: Ia Drang, The Battle That Changed the War in Vietnam* (New York, 1992).

NOTES

LIEUTENANT ANDREW H. FOOTE AND THE AFRICAN SLAVE TRADE

1. Preston to Foote, 28 September 1849, NHCHS; James M. Hoppin, *The Life of Andrew Hull Foote, Rear Admiral, United States Navy* (New York: Harper & Brothers, 1874), 66, 75–76.
2. Henry Steele Commager, ed., *Documents of American History*, 3d edition (New York: F. S. Crofts, 1946), 197; *The United States Statutes at Large*, III: 532–33; 600–1.
3. Edwin M. Hall, *"Smith Thompson," American Secretaries of the Navy*, Vol. 1: 1775–1913, Paolo Coletta, ed. (Annapolis: Naval Institute Press, 1980), 125. The best short treatment of the subject is George M. Brooke, Jr., "The Role of the United States Navy in the Suppression of the African Slave Trade," *American Neptune* 21 (1961): 28–41.
4. W. Patrick Strauss, "James Kirke Paulding," *American Secretaries of the Navy*, Vol 1: 1715–1913, 169; Adams quoted in J. Scott Harmon, "The United States Navy and the Suppression of the Illegal Slave Trade, 1830–1850," *New Aspects of Naval History. Selected Papers Presented at the Fourth Naval History Symposium*, Craig L. Symonds, ed. (Annapolis: Naval Institute Press, 1981), 212.
5. James Tertius de Kay, *Chronicles of the Frigate Macedonian, 1809–1922* (New York: W. W. Norton, 1995), 214–15.
6. Hugh Soulsby, *The Right of Search and the Slave Trade in Anglo-American Relations, 1814–1862* (Baltimore: Johns Hopkins Press, 1933), 42–49; Brooke, "The Role of the United States Navy," 37–38; Andrew H. Foote, *Africa and the American Flag* (New York: D. Appleton, 1854), 152.
7. Hoppin, *Life of Admiral Foote*, 73.
8. John R. Spears, *The American Slave-Trade, an Account of its Origin, Growth, and Suppression* (New York: Charles Scribner's Sons, 1900), 38–39; Strauss, "James Kirke Paulding," 169.
9. Brooke, "Role of the United States Navy," 33; Commager, *Documents of American History*, 300; Paolo E. Coletta, "Abel Parker Upshur," *American*

Secretaries of the Navy, Vol 1: 1715–1913, 189; A. P. Upshur to Commander M. C. Perry, 30 March 1843, House Executive Documents, 35th Cong., 2d Sess., Ser. 1008, Exec. Doc. 104; Samuel Elliot Morison, "Old Bruin," *Commodore Matthew Calbraith Perry* (Boston: Little, Brown, 1967), 164–78; Brooke, "Role of the United States Navy," 33–34.

10. "List of Captures by U.S. Squadron," under Article 8 of August 9, 1842 Treaty, House Executive Documents, 35th Cong., 2d Sess., Ser. 1008, Exec. Doc. 104; Hoppin, *Life of Foote*, 72–74; Brooke, "Role of the United States Navy," 38. Brooke points out that throughout the period the US maintained an average of fewer than the number of guns required, while the British maintained an average far in excess of the treaty minimum.

11. Foote to Senator Truman Smith, 15 November 1852, Foote Papers, LC.

12. Jay Slagle, *Ironclad Captain: Seth Ledyard Phelps and the U.S. Navy, 1841–1864* (Kent, Ohio and London: Kent State University Press, 1996), 39.

13. Morison, "Old Bruin," 164.

14. Howard I. Chapelle, *The History of the American Sailing Navy: The Ships and Their Development* (New York: W. W. Norton, 1949), 450, 452, 549; *Perry* station bill, Foote Papers, LC.

15. Foote's journal on the *Perry*, 29 November; 3, 4, 5, 21, 25 December 1849; 1 January 1850; Foote to Secretary of the Navy Preston, 21 December 1849, Foote Papers, LC.

16. Andrew H. Foote, *The African Squadron: Ashburton Treaty: Consular Sea Letters: Reviewed in an Address by Commander A. H. Foote* (Philadelphia: William F. Geddes, 1855), 9; Foote, *Africa and the American Flag*, 254–57; Foote journal, 31 December 1849; Foote Papers, LC. Secretary of the Navy Preston's general order concerning "Sanatary Regulations for the U.S. Squadron on the Coast of Africa," 23 January 1850, is in Foote Papers, LC.

17. Foote journal, 12 January 1850, Foote Papers, LC.

18. Foote to Gregory, 23 January and to Secretary of the Navy Preston, 24 January 1850, Foote Papers, LC; Captain John Marston of the Yorktown to Foote, 21 January 1850, Foote Papers, NHCHS; Foote, Africa and the American Flag, 257.

19. Foote, *Africa and the American Flag*, 197–99, 205; Foote Journal, 7 January 1851, Foote Papers, LC.

20. Foote to Secretary of the Navy Preston, 7 March 1850, Foote Papers, LC; Foote journal, 8 January, 3 April, 29 May 1850, Foote Papers, LC; Foote, *Africa and the American Flag*, 257.

21. Foote journal, 29 January, 2 and 9 February 1950, Foote to Secretary of the Navy Preston and Simons to Secretary of the Navy Preston, 12 March 1850, Foote Papers, LC.

22. Foote, *Africa and the American Flag*, 257–60.

23. Hoppin, *Life of Admiral Foote*, 81; Foote, *Africa and the American Flag*, 67–70, 259–64.

24. Foote to Secretary of the Navy Preston, 21 March 1850, Foote Papers, LC; Foote, *Africa and the American Flag*, 258–262.

25. Foote to Secretary of the Navy Preston, 27 March 1850 and to Commander Levin M. Powell, to April 1850; Foote Journal, 29 May 1850, Foote Papers, LC; Foote, *Africa and the American Flag*, 258–60.

26. Foote to Gregory, 12 August 1850; G. Hastings to Foote, 24 March 1850; Commander John Tudor of the *Firefly* to Foote, 26 March 1850; Foote journal, 27 March, 5 April 1850; Perry log book, 24 March 1850, Foote Papers, LC; Foote, *Africa and the American Flag*, 271, 277, 337; Hoppin, *Life of Admiral Foote*, 81.

27. Foote journal, 2 February; 1, 2, 5 April; 29 May 1850, Foote Papers, LC.

28. Foote to Gregory, 27, 29 April 1850; Gregory to Foote, 2 May 1850, Foote Papers, LC., *Africa and the American Flag*, 282–284.

29. Foote journal, 29 May 1850, Foote Papers, LC; Foote, *Africa and the American Flag*, 283–84.

30. Gregory to Foote, 6 May 1850, Foote Papers, LC; Foote, *Africa and the American Flag*, 285–86.

31. Foote journal, 21 June 1850, Foote Papers, LC.

32. Foote's order, 1 July 1850, Foote Papers, LC.

33. Foote to Gregory, 7 and 12 June 1850; and Foote to Rush and Simons, both 7 June 1850; Foote journal, 17 June 1850; Perry logbook, 7 and 8 June 1850, Foote Papers, LC; Foote, *Africa and the American Flag*, 286–92; Hoppin, *Life of Admiral Foote*, 82–83; Gerard A. Forlenza, "A Navy Life: The pre-Civil War Career of Rear Admiral Andrew Hull Foote" (unpublished doctoral dissertation, Claremont Graduate School, 1991), 201.

34. Foote journal, 17 June 1850; Foote to Gregory, 5 August 1850, Foote Papers, LC.

35. Foote journal, 17 June 1850, Foote Papers, LC; Perry log, 3 and 9 August 1850, Foote Papers, LC.

36. Foote, *Africa and the American Flag*, 296–300; 339–40.

37. Foote Journal, 3 October 1850, Foote Papers, LC; the two-year period is in Foote, *Africa and the American Flag*, 260.

38. Foote to Renshaw, 17 August 1850; Hastings to Foote, 12 August 1850, containing report from Commander Hastings of the Rattler concerning the Chatsworth, Foote Papers, LC; Foote journal, 3 October 1850, Ibid.; Foote, *Africa and the American Flag*, 301–5.

39. Foote to Acting Lieut. Edmund Selden, 5 September 1850, Foote Papers, LC.

40. Foote to Gregory, 11 September 1850, Foote Papers, LC.

41. Foote to Gregory, 14 September 1850; to Allen, 12 September 1850; to Shepherd, 14 September 1850; to Secretary of the Navy Preston with enclosures, 17 September 1850; Serralunga to Foote, 11 and 14 September 1850; Foote journal, 3 October 1850, Foote Papers, LC; Foote, *Africa and the American Flag*, 318–23; Theodore Canot, *Adventures of an African Slaver*, Malcolm Cowley, ed. (New York: Albert & Charles Boni, 1928), xix, 375–36; Hoppin, *Life of Admiral Foote*, 84.

42. Foote to Gregory, 20 October 1850; Foote journal, 10 December 1850, 12 June 1851, Foote Papers, LC; Foote, *Africa and the American Flag*, 326–35.

43. Foote to Preston, 2 November 1850, Foote Papers, LC; Foote, *Africa and the American Flag*, 336.

44. Perry log, 8 and 22 November 1850, Foote Papers, LC; Foote journal, 1 January 1851, Foote Papers, LC.

45. Foote to Gregory, 8 and 24 January 1851; Foote to Skinner, 22 December 1849, and undated letter; Perry log, 8 January 1851, Foote Papers, LC.

46. Foote journal, 7 January and 13 March 1851; Foote to Gregory, 24 January 1851; Perry log, 8 June 1851, Foote Papers, LC.

47. Foote to Gregory, 3, 4, and 5 February 1851; Gregory to Foote, 4 and 5 February 1851; Foote Papers, LC.

48. Foote to Gregory, 17 April 1851; to Joseph Smith, 17 April 1851; to Secretary of the Navy Graham, 17 May 1851; Foote Journal, 22 May 1851, Foote Papers, LC; Foote, *Africa and the American Flag*, 344–351.

49. Foote to Secretary of the Navy Graham, 1 June 1851; Foote journal, 23 May, 12 June 1851, Foote Papers, LC; Foote, *Africa and the American Flag*, 355.

50. Foote to Secretary of the Navy Graham, 9 July 1851; Foote journal, 14 July 1851; *Perry* log, March–July 1851; Foote Papers, LC; Foote, *Africa and the American Flag*, 369–70.

51. Foote journal, 14 July 1851, Foote Papers, LC; Foote, *Africa and the American Flag*, 16–17.

52. Foote to Lavallette, 1 October 1851; Foote journal, 17 November, 12 December 1851, Foote Papers, LC; Forlenza, "A Navy Life," 216.

53. Perry log, 23 December 1851, Foote Papers, LC; Hoppin, *Life of Admiral Foote*, 88; Foote, *Africa and the American Flag*, 377; Forlenza, "A Navy Life," 216.

54. Hoppin, *Life of Admiral Foote*, 86–87; Foote, *Africa and the American Flag*, 377–378.

55. Foote's remarks to the American Colonization Society, 18 January 1855, in Hoppin, *Life of Admiral Foote*, 88; US, House Executive Documents, 31st Congress, 1st Session, IX, No. 73, 1–2; Brooke, "Role of the United States Navy," 39.

56. Foote, "The African Squadron: Ashburton Treaty Consular Sea Letters," 7; Lloyd, *The Navy and the African Slave Trade*, 288.

57. Foote to William Graham, 7 April 1852, Foote Papers, LC; Hoppin, *Life of Admiral Foote*, 88, 96.

58. *Sailor's Magazine* 24 (1852): 587–88; 619–20; Hoppin, *Life of Admiral Foote*, 97–99.

59. Foote Journal, 29 January 1850; 11 December 1850; 7 January 1851, Foote Papers, LC; Hoppin, *Life of Admiral Foote*, 98–99; Foote, *Africa and the American Flag*, 105, 195–99, 205–9, 388.

60. Foote to Secretary of the Navy Dobbin, 29 June 1854, Foote Papers, LC; Elliot Cresson to Foote, 10 June 1851, Foote Papers, NHCHS; Soulsby, *American The Right of Search and the Slave Trade*, 135; Warren S. Howard, *American Slavers and the Federal Law*, 1837–1862 (Los Angeles: University of California Press, 1963), 48; Hoppin, *Life of Admiral Foote*, 98.

61. James L. Lardner to Foote, 9 April 1853, Foote Papers, LC.

62. Foote journal, 11 January 1850; 2 April 1850; 11 January and 14 July 1851, Foote Papers, LC; Hoppin, *Life of Admiral Foote*, 96; Forlenza, "A Navy Life," 237.

63. Foote, *Africa and the American Flag*, 15–16.

64. Foote, *Africa and the American Flag*, 379–90; Howard, *American Slavers and the Federal Law*, 48–49; Soulsby, *American The Right of Search and the Slave Trade*, 133.

65. Foote, *Africa and the American Flag*, 15, 103–5, 109, 178–79, 196–99.

66. Howard, *American Slavers and the Federal Law*, 48–49; Soulsby, *American The Right of Search and the Slave Trade*, 133; Hoppin, *Life of Admiral Foote*, 100; "Report of the Secretary of the Navy, 1853," House Exec. Docs., I, Pt. 3, 33d Cong., 1st Sess., 299; various letters to Foote acknowledging receipt of his book, NHCHS.

67. Andrew Hull Foote, "The African Squadron: Ashburton Treaty: Consular Sea Letters. Reviewed, in an Address by Commander A. H. Foote, U.S.N." (Philadelphia: William F. Geddes, 1855), 1–16.

68. Foote to Toucey, 14 July 1859, Foote Papers, LC.

69. Foote to Fox, 10 June 1862, Gustavus Fox, Confidential Correspondence of Gustavus Vasa Fox, Assistant Secretary of the Navy, 1861–1865, Robert Means Thompson and Richard Wainwright, eds.; New York: De Vinne Press, 1918), II: 54; Foote to Welles, 13 June 1862, in Hoppin, *Life of Admiral Foote*, 328–29.

THE F-15 EAGLE: ORIGINS AND DEVELOPMENT: 1964–1972

The author thanks Dr. Priscilla D. Jones, Contract Histories Manager at the Air Force History Support Office, for her editorial assistance in compressing portions of the original monograph into this article. He also thanks Dr. Grant T. Hammond, Director of the Center for Strategy and Technology at the Air War College, for his perceptive comments in reviewing the article.

1. Gen Bruce K. Holloway, "Air Superiority in Tactical Air," *Air University Review* (Mar–Apr 68), p 8.

2. Lt Gen Gabriel P. Disosway, "Tactical Airpower: Past Present and Future," *Sup to AF Pol Ltr for Comdrs*, Jun 63, p 10.

3. George F. Lemmer, *Strengthening USAF General Purpose Forces, 1961–1964* (USAF Hist Div Liaison Ofc, Jun 66), p 37n.

4. Intvw, Denys Volan, ADC Historian, with Lt Gen Arthur C. Agan (Ret), 2 Nov 70; intvw, author with Gen Agan, 2 Oct 73.

5. Alain C. Enthoven and K. Wayne Smith, *How much is Enough? Shaping the Defense Program, 1961–1969* (New York, 1971), p 216.

6. Gen John P. McConnell, "Air Force Doctrine on Air Superiority," in *Sup to AF Pol Ltr to Cmdrs*, Jun 65, pp 24–25. The policy statement also appeared in a letter sent to all major commands and separate operating agencies on May 3, 1965.

7. Memos, Eugene M. Zuckert, SAF, to Robert S. McNamara, SECDEF, subj: COIN Aircraft, 5 Dec 64; McNamara to Zuckert, subj: Close Support and SAW Aircraft, 7 Jan 65.

8. Memo, Zuckert to McNamara, subj: Close Support and SAW Aircraft, 2 Feb 65.

9. Study, DCS Plans & Ops, "Force Options for Tactical Air, Mar 1, 1965; ltr, Maj. Gen. John K. Hester, Asst VCSAF, to Air Staff, subj: TAC Force Structure Options, Jun 23, 1964; ltr, Maj. Gen. Horace M. Wade, Asst

DCS/Plans & Ops, to Air Staff, subj: Force Options for Tactical Air, Aug. 11, 1964.

10. Hist, Dir/Plans & Ops, Jan–Jun 1965, p. 85.

11. Ltr, McDonnell to Zuckert, subj: USAF Study of Force Options, 15 Mar 65.

12. Memos, Zuckert to McNamara, subj: HQ USAF Study on "Force Options for Taçtical Air," 16 Mar 65; Zuckert to McNamara, subj: Air Force Tactical Aircraft, 2 Apr 65.

13. Study, "Tactical Fighter Ground Attack Aircraft," Dir/Opl Rqmts, nd, atch to memo, Zuckert to McNamara, subj: Close Support and SAW Aircraft, 14 Jun 65.

14. MR, Gen Catton, subj: Tactical Fighter Ground Attack Briefing for SAF-OS, 30 Apr 65.

15. MR, Maj Gen A. J. Kinney, Asst DCS/R&D, subj: Conference with Dr. Brown re Tactical Aircraft, 2 Apr 65.

16. MR, Charles H. Christenson, Science Advisor to DCS/R&D, subj: F-X Tactical Support Aircraft, 9 Apr 65; intvw, author with Heinrich J. Weigand, Science Advisor to Dir/Space, 2 Mar 73.

17. MR, Lt Col Fred D. Shipley, Dir/Opl Rqmts & Dev Plans, subj: Second Mtg USAF-AFSC, F-X Working Gp, 9 Jul 65; MR, Lt Col Leonard Volet, Dir/Opl Rqmts & Dev Plans, subj: The Initiation of F-X Program, 12 Jul 65.

18. Rpt, Air Staff Board Mtg 65-19, subj: Tactical Fighter (Ground Attack) Study, 22 Apr 65, atch to ltr, Col Campbell Palfrey, Jr., Exec Sec ASB to ASB, subj: Rpt of Air Staff Bd Mtg 65-19, 23 Apr 65; ltr, Gen Catton to Lt Gen James Ferguson, DSC/R&D, subj: F-X Tactical Support Aircraft, 28 Apr 65.

19. Intvws, author with Maj Gen John J. Burns, Dir/Opl Rqmts & Dev Plans, 22 Mar 73; memo, Brockway McMillan, Under SAF, to Dr Brown, DDR&E, subj: Study Funds, F-X Aircraft, 12 Aug 65.

20. Dr R. F. Futrell, *A Chronology of Significant Airpower Events in Southeast Asia, 1950–1968* (Project Corona Harvest, Maxwell AFB, Ala, 1 May 69), p 90.

21. Intvw, author with Charles E. Myers, 18 Jul 73.

22. Ltr, Gen Ferguson to AFSC, subj: F-X Tactical Support Aircraft, 29 Apr 65; hist, ASD, Jan–Dec 65, 1A.

23. Intvw, author with Brig Gen William F. George, Ch International Negotiations Div, J-5 JCS, 5 Jun 73.

24. Intvws, author with Gen Burns, 22 Mar 73, and Gen George, 5 Jun 73; ltr, Maj Gen Gordon M. Graham, Dir/Ops, Hq TAC to HQ USAF Dir/Opl Rqmts & Dev Plans, *et al.*, subj: Qualitative Opl Rqmt for a STOL Fighter Aircraft Weapon System (TAC QOR 65 E), 6 Oct 65.

25. Memo, McNamara to Zuckert, subj: USAF Tactical Fighter Force, 1 Jul 65.

26. Memo, Brown to McNamara, subj: Interim Buy Tactical Fighters, 5 Nov 65; intvw, author with Calvin B. Hargis, Jr., Dep for Dev SAF (R&D), 21 Mar 73; rpt subj: Jt AF/OSD Effort, Vol III: Analysis and Conclusions, 1 Dec 65; intvw, author with Gen Agan, 2 Oct 73.

27. Ltr, Gen Catton to AFSC, subj: Statement of Work, F-X Studies, 26 Nov 65; intvw, author with Cyrus W. Hardy, Dir/Gen Purpose Planning HQ ASD, 15 Feb 65; hist, ASD, Jan–Dec 65, 1A, pp 117–119.
28. Ltrs, Gens Disosway, Hunter Harris, and Bruce K. Holloway to Gen Mc-Connell, subjs: Future Tactical Fighter Aircraft; Near Term Fighter Improvement; and V/STOL Fighter Aircraft, 11 Feb 66; intvw, author with Lt Gen Albert P. Clark, Supt, Air Force Academy, 17 May 73.
29. Intvw, Gen Burns, 22 Mar 73.
30. Ltr, Gen Ferguson to Gen Disosway, Subj: Joint TAC/PACAF/USAFE Position Papers, with 7 atchs, 11 Mar 66.
31. Hist, ASD, Jan–Dec 66, I, pp 207–209.
32. Hist, ASD, Jan–Dec 66, I, pp 207–209.
33. Intvw, author with Col John R. Boyd, Dep Dir/Dev Plans and Analysis Gp, 23 May 73; rpt, APGC TDR 64-35, "Energy Maneuverability Theory," May 64.
34. Intvw, author with Thomas Christie, Dep Tactical Air, Dir/Defense Program Analysis and Evaluation (OSD), 3 Oct 73.
35. Dickey Study, pp 20–21; intvw, Col Boyd, 23 May 73; intvw, Sprey, 12 Jun 73.
36. See note above.
37. CFP, Advanced Tactical Fighter (F-X), AFRDQ/ANSER, Rev 1, 1 Aug 67, p I-56.
38. Memo, Brown to McNamara, subj: Advanced Tactical Fighter (F-X), 30 Aug 67.
39. Hist, Dir/Opnl Reqs and Dev Plans, 1 Jan–30 Jun 66.
40. Memo, Robert A. Frosch, Asst Sec Navy (R&D), and Alexander H. Flax, Asst SAF (R&D), to Foster, subj: Combined VFAX-F-X Concept Formulation, 1 Dec 67.
41. Intvw, Gen Clark, 17 May 63; ltr, Gen Disosway to Gen Holloway, no subj, 1 Mar 68.
42. Testimony of Gen McConnell, 28 May 68, in Hearings before Sen Amd Svcs Preparedness Investigating Subcommittee, 90th Cong, 2d sess, *U.S. Tactical Air Power Program*, pp 92–93, 103.
43. Msg, Gen McConnell to Gen Ferguson, no subj, 17/2157Z May 68.
44. Memo, Lt Gen Charles H. Terhune, Jr, Vice Cmdr AFSC, to Maj Gens Glenn A. Kent and John L. Zoeckler, HQ/AFSC, subj: The F-X, 17 May 68.
45. MR, Brig Gen F. M. Rogers. Asst DCS/Dev Plans (AFSC), subj: F-X Program, 12 Jun 68.
46. Intvw, author with Maj Gen Roger K. Rhodarmer, Cmdr 9AF, 22 Jun 73.
47. Hist, ASD, Jan 67–Jun 68, p 307.
48. CFP, Advanced Tactical Fighter (F-X), AFRDQ/ASZQ, Sup, 9 Aug 68, p 54.
49. Memo, Gen McConnell to Brown, subj: FX Source Selection Plans, 15 Aug 68; memo, Brown to Gen McConnell, subj: FX Source Selection Plans, 25 Sep 68.
50. DCP, No. 19, "New Air Force Tactical Counter Air Fighter (F-X)," DDR&E, 28 Sep 68.

51. Ibid.
52. Ibid.
53. Memo, Foster to Brown, subj: Development Concept Paper, 30 Oct 68.
54. DCP, No. 19, "New Air Force Tactical Counter Air Fighter (F-X)," DDR&E, 28 Sep 68; memo, Foster to Brown, subj: Development Concept Paper, 30 Oct 68.
55. Hist, ASD, FY 69, p 322.
56. Memo, Flax to Gen McConnell, no subj, 20 Feb 69; memo, Seamans to Gen Goldsworthy, Chairman SSAC, subj: Source Selection for the F-15, 25 Feb 69.
57. MR, Grant L. Hansen, Asst SAF (R&D), subj: F-15 Development Schedule, 8 Apr 69.
58. Ltr, Gen Goldsworthy to Gen Ferguson, subj: F-X Procurement Approach, 1 Oct 68; study, Capt Arthur R. Charles, Graduate School of Business, Wright State Univ, Dayton, Ohio, "The Procurement information System for a Major Weapon System," 22 May 72, pp 3–5. Hereafter, Charles Study.
59. Ibid.
60. Memo, Seamans to Packard, subj: F-15 Procurement, 2 Apr 69; memo, Seamans to Packard, subj: F-15 Procurement, with atch: RFP F33657-69-R-0101, 13 May 69.
61. Memo, Foster to Seamans, subj: F-15 Procurement Contract Considerations, 13 May 69.
62. Memo, Col Irving B. Schoenberg, Exec Asst SAF (I&L) to Philip N. Whittaker, Asst SAF (I&L), no subj, 4 Jun 69; MR, Col W. Y. Smith, Mil Asst SAF, no subj, 9 Jun 69; memo, Col Clarence Chamberlain, Asst Manned Systems Asst SAF (I&L), to Whittaker, subj: F-15, 10 Jun 69.
63. Memo, Seamans to Gen McConnell, subj: F-15 Development Program, w/atch: Guidance to F-15 System Program Director, 11 Jun 69.
64. Memo, Foster to Seamans, subj: F-15 Acquisition, 11 Jun 69.
65. Memo, Hansen to Seamans, subj F-15 Acquisition, 23 Jun 69.
66. Memo, Seamans to Packard, subj: F-15 Procurement, 27 Jun 69 [Packard penned-in his approval on this memorandum.]; MR, Gen Ferguson, subj: F-15 Contract and Management, 27 Jun 69.
67. MR, Harvey J. Gordon, Asst SAF (I&L), subj: Visit to Wright-Patterson AFB, 4–5 Nov 69; Task Group initial Review of F-15 Model Contract, 13 Nov 69.
68. Hist, ASD, Jan–Dec 66, I, p 207; memo, AFSC to ASD, 23 Jun 66.
69. Intvw, author with Col Lloyd M. N. Wenzel, Proj Mgr JEPO, 16 Feb 73.
70. Eads Study, pp 27–28.
71. Study, Maj Jens Teal, DSMS, "USAF F-15 Fighter Program and Lessons Learned," Nov 72.
72. Islin Study, p 19.
73. Ltr, Gen Ferguson to J. Leland Atwood, Pres, North American Rockwell Corp, no subj, 25 Sep 69; ltr, Gen Ferguson to Gen Ryan, no subj, 30 Sep 69; memo, Seamans to Packard, subj: The F-15 Program, 9 Oct 69; memo, Packard to Seamans, subj: Visit to F-15 Contractors, 27 Oct 69.

74. Ltr, Gen Ferguson to Gen Goldsworthy, subj: F-15 Configuration Control, 18 Apr 69.

75. Ltr, Gen Ferguson to Gen Ryan, subj: Management of Research, Development and Acquisition, 30 Jun 69; MR, Gen Ferguson, subj: Management of Research, Development and Acquisition, 1 Jul 69; ltr, Lt Gen Seth J. McKee, Asst Vice CSAF, to Air Staff, subj: Transfer of F-15 Function, 3 Jul 69.

76. Memo, Seamans to OSAF, subj: Management Procedures, 23 Jul 69.

77. Intvw, author with Col Richard K. McIntosh (Ret), 6 Mar 73.

78. Al Delugach, "Long Preparation Paid Off for McDonnell on the F-15," *St. Louis Post-Dispatch*, 11–13 Jan 70; Herb Cheshire, "The Dogfight over the F-15," *Business Week*, 20 Dec 69, pp 96–98; rpt, "Advanced Tactical Fighter, F-15," *SAC Proposal Analysis*, ASD, 25 Dec 69.

79. Memo, Seamans to Gen Ryan, subj: F-15 Program, 29 Oct 69; memo, Seamans to Packard, subj: F-15 Souce Selection Schedule, 4 Nov 69.

80. Memo, Foster to Packard, subj: F-15 Management Review, 9 Sep 1969, Report of 9 Oct 69.

81. Memo, Lt Col W. H. Heermans, III, Ch Prog Control Div F-15 SPO, to F-15 SPO, subj: Program Evaluation Group, 1 Oct 69.

82. Rpt, subj: Analysis of the F-15 Aircraft Program, U.S. Compt-Gen, 7 Jul 70; DCP, No. 19, "F-15 Tactical Counter Air Fighter," Rev A, DDR&E, 4 Nov 70.

83. Eads Study, p 29.

84. Memo, Seamans to Maj Gen Lee V. Gossick, Comdr ASD, subj: F-15 Source Selection, 23 Dec 69; Press Conference, Seamans, 24 Dec 69; Press Release, Gen Bellis, 24 Dec 69.

85. Al Delugach, "Long Preparation Paid Off for McDonnell on the F-15," *St. Louis Post-Dispatch*, 11–12 Jan 70; "Superiority in the '70s," *Time*, 5 Jan 70.

86. MR, Brig Gen James O. Frankosky, Dep Dir/ Opnl Reqs and Dev Plans, subj: Congressional Inquiry on F-15 Source Selection Factors, 16 Jul 69, with atch; Request from Armed Services Committee, 9 Jul 69; memo, Whittaker to Seamans, no subj, 15 Aug 69; ltr, L. Mendel Rivers, Ch House Amd Svs Cmte, to Seamans, no subj, 8 Aug 69; ltr, Maj Gen John R. Murphy, Dep Dir/L&L, to Rivers, no subj, 19 Aug 69; memo, Gen Murphy to Rivers, subj: Congressional Request for Source Selection Documents, 31 Dec 69; memo, Whittaker to Murphy, subj: Congressional Request for Source Selection Documents, 2 Jan 70.

87. Memo, Whittaker to Gen Murphy, subj: F-15 Source Selection Material Requested by House Armed Services Investigating Committee, 12 Feb 70.

88. "Source Selection: What the Law Requires," *Armed Forces Journal*, 22 Nov 69, p 14.

89. Ltr, Seamans to Rivers, no subj, 9 Dec 69, with atch: Memorandum of Law, 9 Dec 69.

90. Ltr, Elmer B. Staats, U.S. Compt-Gen, to Rivers, no subj, 19 Jan 70; memo, Jack L. Stempler, Gen Counsel, to Seamans, no subj, 11 Feb 70.

91. Memo, Flax and Frosch to Foster, subj: Combined VFAX/F-X Concept Formulation, 1 Dec 67.

92. Study, Lt Col Joseph D. Mirth, ICAF SP 72–84, "The Advanced Technology Engine Development," 1 May 72, pp 3–5. Hereafter Mirth Study 84.

93. Memo, Flax to Brown, subj: F-X/VFAX Engine Program, 23 Mar 68.

94. Memo, Flax and Frosch to Foster, subj: F-X/VFAX Engine Program, 5 Apr 68; memo, Foster to Flax and Frosch, subj: F-X/VFAX Engine Program, 6 Apr 68.

95. OSD News Release No. 341-68, 15 Apr 68; Mirth Study 84, Chap V; memo, Flax and Frosch, subj: Memorandum of Understanding—F-X/VFAX (VFX-2) Engine Developments, 2 Nov 68.

96. Memo, Joe Jones, Dep Asst SAF (R&D), to Foster, subj: FX/VFAX Engine Program, 20 Aug 68; memo, Foster to Flax and Forsch, subj: FX/VFAX (VFX-2), 23 Aug 68; Mirth Study 84, pp 12–13.

97. Memo, Packard to Chafee and Seamans, subj: DSARC Action on the Advanced Technology Engine for the F-14/F-15 Aircraft, 21 Feb 70; memo, Seamans to Packard, no subj, 26 Feb 70; Mirth Study 84, p 14 and Chap V.

98. Mirth Study 84, pp 3–5.

99. Ibid, Chap VII; testimony of Gen Bellis, Apr 72, in Hngs before House Cmte on Amd Svcs, 92d Cong, 2d sess, *Military Posture and H.R. 12604*, pt 1, p 9195.

100. Mirth Study 84, Chap VII; ltr, F. Edward Hebert, Ch House Amd Svcs Cmte, to Laird, no subj, 23 Dec 71; ltr, Packard to Hebert, no subj, 23 Jun 71; testimony of Lt Gen Otto J. Glasser, DCS/R&D, Mar 72, in Hngs before House Sbcmte of the Cmte on Appns, 92d Cong, 2d sess, *Department of Defense Appropriation for 1973*, pt 4, p 654.

101. Mirth Study 84, Chap VII; testimony of Gen Bellis, Apr 72, in Hngs before House Cmte on Amd Svcs, 92d Cong, 2d sess, *Military Posture and H.R. 12604*, pt 1, p 9225.

102. See note above; Islin Study, pp 23–24.

103. "F-15 Avionics to have austere touch," *Electronics*, 2 Feb 70, pp 37–38.

104. "USAF Cancels AIM-82A Missile," *Aviation Week and Space Technology*, 7 Sep 70, p 9; rpt (S/AFEO), subj: F-15 Avionics and Armament Mission Requirements Analysis, AFSC, 17 Aug 70; MR, Lt Gen John W. O'Neill, Vice Comdr AFSC, subj: F-15 Avionics and Armament Study, 16 Jul 70.

105. Herb Cheshire, "Competitors Scramble to Replace Old Fighter," *Business Week*, 17 May 69, pp 110–111; USAF News Release No. 79-70, 20 Mar 79.

106. Memo, Joe C. Jones, Dep Asst SAF (R&D), to Asst SECDEF (Comptr), subj: GAO Report to the Chairman, Preparedness Investigating Subcommittee, Committee on Armed Services, United States Senate, dated July 7, 1970, "Analysis of the F-15 Aircraft Program," 8 Sep 70.

107. Testimony of Pierre M. Sprey, 8 Dec 71, in Hngs before Sen Cmte on Amd Svcs, 92d Cong, 1st sess, Weapon System Acquisition Process, pp 239–89.

108. Intvw, Sprey, 12 Jun 73; Dickey Study, pp 43–44.

109. "F-15 Won't Meet Soviet Threat, Experts Feel," *Aerospace Daily*, 18 Feb 69, pp 204–205; ltr, Sen Milton R. Young (D-N.D.) to Laird, no subj, 25 Feb 69; memo (1), Joseph J. F. Clark, Dep Dir/L&L, to Seamans, subj: F-15, 18 Feb 69; ltr, Gen Murphy, Dir/L&L, to Earl J. Morgan, House Amd Svcs Cmte, no subj, 7 Mar 69.

110. Memo, Gen Glasser to Gen McConnell, subj: Unsolicited Proposal for Aricraft Development Study, 7 Feb 69; ltr, Flax to Clarence L. Johnson, Vice Pres, Lockheed Aircraft, no subj, 26 Feb 69; memo, Brig Gen John C. Giraudo, Dep Dir/L&L, to Seamans and Gen McConnell, subj: Congressional Briefing on F-15, 12 Feb 69; MR, Col Robert B. Tanguy, Dir/L&L, subj: F-15 Briefing to the Preparedness Investigating Subcommittee (SASC), 19 Feb 69; "F-15 Decision Nears," *Armed Forces Journal*, 5 Jul 69, p 19.

111. "F-14 vs. F-15: Will It Come to a Shootout?" *Armed Forces Journal*, 28 Feb 70, pp 20–21; intvw, Gen Rhodarmer, 22 Jun 73; rpt, subj: Analysis of the House Appropriations Committee Surveys & Investigations Report on the Comparison of the F-14 and F-15, L&L, Apr 71.

112. TAC News Release, 6 Jul 72; William P. Schlitz, "Aerospace World," *Air Force Magazine*, Sep 72, p 33; AF News Service Release No. 630, 11 Feb 73.

No Master Plan: The Employment of Artillery in the Indian Wars, 1860–1890

1. The most comprehensive study on this subject is Larry Don Roberts. "The Artillery with the Regular Army in the West from 1866 to 1890," Ph.D. dissertation, Oldahoma State University, 1981. However, as its title indicates, it does not treat the use of artillery by irregular forces such as state militia or volunteers.

2. Fairfax Downey, *Sound of the Guns: The Story of American Artillery* (New York: David McKay Company, 1955), 86; the book covers artillery history from the ancient and honorable company to the atom cannon and guided missile.

3. "A century of Indian Warfare . . . should have taught us much about people who did not fight in conventional ways, and our military might reasonably have been expected to reflect the lessons thus learned. Some were not without relevance in Vietnam." Robert M. Utley, *Soldiers West: Biographies from the Military Frontier* (Lincoln, Nebraska: University of Nebraska Press, 1987), 3.

4. Roberts, 32–34.

5. Downey, 174.

6. Roberts, 14 28.

7. "Even when doctrinal myopia converted batteries into infantry and cavalry troops, artilleryman served well. Captain Marcus Miller commanded admirably during the Modoc, Nez Perce and Bannock campaigns. He was twice brevetted for gallantry in action against the Indians. Captain Henry Hasbrouck's men hounded Captain Jack's band until the majority surrendered to him. He, too, was brevetted for meritorious conduct and gallantry in action. Lieutenants Hawthorne and Humphrey were awarded Congressional Medals of Honor for Heroism at Wounded Knee and the Clearwater battles, respectively." Ibid., 251–260.

8. Ibid., 259.

9. Ibid., 70.

10. Ibid., 32–28.

11. Ernest Wallace and E. Adamson Hoebel, *The Comanches: Lords of the South Plains* (Norman, Oklahoma: University of Oklahoma Press, 1952, reprint ed. 1985), 306.
12. Downey, 174.
13. David Nevin, *The Soldiers, The Old West* (Alexandria, Virginia: Time-Life Books, 1974), 136–143.
14. Roberts, 50–51.
15. For a thorough comparison of Custer's and Evans' actions, see Ibid., 56–61.
16. Ibid., 71.
17. Ibid., 70.
18. Ibid., 71.
19. Ibid., 70.
20. Ibid., 192.
21. Benjamin Capps, *The Great Chiefs, The Old West* (Alexandria, Virginia: Time-Life Books, 1975), 175.
22. Roberts, 197.
23. Ibid., 201.
24. Ibid., 163–164.
25. Ibid., 182–183.
26. Ibid., 195.
27. Capps, 183.
28. Nevin, 159–167.
29. John P. Langellier, *Redlegs: The U.S. Artillery from the Civil War to the Spanish-American War, 1861–1898*, in the series "G.I.: The Illustrated History of the American Soldier, His Uniform and His Equipment" (London: Greenhill Books, 1998), 7; also see photographic essay in Capps, 226–33.
30. Note: This derogatory terminology was regularly used by whites to describe the various Native American tribes that fought the Army in the west.
31. For a provocative treatment of the recent past, present and likely future environment of war and other violent conflict, see Martin van Creveld, *The Transformation of War* (New York: The Free Press, 1991).
32. For a critical appraisal of current Army doctrine in relation to likely contingencies, see John Kirk, (Brigadier General, US Army, Retired), "Move it on Over," *Armor* (November/December 1999), 14–21.
33. Roberts, 74–75.
34. Robert H. Scales, Jr., *Firepower in Limited War* revised ed. (Novato, California: Presidio Press, 1995), 295.

CLARIFYING THE ORIGINS AND STRATEGIC MISSION OF THE US MARINE CORPS DEFENSE BATTALION, 1898–1941

1. New York *Times*, 29 December 1941, in Gregory J.W. Urwin, 'The Defenders of Wake Island and Their Two Wars, 1941–1945', in Gunter Bischoff and Robert L. Dupont (eds), *The Pacific War Revisited* (Baton Rouge/London: Louisiana State University Press, 1997), 114.
2. For recent works on Wake, see Theodore L. Gatchel, *At the Water's Edge: Defending against the Modern Amphibious Assault* (Annapolis, MD: Naval Institute, 1996), 78–81; Robert J. Cressman, *'A Magnificent Fight': The Battle*

for Wake Island (Annapolis, MD: Naval Institute Press, 1995); Gregory I.W. Unwin, *Facing Fearful Odds: The Seige of Wake Island* (Lincoln, NE: University of Nebraska Press, 1997); and Urwin, 'The Defenders of Wake Island and Their Two Wars', 111–37.

3. For overviews of Marine Corps aviation before Pearl Harbor, see Robert Sherrod, *History of Marine Corps Aviation in World War II* (Baltimore: Nautical and Aviation Publishing, 1987, repr.), 27–33; and 13–29. Neither of these books explains airpower's application to advanced base theory in America's prewar Pacific strategy.

4. The operational application of advanced base theory was called several names including advanced base force, advanced base brigade, advanced base defense regiment, base defense force, defense detachment, and finally defense battalion in 1939.

5. See especially the documents declassified in January and March 1995 in Record Group 80 at the National Archives and Records Administration, Washington, DC [hereafter NARA]: General Board Subject File 1900– 1947, GB 425, Box 135; General Board Subject File 1900–1947, GB 432, Box 132; and General Correspondence of the Chief of Naval Operations and Secretary of the Navy, 1900–1947, Box 54. In Record Group 127, see Division of Plans and Policies War Plans Section 1926–1942; Box 4.

6. See Philip A. Crowl, *The U.S. Marine Corps and Amphibious Warfare: Its Theory and Practice in the Pacific* (Princeton, NJ: Princeton University Press, 1951; Quantico, VA: Marine Corps Association, 1988), 23–9; Louis Morton, 'Origins of Pacific Strategy', *Marine Corps Gazette* [hereafter *MCG*] 41 (August 1957): 36–43; Frank O. Hough et al., *Pearl Harbor to Guadalcanal*, vol. 1, *History of the U.S. Marines in World War I* (Washington: USMC, 1958), 8; Daniel Joseph Costello, 'Planning for War: A History of the General Board of the Navy, 1900–1914' (PhD dissertation, Fletcher School of Law and Diplomacy, 1968), 167–72, 221–4; William Reynolds Braisted, *The United States Navy in the Pacific, 1909–1922* (Austin: University of Texas Press, 1971), 33, 441–52; Graham A. Cosmas and Jack Shulimson, 'Continuity and Consensus: The Evolution of the Marine Advance Base, 1900–1922', in David H. White and John W. Gordon (eds), *Proceedings of the Citadel Conference on War and Diplomacy* (Charleston: Citadel, 1977), 31–5; Allan R. Millett, *Semper Fidelis: The History of the United States Marine Corps*, rev. edn (New York: Free Press, 1991), 267–86, 320–2; and Edwin H. Simmons, *The United States Marine Corps: A History*, 3rd edn (Annapolis, MD: Naval Institute Press, 1998), 82–3.

7. Historians offer a sympathetic view of defense battalions, but none has cited some of the key documents which support my conclusions. For example, see Robert Debs Heinj, Jr., *Soldiers of the Sea: The United States Marine Corps, 1775–1962* (Annapolis, MD: Naval Institute Press, 1962; Baltimore, MD: Nautical and Aviation Publishing, 1991), 301–7; Frank J. Infusino, Jr., 'The United States Marine Corps and War Planning (1900–1941)' (MA thesis, California State University at San Diego, 1973); Nathan N. Prefer, 'An Uncertain Mission: The Role of the U.S. Marine Corps in National Defense, 1880–1947' (PhD dissertation, City University of New York, 1985), 68; Henry I. Shaw, Jr., *Opening Moves: Marines Gear Up For War* (Washington:

Marine Corps Historical Center, 1991), 13–15, 17; Craig M. Cameron, *American Samurai: Myth, Imagination, and the Conduct of Battle in the First Marine Division, 1941–1951* (Cambridge: Cambridge University Press, 1994), 35–7; Naoki Kajiwara, 'The U.S. Marine Corps and the Defense of Advanced Bases: The Evolution of *Tactics and Organizations, 1900–1941* (*unpublished manuscript*, 20 August 1994); Gatchel, *At the Water's Edge*, 78–81; Charles D. Melson, *Condition Red: Marine Defense Battalions in World War II* (Washington DC: Marine Corp Historical Center, 1996).

8. For examples of the established historical view of defense battalions including many of the foremost texts on Marine Corps history, see Holland M. Smith, *The Development of Amphibious Tactics in the U.S. Navy* (Washington: USMC, 1982, repr.); John H. Russell, 'The Birth of the FMF', *United States Naval Institute Proceedings* [hereafter USNIP] 72 (January 1946): 49–51; Isely and Crowl, *The U.S. Marine Corps and Amphibious Warfare*, 3–71; Hough, *Pearl Harbor to Guadalcanal*, 5–8, 13–16, 22, 49–50, 63–9; Kenneth J. Clifford, *Progress and Purpose: A Developmental History of the U.S. Marine Corps* (Washington, DC: USMC, 1973); Ronald H. Spector, *Eagle Against the Sun* (New York: Free Press, 1985), 24–8; Millett, *Semper Fidelis*, 344–8; J. Robert Moskin, *The U.S. Marine Corps Story*, 3rd rev. edn (Boston: Little, Brown & Company, 1992); Allan R. Millett, 'Assault from the Sea: The Development of Amphibious Warfare Between the Wars— The American, British, and Japanese Experiences', in Williamson Murray and Allan R. Millett (eds), *Military Innovations in the Interwar Period* (Cambridge: Cambridge University Press, 1996), 54–9, 70–8; and Simmons, *The United States Marine Corps*, 121–6.

9. For the established historical interpretation and explanation of the defense battalions' prewar strategic importance in relation to amphibious assault, see especially Millett, *Semper Fidelis*, 344–9. Various units including defense battalions are also discussed in detail in Charles L. Updegraph, Jr., *U.S. Marine Corps Special Units of World War II* (Washington: USMC, 1977), 61–73.

10. See Jack Shulimson, *The Marine Corps' Search for a Mission, 1800–1898* (Lawrence, KS: University Press of Kansas, 1993), 11–12, 200–1, 207–10.

11. George Dewey, General Board Report No. 51, 6 October 1900, Marine Corps University Research Archives [hereafter MCURA], author's personal collection; Dion Williams, 'The Defense of Our New Naval Stations' *USNIP* 28 (June 1902): 182–3; Frank H. Schofield and E. H. Ellis, 'Report of Naval War College Committee on Defense of Guam', 14 April 1913, General Board Subject File (GBSF) 1900–47, GB 422, Box 120, Record Group (RG) 80, NARA; President of General Board (GB) to Secretary of the Navy (SecNav), 26 February 1913, in Costéllo, 'Planning for War', 223; A.W. Hinds, 'The Island of Guam as a Naval Base', *USNIP* 41 (May 1915): 449–55; Robert William Neeser, *Our Navy in the Next War* (New York: Charles Scribner & Sons, 1915), 163–5; Cosmas and Shulinson, 'Continuity and Consensus', 31–5; Millett, *Semper Fidelis*, 268–72; Hough, *Pearl Harbor to Guadalcanal*, 7.

12. President of GB to SecNav, 'Duties of Marines and their connection with Advanced Base Outfits', 21 July 1913, George Barnett to SecNav,

8 December 1914, both in GBSF 1900–47, GB 432, Box 163, RG 80, NARA. For a discussion of Culebra, see Graham A. Cosmas and Jack Shulimson, 'The Culebra Maneuver and the Formation of the U.S. Marine Corps' Advance Base Force, 1913–1914', in Robert William Love Jr (ed.), *Changing Interpretations and New Sources in Naval History* (New York: Garland, 1980), 293, 299–306; Millett, *Semper Fidelis*, 273, 382–6; Kajiwara, 'The U.S. Marine Corps and the Defense of Advanced Bases', 2–4; Melson, *Condition Red*, 2–3.

13. Eli K. Cole, lecture, Marine Corps Barracks, Philadelphia, PA, 19 June 1915, File 1975-10, Adjutant and Inspector's Office General Correspondence (A&IOGC) 1913–32, Box 234, RG 127, NARA; Cosmas and Shulimson, 'Continuity and Consensus', 31–5.

14. W.H. Russell, 'Genesis of the FMF Doctrine', *MCG* 39 (November 1955): 18; Earl H. Ellis, *Advanced Base Operations in Micronesia* (Washington: GPO, 1992 [1921]), vi.

15. Joint Board (JB) to the Secretary of War (SecWar), 'Strategy of the Pacific', 18 December 1919, Chief of Naval Operations (CNO) to Major General Commandant (MGC), 'Function of the Marine Corps in War Plans', 28 January 1920, CNO to MGC, 28 January 1920, all in Infusino, 'The United States Marine Corps and War Planning', 140–2, 152–3.

16. Earl H. Ellis, *Navy Bases: Their Location, Resources, and Security* (Washington: GPO, 1992 [1921]), 3–6, 10–23, 30, 48; Ellis, *Advanced Base Operations*, 39–50. Ellis has been a mysterious and controversial figure in Marine Corps history and lore. For a recent reading of his life, see Dirk Anthony Ballendori and Merrill Lewis Bartlett, *Pete Ellis: An Amphibious Warfare Prophet, 1880–1923* (Annapolis, MD: Naval Institute Press, 1997).

17. See J.M. Scammell, 'Our Naval Bases in the Pacific', *Infantry Journal* 30 (January 1927): 19–29; John A. Lejeune, 'The United States Marine Corps, Present and Future', *USNIP* 54 (October 1928): 861; W.C. Neville, 'The Marine Corps', *USNIP* 55 (October 1929): 863–6; Ben H. Fuller, 'The Mission of the Marine Corps', *MCG* 15 (November 1930): 7; E.W. Broadbent, 'The Fleet and the Marines', *USNIP* 57 (March 1931): 369–70; George Richards, 'The Marine Corps and the General Board of the Navy', *MCG* 16 (August 1931): 35; Ernest Lee Jahnke, 'The United State Marine Corps', *MCG* 16 (February 1932): 6; E.B. Miller, 'The Marine Corps: Its Mission, Organization, Power, and Limitation', *MCG* 17 (November 1932): 10–11; GB to SecNav, 'Examination of the Organization and Establishment of the United States Marine Corps', 10 August 1932, GBSF 1900–1947, GB 432, Box 163, RG 80, NARA.

18. David C. Evans and Mark R. Pettie, *Kaigun: Strategy, Tactics, and Technology in the Imperial Japanese Navy, 1887–1941* (Annapolis, MD: Naval Institute Press, 1997), 194–205; Millett, 'Assault from the Sea', 54–9.

19. Joint Army and Navy Basic War Plan—ORANGE', 6 October 1926, in Infusino, 'The United States Marine Corps and War Planning', 145.

20. The most important secondary source on the ORANGE Plan is Edward S. Miller, *War Plan Orange: The U.S. Strategy to Defeat Japan, 1897–1945* (Annapolis, MD: Naval Institute Press, 1991), especially 34–7, 47, 79.

21. 'Joint Action of the Army and Navy, 1927', in E.W. Broadbent, 'The Fleet and the Marines', *USNIP* 57 (March 1931): 370; for more commentary on the 'Joint Action of the Army and Navy, 1927', see MGC to CNO, 'Recommended revisions of Joint Action of Army and Navy, 1935', 11 May 1936, History Amphibious File (HAF) 36, MCURA.

22. See Millett, *Semper Fidelis*, 328; Shulimson, *The Marine Corps' Search*, 206–7.

23. For the Corps' manpower levels and expenditures in both then-year and 1990 dollars, Ulbrich, 'Thomas Holcomb and the Advent of the Marine Corps Defense Battalions', 135–6; see 'Statement 1, Summary of Naval Activities', *Naval Expenditures*, Navy Department, 1933–1939; and Millett *Semper Fidelis*, 654.

24. For various perspectives on the Corps in the early 1930s, see also GB to SecNav, 10 August 1932, 'Examination of the Organization and the Establishment of the United States Marine Corps', GBSF 1900–1947, GB 432, Box 163, RG 80, NARA; Victor Krulak, *First to Fight: An Inside View of the U.S. Marine Corps* (Annapolis, MD: Naval Institute Press, 1984), 142; memoir of Charles G. F. Good, Jr (1970), Marine Corps Oral History Collection, Marine Historical Center (MCOHC), 90; Allan R. Millett, *In Many a Strife: Gerald C. Thomas and the U.S. Marine Corps, 1917–1956* (Annapolis. MD, MD: Naval Institute Press, 1993), 98; Millett, *Assault from the Sea*, 54–9.

25. Spector, *Eagle Against the Sun*, 25; Susan Landrum, 'Carl Vinson: A Study in Military Preparedness' (MA thesis, Emory University, 1966); Calvin William Enders, 'The Vinson Navy' (PhD dissertation, Michigan State University, 1970); John C. Walter, 'Congressman Carl Vinson and Franklin Roosevelt: Naval Preparedness and the Coming the World War II, 1939–1940', *Georgia Historical Quarterly* 64 (Fall 1980): 294–305; Gladys Zehnpfennig, *Melvin J. Maas: Gallant Man of Action* (Minneapolis, MN: T.S. Denison, 1967).

26. Moskin, *The United States Marine Corps Story*, 222. Moskin perpetuates the over-emphasis of the offensive component of the FMF's dual mission. Moskin is not alone in this oversight; see also Spector, *Eagle Against the Sun*, 27; and Hough, *Pearl Harbor to Guadalcanal*, 13–22. Allan R. Millett and Edwin H. Simmons disagree with Moskin and others about the FMF's original purpose. Millett and Simmons acknowledge that the FMF's strategic importance lay in both base seizure and defence. Yet both rarely focuses on the FMF's latter capability again until the defense battalion's formation in 1939. Instead, Millett, for example, emphasises tactical problems facing a successful amphibious assault, such as unity of command, supply, transportation, ship-to-shore landings, air support and naval gunfire support: see Millett, *Semper Fidelis*, 329–44; Simmons, *The United States Marines*, 119.

27. Ralph S. Keyser, 'The Fleet Marine Force', *MCG* 18 (February 1934): 51, 63. For other examples, see MGC to CNO, 'Expeditionary Force', 17 August 1933, and MGC to L. McCarty Little, 'Fleet Marine Force', 5 December 1933: both in File 1975-10, Personnel Department General Correspondence (PDGC), 1933–1938, Box 135, RG 127, NARA; memoir

of William J. Van Ryzin (1975), MCOHC, 74–6. For secondary sources, see Russell, 'Genesis of the FMF Doctrine', 14–22; George W. Baer, *One Hundred Years of Sea Power: The U.S. Navy* (Stanford: Stanford University Press, 1994), 119, 125–7, 138.

28. Marine Corps Schools, *Tentative Manual of Landing Operations*, 1934, Marine Corps Historical Library, Marine Corps Historical Center (MCHL), paragraphs 1-1, 1-2, 1-5, 1-8, 1-22, 3-120; Krulak, *First to Fight*, 81–2; John Breckenridge, reports, 'Some Thoughts on Policy, Strategy, and Comparative Power', and 'A Discussion of Power', 21 November 1934, Julian C. Smith Papers, Marine Corps Personal Paper Collection (MCPPC), Box 29, MCURA. For commentaries on the *Tentative Manual*, see also Gatchel, *At the Water's Edge*, 78–81; Clifford, *Progress and Purpose*, 46–8, 58–9; Hough, *Pearl Harbor to Guadalcanal*, 14–22; Millett, *Semper Fidelis*, 331–7, 343; Millett, *In Many a Strife*, 110–5; Kajiwara, 'The U.S. Marine Corps and the Defense of Advanced Bases', 21–6; Heinl, *Soldiers of the Sea*, 315.

29. Dudley W. Knox 'Bases Mean Ships', *MCG* 18 (February 1934): 1, 11; see also CNO to Director of Ship Movements Division, 17 January 1941, Accession Number (AN) 1277-77-30, Box 1, National Records Center (NRC); although dated much later than the *Tentative Manual*, this 1941 document verified that the Corps' defense battalions were even stationed on island bases as 'permanent garrisons'.

30. See Chairman of GB to SecNav, 7 May 1941, GBSF 1900–1947, GB 432, Box 163, RG 80, NARA; CINCPAC to CNO, 2 December 1941, *Hearings before the Joint Committee on the Investigation of the Pearl Harbor Attack*, 79th Congress, 1st Session, November 1945 to May 31, 1946 (*Hearings*), 2480–5.

31. MGC to CNO, 'Recommended revisions of Joint Action of Army and Navy, 1935', 11 May 1936, HAF 38, MCURA.

32. Ibid.

33. Statutory Board on Submarine, Mine, and Naval Bases, memo for Secretary of the Navy, 1 December 1938, World War II Command File, Operational Archives (WWIICFOA), Box 63, Naval Historical Center (NHC); JCF to Holcomb, 11 February 1939, Thomas Holcomb Papers, MCPPC, Box 3, MCURA; Eliot, *Defending America*, 161–76, 234; Frederick J. Nelson, 'Guam—Our Western Outpost', *USNIP* 66 (January 1940): 83–8. For further explanation, see Millett, *In Many a Strife*, 130–2; Hough, *Pearl Harbor to Guadalcanal*, 59–62; Miller, *War Plan Orange*, 243, 250; Spector, *Eagle Against Sun*, 40–5; John Major, 'The Navy Plans for War, 1937–1941', in *In War and Peace: Interpretations of American Naval History, 1775–1984* (Westport, CT: Greenwood, 1984), 243–5; D. Clayton James, 'American and Japanese Strategies in the Pacific War', in Peter Paret (ed.), *Makers of Modern Strategy from Machiavelli to the Nuclear Age* (Princeton, NJ: Princeton UP, 1986), 706–7.

34. Memo from CNO, 'Report of Hepburn Board—Defense Facilities', 16 February 1939, Division of Plans and Policies War Plans Section General Correspondence (DPPWPSGC) 1926–42, Box 4, RG 127, NARA; unsigned editorial, 'The Idea of a Fleet Marine Force', *MCG* 23 (June 1939): 61; Clyde H. Metcalf, *A History of the United States Marine Corps* (New

York: G.P. Putnam, 1939), 542–3; memoir of Russell N. Jordahl (1970), MCOHC, 13; Heinl, *Soldiers of the Sea*, 306–7; memoir of Omar T. Pfeiffer (1968), MCOHC, 150; Robert D. Heinl, report, 'Defense Battalions', 15 August 1939, DPPWPSGC 1926–42, Box 4, RG 127, NARA.

35. Memo from CNO, 'Report of Hepburn Board—Defense Facilities', 16 February 1939, DPPWPSGC 1926–42, Box 4, RG 127, NARA.

36. Melson, *Condition Red*, 4.

37. Robert D. Heinl, report, 'Defense Battalions', 15 August 1939, unsigned memo, 'Marine Material Requirements for four Defense Battalions—Justification', 15 August 1939, both in DPPWPSGC 1926–42, Box 4, RG 127, NARA; Edwin H. Simmons, 'Director's Page', *Fortitudine* (Summer 1979): 3–4. For the most complete secondary explanation of the defense battalions' tactical organisation, see Kajiwara, 'The U.S. Marine Corps and the Defense of Advanced Bases'.

38. Holcomb to Harry K. Pickett, 12 December 1938, AN 127-77-30, Box 2, NRC; unsigned memo, 'Marine Material Requirements for four Defense Battalions—Justification', 15 August 1939; Robert D. Heinl, report, 'Defense Battalions', 15 August 1939, both in DPPWPSGC 1926–42, Box 4, RG 127, NARA; memoir of William W. Buchanan (1969), MCOHC, 38; memoir, Jordahl, 78; memoir of Samuel G. Taxis (1981), MCOHC, 40–4; memoir of Henry R. Paige (1970), MCOHC, 37–8; memoir, Van Ryzin, 74–7; Miller, *War Plan Orange*, 243; Infusino, 'The United States Marine Corps and War Planning', 99–100.

39. CNO to Department Chiefs, 16 February 1939, DPPWPSGC 1926–42, Box 4, RG 127, NARA; Evans and Pettie, *Kaigun*, 400–1, 426–7, 441–56, 464–7; James, 'American and Japanese Strategies in the Pacific War', 706–7; Spector, *Eagle Against the Sun*, 40–5.

40. Stark to Holcomb, 7 August 1939, George C. Marshall to Franklin D. Roosevelt, 11 August 1939, George V. Strong to Marshall, 11 August 1939: all in DPPWPSGC 1926–42, Box 4, RG 127, NARA; memoir, Paige, 37–8; unsigned memo, 15 August 1939, Holcomb to Stark, 17 August 1939, both in DPPWPSGC 1926–42, Box 4, RG 127, NARA; Eliot, *Defending America*, 230–1; Heinl, *Soldiers of the Sea*, 306–7.

41. J.B. Earle to CNO, 8 September 1939, SecNav to SecWar, 29 September 1939: both in DPPWPSGC 1926–42, Box 4, RG 127, NARA; Simmons, *The United States Marine Corps*, 121; Miller, *War Plan Orange*, 227; Infusino, 'The United States Marine Corps and War Planning', 94–6, 108; Updegraph, *U.S. Marine Corps Special Units*, 62–3.

42. Holcomb, speech, 'The Contribution of the Marine Corps to the National Defense', 27 January 1927, Thomas Holcomb File, Reference Section, MCHC; Holcomb, broadcast transcript, 22 November 1941, Holcomb Papers, MCPPC, Box 5, MCHC; Clayton B. Vogel, speech, 'The Marines and Our First Line of Defense', October 1938, Alexander A. Vandegrift Papers, MCPPC, Box 2, MCURA. For a dated overview of Corps publicity in this time period, see Robert Lindsay, *This High Name: Public Relations and the U.S. Marine Corps* (Madison: University of Wisconsin Press, 1956), 41–51.

43. Henry A. Larsen to Holcomb, 12 October 1939, SecWar to SecNav, 9 October 1939: both in DPPWPSGC 1926–42, Box 4, RG 127, NARA; 'The Defense of Midway', DPPWPSGC 1921–43, Box 33, RG 127, NARA; Robert L. Denig to Holcomb, 26 October 1939, Holcomb Papers, MCPPC, Box 3, MCURA; Alexander A. Vandegrift and Robert B. Asprey, *Once a Marine* (New York: Norton), 92–4; Millett, *Semper Fidelis*, 345; Millett, *In Many a Strife* 132–3; Julius Augustus Furer, *Administration in the Navy Department in World War II* (Washington: GPO, 1959), 41–2, 560–1.

44. One 'unit of fire' was a predetermined amount of ammunition for a given weapon needed for combat. Unsigned memo, 16 July 1940, 'Reflections on certain features of the Far Eastern situation and certain problems of U.S. Far Eastern policy, July 4, 1940', *Hearings*, 1989–97; memo for Holcomb, 16 June 1940, DPPWPSWP 1915–46, Box 14, RG 127, NARA; Vandegrift to John Marston, 29 June 1940, Vandegrift to Leech, 8 July 1940, Vandegrift to Gilder D. Jackson, 10 July 1940, letter to Vandegrift, 22 August 1940: all in Vandegrift Papers, MCPPC, Box 2, MCURA; memoir, Loomis, 98–9; George F. Eliot to Holcomb, 17 August 1940, Holcomb, memo for Eliot, 24 July 1940: both in Holcomb Papers, MCPPC, Box 4, MCURA.

45. James, 'American and Japanese Strategies', 711; Hough, *Pearl Harbor to Guadalcanal*, 63; 'ABC-1 Annex 3', 27 March 1941, *Hearings*, 1504, 1511–3; CNO to Commander in Chief-Pacific Fleet (CINCPAC), Commander in Chief-Atlantic Fleet (CINCLANT), and Commander in Chief-Asian Fleet (CINCAF), 3 April 1941, *Hearings*, 2462–3. The different drafts of the Stark Memorandum later to become Plan DOG can be found in Steven T. Ross (ed.), *American War Plans, 1919–1941* (5 vols), vol. 3, *Plans to Meet the Axis Threat* (New York: Garland, 1992), 225–300. See also Miller, *War Plan Orange*; Mark M. Lowenthal, 'The Stark Memorandum and the American National Security Process, 1940', in *Changing Interpretations and New Sources in Naval History* (New York: Garland, 1980), 355–7.

46. If read in context of my research, the following secondary sources actually confirm the importance of base defense: Miller, *War Plan Orange*, 49; James, 'American and Japanese Strategies', 711; Infusino, 'The United States Marine Corps and War Planning', 97–8; Major, 'The Navy Plans for War', 253–7; Hough, *Pearl Harbor to Guadalcanal*, 64; Updegraph, *U.S. Marine Corps Special Units*, 65.

47. Ingersoll to Holcomb, 10 January 1941, DPPWPSGC, 1926–42, Box 4, RG 127, NARA.

48. 'Plan for the Expansion of U.S. Marine Corps', 6 May 1941, GBSF 1900–47, GB 432, Box 163, RG 80, NARA; 'The Training of Units of the Fleet Marine Force', n.d. [c. March 1941], DPPWPSGC, 1926–42, Box 4, RG 127, NARA; Bureau of Yards and Docks, 1 March 1941, GBSF 1900–47, GB 425, Box 135, RG 80, NARA; Holcomb to J. W. Greenslade, 30 January 1941, GBSF 1900–47, GB 432, Box 163, RG 80, NARA; James H. Reid to Stark, 2 February 1941, A.G. Kirk to Stark, 20 February 1941,

General Correspondence of the CNO and SecNav (GCCNOSN) 1900–47, Box 54, RG 80, NARA. All these primary sources further corroborate note 43. See also Tom Fitzpatrick, 'A Character that Inspires: Major General Charles D. Barrett, USMC, and the USMC, 1909–1943', unpublished manuscript, 1999, in possession of the MCHC; Infusino, 'The United States Marine Corps and War Planning', 96.

49. 'Marine Expeditionary Force', n.d. [c. February 1941], 'Training Units of the Fleet Marine Force', n.d. [c. March 1941], both in GBSF 1900–47, GB 425, Box 135, RG 80, NARA; Ingersoll to Department Chiefs, 28 February 1941, AN 1277-77-30, Box 2, NRC; see also Melson, *Condition Red*, 4–6.

50. Ingersoll to Holcomb, 10 January 1941, DPPWPSGC, 1926–4, Box 4, RG 127.

51. CNO to MGC, 29 April 1941, DPPWPSGC, 1926–1942, Box 4, RG 127, NARA; Chairman of GB to SecNav, 7 May 1941, GBSF 1900–1947, GB 432, Box 163, RG 80, NARA; *Marine Corps Administrative History*, typed manuscript (Washington: Marine Corps Historical Division, 1946), 12.

52. Before the attack on Pearl Harbor, some young men simply wanted 'to be Marines'. Unscientific survey questionnaires were sent by the author to approximately 400 members of the 7th Defense/AAA Battalion Veterans Group and returned to the author from December 1994 until June 1995. Of the 79 respondees, 28 probably joined the Corps before 7 December 1941. According to 25 of the 28, reasons for enlistment included combinations of patriotism, duty, proof of manhood, and sometimes employment. Only 3 chose employment as their main reason for enlisting in the Corps. While the limited size of this survey precludes any concrete conclusions, some young men apparently chose the Corps over a number of alternatives; all in 7th Defense Battalion Questionnaires, World War II Collection, Box 1, MCURA (Questionnaires). For some background, see also Allan R. Millett and Peter Maslowski, *For the Common Defense: A Military History of the United States of America* (New York: Free Press, 1984), 398.

53. James Breckenridge to Vandegrift, 2 April 1941; Charles Price to Vandegrift, 8 May 1941: both in Vandegrift Papers, PPC, Box 2, MCHC; Millett and Maslowski, *For the Common Defense*, 398.

54. Hough, *Pearl Harbor to Guadalcanal*, 56.

55. Homer C. Votaw, 'Wake Island', *USNIP* 67 (January 1941): 52–5; unsigned memo, 'Defense of Bases Established for the Support Force', 13 May 1941, DPPWPSGC 1926–42, Box 1, RG 127, NARA; 9 April 1941, Price to Vandegrift, 8 May 1941, Price to Vandegrift, both in Vandegrift Papers, MCPPC, Box 2, MCURA; CNO to MGC, 29 April, DPPWPSGC 1926–1942, Box 4, RG 127, NARA; Charles H. Petersen, Questionnaire; 'Plan for the Expansion of U.S. Marine Corps', May 6, 1941, GBSF 1900–47, GB 432, Box 135, RG 80, NARA; Infusino, 'The United States Marine Corps and War Planning', 104–6; Hough, *Pearl Harbor to Guadalcanal*, 49–50; Millett, *Semper Fidelis*, 344–8; Millett, *In Many a Strife*, 154–5.

56. MGC to CNO, 5 September 1941, DPPWPSGC 1926–42, Box 4, RG
127, NARA; P. A. del Valle to Holcomb, 22 December 1939, DPPW-
PSGC 1915–46, Box 14, NARARA; memoir, Taxis, 55–6; memoir, Page,
40; memoir, Dessez, 157, 164; memoir of James P.S. Devereux, 92–3;
memoir of Samuel B. Griffiths, II (1970), 30; Benis M. Frank, unpublished
panel comments, 'Pre-War Planning', Siena College World War II Conference, 30 May 1996, author's personal collection.

57. Charles J. Miller, 'Marine Corps Schools, 1934–1935', *MCG* 19 (August
1934): 57–9; Dion Williams, 'The Education of Marine Officer. II. 'The
Marine Corps Schools', *MCG* 18 (August 1933): 17–28; Millett, 'Assault
from the Sea', 74–5; Donald F. Bittner, *Curriculum Evolution: Marine Corps
Command and Staff College, 1920–1988* (Washington: History and Museum
Division, HQMC, 1988), 21-8, and ongoing conversations and correspondence with Bittner in April, August and September 1997.

58. Breckinridge to Vandegrift, 21 April 1941, Vandegrift Papers, PPCC, Box
2, MCHC; Simmons, 'Director's Page', 3–4; Donald F. Bittner to author, 7
October 1997, author's personal collection.

59. Memo, 'Are We Ready III—Additional data on Defense Battalions covering period 1 March 1941 to 15 March 1941', 16 September 1941, DPPW-
PSWP 1939–1940, Box 33, NARA.

60. Husband E. Kimmel to Stark, 26 July 1941; Kimmel to Stark, 12 August
1941; Kimmel to Stark, 15 November 1941: all in *Hearings*, 2240, 2243,
2252–3.

61. Memo from CNO, 24 October 1941; MGC to CNO, 28 October 1941:
both in AN 127-77-30, Box 2, NRC; memoir, Pfeiffer, 169, 179; Miller,
War Plan Orange, 292; Infusino, 'The United States Marine Corps and
War Planning', 102–6

62. Bloch to Kimmel, 17 October 1941, AN 1277-77-30, Box 1, NRC; 'Fortification of Guam', 1 October 1941; G.J. Rowcliff to Stark, 18 October 1941:
both in AN 1277-77-30, Box 2, NRC; CINCPAC to CNO, 2 December
1941, *Hearings*, 2480–501; Kimmel to Stark, 2 December 1941, *Hearings*,
2253–5; Woodrow Kessler, *To Wake and Beyond: Reminiscences* (Washington,
DC: USMC, 1988), 9–12, 23–4, 41–2; John P.S. Devereux, *The Story of Wake
Island* (Philadelphia: Lippincott, 1947), 36–9; see also note 3.

63. Millett, *Semper Fidelis*, 346–8.

64. See Hough, *Pearl Harbor to Guadalcanal*, 63–4; John Breckridge, 'Some
Thoughts on Policy, Strategy, and Comparative Power', n.d. [c. November
1934], Smith Papers, MCPPC, Box 4, MCHC.

MORE THAN NUMBERS: AMERICANS AND THE REVIVAL OF FRENCH
MORALE IN THE GREAT WAR
*At the author's request, the citation of documents in the notes reflects the orthography
used in the originals, even if this is inconsistent. Ed.*

1. B. H. Liddell Hart, *The Real War, 1914–1918* (Boston, 1930), pp. 296, 313,
420, 460; Cyril Falls, *The Great War* (New York, 1959), p. 255; Correlli
Barnett, *The Swordbearers: Supreme Command in the First World War* (New
York, 1964), pp. 233, 239, 274–75, 356.

2. John Keegan, *The First World War* (New York, 1999), pp. 372–427.

3. Keegan, *First World War*, pp. 352, 372, 407, 412, with the quotation on p. 412.

4. For evidence of this friction during the war, see Edward L. Spears, *Prelude to Victory* (London, 1939), p. 67.

5. James Edmonds, ed., *History of the Great War: Military Operations, France and Belgium, 1914–1918*, 14 vols. (London, 1922–48).

6. Tim Travers, *The Killing Ground: The British Army, the Western Front, and the Emergence of Modern Warfare, 1900–1918* (London, 1987), p. 215.

7. See Edmonds's published reviews and other assessments contained in file "French Official History, Tome II, Misrepresentations in—of operations of B.E.F. during Battle of the Marne," file CAB 45/162, Public Records Office, London.

8. Robert A. Doughty, "Viewing the Great War through a Prism," and "Discussion" in Steven Weingartner, ed., *Cantigny at Seventy-Five: A Professional Discussion* (Chicago, 1994), pp. 13–36, 53–54.

9. Keegan, *First World War*, pp. 138–74, 249–56, 301–08, 332–43, 377–92, 429–55, with the quoted words on p. 449. Graydon A. Tunstall, Jr., *Planning for War against Russia and Serbia: Austro-Hungarian and German Military Strategies, 1871–1914* (Boulder, Colo., 1993); Dennis E. Showalter, *Tannenberg: Clash of Empires* (Hamden, Conn., 1991); and Holger H. Herwig, *The First World War: Germany and Austria-Hungary, 1914–1918* (London, 1997), are among the works Keegan cites.

10. Doughty, "Viewing the Great War through a Prism."

11. France, Ministère de la guerre, État-major de l'armée, Service historique, *Les armées françaises dans la grande guerre*, 23 vols. (Paris, 1922–39).

12. G. Q. G. des Armées du Nord et du Nord-Est, S.R. aux armées (contrôle postal), Rapport sur la correspondence des troupes du 27 janvier au 10 février 1917, 15 Feb 1917, carton 16N1485, Service historique de l'armée de terre (henceforth S.H.A.T.), Vincennes, France.

13. G. Q. G. des Armées du Nord et du Nord-Est, S.R. aux armées (contrôle postal), Rapport sur la correspondence des troupes du 10 au 25 avril 1917, 1 May 1917, carton 16N1485, S.H.A.T.

14. S.R. aux armées, Rapport du contrôle postal sur les mutineries, 11 Jun 1917, carton 16N1485, S.H.A.T.

15. G. Q. G. des Armées du Nord et du Nord-Est, S.R. aux armées (contrôle postal), Rapport sur la correspondance des troupes du 10 au 25 avril 1917, 1 May 1917, carton 16N1485, S.H.A.T.

16. Guy Pedroncini, *Les Mutineries de 1917*, 2^d ed. (Paris, 1983), p. 132.

17. John J. Pershing, *My Experiences in the World War*, 2 vols. (New York, 1931), 1: 58–59.

18. James G. Harbord, *Leaves from a War Diary* (New York, 1925), p. 47.

19. Pershing, *Experiences in the World War*, 1: 98, 197.

20. Jean de Pierrefeu, *G. Q. G., Secteur 1: Trois ans au Grand Quartier Général*, 2 vols. (Paris, 1920), 2: 33–37; Pershing, *Experiences in the World War*, 1: 142.

21. "Why France Is Fighting," *Bulletin of the Alliance Française*, no. 66 (17 July 1917), pp. 178–81; Pierrefeu, *G. Q. G., Secteur 1*, 2: 36–37.

22. G. Q. G., Note sur la situation actuelle, 5 Jun 1917, in France, Ministère de la guerre, État-major de l'armée, Service historique, *Les armées françaises*, tome 5, vol. 2, Annex vol. 1, document no. 426, p. 719.

23. G. Q. G. des Armées du Nord et du Nord-Est, S.R. aux armées (contrôle postal), Rapport sur la correspondance des troupes du 10 au 25 mai 1917, 1 Jun 1917; G. Q. G. des Armées du Nord et du Nord-Est, Bureau des services spéciaux, S.R. aux armées (contrôle postal), Rapport de contrôle postal, 18 Sep 1917, both in carton 16N1485, S.H.A.T.

24. État-major général, Huitième rapport de mission du lieutenant-colonel Langlois (Russie et Roumanie), 19 Mar 1917, carton 17N1547, S.H.A.T.; Général de Castelnau à ministre de la guerre, Pétrograd, 2 Feb 1917, carton 5N140, S.H.A.T.; Ministre de la guerre, Rapport du général de division de Curières de Castelnau, Chef de la mission militaire en Russie, 9 Mar 1917, carton 6N68, Fonds Clemenceau, S.H.A.T.

25. G. Q. G. des Armées du Nord et du Nord-Est, S.R. aux armées (contrôle postal), Rapport sur la correspondance des troupes du 10 au 25 mars 1917, 1 Apr 1917, carton 16N1485, S.H.A.T.

26. Mission militaire française près G. Q. G. Russe, Chef mission française, à ministre de la guerre et général commandant en chef, 23 May 1917, in *Les armées françaises*, tome 5, vol. 2, Annex vol. 1, document no. 291, pp. 491–92.

27. Mission militaire française près G. Q. G. Russe, Chef mission militaire à ministre de la guerre et général commandant en chef, 31 May 1917, in ibid., document no. 379, pp. 636–37.

28. Mission militaire française près G. Q. G. Russe, Chef mission française à ministre de la guerre et commandant en chef, 24 Jul 1917, in ibid., tome 5, vol. 2, Annex vol. 2, document no. 800, p. 282.

29. Mission militaire française près G. Q. G. Russe, Chef mission militaire à ministre de la guerre, 29 Jul 1917, in ibid., document no. 833, pp. 326–27; Représentant militaire russe près le G. Q. G., Transmission d'un télégramme du G. Q. G. russe rélatif à la situation sur le front depuis l'offensive du 1er juillet, 7 Aug 1917, in ibid., document no. 886, pp. 407–08.

30. Conference des alliées, Conference militaire du 26 juillet (matin) [1917], carton 6N68, Fonds Clemenceau, S.H.A.T.; Pershing, *Experiences in the World War*, 1: 117, containing the quotation.

31. G. Q. G. des Armées du Nord et du Nord-Est, S.R. aux armées (contrôle postal), Rapport du 10 au 25 mai 1917, 1 Jun 1917.

32. "La Paix ne peut sortir que la Victoire," *Bulletin des armées de la république*, no. 249 (6 Jun 1917), pp. 3–4.

33. Raymond Poincaré, *Au service de la France*, 11 vols. (Paris, 1926–74), 9: 148; Leonard V. Smith, *Between Mutiny and Obedience: The Case of the French Fifth Infantry Division during World War I* (Princeton, 1994), p. 184.

34. G. Q. G., 30 May 1917, in *Les armées françaises*, tome 5, vol. 2, Annex vol. 1, document no. 372, pp. 615–24; S.R. aux armées, Rapport du contrôle postal sur les mutineries, 11 Jun 1917, carton 16N1485, S.H.A.T.

35. Pershing, *Experiences in the World War*, 1: 97.

36. G. Q. G. des Armées du Nord et du Nord-Est, services spéciaux, S.R. aux armées (contrôle postal), Renseignements sur les corps de troupe d'après le

contrôle postal, période du 6 au 26 novembre 1917, carton 16N1485, S.H.A.T.

37. État-major général, Bureau des services spéciaux (contrôle postal), Renseignements sur les corps de troupe d'après le contrôle postal, deuxième quinzaine de décembre, 2 Jan 1918, carton 16N1485, S.H.A.T.

38. G. Q. G., Plan défensif des forces alliées sur le front français pour la fin de 1917 & 1918, 14 Nov 1917, carton 16N172, S.H.A.T.

39. État-major général, Bureau des services spéciaux (contrôle postal), Rapport sur le pessimisme dans le corps de troupes, 15 Dec 1917, carton 16N1485, S.H.A.T.

40. Registre des délibérations du Comité de guerre, 1917–1918 (Ministère Georges Clemenceau), Ière séance, 6 Dec 1917, carton 3N2, S.H.A.T.

41. G. Q. G., Note sur les transports allemands sur le front occidental du Ier janvier au 10 mars, 14 Mar 1918, *Les armées françaises*, tome 6, vol. 1, Annex vol. 1, document no. 455, p. 1053.

42. État-major général, Bureau des services spéciaux (contrôle postal), Renseignements sur les corps de troupe (Ière quinzaine de février), 20 Feb 1918, carton 16N1485, S.H.A.T.

43. État-major général, Bureau des services spéciaux (contrôle postal), Renseignements sur les corps de troupe (Ière quinzaine de février), 20 Feb 1918, carton 16N1485, S.H.A.T.

44. État-major général, Section de renseignements aux armées, contrôle postal, Renseignements sur les corps de troupe d'après le contrôle postal, 6 Apr 1918, carton 16N1485, S.H.A.T.

45. G. Q. G. des Armées du Nord et du Nord-Est, Service des renseignements aux armées, Le moral général de l'armée en avril 1918, 5 May 1918, carton 16N1486, S.H.A.T.

46. État-major général, Section de renseignements aux armées, contrôle postal, Note sur le moral des troupes (d'après le contrôle postal), Ière quinzaine de mai, 15 May 1918, carton 16N1485, S.H.A.T.

47. G. Q. G. des Armées du Nord et du Nord-Est, Service des renseignements aux armées, Le moral général de l'armée en mai 1918, 6 Jun 1918, carton 16N1486, S.H.A.T.

48. IIe Armée, Commandant de génie, Compte-rendu rélatif au moral des troupes, 8 Jul 1918, carton 16N1486, S.H.A.T.

49. Pierrefeu, *G. Q. G.*, *Secteur 1*, 2: 189–90.

50. IIe Armée, État-major, 2me Bureau–S.R., Observation du général cdt. l'armée, 12 Jul 1918, carton 16N1491, S.H.A.T.

51. 6° Armée, État-major, 2° Bureau S.R., Compterendu mensuel rélatif au moral des troupes de la VI° Armée, 15 Jul 1918, carton 16N1486, S.H.A.T.

52. VII° Armée, État-major, 2° Bureau, No. 6133, Compte-rendu sur le moral des troupes, 15 Aug 1918, carton 16N1491, S.H.A.T.

53. IIe Armée, État-major, 2me Bureau–S.R., Observation du général cdt. l'armée, 12 Aug 1918, carton 16N1491, S.H.A.T.

54. IIe Armée, État-major, 2me Bureau–S.R., No. 949, Observation du général cdt. l'armée, 12 Sep 1918, carton 16N1491, S.H.A.T.

55. Général Gerard, Commandant la VIII° Armée, à Monsieur le Général Commandant en Chef, 14 Sep 1918, VIII° Armée, État-major, 2ème Bureau, carton 16N1491, S.H.A.T.
56. Maj Gen Gerard, Cdr, Eighth Army, à Monsieur le Général, Commandant le G.A.E., 14 Oct 1918, VIII° Armée, État-major, 2ème Bureau, S.R., carton 16N1491, S.H.A.T.
57. Ibid.

"Even in Auschwitz . . . Humanity could prevail": British POWs and Jewish Concentration-Camp Inmates at IG Auschwitz, 1943–1945

1. National Archives and Records Administration (NARA), Record Group (RG) 238, Records of the United States Chief of Counsel for War Crimes, Nuremberg Military Tribunals, Relating to Nazi Industrialists, microfilm T-301, roll 101, Nuremberg Industrialist (NI)-12390, frame 1239, Reginald A. Hartland affidavit, 14.11.47, hereafter T-301/101/NI-12390/1239; G. J. Duffree, "The Will to Survive" (unpublished manuscript, 1987), p. 55; Alfred C. Stow, response to my questionnaire, 2.11.94, hereafter responses are cited by name and date. Public Record Office, War Office 309/1063, F. N. Potts, Judge Advocate General's Corps, War Crimes Section to War Crimes Investigation Unit, BAOR/15228/C.3046/JAG, 3.1.47, pp. 1–2. I gratefully acknowledge Crown Copyright. The report reproduces Benno F.'s full name, which I have elected not to print, because it is unclear whether he ever stood trial. NARA, RG 238, *United States of America versus Carl Krauch, et al.*, microfilm M-892, roll 5, frames 717–18, Hartland testimony, 18.11.47, hereafter M-892/5/717–18. Although E715 contained small enclaves of POWs of European descent from Commonwealth countries, notably Australia, New Zealand, and South Africa, I employ the term "British" throughout the paper, because surviving records indicate that most POWs hailed from the British Isles. While the Germans treated the majority of British captives relatively decently, Colonial African POWs formed a noteworthy exception. See David Killingray, "Africans and African Americans in Enemy Hands" in Bob Moore and Kent Fedorowich, eds., *Prisoners of War and Their Captors in World War II* (Oxford: Berg, 1996), pp. 181–204. My thanks go to those who answered specific research queries or commented on earlier drafts of this essay, including Lloyd E. Ambrosius, David Cahan, Gerald H. Davis, Maurice Hatton, Edward L. Homze, Eric Howe, Aaron Kornblum, Peter Morris, the Honorable Shimon Peres, David Silberklang, Mark Sofer, Jeffrey Spinner, Alan E. Steinweis, John Taylor, Jonathon F. Vance, Robert Wolfe, the Zeta Nu Chapter of Phi Alpha Theta at University of Nebraska-Lincoln, and the E715 respondents. For the title citation, see n. 23.
2. On escapes, Ronald Redman, May 1994; and Stow, 2.11.94.
3. Rainer C. Baum, "HOLOCAUST: Moral Indifference as *the* Form of Modern Evil" in Alan Rosenberg and Gerald E. Myers, eds., *Echoes from the Holocaust: Philosophical Reflections on a Dark Time* (Philadelphia: Temple University Press, 1988), p. 57. IG Farbenindustrie in-Abwicklung

served as the legal successor to IG Farben, when founded in 1955 with the blessing of the Federal Republic of Germany. Although intended to be a temporary trusteeship for the disposal of IG Farben's remaining financial assets, the successor firm is still in existence and held its latest shareholder's meeting in August 2000. Holocaust survivors have long demanded the sale of its remaining assets and the division of proceeds among former forced laborers, a principle IG Farben in-Liquidation appears willing finally to embrace. For the complicated history of IG Farben's breakup, see Raymond G. Stokes, *Divide and Prosper: The Heirs of IG Farben Under Allied Authority, 1945–1951* (Berkeley: University of California Press, 1988), esp. pp. 173–79; for the Wollheim suit, see Benjamin B. Ferencz, *Less Than Slaves: Jewish Forced Labor and the Quest for Compensation* (Cambridge: Harvard University Press, 1979), ch. 2; for updates about IG Farben in-Abwicklung, see http://www.kritischeaktionaere.de/Konzernkritik/konzernkritik.html; and "Company to Create Slave Labor Fund," 24.8.00, http://amarillonet.com/stories/082400/usn_slave.shtml.

4. For the cost of IG Auschwitz, see Peter Hayes, *Industry and Ideology: IG Farben in the Nazi Era* (Cambridge: Cambridge University Press, 1989 [1987]), p. 351. On the Reichswerke Hermann Göring, see Richard J. Overy, *War and Economy in the Third Reich* (Oxford: Clarendon Press, 1994), pp. 96–97, 99, 110–14; on Magnitogorsk, see Loren R. Graham, *The Ghost of the Executed Engineer: Technology and the Fall of the Soviet Union* (Cambridge, MA: Harvard University Press, 1993), pp. 56, 58, 60, 74, 103, 106. For technical reasons that led IG Farben to select the site, and problems with the assumption that the availability of concentration-camp labor determined the decision, see Peter J. T. Morris, "The Development of Acetylene Chemistry and Synthetic Rubber by IG Farbenindustrie Aktiengesellschaft, 1926–1945" (unpublished Ph.D. dissertation, University of Oxford, 1982), pp. 330–42. On the putative role that concentration camp Auschwitz's proximity played in IG Farben's decision, compare Joseph Borkin, *The Crime and Punishment of IG Farben* (New York; London: The Free Press, 1978), pp. 115–17; Ferencz, *Less Than Slaves*, p. 9; Robert Simon Yavner, "IG Farben's PetroChemical Plant and Concentration Camp at Auschwitz" (unpublished MA thesis, Old Dominion University, 1984), pp. 31–32; and Bernd C. Wagner, *IG Auschwitz: Zwangsarbeit und Vernichtung von Häftlingen des Lagers Monowitz, 1941–1945*, Darstellungen und Quellen zur Geschichte von Auschwitz (Munich: K. G. Saur, 2000), pp. 46–55; with my own "IG Auschwitz: The Primacy of Racial Politics" (unpublished Ph.D. dissertation, University of Nebraska-Lincoln, 2000), pp. 21–36. Whereas most earlier accounts, including Wagner's, have stressed forced-labor availability as an important factor in the decision, I argue that IG Farben had already decided in favor of the Dwóry site, near Auschwitz, on technical grounds before labor became an issue.

5. For paper and effective strengths of working groups, see M-892/65/813, Dürrfeld Exh. 136, doc. 1505, Five Personnel Charts for IG Auschwitz, 1941–44; quote in Primo Levi, *Survival in Auschwitz: The Nazi Assault on Humanity* (New York: Collier Books, 1961), p. 66.

6. Christopher R. Browning, *Nazi Policy, Jewish Workers, German Killers* (Cambridge: Cambridge University Press, 2000), p. 59; Wagner, *IG Auschwitz*, pp. 141–63; White, "The Primacy of Racial Politics," pp. 36–38, 53–54, 124–52, 184–201.

7. White, "The Primacy of Racial Politics," pp. 96–106; on AELs more generally, see esp. Gerhard Birk, "Arbeitserziehungslager im 'Dritten Reich,'" *Bulletin Faschismus/Zweiter Weltkrieg* (1990): 154–69; and an important new study, Gabriele Lofti, *KZ der Gestapo: Arbeitserziehungslager im Dritten Reich* (Stuttgart: Deutsche Verlags-Anstalt, 2000). The announcement of the column's formation is found in United States Holocaust Memorial Museum Archives (USHMMA), Microfilm RG 11.001 M.03, Zentralbauleitung der Waffen-SS und Polizei Auschwitz Collection, Moscow Central State *Osobyi* (Special) Archives, *fond* (record group) 502, *opis'* (subdivision) 5, *delo* (file) 2, roll 70, IG Auschwitz, Rundschreiben (hereafter R.) Nr. 3011, 30.3.44, Betr.: "Einrichtung einer zbV-Kolonne," p. 248, hereafter RG 11.001 M.03, 502/5/2/70.

8. White, "The Primacy of Racial Politics," pp. 170–72, 178–81, 189–90, 328–42. Management certainly knew a great deal about the killing operations, but who dictated selection criteria inside Monowitz? Although the Nuremberg prosecution argued that they determined selection criteria, plant leaders had preferred to distance themselves as much as possible from the details. The SS set the parameters (such as physical weakness and length of stay in hospital), and used the building project as a rationale for murder. The firm contributed by refusing to expand the camp and hospital to keep up with its incessant labor demands, turning down other requests for improvements, and only sparingly exercising its limited veto over selections. For Monowitz mortality estimates, see Hayes, *Industry and Ideology*, p. 359, n. 144; and Wagner, *IG Auschwitz*, p. 7.

9. T-301/96/NI-11696/664, Charles Joseph Coward affidavit, 24.7.47; NARA, RG 389, Records of the Provost Marshal General, box 2150, Stalag VIII B file, Gabriel Naville, Protecting Power Report No. 3, 29.6.43; quote in ibid., Gabriel Naville, Protecting Power Report No. 4, 15.11.43; ibid., Ruggli, International Committee of the Red Cross (ICRC) Report, 30.10.43; for more on Stalag VIII B, see Oswald Stefan Popiolek and Pawel Barteczko, "Lamsdorf: The Death-Place of About 100 Thousand," *Contemporary Poland* 7 (4.77): 32–4; and esp. Jonathon F. Vance, "The Politics of Camp Life: The Bargaining Process in Two German Prison Camps," *War & Society* 10 (1992): 117–21.

10. The vast majority of E715 POWs who testified either just after the war or fifty years later in response to my questionnaire were captured in North Africa between 1941 and 1942 and spent time in Italian camps. Duffree, "The Will to Survive," pp. 47–48, excoriated his Italian captors for poor treatment, a sentiment common among respondents. Other POWs captured in North Africa and confined in Italy until August and September 1943 included Will Bamford, 10.4.94; Douglas Bond, 8.4.94; Robert Cossar, 5.10.94; W. N. Davis, 5.10.94; G. W. Gardiner, 20.4.94; A. H. Gifford, 10.4.94; Frank Harris, 8.4.94; Hartland, 8.4.94; W. J. Hatch, nd; Cyril Quartermaine, 4.4.94; Redman, May 1994; Cliff Shepherd, sound recording,

1994; Stow, 27.6.94; Richard James Frederick Wellard, sound recording, 2.5.94; T-301/96/NI-11699/693, John Henry Adkin affidavit, 15.6.47; ibid., NI-11698/686, David Innes Alexander affidavit, 19.7.47; ibid., NI-11695/653, Leonard Dales affidavit, 17.6.47; ibid., NI-11694/640, Frederick Davison affidavit, 19.7.47; ibid., 101/NI-12388/1193, Eric James Doyle affidavit, 14.11.47; ibid., 96/NI-11693/626, Robert William Ferris affidavit, 1.7.47; ibid., NI-11692/617, Douglas Tilbrook Frost affidavit, 16.7.47; ibid., NI-11705/746, Dennis Arthur Greenham affidavit, 23.7.47; ibid., 101/NI-12390/1239, Hartland affidavit, 14.11.47; ibid., 96/NI-11704/733, Charles Hill affidavit, 21.7.47; ibid., NI-11703/726, George Harry Longden affidavit, 17.7.47; ibid., NI-11701/708, John Pascoe affidavit, 22.7.47; ibid., NI-11708/769, Albert Victory Seal affidavit, 22.7.47; ibid., NI-11706/752, Frederick Wooley affidavit, 22.7.47.

11. The 1929 Geneva Convention labor provisions are appended to "The Conditions of Employment of Prisoners of War," *International Labour Review* 47 (February 1943): 195–96, hereafter *ILR;* Gerald H. Davis, "Prisoners of War in Twentieth-Century War Economies," *Journal of Contemporary History* 12 (1977): 626, 629–30. For the German definition of "suitable" employment, see M-892/83/55, Defense Doc. PW nr. 10, Wolf Deneke von Weltzien affidavit, 27.5.47. Von Weltzien served in the Office of the Chief of Prisoner of War Affairs and supplied expert testimony for the defense during the IG Farben Trial. "The Employment of Prisoners of War in Germany," *ILR* 48 (September 1943): 320; Jean de Preux, *The Geneva Convention Relative to the Treatment of Prisoners of War,* vol. III in Jean S. Pictet, ed. *The Geneva Conventions of 12 August 1949: Commentary* (Geneva: ICRC, 1960), p. 707.

12. Gardiner, 20.4.94; Davis, 10.5.94; T-301/91/NI-11048/716, IG Farbenindustrie Aktiengesellschaft, Werk Auschwitz, Orientierungsplan, Plan No. 96/44, 20.8.44; ibid., 101/NI-12390/1239, Hartland affidavit, 14.11.47; ibid., 96/NI-11695/653, Dales affidavit, 17.7.47; Doyle testimony, 17.11.47, in United States, Nuremberg Military Tribunals, *Trials of War Criminals Before the Nuremberg Military Tribunals Under Control Council Law No. 10, Nuremberg, October 1946–April 1949,* 15 vols. (Washington: Government Printing Office, 1950–53), VIII: 621; M-892/5/625–26, Hill testimony, 14.11.47; T-301/101/NI-12388/1193, Doyle affidavit, 14.11.47. On the working groups housed in Lager VIII, see M892/66/819, Dürrfeld Exh. 393, Doc. 1413, Helmut Schneider, Gefolgschaftsabteilung/ Lohnempfänger, Wochenbericht Nr. 9 für die Zeit vom 24.2–3.44. Over three hundred Germans, small contingents of Polish males, Italians, Flemings, and male and female Eastern workers also occupied Lager VIII at the time. For aerial photography, see NARA, Records of the United States Strategic Bombing Survey, RG 243, box 124, GS-5612, print 4176, 60 PR 694, 60 Sqdn., 25.8.44, 10.00, F [ocal length] 36", 30,000', hereafter GS-5612, with print and mission information. Lager VIII appears at the southernmost edge of the image. POWs had not occupied that camp for three to four months at the time of photo cover. Duffree, "The Will to Survive," p. 52; Hatch, nd; T-301/96/NI-11696/664, Coward affidavit, 24.7.47; "Official Reports from the Camps," *The Prisoner of War* (British Red Cross Society) 3 (November

1944): 10. Thirty-nine British POWs lost their lives during the first U.S. raid on the plant (20 August 1944), when a bomb struck a splinter-proof trench in Lager VI, which partially accounted for the lowered strength prior to evacuation.

13. "The Conditions of Employment," pp. 183–84. Stuart Erdheim erroneously places Lager VIII inside Auschwitz town and relies upon the often unreliable biography of E715's Man of Confidence Charles Coward to argue that the POWs were transferred on account of Allied psychological warfare leaflets dropped in spring 1944. See his "Could the Allies Have Bombed Auschwitz-Birkenau?" *Holocaust and Genocide Studies* 11:2 (Fall 1997): 160, n. 40; and the Coward biography, John Castle [pseud. Ronald Charles Payne and John William Garrod], *The Password Is Courage* (London: Souvenir, 1954), p. 179; Duffree, "The Will to Survive," p. 54; T-301/96/NI-11696/664, Coward affidavit, 24.7.47; ibid., NI-11693/628, Ferris affidavit, 1.7.47. GS-5612, Print 4173, 60 PR 694, 25.8.44, 10.00, F 36", 30,000', reveals few, if any, obstructions between Lager VI and Monowitz. The AEL, main gate, SS barracks, and garage were closest to the new POW camp, according to the blueprint attached to M-892/65/90–6, Dürrfeld Exh. 14, doc. 102, Rudolf Dömming affidavit, 17.1.48.

14. Duffree, "The Will to Survive," pp. 52–53, 56; Cossar, 5.10.94; Davis, 10.5.94; T-301/96/NI-11695/653, Dales affidavit, 17.7.47; M-892/5/473, Dales testimony, 13.11.47; T-301/96/NI-11693/626, Ferris affidavit, 1.7.47; Bamford, 10.4.94; Alf Denton, 14.4.94; T-301/81/NI-9814/700, Hermann Hausmann affidavit, 24.6.47; John Green, 7.4.94; Hartland, 8.4.94. On German Army labor procedures, M-892/83/59, Defense Doc. PW Nr. 11, Günther Hauntz affidavit, 30.1.48; and "The Employment of Prisoners of War in Germany," p. 321. Shepherd, sound recording, 1994; Wellard, sound recording, 2.5.94; Redman, May 1994; Stow, 2.11.94; T-301/96/NI-11692/617, Frost affidavit, 16.7.47; on POWs in plant administration, RG 11.001 M.03, 502/5/3/70, Franz Peter Niepmann, Abwehrbeauftragte, R. Nr. 7004, 17.7.44, p. 15. For managerial assessments, M-892/65/943–44, Dürrfeld Exh. 161, doc. 1253, Wojis affidavit, 3.11.47; RG 11.001 M.03, 502/5/1/70, Helmut Schneider, Gefolgschaftsabteilung/Lohnempfänger, R. Nr. 5169, Betr.: "Einsatz der Kriegsgefangenen Engländer auf unserer Baustelle," 14.12.43, p. 427; ibid., Schneider, Gefolgschaftsabteilung/Lohnempfänger, R. Nr. 5004, Betr.: "Verhalten des deutschen Aufsichtspersonals gegenüber Kriegsgefangenen," 7.1.44, p. 384; and ibid., Niepmann, Abwehrbeauftragte, R. Nr. 7003, Betr.: "Flucht von entwichenen Kriegsgefangenen in das Ausland," 16.5.44, p. 21 (fragmentary), Quote in "Official Reports from the Camps," *The Prisoner of War* 3 (November 1944): 10; T-301/96/NI-11704/733, Hill affidavit, 21.7.47. On sabotage activities, see Castle, *The Password Is Courage*, pp. 151, 153, 182–83; Davis, 10.5.94; Gardiner, 20.4.94; Hartland, 8.4.94; Harris, 8.4.94; Quartermaine, 4.4.94; and Redman, May 1994; but also the cautionary report, RG 11.001 M.03, 502/5/2/70, Eisfeld, Müller, and Niepmann, R. Nr. 9045, Betr.: "Beschädigungen von Kabeln," 8.7.44, pp. 123–24. Managers had good reason to attribute greater losses of output

to carelessness than intentional damage. But small-scale sabotage was not always reported, as can be seen from the complaint in ibid., 502/5/2/70, Rudolf Brüstle, Abwehrbeauftragte, R. Nr. 7006, Betr.: "Meldungen von Sabotagefällen," 21.8.44, p. 57 (fragmentary).

15. For bodies at the plant, see M-892/5/610, Ferris testimony, 14.11.47; and Harris, 08.04.94; T-301/96/NI-11695/653, Dales affidavit, 17.7.47; for "stripees," ibid., NI-11698/686, Alexander affidavit, 19.7.47, and ibid., NI-11706/752, Wooley affidavit, 22.7.47; for "working corpses," ibid., NI-11700/702, Robert Robertson affidavit, 20.7.47; Shepherd, sound recording, 1994; T-301/96/NI-11697/680, Horace Reginald Charters affidavit, 22.7.47; ibid., NI-11694/640, Davison affidavit, 19.7.47; ibid., NI-11704/733, Hill affidavit, 21.7.47; ibid., NI-11703/726, Longden affidavit, 17.7.47; Wellard, sound recording, 2.5.94.

16. Duffree, "The Will to Survive," p. 54. Walter Laqueur, *The Terrible Secret: Suppression of the Truth About Hitler's "Final Solution"* (Boston: Little, Brown, 1980), pp. 22–23, discusses POW accounts in the context of what IG Auschwitz managers probably knew about the Holocaust.

17. Duffree, "The Will to Survive," p. 52; Bond, 8.4.94; T-301/96/NI-11705/748, Greenham affidavit; Davis, 10.5.94; Cossar, 5.10.94; Gardiner, 20.4.94; Gifford, 10.4.94. Secondhand accounts of gas chambers include: T-301/96/NI-11708/769, Seal affidavit, 22.7.47; ibid., NI-11703/726, Longden affidavit, 17.7.47; ibid., NI-11704/733, Hill affidavit, 21.7.47; ibid., 101/NI-12390/1240, Hartland affidavit, 14.11.47; Stow, 2.11.94; and Harris, 8.4.94; Tamotsu Shibutani, *Improvised News: A Sociological Study of Rumor* (Indianapolis: Bobbs-Merrill, 1966), pp. v–vii, 3–17, 29, 200–12; T-301/96/NI-11706/752, Wooley affidavit, 22.7.47. Churchill quote in Richard Breitman, *Official Secrets: What the Nazis Planned, What the British and Americans Knew* (New York: Hill and Wang, 1998), p. 93.

18. Redman, May 1994; Quartermaine, 4.4.94; T-301/101/NI-12388/1194–95, Doyle affidavit, 14.11.47; ibid., 96/NI-11695/654, Dales affidavit, 17.7.47. For an example of how improvised news circulated from E715 to Monowitz, see Oszkár Betlen, *Leben auf dem Acker des Todes* (Budapest: Corvina; Berlin: Dietz Verlag GmbH, 1962), p. 250, who reported that some "sixty" British POWs lost their lives during the first U.S. raid. The actual death toll was lower, but Betlen could not have learned about the losses at the time by any means other than camp rumor, because he worked in the Monowitz report clerk's office from May to December 1944, not the plant.

19. USHMMA, RG 50.042°0032, Norbert Wollheim interview, 18.2.92, transcript, Wentworth Films, Silver Spring, MD, pp. 20–21, 46–47, 49–50, hereafter RG 50.042°0032, Wollheim interview, 18.2.92. T-301/101/NI-12390/1240, Hartland affidavit, 14.11.47; M-892/5/725, Hartland testimony, 18.11.47; Hartland, 8.4.94. On secret radios at E715, Gardiner, 20.4.94; Gifford, 10.4.94; Green, 7.4.94; Duffree, "The Will to Survive," p. 58; Hartland's news-clipping and photograph collection includes a photograph of him with Coward and Wollheim during the 1962 broadcast. Wollheim sued IG Farben in-Liquidation in the early 1950s, which led the firm to make a class-action settlement with Jewish forced laborers. See Ferencz,

Less than Slaves, ch. 2; *New York Times*, 2./6.3.55; 7.2.57; 18.3.60. Two POWs, Charles Coward and Robert Ferris, appeared as witnesses during the German civil suit.

20. A German affiant at Nuremberg also affirmed the exchange of improvised news among Germans and Britons. See M-892/65/944, Dürrfeld Exh. 161, doc. 1253, Wojis affidavit, 3.11.47. Stow, 2.11.94; Shepherd, sound recording, 1994; T-301/96/NI-11693/627, Ferris affidavit, 1.7.47; M-892/5/624, Ferris testimony, 14.11.47. Duffree, "The Will to Survive," pp. 53–54. Daniel Jonah Goldhagen, *Hitler's Willing Executioners: Ordinary Germans and the Holocaust* (New York: Knopf, 1996), p. 23 and Part IV. If British testimony offers compelling evidence in favor of Goldhagen's insight about the connection between work and anti-semitism, the overall history of IG Auschwitz supplies a telling counterexample to ahistorical approaches.

21. Mrs. Eva Murray (on behalf of the late John Murray), nd; Quartermaine, 4.4.94; Bond, 8.4.94; T-301/96/NI-11705/747, Greenham affidavit, 23.7.47; ibid., NI-11692/617, Frost affidavit, 16.7.47; ibid., NI-11696/664, Coward affidavit, 24.7.47; ibid., NI-11699/693, Adkin affidavit, 15.7.47; Duffree, "The Will to Survive," p. 54. For a comprehensive listing of Red Cross parcel contents, see White, "The Primacy of Racial Politics," pp. 342–44; see also Patrick Gilbo, *The American Red Cross: The First Century* (New York: Harper & Row, 1981), p. 165; A. J. Barker, *Behind Barbed Wire* (London: B. T. Batsford, 1974), p. 164; "Gifts for Allied Prisoners," *American Journal of Nursing* 41 (October 1941): 1150; "Posting for Christmas; This Month Thousands of Puddings Will Be Leaving for the Camps; His Christmas Box Contains," *The Prisoner of War* 1 (July 1942): 3; "Any Questions?" *The Prisoner of War* 1 (August 1942): 14; and "The Editor Writes . . . His Xmas Dinner," *The Prisoner of War* 2 (December 1943): 2. Although disruptions took place in parcel delivery during August and December 1944, the British were marginally better off in material terms than even some Germans for most of their captivity at Auschwitz.

22. R. A. Radford, "The Economic Organisation of a POW Camp," *Economica* XII (November 1945): 190–93, 195–96, 197–99, 200, observes that the Red Cross cigarette was the "normal currency" in POW camps (191). Davis, 10.5.94; Redman, May 1994.

23. Levi, *Survival in Auschwitz*, pp. 61, 90–91, 123, 154, quotes on p. 90; Stow, 2.11.94, reports that he befriended Henri while at the building site, but perhaps incorporated Levi's account into his memory of the event. RG 50.042°0032, Wollheim interview, 18.2.92, pp. 49–50.

24. Harris, 8.4.94; T-301/91/NI-11015/386, Abraham Fuks, Strafmeldung, 21.3.44; ibid., NI-11035/571, Paul Steinberg, Strafmeldung, 9.8.44; ibid., NI-11031/532, Pepo Pitson, Strafmeldung, 9.6.44; ibid., NI-11014/373, Israel Majzlik, Strafmeldung, 28.2.44; Henryk Kuszaj, "Strafen, die von der SS an Häftlingen des Konzentrationslagers Auschwitz vollzogen wurden," *Hefte von Auschwitz* 3 (1960): 7–8, 14–21, hereafter *HvA*; T-301/96/NI-11695/654, Dales affidavit, 17.7.47.

25. T-301/96/NI-11696/667, Coward affidavit, 24.7.47; RG 50.042°0032, Wollheim interview, 18.2.92, p. 49; Redman, May 1994.

26. M-892/5/467, Coward testimony, 13.11.47; USHMMA, RG 19.045 M, roll 14, Archives of the International Committee of the Red Cross, Collection "Jews-Israélites, 1939–1961," file number G59/12/13–367.01, Camp d'Auschwitz, 28.3.1944–27.11.1945, "Rapport du Dr. Rossel, délégé de CICR, au camp d'Auschwitz: Tentative avortée," 29.9.44, frame 193–95, hereafter, "Rapport du Dr. Rossel . . . ," with frame number. A published copy can be found in Comité International de la Croix-Rouge (CICR), *Documents sur l'activité du Comité International de la Croix Rouge en faveur des civils déténus dans les camps de concentration en Allemagne (1939–1945)*, 3rd ed. (Geneva: CICR, Apr. 1947), pp. 91–92.

27. "Rapport du Dr. Rossel . . . ," frame 195; Ronald W. Zweig, "Feeding the Camps: Allied Blockade Policy and the Relief of Concentration Camps in Germany, 1944–1945," *The Historical Journal* 4 (1998): 826–27, 830–31, 841–42. Zweig points out that ICRC circumvented Berlin in regard to relief by bribing individual concentration-camp commandants. Some parcels reached Jewish inmates, despite SS policy.

28. "Rapport du Dr. Rossel . . . ," frame 195. Apart from temporary penal assignment, British POWs had ceased participation in local mining operations beginning in August 1943, a month before E715 became operational and more than a year before the Red Cross inspection. Consequently, Rossel's reference to a "mine" can be discounted as a misunderstanding. Alfred Sulik, "Volkstumspolitik und Arbeitseinsatz: Zwangsarbeiter in der Großindustrie Oberschlesiens" in Ulrich Herbert, ed., *Europa und der "Reichseinsatz": Ausländische Zivilarbeiter, Kriegsgefangene, und KZ-Häftlinge in Deutschland, 1938–1945* (Essen: Klartext, 1991), pp. 118–20, reports that the British normally worked in construction and rarely in the mines. IG Farben's Janina mine deployed them during summer 1943, but requested their removal in August due to disciplinary problems. For their part, the POWs and German Army were dissatisfied with Janina's working and living conditions. See T-301/87/NI-10526/291–93, IG Farben, Janinagrube, 14.8.43; ibid., 96/NI-11696/664, Coward affidavit, 24.7.47; on POW identification of Birkenau, ibid., 101/NI-12390/1240, Hartland affidavit, 14.11.47.

29. Castle, *The Password Is Courage*, pp. 142, 161, 163, 176, 183–84, 221–23. Respondents to my questionnaire sharply divided over Charles Coward's memory. In probing for contemporaneous rumors of his activities, I unwittingly discovered that the Payne and Garrod book was the veterans' equivalent of a Rorschach blot. His detractors had read it, or watched the MGM film, and seemed to resent the attention he had received. Even some of his partisans took issue with one element or another of the book, while still calling him a genuine hero. The division reflected the force of his personality. Several of his partisans either consciously or unconsciously based their responses upon the biography, a dubious source at best. His critics demonstrated by recounting their own exploits that Payne and Garrod came near the mark about E715, though not necessarily about him. While Coward was not the tsar of E715, to say nothing of the "Count of Auschwitz" (159), he and other kriegies quietly upset the Nazi racial hierarchy. In novelistic fashion, Payne and Garrod erred in attributing anti-Nazi activities in E715 to one visionary

leader. The kriegies damaged a pipe here, an axle there, left food for the starving, and wrote letters on behalf of the desperate, without always talking among themselves. Coward died in 1976. Compare Davis, 10.5.94; Denton, 14.4.94; Harris, 8.4.94 and 23.5.94; Quartermaine, 4.4.94; Shepherd, sound recording, 1994; and Stow, 2.11.94; with Bond, 8.4.94; Cossar, 5.10.94; Duffree, "The Will to Survive," passim; Gardiner, 20.4.94, 20.5.94; Gifford, 10.4.94; and Hartland, 8.4.94. T-301/96/NI-11696/665–67, Coward affidavit, 24.7.47; Yad Vashem Archives (YVA), Jerusalem, Israel, Charles Joseph Coward file, 2004/176-T, 31.12.63, pp. 6, 8–9, hereafter, YVA Coward file, with page numbers. The Coward interview took place in December 1962, but the file is dated December 1963. I have assigned the greatest weight to Coward's statements closest to the event, namely the Nuremberg affidavit and testimony.
30. T-301/96/NI-11696/665, Coward affidavit, 24.7.47; Castle, *The Password Is Courage*, pp. 140, 174, credited his letters with leading to an Allied leaflet drop over the area, with a warning to potential war criminals, as assertion that awaits confirmation. M. R. D. Foot and J. M. Langley, *MI 9: The British Secret Service that Fostered Escape and Evasion and Its American Counterpart, 1939–1945*, (London: The Bodley Head, 1979), pp. 105, 111; Lloyd R. Shoemaker, *The Escape Factory: The Story of MIS-X* (New York: St. Martin's, 1992), pp. 19–20.
31. T-301/96/NI-11696/664–65, Coward affidavit, 24.7.47; Castle, *The Password Is Courage*, pp. 184–86, 188–89, 193–94, 196, dated the incident as occurring in September 1944, but other sources are silent.
32. On Coward's escape attempts, YVA Coward file, p. 5. M-892/65/943–44, Dürrfeld Exh. 161, doc. 1253, Wojis affidavit, 3.11.47; ibid., 5/467–69, Coward testimony, 13.11.47; Hartland, 26.5.95; Redman, May 1994.
33. T-301/96/NI-11696/664–65, Coward affidavit, 24.7.47, recalled that the anonymous naval doctor hailed from "Sonderland [sic]"; Castle, *The Password Is Courage*, p. 185, reproduced a copy of the note, absent name and street address; Jan Sehn, *"Concentration and Extermination Camp at Oswiecim (Auschwitz-Birkenau)"* in Central Commission for Investigation of German Crimes in Poland, ed., *German Crimes in Poland* (New York: Howard Fertig, 1982), p. 40, n. 1, identified an "English doctor Sperber" who had been sent from an Oflag, or officers' camp, to Auschwitz on 19.12.42 with inmate number 85512; Antoni Makowski, "Organization, Growth and Activity of the Prisoners' Hospital at Monowitz (KL Auschwitz III)" in Kazimierz Smoleń, ed., *From the History of KL Auschwitz*, trans. Krystyna Michalik, 2 vols. (Auschwitz: Państwowe Muzeum w Oświęcim, 1976), II: 191, identified him as a Monowitz physician and supplied his full name and inmate number. For more about German attempts to segregate Jewish POWs, Yoav Gelber, "Palestinian POWs in German Captivity," *Yad Vashem Studies* XIV (1981): 101–2, 107–8, 111–12, 136.
34. My thanks go to Peter Morris for supplying information about Sperber's postwar career. To this day it is unclear whether Sperber and Coward ever actually met.
35. Castle, *The Password Is Courage*, pp. 164–65, 167; YVA Coward file, pp. 7, 9, quote on p. 7; Shimon Peres, *Battling for Peace: A Memoir*, ed. David

Landau (New York: Random House, 1995), p. 46. Accounts that rely upon
Castle include Arieh L. Bauminger, *Roll of Honour* (Jerusalem: Menora,
1970), pp. 33–35; Eric Silver, *The Book of the Just: The Unsung Heroes Who
Rescued Jews from Hitler* (New York: Grove Press, 1992), pp. 63–64; and
most recently, Alan J. Levine, *Captivity, Flight, and Survival in World War
II* (Westport, CT; London: Praeger, 2000), pp. 83, 224–25. Coward was
not the last Briton to receive the Righteous Medal: Silver (p. 75) lists ten
former British POWs honored in 1989, for protecting Sara Matuson in
1945.

36. Peres, *Battling for Peace*, pp. 14, 45–47; Silver, *The Book of the Just*,
pp. 64–65; Duffree, 31.5.94.

37. YVA, Coward file, pp. 3–9, quotes on pp. 3–4, 5–6; Peres, *Battling for Peace*,
pp. 46–47. Peres secured him a job in Britain through Chaim Morrison.
On the "Israelization" of the Holocaust and the role of resistance, see Tom
Segev, *The Seventh Million: The Israelis and the Holocaust* (New York: Hill
and Wang, 1993), pp. 160, 184–85, 353; Omer Bartov, *Murder in Our
Midst: The Holocaust, Industrial Killing, and Representation* (New York: Oxford University Press, 1996), pp. 175–77; idem, *Mirrors of Destruction: War,
Genocide, and Modern Identity* (New York: Oxford University Press, 2000),
pp. 127–32; and Tim Cole, *Selling the Holocaust: From Auschwitz to
Schindler; How History is Bought, Packaged, and Sold* (New York: Routledge,
1999), pp. 57, 59–60, 125–28, 132, 135.

38. T-301/96/NI-11696/665, Coward affidavit, 24.7.47; Tadeusz Iwaszko,
"Häftlingsfluchten aus dem Konzentrationslager Auschwitz," *HvA* 7
(1964): 30, 49–52. Altogether there were 667 recorded escapes from the
Auschwitz complex between 1940 and 1945.

39. T-301/96/NI-11693/627, Ferris affidavit, 1.7.47. Coward may remind
some of Australian POW Donald C. Watt's problematic account, *Stoker:
The Story of an Australian Soldier Who Survived Auschwitz-Birkenau* (East
Roseville, Australia: Simon & Schuster, 1995). His memoir received a favorable review in a prominent British opinion journal, but specialists have
doubted his claims to having been an inmate of Bergen-Belsen and
Auschwitz-Birkenau, particularly of his having stoked crematory furnaces
in the latter. For the favorable review, see Tom Hiney, "The Price of Silence," *The Spectator* 275 (8.7.95): 36; and a critical assessment, Darren
O'Brien, "Donald Watt's 'Stoker': The Perils of Testimony," (1997), http://
www.genocide.mq.edu.au/watt.htm. A hard copy is found in *Centre for
Comparative Genocide Studies Newsletter* III (1997). The Coward case is better documented. Although Watt's testimony is unreliable, other POWs became concentration-camp inmates following escape attempts, especially in
1944. Designated "XKGF," or "Former Prisoners of War," the inmates
wore black (or "asocial") triangles on their striped uniforms. For a British
testimony, see T-301/96/NI-11702/718–19, Kenneth Clifford Lovell affidavit, 15.7.47; and for Americans, see Lewis H. Carlson, *We Were Each
Other's Prisoners: An Oral History of World War II American and German
Prisoners of War* (New York: Basic, 1997), pp. 181–99.

40. YVA, Coward file, pp. 3–4, 6–9; Stow, 2.11.94; Wellard, sound recording,
2.5.94; Davis, 10.5.94; Gardiner, postcard of theater broadside of *[A] Night*

at an Inn, 13.12.44; Edward J. M. D. P. Dunsany, *A Night at an Inn* in Kenneth Thorpe Rowe, *Write That Play* (New York: Funk & Wagnall's, 1968), pp. 64–86. Set in British India, the original play denigrated South Asians, but contained no reference to Jews. The Lindsay version has so far not turned up except in broadside form. Nechama Tec, *When Light Pierced the Darkness: Christian Rescue of Jews in Nazi-Occupied Poland* (New York: Oxford University Press, 1986), pp. 55–56; Bernard Wasserstein, *Britain and the Jews of Europe, 1939–1945* (New York: Oxford University Press, 1988 [1979]), p. 116; Tony Kushner, *The Persistence of Prejudice: Antisemitism in British Society During the Second World War* (Manchester; New York: Manchester University Press, 1989), pp. 9–10, 49, 92, 101–5, 109–11, 114–15, 122, 124; Maurice Hatton, "The British in Auschwitz" (unpublished manuscript, 1994), p. 3. This manuscript is a synopsis of his documentary film, *Satan at His Best*.

41. Tec, *When Light Pierced the Darkness*, pp. 55–56, 154, 175–76; Kushner, *The Persistence of Prejudice*, p. 92.

42. T-301/96/NI-11699/693, Adkin affidavit, 15.7.47; ibid., NI-11696/667, Coward affidavit, 24.7.47.

43. Duffree, "The Will to Survive," p. 55; Bond, 8.4.94; Gardiner, 20.4.94, 20.5.94; Gardiner, postcard of theater broadside, "FAST and FUNNY," 6./7.1.45; Harris, 23.5.94; Harris copy of Sweeney Todd theater broadside, 2.12.44; Davis, 10.5.94; Gifford, 10.4.94; M-892/65/943, Dürrfeld Exh. 161, doc. 1253, Wojis affidavit, 3.11.47. *Wehrkreis* (military district) VIII banned theatrical performances in POW camps in autumn 1944, but rescinded the order after Swiss complaints. "German Theatre Ban," *The Prisoner of War* 3 (January 1945): 2. In reply to my questionnaire, which in part queried whether anyone had ever asked them to serve as witnesses at Nuremberg, Robert Cossar responded: "Well, you seem to be more concerned than our government. . . ." Cossar, 5.10.94. Unfortunately, British and American television have not shown interest in airing Hatton's documentary. See *The Manchester Guardian*, 24.1.95.

44. T-301/98/NI-11956/409–10, 413, 416, Walther Dürrfeld, "Bericht über die Kriegsereignisse in und um Werk Auschwitz vom 13. Januar bis 24. Januar 1945," Abschrift/D, 7.2.45. A strong camp resistance organization brought Monowitz through the death march with more apparent coherence and order than other concentration camps. See the comments by Emil Carlebach in *The Buchenwald Report* (Boulder: Westview Press, 1995), p. 167. Other important accounts of the Monowitz death march include Elie Wiesel, *Night*, trans. Stella Rodway (New York: Bantam, 1986 [1960]), pp. 79–98, 95–96; and Betlen, *Leben auf dem Acker des Todes*, pp. 346–47. Betlen was in Gleiwitz II when the evacuation began and discovered soon after liberation that the SS had butchered some of his Monowitz comrades on the march.

45. On the evacuation of E715, Gardiner, 20.4.94; Green, 7.4.94; Harris, 8.4.94; Stow, 2.11.94; T-301/96/NI-11705/746, Greenham affidavit, 23.7.47; Duffree, "The Will to Survive," pp. 52, 60–66; Shepherd, sound recording, 1994; Murray, nd. Two POWs Harris and Redman, escaped and were liberated by the Soviets, while Dennis Greenham spent the final

months of the war in a Czech hospital. See Redman, May 1994; and T-301/96/NI-11705/746, Greenham affidavit, 23.7.47. On the correlation between starvation and PTSD, see William Frank Page, *The Health of Former Prisoners of War: Results from the Medical Examination Survey of Former POWs of World War II and the Korean Conflict* (Washington: National Academy Press, 1992), pp. 2, 46–48; and Robert A. Zeiss and Harold R. Dickman, "PTSD 40 Years Later: Incidence and Person-Situation Correlates in Former POWs," *Journal of Clinical Psychology* 45 (1989): 80–87. Historians now apply the PTSD concept to much earlier conflicts. See Eric T. Dean, Jr., *Shook Over Hell: Post-Traumatic Stress, Vietnam, and the Civil War* (Cambridge and London: Harvard University Press, 1999 [1997]).

46. Stephen Davies and Nick Hunt, "Silent Veterans Trapped in the Ruins of a Dead War," *Times Higher Education Supplement* (11.7.97), p. 19a; T-301/101/NI-12388/1194, Doyle affidavit, 14.11.47; Murray, nd.

U.S. ARMY CHAPLAIN MINISTRY TO GERMAN WAR CRIMINALS AT NUREMBERG, 1945–1946

1. Burton C. Andrus, *I Was The Nuremberg Jailer* (New York: Coward-McCann, 1969), 108–109.
2. Earl F. Stover, *Up From Handyman: The United States Army Chaplaincy, 1865–1920* (Washington, DC: Office of the Chief of Chaplains, Department of the Army, 1977), 197.
3. Roger R. Venzke, *Confidence In Battle, Inspiration In Peace: The United States Army Chaplaincy, 1945–1975* (Washington, DC: Office of the Chief of Chaplains, Department of the Army, 1977), 117.
4. Roy J. Honeywell, *Chaplains of the United States Army* (Washington, DC: Office of the Chief of Chaplains, Department of the Army, 1958), 283.
5. Shelby Foote, *The Civil War, A Narrative: Red River to Appomattox* (New York: Random House, 1974), 1032–33.
6. As quoted in, G. M. Gilbert, *Nuremberg Diary* (Farrar, Straus and Company: New York, 1947), 460.
7. Michael R. Marrus, "The Nuremberg Trial: Fifty Years Later," *The American Scholar* (Autumn 1997), 564.
8. "War Crimes," *Encyclopaedia Britannica*, XXIII (Chicago: Encyclopaedia Britannica, Inc., 1972), 206.
9. Ventzke, *Confidence*, 7.
10. Ibid. 7; Gilbert, *Nuremberg Diary*, 4–7.
11. Ibid.; Ventzke, *Confidence*, 8.
12. Matthew H. Imrie, Office of the Chief of Chaplains, to Alfred P. Klausle, "Walther League Messenger," 22 April 1947, Records of the Army Chief of Chaplains, Record Group 47, file 000.76, National Archives, Washington, DC.
13. Henry F. Gerecke, "Assignment With the International Tribunal As Spiritual Advisor," *Army and Navy Chaplain* (July-August 1947), 2.
14. David Strand, "A Witness at Nuremberg," *The Lutheran Witness* (May 1995), 8–9; Ventzke, *Confidence*, 8.
15. As quoted in, Andrus, *Nuremberg Jailer*, 109.

16. As quoted in, Gerecke, "Assignment," 3.
17. Gilbert, *Nuremberg Diary*, 81.
18. As quoted in, Ibid., 87.
19. Robert Cecil, *The Myth of the Master Race: Alfred Rosenberg and Nazi Ideology* (New York: Dodd Mead & Co., 1972), 229–230.
20. Gerecke, "Assignment," 137; Goering quote, Gilbert, *Nuremberg*, 60.
21. As quoted in, Ibid., 125.
22. Andrus, *Nuremberg Jailer*, 185–86.
23. Ibid., 188–89.
24. *Encyclopaedia Britannica*, 206.
25. Andrus, *Nuremberg Jailer*, 182.
26. Gerecke, "Assignment," 20.
27. Ibid.
28. As quoted in, Andrus, *Nuremberg Jailer*, 194.
29. As quoted in, Strand, "Witness," 11.
30. As quoted in, Andrus, *Nuremberg Jailer*, 195.
31. Joe E. Heydecker and Johannes Leeb, *The Nuremberg Trial: A History of Nazi Germany As Revealed Through the Testimony At Nuremberg* (New York: The World Publishing Company, 1962), 385–87.
32. Ibid., 387.
33. Ibid., 387–88.

THE EMERGING BIOCRUISE THREAT

1. Humphry Crum Ewing et al., *Cruise Missiles: Precision and Countermeasures*, Bailrigg Memorandum no. 10 (Lancaster, United Kingdom: Centre for Defence and International Security Studies, 1995), 60.
2. Department of Defense, *Conduct of the Persian Gulf Conflict: Final Report to Congress*, vol. 1 (Washington, D.C.: US Government Printing Office, April 1992), 244.
3. Kori Schake, "Rogue States and Proliferation: How Serious Is the Threat?" in *Strategic Assessment 1999: Priorities for a Turbulent World*, ed. Hans Binnendijk et al. (Washington, D.C.: US Government Printing Office, June 1999), 220. The United States has identified Iran, Iraq, Libya, North Korea, and Syria as rogue nations capable of BW proliferation and believes them to be sponsors of terrorism. No single, universally accepted definition of a rogue nation exists. The Clinton administration defined such states as "recalcitrant and outlaw states that not only choose to remain outside the family [of democracies] but also assault its basic values." See Anthony Lake, "Confronting Backlash States," *Foreign Affairs* 73, no. 2 (March/April 1994): 45–46. Some of the characteristics of rogue nations are that they aggressively pursue unconventional means to threaten US and international interests, do not conform to the norms of international behavior (and are not easily persuaded to do so), and tend to be sponsors of terrorism.
4. Ramesh Thakur, "Arms Control, Disarmament and Non-Proliferation: A Political Perspective," in *Arms Control in the Asia-Pacific Region*, ed. Jeffrey A. Larsen and Thomas D. Miller (Washington, D.C.: US Government Printing Office, August 1999), 43.

5. "Iran, Other Rogue Regimes Developing Cruise Missiles." May 1999, on-line, Internet, 1 February 2000, available from http://www.ourjerusalem.com/documents/febmay99/0412docs.htm.

6. National Intelligence Council, *Foreign Missile Developments and the Ballistic Missile Threat to the United States through 2015*, September 1999, on-line, Internet, 21 January 2000, available from http://www.usconsulate.org.hk/uscn/others/1999/0909.htm.

7. In Joint Publication 1-02, *Department of Defense Dictionary of Military and Associated Terms*, 12 April 2001 (as amended through 25 September 2002), on-line, Internet, 22 January 2003, available from http://www.dtic.mil/doctrine/jel/new_pubs/jp1_02.pdf, a *cruise missile* is defined as a "guided missile, the major portion of whose flight path to its target is conducted at approximately constant velocity; depends on the dynamic reaction of air for lift and upon propulsion forces to balance drag." A *guided missile* is "an unmanned vehicle moving above the surface of the Earth whose trajectory or flight path is capable of being altered by an external or internal mechanism."

8. National Air Intelligence Center, *Ballistic and Cruise Missile Threat*, NAIC-1031-0985-99 (Dayton, Ohio: Wright-Patterson Air Force Base, April 1999), 6.

9. Centre for Defence and International Security Studies, "Cruise Missile Capabilities: An Assessment," on-line, Internet, 1 February 2000, available from http://www.cdiss.com/tabanaly.htm.

10. W. Seth Carus, *Cruise Missile Proliferation in the 1990s* (Westport, Conn.: Praeger, 1992), 15.

11. Ibid.

12. Marshall Brain, "How Cruise Missiles Work," on-line, Internet, 21 September 1999, available from http://www.howstuffworks.com/cruise-missile.htm.

13. Ewing et al., 49 and 51. INS uses gyroscopes and accelerometers to detect changes in speed and direction of the LACM, which can then be used to compute changes in relative positions. Although an INS guidance system has the advantage of being jamproof, the gyroscopes have inherent inaccuracies that result in increasing positional errors (called drift) with increasing LACM flight time. For example, the US TLAM INS drifts by 900 meters per hour. At the TLAM's cruising speed of 800 km per hour, an uncorrected INS would result in a 1.8 km positional error for striking a target at a range of 1,600 km. Thus, to strike targets at long range, the LACM's INS must be supplemented with other guidance systems such as GPS or TERCOM. TERCOM corrects any INS by taking periodic fixes on the terrain features (which must be areas of distinctive topography) over which the LACM is flying. To accomplish this, the TERCOM system uses an on-board computer, in which maps of the relevant terrain, obtained from high-resolution satellite images, are stored, along with a radar altimeter. The computer correlates data received from altimeter readings with elevation data from the stored maps. The system then calculates the corrections needed to put the LACM back on course and provides this information to the missile's autopilot.

14. DSMAC is a two-dimensional map-matching technique that employs an onboard sensor to obtain a sequence of images of the ground directly below the missile. The images are compared to reference data stored in the missile's navigational computer, and position changes are made as needed prior to final target acquisition. DSMAC is a complex technology that significantly improves the terminal accuracy of the cruise missile.

15. This regime was created in 1987 by the G-7 governments of Canada, France, Italy, Japan, United Kingdom, United States, and West Germany. It is an informal, voluntary export-control arrangement with guidelines prohibiting the sale or transfer of certain categories of ballistic and cruise missiles and their related technologies. The regime grew out of the mutual fears of the G-7 nations that rogue states would acquire offensive missiles for use as WMD-delivery platforms. The current membership includes 32 countries.

16. K. Scott McMahon and Dennis M. Gormley, *Controlling the Spread of Land-Attack Cruise Missiles,* AISC Papers, no. 7 (Marina del Rey, Calif.: American Institute for Strategic Cooperation [AISC], January 1995), 22.

17. DGPS is a method of correcting GPS that allows a weapon system to obtain extremely high positional accuracies. The concept of DGPS is as follows: A receiver is placed at a presurveyed location whose position has been determined very accurately. Both the GPS receiver at the known location and the DGPS receiver on the weapon system acquire the same set of GPS signals from the same set of satellites. The errors in the GPS signals are determined by comparing the surveyed site's known position to the position determined using the GPS signals. Correction terms are then calculated and transmitted to the weapon-system DGPS receiver, allowing elimination of most of the errors of the GPS signals. The DGPS technique can yield weapon-system positional accuracies of 1 to 5 m.

18. "IKONOS Satellite Launches into Space," on-line, Internet, 1 October 1999, available from http://www.spaceimage.com/newsroom/releases/1999/inorbit.htm. Space Imaging, a US firm, successfully launched its IKONOS satellite on 24 September 1999. This is the first commercial imaging satellite of its kind, simultaneously collecting panchromatic images of 1 m resolution and multispectral images of 4 m resolution. Space Imaging is now selling and distributing imagery. Many other commercial imaging satellites, both US and foreign, that provide imagery of 1 m resolution were scheduled for launch in 2000, 2001, 2002, and so forth. See also McMahon and Gormley, 24.

19. McMahon and Gormley, 25.

20. Dennis Gormley and Richard Speier, "Cruise Missile Proliferation: Threat, Policy, and Defenses" (presentation to the Carnegie Endowment for International Peace Proliferation Roundtable, 9 October 1998), on-line, Internet, 21 September 1999, available from http://www.ceip.org/programs/npp/cruise4.htm.

21. Dennis M. Gormley, "Hedging against the Cruise-Missile Threat," *Survival,* spring 1998, 92–111, on-line, Internet, 21 September 1999, available from http://www.celp.org/programs/npp/gormley%20survival.htm.

22. National Intelligence Council, *Foreign Missile Developments.*

23. Ewing et al., 50.
24. Carus, 22.
25. David A. Fulghum, "Stealth, Cheap Technology Complicate Defense Schemes," *Aviation Week and Space Technology* 147, no. 2 (14 July 1997): 47.
26. Ibid.
27. Bryan Bender, "Cruise Control," *Jane's Defence Weekly* 30, no. 3 (22 July 1998): 21.
28. Dennis M. Gormley, "Remarks from a Panel on the Missile Proliferation Threat at the Conference on Nuclear Non-Proliferation: Enhancing the Tools of the Trade," 9–10 June 1997, Washington, D.C., on-line, Internet, 29 September 1999, available from http://www.ceip.org/programs/npp/np9715gohtm. See also McMahon and Gormley, 14–18; Amy Truesdell, "Cruise Missiles: The Discriminating Weapon of Choice?" *Jane's Intelligence Review*, February 1997, 87–90; and Carus, 69 and 83.
29. Gormley and Speier.
30. Carus, 25.
31. *Militarily Critical Technologies List (MCTL) Part II: Weapons of Mass Destruction Technologies, Section I—Means of Delivery Technology*, September 1998, II-1-2, on-line, Internet, 10 September 1999, available from http://www.fas.org/lrp/threat/mctl98-2/p2sec01.pdf.
32. Richard K. Betts, "The New Threat of Mass Destruction," *Foreign Affairs* 77, no. 1 (January/February 1998): 28. See also Eugene Gholz, Daryl G. Press, and Harvey M. Sapolsky, "Come Home America: The Strategy of Restraint in the Face of Temptation," *International Security* 21, no. 4 (spring 1997): 7.
33. Betts, 27.
34. Efraim Karsh, "Rational Ruthlessness: Non-Conventional and Missile Warfare in the Iran-Iraq War," in *Non-Conventional-Weapons Proliferation in the Middle East*, ed. Efraim Karsh, Martin S. Navias, and Philip Sabin (New York: Oxford University Press, 1993), 36–42.
35. Robin Ranger and David Wiencek, *The Devil's Brews II: Weapons of Mass Destruction and International Security*, Bailrigg Memorandum no. 17 (Lancaster, United Kingdom: Centre for Defence and International Security Studies, 1997), 16.
36. Betts, 31.
37. Dennis M. Gormley and K. Scott McMahon, "Counterforce: The Neglected Pillar of Theater Missile Defense," on-line, Internet, 29 September 1999, available from http://www.cdiss.org/colsep1.htm.
38. House Committee on Armed Services, *Countering the Chemical and Biological Weapons Threat in the Post-Soviet World*, Special Inquiry into the Chemical and Biological Threat, Report to the Congress (Washington, D.C.: US Government Printing Office, 23 February 1993), 4.
39. Willis Stanley and Keith Payne, "Chapter II. Missile Proliferation: Threat and U.S. Response," *Comparative Strategy* 16, no. 2 (1997): 135.
40. Gormley and Speier.
41. Betts, 32.
42. Edward M. Eitzen, "Use of Biological Weapons," in *Medical Aspects of Chemical and Biological Warfare*, ed. Frederick R. Sidell, Ernest T. Takafuj,

and David R. Franz (Washington, D.C.: Office of the Surgeon General at TMM Publications, 1997), 446.

43. US Congress, Office of Technology Assessment, *Proliferation of Weapons of Mass Destruction: Assessing the Risks*, OTA-ISC-559 (Washington, D.C.: US Government Printing Office, August 1993), 54.

44. World Health Organization Group of Consultants, *Health Aspects of Chemical and Biological Weapons* (Geneva, Switzerland: World Health Organization, 1970), 98–99.

45. Lester C. Caudle, "The Biological Warfare Threat," in *Medical Aspects of Chemical and Biological Warfare*, 437–50.

46. Biological agents are either replicating agents (bacteria or viruses) or non-replicating materials (toxins or physiologically active proteins or peptides) that can be produced by living organisms. The replicating nature and extreme infectivity at low doses of pathogens such as *Bacillus anthracis* (the organism that causes anthrax) and *Yersinia pestis* (the organism that causes plague) make them, weight-for-weight, more deadly than CW nerve agents. Additionally, toxins such as the staphylococcal enterotoxins and botulinum toxins are extraordinarily toxic—1,000- to 10,000-fold more toxic than classic nerve agents. For further information, see *The Biological and Chemical Warfare Threat* (Washington, D.C.: US Government Printing Office, 1999), 1–23: Frederick R. Sidell and David R. Franz, "Overview: Defense against the Effects of Chemical and Biological Warfare Agents," in *Medical Aspects of Chemical and Biological Warfare*, 1–7; and Eitzen, 437–50.

47. Caudle, 458. See also Lord Lyell, "Chemical and Biological Weapons: The Poor Man's Bomb," 4 October 1996, on-line, Internet, 11 May 2000, available from http://www.pgs.ca/pages/cw/cw980327.htm. Lyell states that "a more specific assessment suggests that the development of biological weapons would cost less than $100,000, require five biologists, and take just a few weeks using equipment that is readily available."

48. *The Biological and Chemical Warfare Threat*, 1.

49. Jonathan B. Tucker. "The Future of Biological Warfare," in *The Proliferation of Advanced Weaponry: Technology, Motivations, and Responses*, ed. W. Thomas Wander and Eric H. Arnett (Washington, D.C.: American Association for the Advancement of Science, 1992), 67.

50. W. Seth Carus, *Bioterrorism and Biocrimes: The Illicit Use of Biological Agents in the 20th Century* (Washington, D.C.: Center for Counterproliferation Research. National Defense University. August 1998 [March 1999 revision]), 25.

51. Carus, *Bioterrorism and Biocrimes*, 24.

52. Tucker, 67.

53. Carus, *Bioterrorism and Biocrimes*, 25.

54. Ibid., 26.

55. Milton Leitenberg. "Deadly Unknowns about Iraq's Biological Weapons Program," 9 February 2000, on-line, Internet, 14 February 2000, available from http://www.isis.online.org/publications/iraq/leitenberg.html.

56. National Intelligence Council, *Foreign Missile Developments*.

57. Judith Miller, "U.S. Intelligence: Flying Blind in a Dangerous World," *New York Times*, 6 February 2000, D5.

THE LOOMING BIOLOGICAL WARFARE STORM: MISCONCEPTIONS AND PROBABLE SCENARIOS

1. Roberta Wohlstetter, *Pearl Harbor: Warning and Decision* (Stanford, Calif.: Stanford University Press, 1962), vii.
2. Anthony H. Cordesman, *Trends in US Military Forces and Defense Spending: Peace Dividend or Underfunding?* (Washington, D.C.: Center for Strategic and International Studies, 26 July 1999), 4, on-line, Internet, 11 September 2001, available from http://www.csis.org.
3. James E. Gibson, *Dr. Bodo Otto and the Medical Background of the American Revolution* (Baltimore, Md.: George Banta Publishing Company, 1937), 88–89; and Jonathan B. Tucker, *Scourge: The Once and Future Threat of Smallpox* (New York: Atlantic Monthly Press, 2001), 18–22.
4. Sheldon H. Harris, *Factories of Death: Japanese Biological Warfare, 1932–45, and the American Cover-up* (New York: Routledge, 1994), 74–76.
5. Ken Alibek with Stephen Handelman, *Biohazard* (New York: Random House, 1999), 29–31.
6. Frederick R. Sidell, Ernest T. Takafuji, and David R. Franz, eds., *Textbook of Military Medicine: Medical Aspects of Chemical and Biological Warfare* (Washington, D.C.: Office of the Surgeon General, US Army, 1997), 656.
7. W. Seth Carus, *Bioterrorism and Biocrimes: The Illicit Use of Biological Agents in the 20th Century*, rev. ed. (Washington, D.C.: National Defense University, Center for Counterproliferation Research, 1998), 58; Jessica Stern, *The Ultimate Terrorists* (Cambridge, Mass.: Harvard University Press, 1999), 63; and Dean A. Wilkening, "BCW in Attack Scenarios," in *The New Terror: Facing the Threat of Biological and Chemical Weapons* (Stanford, Calif.: Hoover Institution Press, 1999), 91–93.
8. W. Seth Carus, "The Rajneeshees (1984)," in *Toxic Terror: Assessing Terrorist Use of Chemical and Biological Weapons*, ed. Jonathan B. Tucker (Cambridge, Mass.: MIT Press, 2000), 115–37.
9. David E. Kaplan, "Terrorism's Next Wave, Nerve Gas and Germs Are the New Weapons of Choice," *U.S. News and World Report*, 17 November 1997, on-line, Internet, 17 November 1997, available from http://www.inforwar.com/CLASS_3/class3_112897b.html-ssi.
10. Dr. Tara O'Toole, "Medical and Public Health Aspects of Bioterrorism," presentation, Johns Hopkins University, Baltimore, Md., 25 June 2001.
11. Uncle Fester, *Silent Death*, 2d ed. (Unknown, Uncle Fester, 1997), available for sale on Internet only, on-line, Internet, 25 January 2003, available from http://www.crbbooks.com/catalog_2_item_nl/uncle-silent.htm.
12. O'Toole; Michael T. Osterholm and John Schwartz, *Living Terrors: What America Needs to Know to Survive the Coming Bioterrorist Catastrophe* (New York: Random House, Inc., 2000), 37–39; and Judith Miller, Stephen Engelberg, and William Broad, *Germs: Biological Weapons and America's Secret War* (New York: Simon and Schuster, 2001), 316.
13. Wilkening, 91–93; and David E. Kaplan and Andrew Marshall, *The Cult at the End of the World* (New York: Crown Publishers, 1996), 1–283.
14. O'Toole: Osterholm, 37–39; and Miller, 316.
15. Stern, 81–83.

16. Simon Reeve, *The New Jackals; Ramzi Yousef, Osama bin Laden and the Future of Terrorism* (Boston, Mass.: Northeastern University Press, 1999), 24.
17. James Phillips, "After World Trade Center Bombing, U.S. Needs Stronger Anti-Terrorism Policy." *The Heritage Foundation Backgrounder,* 22 February 1995, 240, on-line, Internet, 12 September 2001, available from http://www.heritage.org/library/categories/natsec/bgu240.html.
18. "Sentenced To Die," *Online NewsHour with Jim Lehrer,* 13 June 1997, n.p., on-line, Internet, 12 September 2001, available from http://www.pbs.org/newshour/bb/law.
19. "Deadly Explosion," *Online NewsHour with Jim Lehrer,* 19 April 1995, n.p., on-line, Internet, 12 September 2001, available from http://www.pbs.org/newshour/bb/law.
20. "September 11, 2001 Victims," *American Liberty Partnership.* 2 February 2002, on-line, Internet, 5 February 2002, available from http://www.september11victims.com.
21. John Pike, "Administrative Support Unit Southwest Asia (ASU SWA) Manama, Bahrain," *FAS Military Analysis Network,* on-line, Internet, 12 September 2001, available from http://www.fas.org/man/dod-101/fac/port/manama.htm.
22. "World Population," *PBS,* 12 September 2001, n.p., on-line, Internet, 12 September 2001, available from http://www.pbs.org/kqed/population_bomb/hope/worldp.html.
23. "Responding to the Threat of Agroterrorism: Specific Recommendation for the United States Department of Agriculture," Belfer Center for Science and International Affairs (BCSIA) Discussion Paper 2000–29, Executive Session on Domestic Preparedness (ESDP) Discussion Paper 2000–04 (Cambridge, Mass.: John F. Kennedy School of Government, Harvard University, October 2000), 12.
24. Mark Wheelis, *Agricultural Biowarfare & Bioterrorism: An Analytical Framework & Recommendations for the Fifth BTWC Review Conference,* September 1999, n.p., on-line, Internet, 2 February 2002, available from http://www.fas.org/bwc/agr/agwhole.htm.
25. "The 'Hidden' Epidemic of Foot-and-Mouth Disease," *News and Highlights—Food and Agriculture Organization of the United Nations,* 29 May 2001, n.p., on-line, Internet, 12 September 2001, available from http://www.fao.org/News/2001/010508-e.htm.
26. Steve Goldstein, "U.S. Officials Awakening to Threat of Agroterror," *Dallas Morning News,* 27 June 1999, n.p., on-line, Internet, 12 September 2001, available from http://www.dallasnews.com/national/ 0627nat4agroterror.htm.
27. Ibid.
28. Ibid.
29. "Chemical and Biological Weapons: Possession and Programs Past and Present," *Center for Nonproliferation Studies* (Chemical and Biological Weapons Resource Page), 4 September 2002, n.p., on-line, Internet, 25 January 2003, available from http://cns.miis.edu/research/cbw/possess.htm.

30. Rex R. Kiziah, *Assessment of the Emerging Biocruise Threat*, Future Warfare Series no. 6 (Maxwell AFB, Ala.: USAF Counter-proliferation Center, August 2000), n.p., on-line, Internet, 25 January 2003, available from http://www.au.af.mil/au/awc.

WHAT CAN WE LEARN FROM ENDURING FREEDOM?
1. "Die Jagd auf ein Phantom," *Der Spiegel*, 22 April 2002, p. 137.
2. Lothar Ruehl, "Amerikas 'langer Arm' zwischen den Kontinenten," *Neue Zuercher Zeitung*, 8 December 2001.
3. Tom Bowman, "Studying Lessons of Battle Success," *Baltimore Sun*, 17 December 2001.
4. Bryan Bender, et al., "Afghanistan: First Lessons," *Jane's Defence Weekly*, 19 December 2001.
5. Richard Hart Sinnreich, "The Long Arm of Command," *The Washington Post*, 31 December 2001, p. A17.
6. Sinnreich, "The Long Arm of Command," p. A17.
7. Joseph Fitchett, "High-Tech Weapons Change the Dynamics and the Scope of Battle," *International Herald Tribune*, 28 December 2001.
8. Benjamin S. Lambeth, *NATO's Air War for Kosovo; A Strategic and Operational Assessment*, (Santa Monica, CA: RAND Corporation, 2001), p. xix.
9. William M. Arkin, "Fear of Civilian Deaths May Have Undermined Effort," *Los Angeles Times*, 16 January 2002.
10. Esther Schrader, "War, On Advice of Counsel," *Los Angeles Times*, 15 February 2002, p. 1.
11. William M. Arkin, "Fear of Civilian Deaths."
12. "Turning the Tide in Afghanistan," *Boston Globe*, 31 December 2001, p. 1.
13. "Why Osama Escaped," *Boston Globe*, 19 April 2002, p. 18.
14. Edward Cody, "Taliban's 'Hide-and-Wait' Strategy Failed," *The Washington Post*, 23 December 2001, p. A12.
15. Loren B. Thompson, "The Limits of Transformation: Some Words of Caution about Rumsfield's Revolution," *Defense Week*, 22 April 2002, p. 1.

COMBAT SEARCH AND RESCUE: A LONGER LOOK
1. James C. Humes, *Churchill: Speaker of the Century* (New York: Scarborough Books, 1982), 269.
2. This data comes from the joint CSAR Joint Test and Evaluation recently completed at Nellis AFB, Nevada.
3. Joint Services S.E.R.E. Agency, *F-16 Lessons Learned: Introduction*, 3 December 1999, 17. (Secret) Information extracted is unclassified.
4. Robert F. Futrell, *The United States Air Force in Korea, 1950–1953* (Washington, D.C.: Office of Air Force History, 1983), 583.
5. *F-16 Lessons Learned*, 14. (Secret) Information extracted is unclassified.
6. Futrell, 583.
7. Robert J. Cressman, "Rescue from Truk Lagoon," *The Hook*, Winter 1993, 24.
8. Battleship *North Carolina*: Kingfisher Truk Rescue, 30 April 1944; on-line, Internet, 16 March 2000, available from http://www.battleshipnc.com/kingfisher_truk_rescue.htm.

9. Futrell, 578–79.
10. Jeffrey Ethell and Alfred Price, "Man on the Run," *Air Power History*, Fall 1989, 45.
11. See Darrel Whitcomb, *The Rescue of Bat 21* (Annapolis, Md.: US Naval Institute Press, 1998).
12. Ibid., 152.
13. Lt Col Tom Trask, interviewed by author, 17 February 2000.
14. Adm Leighton Smith, press conference, Naples, Italy, 22 September 1995; on-line, Internet, 4 January 2000, available from http://www.hri.org/news/misc/misc-news/95-09-22.misc.html.
15. Earl Tilford, *Search and Rescue in Southeast Asia: 1961–1975* (Washington, D.C.: Office of Air Force History, 1980), 119.
16. Joint Publication 3-50.21, *Joint Tactics, Techniques, and Procedures for Combat Search and Rescue*, 23 March 1998, I-1.
17. Ibid., II-12.
18. Tilford, 5–7.
19. John Warden, *The Air Campaign: Planning for Combat* (Washington, D.C.: National Defense University Press, 1988), 49.
20. Gen Hugh Shelton, remarks at the Department of Defense Personnel Recovery Conference, Fort Belvoir, Va., 27 October 1999; on-line, Internet, 3 November 1999, available from http://www.defenselink.mil/news/ #News Articles.
21. Air Force Doctrine Document 2-1.6, *Combat Search and Rescue*, 30 September 1998, 4.
22. Tilford, 3.
23. See, for example, *Band of Brothers: E Company, 506th Regiment, 101st Airborne from Normandy to Hilter's Eagle's Nest* (New York: Simon and Schuster, 1992).
24. Carl von Clausewitz, *On War*, ed. and trans. Michael Howard and Peter Paret (Princeton, N.J.: Princeton University Press, 1976), 87.
25. Ibid., 92.
26. Whitcomb, 142.
27. Dick Keresey, "Farthest Forward," *American Heritage*, July/August 1998, 60.
28. Shelton remarks.
29. Winston S. Churchill, *The Second World War* (New York: Time Inc., 1950), 72.
30. "Jolly Green Funeral Ceremony," Headquarters United States Air Force TV Center, 11th Communications Squadron, Pentagon, Washington, D.C., 25 November 1997.

NOTES ON
CONTRIBUTORS

MARTIN BLUMENSON was a former professor at the Army War College. A graduate of both Bucknell and Harvard Universities, he served as an instructor in the U.S. Merchant Marine Academy; Hofstra College. Historical Officer, European theater, World War II; Commanding Officer, 3d Historical Detachment, Korean War; Historian, Joint Task Force SEVEN. Bronze Star Medal, Commendation Ribbon. Captain, U.S. Army Reserve. He is the author of dozens of military history books, including *Patton: The Man Behind the Legend 1885–1945, Breakout and Pursuit* and *Salerno to Cassino; Anzio: The Gamble That Failed; Rommel's Last Victory; Operation RED-WING: The Atomic Weapons Tests in the Pacific, 1956;* and numerous articles in military and historical journals.

BRIGADIER GENERAL JOHN S. BROWN has been chief of military history at the Center of Military History since 1998. He commanded the Second Battalion, 66th Armor Division in Iraq and Kuwait during the Gulf War. He holds a doctorate in history from Indiana University and is the author of *Draftee Division: The 88th Infantry Division in World War II.*

ROBERT J. BUNKER, Ph.D., attended California State Polytechnic University at Pomona, and the Clairemont Graduate University. He holds a doctorate in political science, a master's degree in government, and bachelor's degrees in anthropology/geography, social science, behavioral science, and history. Dr. Bunker is Adjunct Professor, National Securities Studies Program, California State University, San Bernardino, and Professor, Unconventional Warfare, American Military University, Manassas Park, Virginia. He has served as a consultant to both the military and law enforcement communities. His research focus is on the influence of technology on warfare and political organization and on the national security implications of emerging forms of warfare. Dr. Bunker's works have appeared in *Parameters, Special Warfare, Army RDA, Military Intelligence, Red Thrust Star, Airpower Journal, Marine Corps Gazette, Institute of Land Warfare Papers, Institute for National Security Studies Occasional Papers,* and various law enforcement publications, military encyclopedias, and in book chapters.

EDWARD L. "TED" BYRNES was born and raised in Syracuse, New York. He received an Associate's degree in Journalism from Morrisville College, Morrisville, New York, and a Bachelor of Arts degree in English/Writing from Potsdam State University, Potsdam, New York. The bulk of his writing has been for corporate employers in several diverse industries, including animal agriculture, health care, religion and military aviation. He is a former managing editor and art director of *Foundation* magazine, published by the Naval Aviation Museum Foundation for the National Museum of Naval Aviation at Naval Air Station Pensacola, Florida. He currently resides in Syracuse.

COLONEL (DR.) JIM A. DAVIS is the Deputy Director to the USAF Counterproliferation Center and a Professor in Chemical-Biological Warfare (CBW) at the Air War College. Colonel Davis started his career with a Bachelor and Doctorate of Veterinary Medicine from Texas A&M. He then served four years in the Army Veterinary Corps in various capacities several of which dealt with defensive CBW. During a break in active military service, Colonel Davis practiced veterinary medicine for six years but stayed in the Army Reserves. In 1987, Colonel Davis joined the USAF as a Public Health Officer. While in the USAF he has earned a Master and a Doctorate of Public Health from the University of Texas. He is board certified with the American College of Veterinary Preventive Medicine and is a Foreign Animal Disease Diagnostician. He is also a graduate of the Air Command and Staff College and Air War College. Colonel Davis's CBW experiences have included overseeing stored chemical agents, teaching emergency wartime medicine in surgical labs, leading decon teams, briefings to city and state officials, research and publishing, assisting in exercises, assisting OSD and CENTCOM in international environments. Before assuming his current position, he was the USAF Surgeon General's Chair to Air University. Colonel Davis was the Commander, 48th Aerospace Medicine Squadron at RAF Lakenheath, UK. As commander, he was responsible for the largest Aerospace Medicine Squadron in Europe, which directed flight medicine, optometry, preventive medicine, health promotion, public health, industrial hygiene and bioenvironmental engineering. His areas of expertise include chemical and biological warfare and terrorism, and the Middle East.

COLONEL ROBERT A. DOUGHTY has been the head of the Department of History at West Point since August 1985. He graduated from the Military Academy in 1965 and received his Ph.D. from the University of Kansas in 1979. Among his publications are "Seeds of Disaster: The Development of French Army Doctrine, 1919–1939" and "The Breaking Point: Sedan and the Fall of France, 1940." He currently is working on a book tentatively entitled "Pyrrhic Victory: French Strategy and Operations in the Great War." He received the Birdsall Prize in 1986 from the American Historical Association, and his awards and decorations include the Silver Star and Combat Infantryman's Badge.

THOMAS FLEMING is a distinguished historian and the author of numerous critically acclaimed and bestselling novels. His masterpiece, *The Officers' Wives*, was an international bestseller with over two million copies sold. His novels *Time and Tide* and *Liberty Tavern* were both *New York Times* bestsellers. He is also the author to the award-winning PBS miniseries *Liberty! The American Revolution*. A decade ago Fleming was elected a Fellow of the Society of American Historians. He writes frequently for *American Heritage Magazine* and is contributing editor of the *Quarterly Journal of Military History*. His most recent nonfiction book is *Duel: Alexander Hamilton, Aaron Burr, and the Future of America*. Thomas Fleming lives in New York City.

COMMANDER STEPHEN E. FLYNN, USCG, is the nation's leading expert on port and container security and a noted authority on Homeland Security. Dr. Flynn is a consultant to the Ports of New York and New Jersey, Los Angeles, Seattle, and Tacoma, and an advisor to the Council on Competitiveness. He served as Director of the Office of Global Issues, National Security Council, was a Consultant to both the U.S. Commission on National Security/21st Century (the Hart-Rudman Commission), and the White House Office of Emergency Operations. Dr. Flynn was Executive Assistant to General Charles C. Krulak, USMC, at the White House Military Office, and an Associate Professor of International Relations at the U.S. Coast Guard Academy, responsible for curriculum development and instruction in International Relations, National Security Policy, Drugs Policy, and Global Policy Studies. An author of countless articles, monographs, book chapters, and papers, Dr. Flynn is one of the nation's most sought-after experts in the fields of Homeland Security, Port Security, Container Security,

Border Management, and the Global Drug Trade. He has organized numerous conferences, panels, and workshops and presented papers throughout the world to a variety of organizations, including the United Nations, the U.S. Congress, the Department of Transportation, the National Academy of Sciences, the universities of Harvard, Princeton, and Pennsylvania, the U.S. Naval War College, and the National Defense University. A 1982 graduate of the U.S. Coast Guard Academy, Dr. Flynn retired with the rank of Commander after twenty years of active-duty service.

LIEUTENANT COLONEL RAYMOND H. FREDETTE, USAF (Ret.), is a native of Massachusetts. He earned degrees in history and international relations from Tufts University and the Fletcher School of Law and Diplomacy. During World War II, he flew thirty-one combat missions over Germany with the Eighth Air Force. Recalled to active duty in 1951, Fredette served as an intelligence officer in Morocco, Germany, and Vietnam. He also had teaching assignments with AFROTC and the Defense Intelligence School in Washington, D.C. Shortly after retiring, he met Charles Lindbergh, who agreed to cooperate in the writing of a book about his military activities. Colonel Fredette has written many articles on aviation history and a book on the origins of strategic bombing in World War I, *The Sky on Fire*, which has been reissued as a volume in the Smithsonian History of Aviation Series.

PHILIP HANDLEMAN has been a pilot for thirty-one years. He is the author/editor of seventeen aerospace-related books, including *Brassey's Air Combat Reader* (with retired Colonel Walter J. Boyne, USAF) and, most recently, *Air Racing Today*. Also, his photograph of the Air Force Thunderbirds air demonstration was featured on the U.S. postage stamp commemorating the fiftieth anniversary of the Air Force in 1997.

ADAM J. HEBERT is the senior correspondent for InsideDefense.com, an Internet-based defense information site, and contributing editor for *Inside the Air Force*, a Washington, D.C.–based newsletter.

MAJOR PRISCO R. HERNANDEZ was born in Rio Piedras, Puerto Rico. He is an Army National Guard officer with over seventeen years of service and is currently serving on active duty at Fort Sill, Oklahoma. He has published several award-winning articles on military history. His article "No Master Plan: The Employment of Artillery in the Indian Wars, 1860–1890" was selected by the Army Historical Foundation as the most distinguished piece of professional military writing for the year 2000. He has also published the results of his field research into Puerto Rican folk music and several papers on medieval Spanish poetry and song in various scholarly journals. Dr. Hernandez holds a Ph.D. in the history of music from the University of Wisconsin at Madison with a minor in medieval Spanish literature. His dissertation, "Spanish and Portuguese Song at the End of the Middle Ages and the Beginning of the Renaissance (1466–1520): A Contextual Study," is an important contribution to a little-known area of Hispanic cultural history. He is an experienced translator, lecturer, and also an accomplished musician and military miniatures painter. Prisco and his wife, Anilia, have two wonderful daughters: Ana Julia and Priscila.

WILLIAM J. HOURIHAN, Ph.D., serves as the Army Chaplain Branch historian. He is located at the U.S. Army Chaplain Center and School, Fort Jackson, S.C.

LIEUTENANT COLONEL REX R. KIZIAH (B.S., U.S. Air Force Academy; Ph.D., University of Texas at Austin) is currently the deputy chief, Theater Air Defense Division in the Air Staff's Directorate of Global Air Power Programs. Previous assignments include serving as the Air Force Research's Laboratory commander's representative to the National Reconnaissance Office; deputy program manager of the Office of the Secretary of Defense Counterproliferation Support Program; special assistant for research and technology for the assistant to the Secretary of Defense for Nuclear, Chemical, and Biological Defense Programs; associate professor of physics at the USAFA; and section chief and neutral particle beam research officer at the Air Force Weapons Laboratory. He is a graduate of Squadron Officer School, Air Command and Staff College, a 1998 graduate of the Defense Systems Management College, and a 2000 graduate of the Air War College.

JACOB NEUFELD is the editor of *Air Power History* magazine, and has worked in the Office of Air Force History. He is also the author, editor, and contributor to several books, including *An Illustrated Guide to the Air War over Vietnam*, *The U.S. Air Force in Space: 1945 to the 21st Century*, and *Development of Ballistic Missiles in the U.S. Air Force, 1945–1960*.

BARRETT TILLMAN is the author of four novels, including *Hellcats*, which was nominated for the Military Novel of the Year in 1996; twenty nonfiction historical and biography books, and more than four hundred military and aviation articles in American, European, and Pacific Rim publications. He received his bachelor's degree in journalism from the University of Oregon in 1971, and spent the next decade writing freelance articles. He later worked with the Champlain Museum Press and as the managing editor of

The Hook magazine. In 1989 he returned to freelance writing, and has been at it ever since. His military nonfiction has been critically lauded, and garnered him several awards, including the U.S. Air Force's Historical Foundation Award, the Nautical and Oceanographic Society's Outstanding Biography Award, and the Arthur Radford Award for Naval History and Achievement. He is also an honorary member of the Navy fighter squadrons VF-111 and VA-35. He lives and works in Mesa, Arizona.

SPENCER C. TUCKER holds the John Biggs Chair of Military History and has been at VMI since 1997. He graduated from VMI with a B.A. degree in 1959, studied in France on a Fulbright at the University of Bordeaux during 1959–1960, and received his M.A. and Ph.D. degrees from the University of North Carolina at Chapel Hill in 1962 and 1966. He served as a captain in Army Intelligence during 1965–67 and was professor of history at Texas Christian University from 1967 to 1997 and chair of the department from 1992 to 1997. During 1969–1970 he was a visiting research associate at the Smithsonian Institute.

DAVID J. ULBRICH is currently a doctoral candidate in history at Temple University, where he studies with Professor Gregory J. W. Urwin. Ulbrich's article reprinted in this volume received the 2000 Heinl Award from the Marine Corps Heritage Foundation. He has also published in *Journal of Asian Studies, Journal of Men's Studies, Journal of Military History, Marine Corps Gazette,* and *War and History.* Most recently, his "Research Note: 'A Program for Covert Action Against the Castro Regime, 16 March 1960'" appeared in the *SHAFER Newsletter* (2002). Ulbrich is an adjunct instructor of history at the University of Delaware.

DR. MILAN VEGO is Professor of Operations, Joint Military Operations Department, at the Naval War College, Newport, Rhode Island. He has also written several books about strategy and tactics, including *Soviet Naval Tactics, Naval Strategy and Operations in Narrow Seas,* and *Austro-Hungarian Naval Policy 1904–1914.*

COLONEL DARREL WHITCOMB, USAF (RET.), is a contractor analyst with the MARC Corporation at the Joint Personnel Recovery Agency. He served three tours as a cargo pilot and forward air controller in Southeast Asia, and subsequently flew the A-37 and A-10 with the 926th Fighter Wing and the 442nd Fighter Wing. He also served tours in fighter plans on the Air Staff and in mobilization plans on the Joint Staff. Most recently, he served on the faculty at Air Command and Staff College and as the mobilization assistant to the commander of the Air Force Doctrine Center at Maxwell AFB, Alabama. A previous contributor to *Aerospace Power Journal*, he has been published in several other journals, and is the author of *The Rescue of Bat 21*. Colonel Whitcomb attended Squadron Officer School, Army Command and General Staff College, and the National War College.

JOSEPH ROBERT WHITE is a Postdoctoral Fellow at the Center for Advanced Holocaust Studies. He has written many articles about the Holocaust, including "Target Auschwitz: Historical and Hypothetical German Responses to Allied Attack." He lives and works in Washington, D.C.

INDEX